a middle english anthology

a middle english anthology

Edited by Ann S. Haskell

WAYNE STATE UNIVERSITY PRESS
DETROIT

Manufactured in the United States of America.

96 95 94 93 92   7 6 5 4 3

Library of Congress Cataloging-in-Publication Data

A Middle English anthology / edited by Ann S. Haskell.
　　p.　　cm.
　　Bibliography: p.
　　Includes index.
　　ISBN 0-8143-1798-7 (alk. paper)
　　1. English literature—Middle English, 1100-1500.　I. Haskell,
Ann S. (Ann Sullivan)
[PR1120.M52　1989]
820′.8′001—dc19　　　　　　　　　　　　　　　　89-5595
　　　　　　　　　　　　　　　　　　　　　　　　　　CIP

CONTENTS

PREFACE

This book first appeared in print in 1969. The period of time that has elapsed since then has been remarkable in several ways, and the changes that have resulted touch every aspect of our society, including its literature and scholarship. The amount of research that has been done on this book's twenty-nine texts over the last sixteen years is formidable. The publications that have resulted from that mammoth effort are impressive not only for their numbers but also for the directions their inquiry has taken.

All the texts in this book have attracted recent scholarly attention, and the studies listed in the addendum to the bibliography were selected from that body of work. But a few texts—most notably *Piers Plowman* and *Sir Gawayn and the Grene Knyght*—have generated such a gargantuan outpouring of books and articles that it has been impossible to choose a modest number from among them. Therefore, recent bibliographies of the scholarship on those works represent them here.

But the most significant characteristic of the literature in this volume is independent of research and publication. It is that with the passage of time its aesthetic attraction—for new acquaintances and long-faithful lovers alike—never stops growing.

ACKNOWLEDGMENTS

Though I wish to thank several people who have helped me with this edition, my greatest debt is owed to Patricia Anderson, who put aside her own work in medieval literature to prepare the new bibilography.

I would also like to thank Erwin Ford II and numerous members of the staff of the Lockwood Memorial Library who so generously gave me their help, the Department of English at the State University of New York at Buffalo for providing research assistance, and the students in my medieval literature seminars who have made invaluable suggestions.

This book is especially for my children—Dean, Mark, Peter, and Gretl—and now for John.

A.S.H.

Buffalo, New York
April, 1985

INTRODUCTION

This anthology was edited on the following premises: that the primary purpose of literature is pleasure; hence the glosses are marginal or on facing pages, rather than buried in the back of the book; that each professor is entitled to teach his own course; therefore the apparatus accompanying the texts is minimal and the selections numerous enough for variation from course to course; that literature is only a part of the whole cultural context in which it was written and should not be excised from that milieu; for this reason, the supplementary references include comparative media.

The material in this book is presented with frank subjectivity. The texts are those which I enjoy, those which I teach. They are deliberately not given any particular order, though no text is prerequisite to another and a chronological reading sequence—backward or forward in time—is quite possible. Similarly, the supplementary material selections are those which I have used to illuminate the various Middle English texts and are in no way to be construed as comprising a comprehensive list. They are presented simply to suggest ways of examining the literature. It is hoped that the lack of strictures in the book will give its users, both students and instructors, the freedom to approach Middle English literature according to individual tastes.

I have made no attempt to pour the language of this book's twenty-nine selections into a common linguistic mold, from which it would all emerge as Chaucerian Londonese or Pearl-poet patois. A medieval text without its beguiling irregularities is as unexciting as a machine-made oriental rug. Individualizing textual features constitute much of the aesthetic appeal, visual as well as aural, of medieval literature. I have not tampered with the dialectal differences of the texts at all.

Since the appearance of a medieval text can be overwhelming to the inexperienced reader, I have supplied punctuation, capitalization, and accent marks where they seem necessary. Also, I have converted medieval symbols to their modern equivalents. My criterion for such modernization has been comprehension and the presentation of an enjoyable text as opposed to a forbidding one. On the other hand, vagaries of text, where they do not seriously hamper understanding, have been respected.

I have regularly converted þ and ð to *th*, and ʒ to *gh, g, y,* and occasionally *w*. I have regularized the interchangeable *u*'s and *v*'s, since their vocalic and consonantal use can be confused. *I*, *y*, and *j*, however, seem less ambiguous and have been left unchanged. I have generally adopted time-honored emendations without comment, though for some texts, such as *Wynnere and Wastoure*, I have rejected many of them.

I feel strongly that the glosses should not be tools for smooth translations into modern English, but rather aids in understanding the Middle English. Consequently I have avoided the definition in favor of the cognate, if the price is no more than a shade of meaning; the use of a word in half a dozen contexts will usually reveal its meaning better than an explanation, no matter how extensive. Where no modern equivalent of a word exists, I have frequently given similar constructions or related terms to reinforce a Middle English word. Where etymologies are amply explanatory I have preferred them to definitions.

I will make no attempt to condense Baugh's language history or Sisam's fourteenth-century Middle English appendix into a single paragraph of this introduction. The linguistic references in section B of the bibliography are intended to provide this background material.

My bases for these editions have been reproductions of the original manuscripts, wherever possible, with reference to the editions noted in the bibliography. In some instances (notably the lyrics), however, collations of several reliable editions of a manuscript have formed the basis of the text. I gratefully acknowledge my debt to previous editors whose scholarship can be fully appreciated only by someone following in their wake.

ABBREVIATIONS

auxil.	auxiliary
bibl.	bibliography
cf.	compare
constr.	construction
f., fol.	following
fr.	from
Fr.	French
freq.	frequently
GGK	*Sir Gawayn and the Grene Knyght*
Gk.	Greek
l.	line (used with numbers in gloss to refer to previous use of a word within a single poem)
lit.	literally
M.E.	Middle English
M.E.D.	*Middle English Dictionary*
n.	noun; following a number, note
N.E.	modern English
neg.	negative, *ne,* frequently pleonastic
N.Fr.	modern French
N.G.	modern German
O.E.	Old English
O.E.D.	*Oxford English Dictionary*
O.Fr.	Old French
O.H.G.	Old High German
O.N.	Old Norse
pl.	plural
poss.	possible, -ly
prob.	probably
pron.	pronoun
rel.	relative, related
Shks.	Shakespearean usage
vb.	verb

SCOTLAND

NORTH
SEA

IRELAND

IRISH SEA

York

□ Wakefield
Plays

○ Richard
Rolle

△ Land
of
Cokaygne

Chester

○ Gawayn
Pearl

○ Mannyng

○ Wynnere and Wastoure
Parlement of Thre Ages

△ Layamon
Brut

Cambridge

○ Piers Plowman
Malvern Hills

WALES

Oxford

□ Caxton-Malory
London

○ Mandeville

○ Chaucer

○ Sir
Orfeo

Dover

□ Sir
Launfal

△ Owl and
Nightingale

Hastings

ENGLISH CHANNEL

△ 12-13th CENTURY   ○ 14th CENTURY   □ 15th CENTURY

A LITERARY MAP OF MIDDLE ENGLISH

A MIDDLE
ENGLISH
ANTHOLOGY

SIR GAWAYN
AND THE
GRENE KNYGHT

SIR GAWAYN AND THE GRENE KNYGHT

PART I

1

Sithen the sege and the assaut was sesed at Troye,
The borgh brittened and brent to brondes and askes,
The tulk that the trammes of tresoun ther wroght
Was tried for his tricherie, the trewest on erthe—
Hit was Ennias the athel and his highe kynde,   5
That sithen depreced provinces and patrounes bicome
Welneghe of al the wele in the west iles.
Fro riche Romulus to Rome ricchis hym swythe,
With gret bobbaunce that burghe he biges upon fyrst,
And nevenes hit his aune nome, as hit now hat.   10
Ticius to Tuskan and teldes bigynnes,
Langaberde in Lumbardie lyftes up homes,
And fer over the French flod Felix Brutus
On mony bonkkes ful brode Bretayn he settes
     wyth wynne,   15
     Where werre and wrake and wonder
     Bi sythes has wont therinne,
     And oft bothe blysse and blunder
     Ful skete has skyfted synne.

2

Ande quen this Bretayn was bigged by this burn rych,   20
Bolde bredden therinne, baret that lofden,
In mony turned tyme tene that wroghten.
Mo ferlyes on this folde han fallen here oft
Then in any other that I wot syn that ilk tyme.
Bot of alle that here bult of Bretaygne kynges   25
Ay was Arthur the hendest, as I haf herde telle.

1 *ceased*
2 *burg/broken/burnt/brands/ashes*
3 *man/trammels, web**
4 *treachery*
5 *noble*
6 *depressed, overcame*
7 *well nigh/weal*
8 *Afterward (from that time)/goes/swiftly*
9 *pomp/builds*
10 *names/own/name/is called*
11 *(goes) to/buildings*
12 *raises*
13 *far/sea*
14 *banks, shores/settles*
15 *joy*
16 *war/wrack*
17 *betimes/dwelled*

19 *quickly/shifted/since*

20 *when**/man/noble*
21 *bold (ones)/battle/loved*
22 *past/trouble*
23 *marvels/land/have*
24 *know/same*
25 *dwelt*
26 *Always/most noble, courteous*

---

3 Fr. O.Fr. for 'woof.'
20 *Qu-* frequently = *wh-*.

Forthi an aunter in erde I attle to schawe*
That a selly in sight summe men hit holden,
And an outtrage awenture of Arthures wonderes.
If ye wyl lysten this laye bot on littel quile,   30
I schal telle hit astit, as I in toun herde,
   with tonge,
    As hit is stad and stoken
    In stori stif and stronge,
    With lel letteres loken,   35
    In londe so has ben longe.

3

This kyng lay at Camylot upon Krystmasse
With mony luflych lorde, ledes of the best,
Rekenly of the Rounde Table alle tho rich brether,
With rych revel oryght and rechles merthes.   40
Ther tournayed tulkes by tymes ful mony,
Justed ful jolilé thise gentyle knightes,
Sythen kayred to the court caroles to make.
For ther the fest was ilyche ful fiften dayes,
With alle the mete and the mirthe that men couthe avyse.   45
Such glaum ande gle glorious to here,
Dere dyn upon day, daunsyng on nyghtes,
Al was hap upon heghe in halles and chambres
With lordes and ladies, as levest him thoght.
With alle the wele of the worlde they woned ther samen,   50
The most kyd knyghtes under Krystes selven,
And the lovelokkest ladies that ever lif haden,
And he the comlokest kyng that the court haldes.
For al was this fayre folk in her first age,
   on sille,   55
    The hapnest under heven,
    Kyng hyghest mon of wylle;
    Hit were now gret nye to neven
    So hardy a here on hille.

4

Wyle Nw Yer was so yep that hit was nwe cummen,   60
That day doubble on the dece was the douth served,

---

27 "Therefore an adventure on earth I intend to show."

28 *marvel*
29 *strange adventure*

31 *immediately*

33 *standing/stuck, set down*

35 *loyal/locked*

38 *gracious/men*

40 *aright*

42 *Jousted*
43 *rode, proceeded**
44 *alike*
45 *devise*
46 *joyful noise*

48 *happiness on high*
49 *dearest**
50 *dwelled/together*
51 *known, renowned*
52 *loveliest*

54 *in their* youth*
55 *sill, floor*
56 *luckiest*

58 *(it would be) hard/name* (1. 10)
59 *host*

60 *keen, fresh*
61 *dais/company*

---

43 O.N. *keyra*, found freq. in M.E. as *kayre, cayre*.
49 Fr. O.E. *lēof* 'love'; M.E. *leve, lef* 'dear, beloved' freq.
54 Pl. pron. forms freq. throughout with initial *h-*; cf. l. 67.

Fro the kyng was cummen with knyghtes into the halle,
The chauntré of the chapel cheved to an ende.
Loude crye was ther kest to clerkes and other,
Nowel nayted onewe, nevened ful ofte.   65
And sythen riche forth runnen to reche hondeselle,
Yeyed yeres-giftes on high, yelde hem bi hond,
Debated busyly aboute tho giftes.
Ladies laghed ful loude, thogh they lost haden,
And he that wan was not wrothe, that may ye wel trawe.   70
Alle this mirthe thay maden to the mete tyme.
When thay had waschen worthyly thay wenten to sete,
The best burne ay abof, as hit best semed,
Whene Guenore, ful gay, graythed in the myddes,
Dressed on the dere des, dubbed al aboute,   75
Smal sendal bisides, a selure hir over
Of tryed tolouse, of tars tapites innoghe,
That were enbrawded and beten wyth the best gemmes
That myght be preved of prys wyth penyes to bye,
    in daye.   80
The comlokest to discrye
Ther glent with yghen gray,
A semloker that ever he syghe,
Soth moght no mon say.

5

Bot Arthure wolde not ete til al were served,   85
He was so joly of his joyfnes, and sumquat childgered:
His lif liked hym lyght, he lovied the lasse
Auther to longe lye or to longe sitte,
So bisied him his yonge blod and his brayn wylde.
And also an other maner meved him eke   90
That he thurgh nobelay had nomen, he wolde never ete
Upon such a dere day er hym devised were
Of sum aventurus thyng an uncouthe tale
Of sum mayn mervayle, that he myght trawe,
Of alderes, of armes, of other aventurus,   95
Other sum segg hym bisoght of sum siker knyght
To joyne wyth hym in iustyng, in jopardé to lay,
Lede lif for lyf, leve uchon other,
As fortune wolde fulsun hom, the fayrer to have.
This was kynges countenaunce where he in court were,   100

63 (mass) chanting/achieved
64 cast
65 proclaimed/anew
66 rich, noble (ones)/gifts
67 Announced/yielded, repaid

70 won/believe

73 man/above, ahead (in order of rank)
74 Queen Guenivere/seated
75 dais (l. 61)
76 Fine silk/canopy
77 Toulouse/Tharsia/tapestries

79 proved/price, value

82 glinted/eyes
83 (might) see
84 might

86 child-mannered
87 less
88 Either

90 moved/also
91 taken, adopted
92 told
93 strange
94 mighty marvel
95 noblemen
96 Or/man/sure
97 jousting
98 each one
99 aid them
100 custom

At uch farand fest among his fre meny
   in halle.
  Therfore of face so fere
  He stightles stif in stalle,
  Ful yep in that Nw Yere   105
  Much mirthe he mas with alle.

7

Thus ther stondes in stale the stif kyng hisselven,
Talkkande bifore the hyghe table of trifles ful hende.
There gode Gawan was graythed Gwenore bisyde,
And Agravayn a la dure mayn on that other syde sittes,   110
Bothe the kynges sistersunes and ful siker knightes.
Bischop Bawdewyn abof bigines the table,
And Ywan, Uryn son, ette with hymselven.
Thise were dight on the des and derworthly served,
And sithen mony siker segge at the sidbordes.   115
Then the first cors come with crakkyng of trumpes,
Wyth mony baner ful bryght that therbi henged.
Nwe nakryn noyse with the noble pipes,
Wylde werbles and wyght wakned lote,
That mony hert ful highe hef at her towches.   120
Dayntés dryven therwyth of ful dere metes,
Foysoun of the fresche and on so fele disches
That pine to fynde the place the peple biforne
For to sette the sylveren that sere sewes halden
   on clothe.   125
  Iche lede as he loved hymselve
  Ther laght withouten lothe.
  Ay two had disches twelve,
  Good ber and bryght wyn bothe.

8

Now wyl I of hor servise say yow no more,   130
For uch wyghe may wel wit no wont that ther were.
An other noyse ful newe neghed bilive,
That the lude myght haf leve liflode to cach,
For unethe was the noyce not a whyle sesed,
And the fyrst cource in the court kyndely served,   135
Ther hales in at the halle dor an aghlich mayster,

101 *glorious**/noble/retinue

104 "He stands stalwartly"
105 keen, fresh (l. 60)
106 makes

108 courteous (l. 26)
109 seated (l. 74)

111 nephews (lit. sister-sons)

114 placed
115 afterward (ll. 1, 6, 43)

118 kettledrums
119 loud/sound
120 heaved

122 plenty/many

124 various stews

126 Each/man (l. 38)
127 latched, took

131 person/know/lack, n.
132 nighed, neared/quickly
133 (So) that/people/food/take, get
134 scarcely

136 terrible

---

101 The suffix -and = -ing freq.

On the most on the molde on mesure hyghe
Fro the swyre to the swange so sware and so thik,
And his lyndes and his lymes so longe and so grete,
Half etayn in erde I hope that he were,   140
Bot mon most I algate mynn hym to bene,
And that the myriest in his muckel that myght ride;
For of bak and of brest al were his bodi sturne,
Both his wombe and his wast were worthily smale,
And alle his fetures folwande, in forme that he hade,   145
    ful clene;
For wonder of his hwe men hade,
Set in his semblaunt sene,
He ferde as freke were fade,
And overal enker grene.   150

9

Ande al graythed in grene this gome and his wedes:
A strayt cote ful streght, that stek on his sides,
A meré mantile abof, mensked withinne
With pelure pured apert, the pane ful clene
With blythe blaunner ful bryght, and his hod bothe,   155
That was laght fro his lokkes and layde on his schulderes;
Heme wel-haled hose of that same grene,
That spenet on his sparlyr, and clene spures under
Of bryght golde, upon silk bordes barred ful ryche,
And scholes under schankes there the schalk rides;   160
And alle his vesture verayly was clene verdure,
Bothe the barres of his belt and other blythe stones,
That were richely rayled in his aray clene
Aboutte hymself and his sadel, upon silk werkes,
That were to tor for to telle of tryfles the halve   165
That were enbrauded abof, wyth bryddes and flyes
With gay gaudi of grene, the golde ay inmyddes.
The pendauntes of his payttrure, the proude cropure,
His molaynes and alle the metail anamayld was thenne,
The steropes that he stod on stayned of the same,   170
And his arsouns al after and his athel sturtes,
That ever glemered and glent al of grene stones.
The fole that he ferkkes on fyn of that ilke,
    sertayn,
A grene hors gret and thikke,   175
A stede ful stif to strayne,

137 *One of the tallest on earth*
138 *neck/waist/square*
139 *loins*
140 *giant/earth/think*
141 *biggest/always/remember*
142 *size*

144 *belly*
145 *following, likewise*

147 *hue*
148 *appearance*
149 *fared/man/bold*
150 *very*

151 *arrayed/man/clothes*

153 *decorated*
154 *fur/purified* = *trimmed/evident*
155 *white fur*
156 *latched, pulled back*
157 *Neat/well-drawn up*
158 *clung/calves*

160 *shoes* (*or ?shoeless*)/*man*
161 *green*

163 *arrayed*

165 *too difficult*
166 *embroidered/birds*
167 *beads/in the middle*
168 *horse's neck-cover*
169 *ornaments on the bit/enameled*

171 *saddlebows/noble/saddle harness*

173 *horse/goes/same*

176 *restrain*

In brawden brydel quik—
To the gome he was ful gayn.

10

Wel gay was this gome gered in grene,
And the here of his hed of his hors swete,   180
Fayre fannand fax umbefoldes his schulderes.
A much berd as a busk over his brest henges,
That with his highlich here that of his hed reches
Was evesed al umbetorne abof his elbowes,
That half his armes ther-under were halched in the wyse   185
Of a kynges capados that closes his swyre;
The mane of that mayn hors much to hit lyke,
Wel cresped and cemmed, wyth knottes ful mony
Folden in wyth fildore aboute the fayre grene,
Ay a herle of the here, an other of golde.   190
The tayle and his toppyng twynnen of a sute,
And bounden bothe wyth a bande of bryght grene,
Dubbed wyth ful dere stones, as the dok lasted,
Sythen thrawen wyth a thwong a thwarle knot alofte,
Ther mony belles ful bryght of brende golde rungen.   195
Such a fole upon folde, ne freke that hym rydes,
Was never sene in that sale wyth syght er that tyme
     with yghe.
   He loked as layt so lyght
   So sayd al that hym syghe.   200
   Hit semed as no mon myght
   Under his dynttes dryghe.

11

Whether hade he no helme ne hawbergh nauther
Ne no pysan ne no plate that pented to armes,
Ne no schafte ne no schelde to schwue ne to smyte,   205
Bot in his on honde he hade a holyn bobbe,
That is grattest in grene when greves ar bare,
And an ax in his other, a hoge and unmete,
A spetos sparthe to expoun in spelle, quoso myght.
The hede of an elnyerde the large lenkthe hade,   210
The grayn al of grene stele and of golde hewen,
The bit burnyst bryght, wyth a brod egge

177 *lively* (cf. *"the quick and the dead"*)
178 *man/ready*

180 *hair* (*of man and horse*)/*matched* (O.Fr. *siute*)
181 *fanning* (l. 101, n.)/*hair*/*folds around**
182 *great/bush*
183 *glorious*
184 *clipped*
185 *enclosed/manner*
186 *hooded cape/neck* (l. 138)
187 *mighty* (l. 94, cf. *"might and main"*)
188 *crisped, curled/combed*
189 *O.Fr. fil d'or* 'gold thread'
190 *strand*
191 *twined/suit, the same* (l. 180)

193 *the length of the dock*
194 *twisted/thong/complicated*
195 *Where**/*burnt*
196 *horse* (l. 173)/*earth* (l. 23)/*man* (l. 149)
197 *hall* (cf. Fr. *salle*, N.E. *salon*, etc.)
198 *eye*
199 *lightning*
200 (*might*) *see* (l. 83)

202 *dints/endure*

204 *neck armor* (*of Pisa*)/*appended*
205 *shove, thrust*
206 *one/holly*
207 *groves*
208 *huge/unmeasurable* (*one*)
209 *spiteful, cruel/battle-ax/tale* (cf. *gospel*)
210 *ell-yard* (45″) *measure*
211 *blade*
212 *edge*

---

181 The prefix *umbe-* 'around' freq.; cf. l. 184.
195 *Ther* as both 'where' and 'there' freq.

As wel schapen to schere as scharp rasores,
The stele of a stif staf the sturne hit by grypte,
That was wounden wyth yrn to the wandes ende,   215
And al bigraven with grene in gracios werkes.
A lace lapped aboute, that louked at the hede,
And so after the halme halched ful ofte
Wyth tryed tasseles therto tacched innoghe
On botouns of the bryght grene brayden ful ryche.   220
This hathel heldes hym in and the halle entres,
Drivande to the heghe dece, dut he no wothe,
Haylsed he never one, bot heghe he over loked.
The fyrst word that he warp, 'Wher is,' he sayd,
'The governour of this gyng? Gladly I wolde   225
Se that segg in syght, and with himself speke
     raysoun.'
     To knyghtes he kest his yghe,
     And reled hym up and doun;
     He stemmed and con studie   230
     Quo walt ther most renoun.

          12

Ther was lokyng on lenthe the lude to beholde,
For uch mon had mervayle quat hit mene myght,
That a hathel and a horse myght such a hwe lach,
As growe grene as the gres and grener hit semed,   235
Then grene aumayl on golde glowande bryghter.
Al studied that ther stod and stalked hym nerre
Wyth al the wonder of the worlde what he worch shulde.
For fele sellyes had they sen bot such never are;
Forthi, for fantoum and fayrye the folk there hit demed.   240
Therfore to answare was arghe mony athel freke
And al stouned at his steven and stonstil seten
In a swoghe sylence thurgh the sale riche.
As al were slypped upon slepe, so slaked hor lotes
     in hyghe—   245
     I deme hit not al for doute,
     Bot sum for cortaysye—
     Bot let hym that al schulde loute
     Cast unto that wyghe.

          13

Thenn Arthour bifore the high dece that aventure byholdes,   250
And rekenly hym reverenced, for rad was he never,

214 *stem/stern (one)*
215 *iron*

217 *locked*
218 *fastened* (l. 185)

221 *man/goes*
222 *doubted, feared/danger*
223 *hailed*
224 *warped, cast*
225 *gang, company*
226 *man* (ll. 96, 115)

228 *cast/eye* (ll. 82, 198)
229 *reeled, rolled/them*
230 *stopped/did*
231 *Who/wielded, possessed*

232 *man*

234 *man/hue/latch, possess*

236 *enamel*
237 *nearer*
238 *work, do*
239 *many/marvels* (l. 28)/*ere, before*
240 *Therefore* (l. 27)
241 *afraid/noble/man* (l. 149)
242 *astounded/voice/stone-still*
243 *swoon-like/hall* (l. 197)
244 *As (if)/slacked/cries*

248 *bow* (cf. N.E. *lute*)
249 *wight, man*

251 *afraid*

And sayde, 'Wyghe, welcum iwys to this place,
The hede of this ostel Arthour I hat.
Light luflych adoun and lenge, I the praye,
And quat-so thy wylle is we schal syt after.'   255
'Nay, as help me,' quoth the hathel, 'he that on hyghe syttes,
To wone any quyle in this won, hit was not myn ernde;
Bot for the los of the, lede, is lyft up so hyghe,
And thy burgh and thy burnes best ar holden
Stifest under stel-gere on stedes to ryde,   260
The wyghtest and the worthyest of the worldes kynde,
Preve for to play with in other pure laykes,
And here is kydde cortaysye, as I haf herd carp,
And that has wayned me hider, iwyis, at this tyme.
Ye may be seker by this braunch that I bere here   265
That I passe as in pes and no plyght seche;
For had I founded in fere in feghtyng wyse,
I have a hauberghe at home and a helme bothe,
A schelde and a scharp spere, schinande bryght,
Ande other weppenes to welde, I wene wel, als;   270
Bot for I wolde no were, my wedes ar softer.
Bot if thou be so bold as alle burnes tellen,
Thou wyl grant me godly the gomen that I ask
    bi ryght.'
        Arthour con onsware,   275
        And sayd, 'Sir cortays knyght,
        If thou crave batayl bare,
        Here fayles thou not to fyght.

        14

'Nay, frayst I no fyght, in fayth I the telle,
Hit arn aboute on this bench bot berdles chylder.   280
If I were hasped in armes on a heghe stede,
Here is no mon me to mach, for myghtes so wayke.
Forthy I crave in this court a Crystemas gomen,
For hit is Yol and Nwe Yer and here are yep mony;
If any so hardy in this hous holdes hymselven,   285
Be so bolde in his blod, brayn in his hede,
That dar stifly strike a strok for an other,
I schal gif hym of my gyft thys giserne ryche,
This ax, that his hevé innogh, to hondele as hym lykes,
And I schal bide the fyrst bur as bare as I sitte.   290
If any freke be so felle to fonde that I telle,

252 *indeed*
253 *hostel/am called* (l. 10)
254 *graciously* (l. 38)/*linger*
255 *know*

257 *dwell/dwelling/errand*
258 *fame of thee, man*
259 *men*

261 *manliest*
262 *Valiant/games*
263 *made known/carped, told*
264 *brought*
265 *certain* (l. 115)
266 *peace/seek*
267 *traveled/company*

270 *think/also*
271 *because I wished/war/clothes* (l. 151)

273 *game*

275 *did* (l. 230, freq. auxil.)/*answer*

277 *actual*

279 *ask*
280 *are/beardless children*

282 *weak*

284 *Yule/bold* (l. 105)

286 *turbulent*

288 (O.Fr. *guiserne*) *ax*

290 *blow*
291 *man/fierce/test*

Lepe lyghtly me to and lach this weppen,
I quit-clayme hit for ever, kepe hit as his auen,
And I schal stonde hym a strok, stif on this flet;
Elles thou wyl dight me the dom to dele hym an other,   295
    barlay,
And yet gif hym respite,
A twelmonyth and a day;
Now hyghe and let se tite
Dar any herinne oght say.'   300

15

If he hem stowned upon fyrst, stiller were thanne
Alle the heredmen in halle, the hygh and the lowe.
The renk on his rouncé hym ruched in his sadel,
And runischly his rede yghen he reled aboute,
Bende his bresed browes, blycande grene,   305
Wayved his berde for to wayte quo-so wolde ryse.
When non wolde kepe hym with carp, he coghed ful hyghe.
Ande rimed hym ful richley, and ryght hym to speke:
'What, is this Arthures hous,' quoth the hathel thenne,
'That al the rous rennes of thurgh ryalmes so mony?   310
Where is now your sourquydrye and your conquestes,
Your gryndellayk and your greme, and your grete wordes?
Now is the revel and the renoun of the Rounde Table
Overwalt wyth a worde of on wyghes speche,
For al dares for drede withoute dynt schewed!'   315
Wyth this he laghes so loude that the lorde greved.
The blod schot for scham into his schyre face
    and lere.
    He wex as wroth as wynde,
    So did alle that ther were.   320
    The kyng as kene bi kynde
    Then stod that stif mon nere,

16

Ande sayde, 'Hathel, by heven, thyn askyng is nys,
And as thou foly has frayst, fynde the behoves.
I know no gome that is gast of thy grete wordes;   325
Gif me now thy geserne, upon Godes halve,
And I schal baythen thy bone that thou boden habbes.'
Lyghtly lepes he hym to, and laght at his honde.
Then feersly that other freke upon fote lyghtis.

293 *own*
294 *flat, floor*
295 *grant/judgment*
296 (unknown)

299 *hie, hasten/quickly*
300 *a whit, anything*

301 *astounded* (l. 242)
302 *retainers*
303 *man/rouncy horse/turned*
304 *furiously*
305 *Bent/bristling/shining*
306 *await/whosoever*
307 *keep up conversation with him* (l. 263)
308 *stood/began (to speak)*

310 *talk/runs/realms*
311 *pride*
312 *fierceness/wrath*

314 *overturned*
315 *cower in fear without a blow shown*

317 *shot/shame/fair*
318 *cheek*

321 *by nature*

323 *nice = foolish*
324 *folly/asked* (l. 279)/*(to) find (it)*
325 *aghast*
326 *battle-ax* (l. 288)/*behalf*
327 *bid/boon/begged/have*
328 *latched, caught*
329 *man* (ll. 149, 241)

Now has Arthure his axe, and the halme grypes,   330
And sturnely stures hit aboute, that stryke wyth hit thoght.
The stif mon hym bifore stod upon hyght,
Herre then ani in the hous by the hede and more.
Wyth sturne schere ther he stod he stroked his berde,
And wyth a countenaunce dryghe he drogh doun his cote,   335
No more mate ne dismayd for hys mayn dintes
Then any burne upon bench hade broght hym to drynk
    of wyne.
    Gawan, that sate by the quene,
    To the kyng he can enclyne,   340
    'I beseche now with sawes sene,
    This melly mot be myne.'

                17

'Wolde ye, worthilych lorde,' quoth Wawan to the kyng,
'Bid me bowe fro this benche, and stonde by yow there,
That I wythoute vylanye myght voyde this table,   345
And that my legge lady lyked not ille,
I wolde com to your counseyl bifore your cort ryche.
For me think hit not semly, as hit is soth knawen,
Ther such an askyng is hevened so hyghe in your sale,
Thagh ye yourself be talenttyf to take hit to yourselven,   350
Whil mony so bolde yow aboute upon bench sytten,
That under heven, I hope, non hayerer of wylle,
Ne better bodyes on bent ther baret is rered.
I am the wakkest, I wot, and of wyt feblest,
And lest lur of my lyf, quo laytes the sothe,   355
Bot for as much as ye ar myn em I am only to prayse,
No bounté bot your blod I in my bodé knowe;
And sythen this note is so nys that noght hit yow falles,
And I have frayned hit at yow fyrst, foldes hit to me,
And if I carp not comlyly, let alle this cort rych   360
    bout blame.'
    Ryche togeder con roun,
    And sythen thay redden alle same
    To ryd the kyng with croun,
    And gif Gawan the game.   365

        18

Then comaunded the kyng the knyght for to ryse;
And he ful radly upros and ruchched hym fayre,

330 *shaft*
331 *stirs, waves*

333 *Higher*
334 *chere, expression*
335 *unchanging/drew*
336 *disturbed/mighty* (ll. 94, 187)
337 *Than (if)/man*

340 *did* (l. 275)
341 *sayings* (cf. N.E. *"old saws")/seen*, i.e., *clear*
342 *melee, battle/might*

343 *Gawayn*
344 *bend, proceed*
345 *villainy/leave*
346 *liege*

349 *heaved*
350 *desirous*

352 *handier, more skilful*
353 *field/battle* (l. 21)
354 *weakest/know*
355 *loss/seeks*
356 *uncle*

358 *business/foolish* (l. 323)
359 *asked/befits*

361 *but*
362 *whisper* (cf. *rune* 'secret writing')
363 *advised*

367 *promptly/proceeded* (l. 303)

Kneled doun bifore the kyng and caches that weppen,
And hè luflyly hit hym laft, and lyfte up his honde,
And gef hym Goddes blessyng and gladly hym biddes   370
That his hert and his honde schulde hardi be bothe.
'Kepe the, cosyn,' quoth the kyng, 'that thou on kyrf sette,*
And if thou redes hym ryght, redly I trowe
That thou schal byden the bur that he schal bede after.'
Gawan gos to the gome with giserne in honde,   375
And he baldly hym bydes, he bayst never the helder.
Then carppes to Sir Gawan the knyght in the grene,
'Refourme we oure forwardes, er we fyrre passe.
Fyrst I ethe the, hathel, how that thou hattes,
That thou me telle truly, as I tryst may.'   380
'In god fayth,' quoth the goode knyght, 'Gawan I hatte,
That bede the this buffet, quat-so bifalles after,
And at this tyme twelmonyth take at the an other
Wyth what weppen so thou wylt and wyth no wygh elles
    on lyve.'   385
    That other onswares agayn,
    'Sir Gawan, so mot I thryve,
    As I am ferly fayn
    This dint that thou schal dryve.'

19

'Bigog,' quoth the grene knyght, 'Sir Gawan, me lykes   390
That I schal fange at thy fust that I haf frayst here.
And thou has redily rehersed, by resoun ful trwe,
Clanly al the covenaunt that I the kynge asked,
Saf that thou schal siker me, segge, bi thi trawthe,
That thou schal seche me thiself, where-so thou hopes   395
I may be funde upon folde and foch the such wages
As thou deles me to-day bifore this douthe ryche.'
'Where schulde I wale the,' quoth Gauan, 'where is thy place?
I wot never where thou wonyes, bi hym that me wroght,
Ne I know not the, knyght, thy cort ne thi name.   400
Bot teche me truly therto and telle me howe thou hattes,
And I schal ware alle my wyt to wynne me theder,
And that I swere the for sothe, and by my seker traweth.'
'That is innogh in New Yer, hit nedes no more,'
Quoth the gome in the grene to Gawan the hende,   405
'Yif I the telle trwly, quen I the tape have

_____

372 "Watch out, cousin," said the king, "that you concentrate on the blow"
(_cut_; cf. N.E. _carve_).

369 *left*

373 *advise* (l. 363)/*promptly* (l. 367)
374 *blow* (l. 290)
375 *man/ax* (l. 288)
376 *boldly/was disturbed* (cf. N.E. *abased*)/*more*

378 *repeat/pact/further*
379 *ask* (cf. N.E. *oath*)/*are called*
380 *believe*

384 *man* (l. 314)
385 *alive*

388 *marvelously* (l. 23)

391 *take/fist/asked* (ll. 279, 324)

393 *cleanly, clearly*
394 *certain, assure* (l. 265)
395 *believe* (l. 140)
396 *found/earth* (l. 196)/*fetch*
397 *assemblage*
398 *seek*
399 *dwell* (cf. l. 257)

401 *are called* (l. 379)
402 *use/thither*
403 *trusty, certain* (l. 265, etc.)

406 *tap*

And thou me smothely has smyten, smartly I the teche
Of my hous and my home and myn owen nome,
Then may thou frayst my fare and forwardes holde;
And if I spende no speche, thenne spedes thou the better,   410
For thou may leng in thy londe and layt no fyrre—
        bot slokes!
    Ta now thy grymme tole to the,
    And let se how thou cnokes.
    'Gladly, sir, for sothe,'   415
    Quoth Gawan. His ax he strokes.

            20

The grene knyght upon grounde graythely hym dresses,
A littel lut with the hede, the lere he discoveres,
His longe lovelych lokkes he layd over his croun,
Let the naked nec to the note schewe.   420
Gauan gripped to his ax, and gederes hit on hyght,
The kay fot on the fold he before sette,
Let hit doun lyghtly lyght on the naked,
That the scharp of the schalk schyndered the bones,
And schrank thurgh the schyire grece and schade hit in twynne,   425
That the bit of the broun stel bot on the grounde.
The fayre hede fro the halce hit to the erthe,
That fele hit foyned wyth her fete, there hit forth roled;
The blod brayd fro the body, that blykked on the grene;
And nawther faltered ne fel the freke never the helder,   430
Bot stythly he start forth upon styf schonkes,
And runyschly he raght out, there as renkkes stoden,
Laght to his lufly hed and lyft hit up sone;
And sythen bowes to his blonk, the brydel he cachches,
Steppes into stelbawe and strydes alofte,   435
And his hede by the here in his honde haldes;
And as sadly the segge hym in his sadel sette
As non unhap had hym ayled, thagh hedles he were
        in stedde.
    He brayde his bulk aboute,   440
    That ugly bodi that bledde;
    Moni on of hym had doute,
    Bi that his resouns were redde.

        21

For the hede in his honde he haldes up even,

411 *linger/seek/further* (l. 378)
412 *stop*
413 *Take/tool*
414 *knocks*

417 *readily/prepares*
418 *bowed* (cf. l. 248)/*flesh/uncovers*

420 *business* (l. 358)
421 *gathers*
422 *left*

424 *man* (l. 160)/*cleft*
425 *sank/fair/grease, fat/severed/two*
426 *bit*
427 *neck* (cf. N.E. *halter*)
428 *many/kicked*
429 *spurted/shown* (l. 305)
430 *more* (l. 376)
431 *stoutly/shanks*
432 *furiously* (l. 304)/*reached/men* (l. 303)
433 *Latched on* (l. 328)
434 *horse*
435 *steel-bow, stirrup*

437 *firmly*
438 *As* (*if*)/*mishap* (ll. 48, 56)

440 *drew*

443 *declared*

Toward the derrest on the dece he dresses the face,   445
And hit lyfte up the yghe-lyddes and loked ful brode,
And meled thus much with his muthe, as ye may now here:
'Loke, Gawan, thou be graythe to go as thou hettes,
And layte as lelly til thou me, lude, fynde,
As thou has hette in this halle, herande thise knyghtes;   450
To the grene chapel thou chose, I charge the, to fotte
Such a dunt as thou has dalt—disserved thou habbes
To be yederly yolden on Nw Yeres morn.
The knyght of the grene chapel men knowen me mony;
Forthi me for to fynde if thou fraystes, fayles thou never.   455
Therfore com, other recreaunt be calde the behoves.'
With a runisch rout the raynes he tornes,
Halled out at the hal dor, his hed in his hande,
That the fyr of the flynt flaghe fro fole hoves.
To quat kyth he becom knwe non there,   460
Never more then thay wyste fram quethen he was wonnen.
      What thenne?
   The kyng and Gawen thare
   At that grene thay laghe and grenne,
   Yet breved was hit ful bare   465
   A mervayl among tho menne.

22

Thagh Arther the hende kyng at hert hade wonder,
He let no semblaunt be sene, bot sayde ful hyghe
To the comlych quene wyth cortays speche,
'Dere dame, to-day demay yow never;   470
Wel bycommes such craft upon Cristmasse,
Laykyng of enterludes, to laghe and to syng,
Among thise kynde caroles of knyghtes and ladyes.
Never the lece to my mete I may me wel dres,
For I haf sen a selly, I may not forsake.'   475
He glent upon Sir Gawen, and gaynly he sayde,
'Now sir, heng up thyn ax, that has innogh hewen';
And hit was don abof the dece on doser to henge,
Ther alle men for mervayl myght on hit loke,
And bi trwe tytel therof to telle the wonder,   480
Thenne thay bowed to a borde thise burnes togeder,
The kyng and the gode knyght, and kene men hem served
Of alle dayntyes double, as derrest myght falle;
Wyth alle maner of mete and mynstralcie bothe,

445 *dearest/addresses*

447 *spoke/mouth*
448 *prompt/promised*
449 *seek* (l. 411)/*loyally/man* (l. 232)
450 *within hearing of*
451 *choose* (*your way*)/*fetch*
452 *dint/dealt*
453 *promptly/yielded*

456 *or*
457 *rough* (cf. l. 432)/*jerk*

459 *fire/flew/horse's* (l. 196)
460 *land/becomes, befits*
461 *knew/whence/had come*

464 *laughed/grinned*
465 *recorded/completely* (cf. l. 277)

470 *dismay*

472 *Playing* (cf. l. 262)

474 *less/address, direct* (l. 445)
475 *marvel* (l. 239)
476 *glanced*

478 *tapestry*

Wyth wele walt thay that day, til worthed an ende   485
    in londe.
  Now thenk wel, Sir Gawan,
  For wothe that thou ne wonde
  This aventure for to frayn
  That thou has tan on honde.   490

485 *weal/wielded/came*

488 *danger* (l. 222)/*neglect*
489 *ask* (l. 359)
490 *taken*

PART II

23(1)

This hanselle has Arthur of aventurus on fyrst
In yonge yer, for he yerned yelpyng to here.
Thagh hym wordes were wane when thay to sete wenten,
Now ar thay stoken of sturne werk, stafful her hond.
Gawan was glad to begynne those gomnes in halle,⁣   495
Bot thagh the ende be hevy, haf ye no wonder;
For thagh men ben mery in mynde quen thay han mayn drynk,
A yere yernes ful yerne and yeldes never lyke,
The forme to the fynisment foldes ful selden.
Forthi this Yol overyede, and the yere after,⁣   500
And uche sesoun serlepes sued after other:
After Crystenmasse com the crabbed lentoun,
That fraystes flesch wyth the fysche and fode more symple;
Bot thenne the weder of the worlde wyth wynter hit threpes,
Colde clenges adoun, cloudes uplyften,⁣   505
Schyre schedes the rayn in schowres ful warme,
Falles upon fayre flat, flowres there schewen,
Bothe groundes and the greves grene ar her wedes,
Bryddes busken to bylde and bremlych syngen
For solace of the softe somer that sues therafter⁣   510
    bi bonk;
    And blossumes bolne to blowe
    Bi rawes rych and ronk,
    Then notes noble innoghe
    Ar herde in wod so wlonk.⁣   515

24(2)

After, the sesoun of somer wyth the soft wyndes,
Quen Zeferus syfles hymself on sedes and erbes;
Wela wynne is the wort that waxes theroute,
When the donkande dewe dropes of the leves
To bide a blysful blusch of the bryght sunne.⁣   520
Bot then hyghes hervest and hardenes hym sone,
Warnes hym for the wynter to wax ful rype.
He dryves wyth droght the dust for to ryse,
Fro the face of the folde to flyghe ful hyghe;
Wrothe wynde of the welkyn wrasteles with the sunne,⁣   525

491 *gift* (l. 66)
492 *boasting*
493 *lacking*
494 *stocked/jam-full*

497 *"have strong drink"* (ll. 187, 336)
498 *passes/quickly*
499 *first/finish/matches/seldom*
500 *over-passed, went by*
501 *in turn/followed*
502 *Lent*
503 *tests*
504 *contests*

506 *Fair* (l. 317)/*sheds*
507 *plain*
508 *groves* (l. 207)
509 *Birds/bustle/brilliantly*
510 *bliss*
511 *bank* (l. 14)
512 *bulge/bloom*
513 *rows/rank*

515 *lovely*

517 *blows*
518 *Very/joyous/plant*
519 *dampening* (cf. N.E. *dank*)

525 *heaven*

The leves lancen from the lynde and lyghten on the grounde,
And al grayes the gres that grene was ere;
Thenne al rypes and rotes that ros upon fyrst,
And thus yirnes the yere in yisterdayes mony,
And wynter wyndes agayn, as the worlde askes,   530
   no fage,
  Til Meghelmas mone
  Was cumen wyth wynter wage;
  Then thenkkes Gawan ful sone
  Of his anious vyage.   535

25(3)

Yet quyl Al-hal-day with Arther he lenges;
And he made a fare on that fest for the frekes sake,
With much revel and ryche of the Rounde Table.
Knyghtes ful cortays and comlych ladies
Al for luf of that lede in longynge thay were,   540
Bot never the lece ne the later thay nevened bot merthe:
Mony ioyles for that ientyle iapes ther maden.
For aftter mete with mournyng he meles to his eme,
And spekes of his passage and pertly he sayde,
'Now, lege lorde of my lyf, leve I yow ask;   545
Ye knowe the cost of this cace, kepe I no more
To telle yow tenes therof, never bot trifel;
Bot I am boun to the bur barely to-morne
To sech the gome of the grene, as God wyl me wysse.'
Thenne the best of the burgh bowed togeder,   550
Aywan, and Errik, and other ful mony,
Sir Doddinaval de Savage, the duk of Clarence,
Launcelot, and Lyonel, and Lucan the gode,
Sir Boos and Sir Bydver, big men bothe,
And mony other menskful, with Mador de la Port.   555
Alle this compayny of court com the kyng nerre
For to counseyl the knyght, with care at her hert.
There was much derve doel driven in the sale
That so worthé as Wawan schulde wende on that ernde
To dryghe a delful dynt and dele no more   560
   wyth bronde.
  The knyght mad ay god chere,
  And sayde, 'Quat schuld I wonde?
  Of destinés derf and dere
  What may mon do bot fonde?'   565

526 *tree*

528 *rots*
529 *runs*
530 *needs*
531 *honestly*
532 *Michaelmas moon*

535 *troublesome trip*

536 *while, until/All Hallows' Day/lingers* (l. 411)

541 *nevertheless/named* (l. 65)
542 *joyless/gentle* (*one*)/*jests*
543 *speaks* (l. 447)/*uncle* (l. 356)

547 *troubles* (l. 22)
548 *blow* (l. 374)
549 *guide*

555 *courteous* (*ones*)

558 *sad/sorrowing, dole*
559 *Gawayn/go/errand*
560 *endure/doleful*

563 *fear* (l. 488)
564 *grievous* (l. 558)/*gentle*
565 *try*

26(4)

He dowelles ther al that day and dresses on the morn,
Askes erly hys armes and alle were thay broght.
Fyrst a tulé tapit tyght over the flet,
And miche was the gyld gere that glent theralofte;
The stif mon steppes theron and the stel hondeles,   570
Dubbed in a dublet of a dere tars,
And sythen a crafty capados, closed aloft,
That wyth a bryght blaunner was bounden withinne.
Thenne set thay the sabatouns upon the segge fotes,
His leges lapped in stel with luflych greves,   575
With polaynes piched therto, policed ful clene,
Aboute his knes knaged with knotes of golde;
Queme quyssewes then, that coyntlych closed
His thik thrawen thyghes, with thwonges to tachched;
And sythen the brawden bryné of bryght stel rynges   580
Umbeweved that wygh upon wlonk stuffe,
And wel bornyst brace upon his bothe armes,
With gode cowters and gay and gloves of plate,
And alle the godlych gere that hym gayn schulde
        that tyde;   585
    Wyth ryche cote-armure,
    His gold spores spend with pryde,
    Gurde wyth a bront ful sure
    With silk sayn umbe his syde.

27(5)

When he was hasped in armes, his harnays was ryche—   590
The lest lachet other loupe lemed of golde.
So harnayst as he was he herknes his masse,
Offred and honoured at the heghe auter.
Sythen he comes to the kyng and to his cort-feres,
Laches lufly his leve at lordes and ladyes,   595
And thay hym kyst and conveyed, bikende hym to Kryst.
Bi that was Gryngolet grayth and gurde with a sadel
That glemed ful gayly with mony golde frenges,
Ayquere naylet ful nwe, for that note ryched;
The brydel barred aboute, with bryght golde bounden;   600
The apparayl of the payttrure and of the proude skyrtes,
The cropore and the covertor, acorded wyth the arsounes;

566 *dwells*

568 *Toulousian/tapestry/placed/floor* (l. 294)
569 *much/gilt*
570 *handles, touches*
571 *Tharsian fabric*
572 *hooded cape* (l. 186)
573 *fur*
574 *shoes/man's*

576 *knee armor/pitched, set/polished*
577 *pegged*
578 *Fine/leg armor/quaintly, skilfully/enclosed*
579 *twisted/thongs/attached*
580 *tunic of mail*
581 *Enveloped* (l. 181n.)/*fine* (l. 515)
582 *burnished*
583 *elbow armor*

587 *fastened*
588 *brand*
589 *girdle* (O.Fr. *ceint*, cf. N.E. *cinch*)

591 *least = smallest/or/gleamed*
592 *hears*
593 *altar*
594 *companions* (cf. l. 267)
595 *"Takes . . . leave from"*
596 *escorted/commend*
597 *ready* (l. 448)

599 *Everywhere/nailed/business/readied*

601 *breast gear* (l. 168)
602 *cover-cloth/saddlebows* (l. 171)

And al was rayled on red ryche golde nayles,
That al glytered and glent as glem of the sunne.
Thenne hentes he the helme and hastily hit kysses,   605
That was stapled stifly and stoffed wythinne.
Hit was hyghe on his hede, hasped bihynde,
Wyth a lyghtly urysoun over the aventayle,
Enbrawden and bounden wyth the best gemmes
On brode sylken borde, and bryddes on semes   610
As papiayes paynted pervyng bitwene,
Tortors and trulofes entayled so thyk
As mony burde theraboute had ben seven wynter
    in toune.
    The cercle was more o prys   615
    That umbeclypped hys croun,
    Of diamauntes a devys
    That bothe were bryght and broun.

        28(6)

Then thay schewed hym the schelde, that was of schyr goules
Wyth the pentangel* depaynt of pure golde hwes.   620
He braydes hit by the bauderyk, aboute the hals kestes,
That bisemed the segge semlyly fayre.
And quy the pentangel apendes to that prynce noble
I am intent yow to telle, thof tary hyt me schulde:
Hit is a syngne that Salamon set sumquyle   625
In bytoknyng of trawthe, bi tytle that hit habbes,
For hit is a figure that haldes fyve poyntes,
And uche lyne umbelappes and loukes in other,
And ayquere hit is endeles, and Englych hit callen
Overal, as I here, the endeles knot.   630
Forthy hit acordes to this knyght and to his cler armes,
For ay faythful in fyve and sere fyve sythes
Gawan was for gode knawen and as golde pured
Voyded of uche vylany wyth vertues ennourned
    in mote.   635
    Forthy the pentangel nwe
    He ber in schelde and cote,
    As tulk of tale most trwe
    And gentylest knyght of lote.

---

620 Gawain's emblem, the pentangle, was a five-pointed figure made with a
single, unbroken—endless—stroke, signifying perfection.

603 *arrayed* (l. 163)

605 *seizes*

608 *silk ban/metal helmet guard*

610 *band/birds* (l. 509)
611 *popinjays/periwinkle*
612 *Turtles (doves)/trueloves*
613 *maids, embroiderers*
614 *in the town (engaged in the making of it)*
615 *of price, precious*
616 *surrounded*

619 *fair* (l. 506)/*gules, red*
620 *painted*
621 *draws/neck* (l. 427)/*casts*

624 *though*
625 *sign/somewhile, once*

632 *each/times*

634 *adorned*
635 *moat = castle*

638 *man*
639 *saying* (l. 244)

29(7)

Fyrst he was funden fautles in his fyve wyttes,   640
And efte fayled never the freke in his fyve fyngres.
And alle his afyaunce upon folde was in the fyve woundes
That Cryst kaght on the croys, as the crede telles;
And quere-so-ever thys mon in melly was stad,
His thro thoght was in that, thurgh alle other thynges,   645
That alle his forsnes he feng at the fyve joyes
That the hendé heven quene had of hir chylde;
At this cause the knyght comlyche hade
In the inore half of his schelde hir ymage depaynted,
That quen he blusched therto his belde never payred.   650
The fyft fyve that I finde that the frek used
Was fraunchyse and felawschyp forbe al thyng,
His clannes and his cortaysye croked were never,
And pité, that passes alle poyntes, thyse pure fyve
Were harder happed on that hathel then on any other.   655
Now alle these fyve sythes, for sothe, were fetled on this knyght,
And uchone halched in other, that non ende hade,
And fyched upon fyve poyntes that fayld never,
Ne samned never in no syde, ne sundred nouther,
Withouten ende at any noke aiquere, I fynde,   660
Whereever the gomen bygan, or glod to an ende.
Therfore on his schene schelde schapen was the knot
Ryally wyth red golde upon rede gowles,
That is the pure pentaungel wyth the peple called
         with lore.   665
   Now graythed is Gawan gay,
   And laght his launce ryght thore,
   And gef hem alle goud day,
   He wende for ever more.

30(8)

He sperred the sted with the spures and sprong on his way,   670
So stif that the ston-fyr stroke out therafter.
Al that segh that semly syked in hert,
And sayde sothly al same segges til other,
Carande for that comly, 'Bi Kryst, hit is scathe
That thou, leude, schal be lost, that art of lyf noble!   675
To fynde hys fere upon folde, in fayth, is not ethe.
Warloker to haf wroght had more wyt bene,

640 *found/faultless*

642 *trust* (cf. N.E. *affiance*)
643 *caught, received/cross*
644 *melee* (l. 342)/*placed*
645 *intense*
646 *forcefulness/took* (l. 391)

649 *inner*
650 *when/looked/courage/(was) impaired*

652 *generosity/before*
653 *cleanness, purity*

655 *clamped* (cf. N.E. *hasp*)/*knight* (l. 323, etc.)
656 *fixed*
657 *held* (l. 218)
658 *fixed*
659 *joined*
660 *nook, spot/everywhere* (ll. 599, 629)
661 *device* (*game*)/*glided*

663 *gules* (l. 619)

667 *latched, took* (l. 127, etc.)/*there*

671 *struck*
672 *saw/seemly* (*one*)/*sighed*
673 *to*
674 *shame*
675 *man*
676 *equal/earth/easy*
677 *more wary*

And haf dyght yonder dere a duk to have worthed;
A lowande leder of ledes in londe hym wel semes,
And so had better haf ben then britned to noght,   680
Hadet wyth an alvisch mon, for angardes pryde.
Who knew ever any kyng such counsel to take
As knyghtes in cavelaciouns on Crystmasse gomnes!'
Wel much was the warme water that waltered of yghen,
When that semly syre soght fro tho wones   685
    thad daye.
  He made non abode,
  Bot wyghtly went hys way;
  Mony wylsum way he rode,
  The bok as I herde say.   690

31(9)

Now rides this renk thurgh the ryalme of Logres,
Sir Gauan, on Godes halve, thagh hym no gomen thoght.
Oft leudles alone he lenges on nyghtes,
Ther he fonde noght hym byfore the fare that he lyked.
Hade he no fere bot his fole bi frythes and dounes,   695
Ne no gome bot God bi gate wyth to karp,
Til that he neghed ful neghe into the Northe Wales.
Alle the iles of Anglesay on lyft half he haldes,
And fares over the fordes by the forlondes,
Over at the Holy Hede, til he hade eft bonk   700
In the wyldrenesse of Wyrale; wonde ther bot lyte
That auther God other gome wyth goud hert lovied.
And ay he frayned, as he ferde, at frekes that he met,
If thay hade herde any karp of a knyght grene,
In any grounde theraboute, of the grene chapel;   705
And al nykked hym wyth nay, that never in her lyve
Thay seghe never no segge that was of suche hwes
    of grene.
  The knyght tok gates straunge
  In mony a bonk unbene,   710
  His cher ful oft con chaunge
  That chapel er he myght sene.

32(10)

Mony klyf he overclambe in contrayes straunge,
Fer floten fro his frendes, fremedly he rydes.
At uche warthe other water ther the wyghe passed   715

678 *bedight, dubbed/duke/become*
679 *brilliant*
680 *broken* (l. 2)
681 *Beheaded/elvish/excessive*

683 *cavilations, disputes*
684 *weltered/eyes*
685 *dwelling*

687 *stop*

689 *wandering*

692 *game*
693 *man-less, without companion/stays, lingers* (l. 536)

695 *horse/woods/downs*
696 *man/(the) way/talk* (l. 377)

698 *"he keeps on the left"*

700 *afterward, again/bank* (ll. 14, 511)
701 *lived* (l. 50)*/little*
702 *either/or*
703 *"asked . . . of"/went*

706 *denied*

710 *unfair* (cf. Fr. *bien*, N.E. *benefit*, etc.)
711 *expression* (l. 334)*/did* (l. 362)

713 *climbed over*
714 *Far/fleeted/as a stranger*
715 *ford*

He fonde a foo hym byfore, bot ferly hit were,
And that so foule and so felle that feght hym byhode.
So mony mervayl bi mount ther the mon fyndes,
Hit were to tore for to telle of the tenthe dole.
Sumwhyle wyth wormes he werres and with wolves als,   720
Sumwhyle wyth wodwos, that woned in the knarres,
Bothe wyth bulles and beres and bores otherquyle,
And etaynes that hym anelede of the heghe felle;
Nade he ben dughty and dryghe and dryghtyn had served,
Douteles he hade ben ded and dreped ful ofte.   725
For werre wrathed hym not so much that wynter was wors,
When the colde cler water fro the cloudes schadde,
And fres er hit falle myght to the fale erthe;
Ner slayn wyth the slete he sleped in his yrnes
Mo nyghtes then innoghe in naked rokkes,   730
Ther as claterande fro the crest the colde borne rennes,
And henged heghe over his hede in hard iisse-ikkles.
Thus in peryl and payne and plytes ful harde
Bi contray caryes this knyght, tyl Krystmasse even,
      al one.   735
   The knyght wel that tyde
   To Mary made his mone,
   That ho hym red to ryde
   And wysse hym to sum wone.

33(11)

Bi a mounte on the morne meryly he rydes   740
Into a forest ful dep that ferly was wylde,
Highe hilles on uche a halve and holtwodes under
Of hore okes ful hoge a hundreth togeder;
The hasel and the hawthorne were harled al samen,
With roghe raged mosse rayled aywhere,   745
With mony bryddes unblythe upon bare twyges,
That pitosly ther piped for pyne of the colde.
The gome upon Gryngolet glydes hem under,
Thurgh mony misy and myre, mon al hym one,
Carande for his costes, lest he ne kever schulde   750
To se the servyse of that syre, that on that self nyght
Of a burde was borne oure baret to quelle;
And therfore sykyng he sayde, 'I beseche the, lorde,
And Mary, that is myldest moder so dere,
Of sum herber ther heghly I myght here masse,   755

716 *foe/wondrous*
717 *fierce/behoved*

719 *difficult* (l. 165)/*deal, part*
720 *dragons/wars*
721 *satyrs/dwelled* (l. 701)/*crags*

723 *giants* (l. 140)/*pursued/cliff*
724 *Hadn't/constant* (l. 335)/(*the*) *Lord*
725 *killed*

727 *shed*
728 *froze/faded*
729 *irons* (l. 215)

731 *stream/runs*
732 *icicles*

734 *rides* (l. 43)

737 *moan*
738 *she/would advise*
739 *direct/dwelling* (l. 257)

741 *wondrously*

743 *oaks/huge*
744 *intertwined/together* (l. 673)

749 *swamp/alone*
750 *condition/cover, manage*
751 *same*
752 *maid* (l. 613)/*strife* (l. 353)
753 *sighing* (l. 672)

755 *harbor/highly, devoutly*

Ande thy matynes to-morne, mekely I ask,
And therto prestly I pray my *pater* and *ave*
   and crede.'
   He rode in his prayere,
   And cryed for his mysdede,   760
   He sayned hym in sythes sere,
   And sayde 'Cros Kryst me spede!'

34(12)

Nade he sayned hymself, segge, bot thrye,
Er he was war in the wod of a won in a mote,
Abof a launde, on a lawe, loken under boghes,   765
Of mony borelych bole aboute bi the diches:
A castel the comlokest that ever knyght aghte,
Pyched on a prayere, a park al aboute,
With a pyked palays pyned ful thik,
That umbetewe mony tre mo then two myle.   770
That holde on that on syde the hathel avysed,
As hit schemered and schon thurgh the schyre okes;
Thenne has he hendly of his helme, and heghly he thonkes
Jesus and sayn Gilyan, that gentyle ar bothe,
That cortaysly had hym kydde, and his cry herkened.   775
'Now bone hostel,' cothe the burne, 'I beseche yow yette!'
Thenne gerdes he to Gryngolet with the gilt heles,
And he ful chauncely has chosen to the chef gate,
That broght bremly the burne to the bryge ende
   in haste.   780
   The bryge was breme upbrayde,
   The yates wer stoken faste,
   The walles were wel arayed,
   Hit dut no wyndes blaste.

35(13)

The burne bode on bonk, that on blonk hoved,   785
Of the depe double dich that drof to the place;
The walle wod in the water wonderly depe,
Ande eft a ful huge heght hit haled up on lofte
Of harde hewen ston up to the tables,
Enbaned under the abataylment in the best lawe;   790
And sythen garytes ful gaye gered bitwene,
Wyth mony luflych loupe that louked ful clene.
A better barbican that burne blusched upon never.

756 *matins*
757 *promptly* (cf. *presto*)

761 *signed/several* (l. 632)

763 *Had not* (l. 724)/*signed, crossed/thrice*
764 *aware/dwelling* (l. 739)/*moat* (l. 635)
765 *knoll*
766 *strong, burly/tree trunks*
767 *owned*
768 *Pitched/meadow* (cf. N.E. *prairie*)
769 *piked, spiked/enclosed*
770 *surrounded*

774 *St. Julian*
775 *shown*
776 O.Fr. *bon hostel* 'Good lodging'/*quoth*
777 *girds/heels*
778 *chosen* (*his way*)
779 *quickly/bridge*

781 *stoutly/drawn up*
782 *gates/stuck, shut*

784 *feared*

785 *horse/halted, hove* (*to*)

787 *waded*

789 *cornices*
790 "*With horn-work below the battlement . . ."/style*
791 *turrets*
792 *loop(holes)/locked*
793 *outer fortification*

And innermore he behelde that halle ful hyghe,
Towres telded bytwene, trochet ful thik,   795
Fayre fylyoles that fyghed and ferlyly long,
With corvon coprounes craftyly sleghe.
Chalkwhyt chymnees ther ches he innoghe
Upon bastel roves, that blenked ful quyte;
So mony pynakle payntet was poudred ayquere,   800
Among the castel carneles clambred so thik,
That pared out of papure purely hit semed.
The fre freke on the fole hit fayr innoghe thoght,
If he myght kever to com the cloyster wythinne,
To herber in that hostel whyl halyday lested,   805
    avinant.
    He calde and sone ther com
    A porter pure plesaunt,
    On the wal his ernd he nome,
    And haylsed the knyght erraunt.   810

36(14)

'Gode sir,' quoth Gawan, 'woldes thou go myn ernde
To the hegh lorde of this hous, herber to crave?'
'Ye, Peter,' quoth the porter, 'and purely I trowee
That ye be, wyghe, welcum to won quyle yow lykes.'
Then yede the wyghe agayn swythe,   815
And folke frely hym wyth, to fonge the knyght.
Thay let doun the grete draght and derely out yeden,
And kneled doun on her knes upon the colde erthe
To welcum this ilk wygh as worthy hom thoght;
Thay yolden hym the brode yate, yarked up wyde,   820
And he hem raysed rekenly and rod over the brygge.
Sere segges hym sesed by sadel, quel he lyght,
And sythen stabeled his stede stif men innoghe.
Knyghtes and swyeres comen doun thenne
For to bryng this buurne wyth blys into halle;   825
Quen he hef up his helme, ther highed innoghe
For to hent hit at his honde, the hende to serven;
His bronde and his blasoun bothe thay token.
Then haylsed he ful hendly tho hatheles uchone,
And mony proud mon ther presed that prynce to honour.   830
Alle hasped in his hegh wede to halle thay hym wonnen,
Ther fayre fyre upon flet fersly brenned.
Thenne the lorde of the lede loutes fro his chambre

795 pitched/pinnacled
796 pinnacles/fitted/marvelously (l. 716)
797 carved/capitals/made slyly, skilfully
798 chose, picked out
799 bastille/roofs/white
800 powdered, set around
801 battlement embrasures
802 paper
803 noble (l. 101)
804 cover, manage (l. 750)

806 fittingly

809 errand (l. 559)/took
810 hailed (l. 223)

813 St. Peter (oath, approp. for a gatekeeper)
814 dwell (l. 701)
815 went/quickly (l. 8)
816 receive (l. 391)
817 drawbridge
818 their
819 same/them
820 yielded/gate/set
821 motioned to rise/courteously
822 Several (l. 761)/seized/while/lighted (down)

824 squires
825 man
826 hied (l. 521)
827 take (l. 605)
828 shield

831 weeds, clothes/brought
832 floor (l. 568)/burned
833 people/turns (l. 248)

For to mete wyth menske the mon on the flor;
He sayde, 'Ye ar welcum to welde as yow lykes;   835
That here is, al is yowre awen, to have at yowre wylle
    and welde.'
'Graunt mercy,' quoth Gawayn,
'Ther Kryst hit yow foryelde';
As frekes that semed fayn   840
Ayther other in armes con felde.

37(15)

Gawayn glyght on the gome that godly hym gret,
And thught hit a bolde burne that the burgh aghte,
A hoge hathel for the nones, and of hyghe eldee;
Brode, bryght, was his berde, and al bever-hwed,   845
Sturne, stif on the strythe on stalworth schonkes,
Felle face as the fyre, and fre of hys speche;
And wel hym semed, for sothe, as the segge thught,
To lede a lortschyp in lee of leudes ful gode.
The lorde hym charred to a chambre and chefly cumaundes   850
To delyver hym a leude, hym loghly to serve;
And there were boun at his bode burnes innoghe,
That broght hym to a bryght boure, ther beddyng was noble,
Of cortynes of clene sylk wyth cler bolde hemmes,
And covertores ful curious with comlych panes,   855
Of bryght blaunner above enbrawded bisydes,
Rudeles rennande on ropes, red golde rynges,
Tapites tyght to the wowe of tuly and tars,
And under fete, on the flet, of folwande sute.
Ther he was dispoyled, wyth speches of myerthe,   860
The burn of his bruny and of his bryght wedes.
Ryche robes ful rad renkkes hym broghten,
For to charge and to chaunge and chose of the best.
Sone as he on hent, and happed therinne,
That sete on hym semly wyth saylande skyrtes,   865
The ver by his visage verayly hit semed
Welnegh to uche hathel, alle on hwes,
Lowande and lufly alle his lymmes under,
That a comloker knyght never Kryst made
    hem thoght.
        Whethen in worlde he were,   870
        Hit semed as he moght

834 *courtesy* (l. 834)
835 *wield, use*
836 *own*

839 *repay*

841 *Each/did/fold*

842 *glanced*
843 *owned*
844 *huge/indeed/high, advanced/age* (cf. N.E. *elder*)

846 *stance*
847 *fierce* (l. 717)

849 *protection* (cf. N.E. *alee, leeward*)
850 *took*
851 *lowly, humbly*
852 *ready*
853 *bower*
854 *curtains*
855 *coverlets* (l. 602)
856 *fur* (l. 573)
857 *Curtains/running*
858 *Tapestries/tied/wall/Toulousian and Tharsian fabrics* (ll. 568, 571)
859 *following/suit*
860 *stripped*
861 *mail shirt* (l. 580)
862 *promptly*

864 *one/took* (l. 827)/*wrapped* (l. 655)
865 *sailing*
866 *spring*

868 *gleaming* (l. 236)

871 *Wherever*

Be prynce withouten pere
In felde ther felle men foght.

38(16)

A cheyer byfore the chemné, ther charcole brenned,   875
Was graythed for Sir Gawan graythely with clothes,
Whyssynes upon queldepoyntes that koynt wer bothe;
And thenne a meré mantyle was on that mon cast
Of a broun bleeaunt, enbrauded ful ryche
And fayre furred wythinne with felles of the best,   880
Alle of ermyn inurnde, his hode of the same;
And he sete in that settel semlych ryche,
And achaufed hym chefly, and thenne his cher mended.
Sone was telded up a tabil on trestes ful fayre,
Clad wyth a clene clothe that cler quyt schewed,   885
Sanap and salure and sylverin spones.
The wyghe wesche at his wylle and went to his mete.
Segges hym served semly innoghe
Wyth sere sewes and sete, sesounde of the best,
Double-felde, as hit falles, and fele kyn fisches,   890
Summe baken in bred, summe brad on the gledes,
Summe sothen, summe in sewe savered with spyces,
And ay sawes so sleghe that the segge lyked.
The freke calde hit a fest ful frely and ofte
Ful hendely, quen alle the hatheles rehayted hym at ones   895
    as hende:
'This penaunce now ye take,
And eft hit schal amende.'
That mon much merthe con make,
For wyn in his hed that wende.   900

39(17)

Thenne was spyed and spured upon spare wyse
Bi prevé poyntes of that prynce, put to hymselven,
That he beknew cortaysly of the court that he were,
That athel Arthure the hende haldes hym one,
That is the ryche ryal kyng of the Rounde Table,   905
And hit was Wawen hymself that in that won syttes,
Comen to that Krystmasse, as case hym then lymped.
When the lorde hade lerned that he the leude hade,
Loude laghed he therat, so lef hit hym thoght,
And alle the men in that mote maden much joye   910

875 *chair*
876 *coverings*
877 *Cushions/quilted covers/skilful* (l. 578)

879 *costly fabric*
880 *skins*
881 *decorated*
882 *seat*
883 *warmed* (cf. N.E. *chafing dish*, etc.)
884 *pitched, set* (l. 795)/*trestles*

886 *Overcloth/salt dish*
887 *washed* (l. 72)

889 *soups/excellent*
890 *Doublefold/many*
891 *grilled/coals*
892 *boiled*
893 *sauces/subtle* (l. 797)

895 *exhorted*

901 *asked/sparing, discreet*
902 *polite*
903 *revealed*
904 *noble*

907 *chance/happened*

909 *dear* (l. 49n.)
910 *moat* = *castle* (l. 635)

To apere in his presense prestly that tyme,
That alle prys and prowes and pured thewes
Apendes to hys persoun and praysed is ever,
Byfore alle men upon molde his mensk is the most.
Uch segge ful softly sayde to his fere: 915
'Now schal we semlych se sleghtes of thewes
And the teccheles termes of talkyng noble,
Wich spede is in speche unspurd may we lerne,
Syn we haf fonged that fyne fader of nurture.
God has geven uus his grace godly for sothe,   920
That such a gest as Gawan grauntes uus to have,
When burnes blythe of his burthe schal sitte
      and synge.
   In menyng of maneres mere
   This burne now schal uus bryng,   925
   I hope that may hym here
   Schal lerne of luf-talkyng.'

                    40(18)

Bi that the diner was done and the dere up,
Hit was negh at the niyght neghed the tyme.
Chaplaynes to the chapeles chosen the gate,   930
Rungen ful rychely, ryght as thay schulden,
To the hersum evensong of the hyghe tyde.
The lorde loutes therto and the lady als,
Into a cumly closet coyntly ho entres.
Gawan glydes ful gay and gos theder sone;   935
The lorde laches hym by the lappe and ledes hym to sytte,
And couthly hym knowes and calles hym his nome,
And sayde he was the welcomest wyghe of the worlde;
And he hym thonkked throly and ayther halched other,
And seten soberly samen the servise quyle.   940
Thenne lyst the lady to loke on the knyght,
Thenne com ho of hir closet with mony cler burdes.
Ho was the fayrest in felle, of flesche and of lyre,
And of compas and colour and costes, of alle other,
And wener then Wenore, as the wyghe thoght.   945
He ches thurgh the chaunsel to cheryche that hende.
An other lady hir lad bi the lyft honde,
That was alder then ho, an auncian hit semed,
And heghly honowred with hatheles aboute.
Bot unlyke on to loke tho ladyes were,   950

911 *quickly* (l. 757)
912 *price, worth/prowess/customs*

914 *honor* (l. 834)
915 *companion* (l. 695)
916 *skills* (cf. N.E. *sleight of hand*)
917 *flawless*
918 *unasked* (cf. l. 901)
919 *received, welcomed* (ll. 391, 816)

921 *guest*

929 *nigh/neared, drawn* (cf. l. 697)
930 *way* (cf. l. 778)

932 *devout/season*

934 *pew/she*

936 *lapel*
937 *obviously*

939 *intensely* (l. 645)/*together/hugged* (l. 657)
940 *while, time* (*of*)

942 *maids* (l. 752)
943 *skin* (l. 880)/*face* (l. 318)
944 *formation/disposition*
945 *lovelier/Guenivere*
946 *chose* (*his way*)/*chancel/cherish*
947 *led*

For if the yonge was yep, yolwe was that other;
Riche red on that on rayled ayquere,
Rugh ronkled chekes that other on rolled;
Kerchofes of that on, wyth mony cler perles,
Hir brest and hir bryght throte bare displayed,   955
Schon schyrer then snawe that schedes on hilles;
That other wyth a gorger was gered over the swyre,
Chymbled over hir blake chyn with chalkquyte vayles,
Hir frount folden in sylk, enfoubled ayquere,
Toret and treleted with tryfles aboute,   960
That noght was bare of that burde bot the blake browes,
The tweyne yghen and the nase, the naked lyppes,
And those were soure to se and sellyly blered;
A mensk lady on molde mon may hir calle,
       for Gode!   965
  Hir body was schort and thik,
  Hir buttokes balgh and brode,
  More lykkerwys on to lyk
  Was that scho hade on lode.

41(19)

When Gawayn glyght on that gay, that graciously loked,   970
Wyth leve laght of the lorde he went hem agaynes;
The alder he haylses, heldande ful lowe,
The loveloker he lappes a lyttel in armes,
He kysses hir comlyly and knyghtly he meles.
Thay kallen hym of aquoyntaunce and he hit quyk askes   975
To be her servaunt sothly, if hemself lyked.
Thay tan hym bytwene hem, wyth talkyng hym leden
To chambre, to chemné, and chefly thay asken
Spyces, that unsparely men speded hom to bryng,
And the wynnelych wyne therwith uche tyme.   980
The lorde luflych aloft lepes ful ofte,
Mynned merthe to be made upon mony sythes,
Hent heghly of his hode and on a spere henged,
And wayved hom to wynne the worchip therof,
That most myrthe myght meve that Crystenmas whyle—   985
'And I schal fonde, bi my fayth, to fylter wyth the best,
Er me wont the wede with help of my frendes.'
Thus wyth laghande lotes the lorde hit tayt makes,
For to glade Sir Gawayn with gomnes in halle
       that nyght,   990

951 *fresh* (l. 284)/*yellow*
952 *one/arrayed* (l. 745)
953 *Rough/wrinkled*
954 *Kerchiefs*

956 *fairer* (l. 702)/*sheds* (l. 506)
957 *gorget, throat scarf/neck* (l. 186)
958 *Wrapped*
959 *enveloped*
960 *Towering/trellised*

963 *strangely* (l. 475)/*bleared*
964 *honored* (l. 834)

967 *rounded, bulging*
968 *delicious*
969 *lead, leading*

971 *against, toward*
972 *bowing*

974 *speaks* (l. 543)

977 *take/lead*

979 *them*
980 *delightful* (cf. l. 518)

982 *Commanded*
983 *off/hood*
984 *ownership*

986 *try* (l. 565)/*contend*
987 *lack*
988 *words* (l. 639)/*merry*

Til that hit was tyme
The lord comaundet lyght;
Sir Gawen his leve con nyme
And to his bed hym dight.

42(20)

On the morne, as uche mon mynes that tyme   995
That Dryghtyn for oure destyné to deye was borne,
Wele waxes in uche a won in worlde for his sake;
So did hit there on that day thurgh dayntés mony:
Bothe at mes and at mele messes ful quaynt
Derf men upon dece drest of the best.   1000
The olde auncian wyf heghest ho syttes,
The lorde lufly her by lent, as I trowe;
Gawan and the gay burde togeder thay seten,
Even inmyddes, as the messe metely come,
And sythen thurgh al the sale, as hem best semed,   1005
Bi uche grome at his degré graythely was served.
Ther was mete, ther was myrthe, ther was much ioye,
That for to telle therof hit me tene were,
And to poynte hit yet I pyned me paraventure.
Bot yet I wot that Wawen and the wale burde   1010
Such comfort of her compaynye caghten togeder
Thurgh her dere dalyaunce of her derne wordes,
Wyth clene cortays carp, closed fro fylthe,
That hor play was passande uche prynce gomen,
      in vayres.   1015
   Trumpes and nakerys,
   Much pypyng ther repayres;
   Uche mon tented hys,
   And thay two tented thayres.

43(21)

Much dut was ther dryven that day and that other,   1020
And the thryd as thro thronge in therafter;
The ioye of sayn Jones day was gentyle to here,
And was the last of the layk, leudes ther thoghten.
Ther wer gestes to go upon the gray morne,
Forthy wonderly thay woke, and the wyn dronken,   1025
Daunsed ful dreghly wyth dere caroles.
At the last, when hit was late, thay lachen her leve,
Uchon to wende on his way that was wyghe stronge.

993 *take*
994 *went*

995 *remembers*
996 *Lord* (l. 724)/*die*

999 *mess, table*
1000 *Bold* (l. 564)

1002 *went*

1004 *in the middle*

1008 *trouble* (l. 547)

1010 *choice* (l. 398)
1011 *caught, got*
1012 *conversation/private*
1013 *talk* (l. 704)
1014 *surpassing/princely*
1015 *truth*
1016 *Trumpets/drums*
1017 *piping/is present*
1018 *attended/his* (*own affairs*)

1020 *delight*
1021 *intense* (l. 645)
1022 *St. John's*
1023 *amusement* (ll. 262, 472)
1024 *guests*

1026 *unceasingly* (l. 724)

1028 "*not of the household*"

Gawan gef hym god day, the god mon hym lachches,
Ledes hym to his awen chambre, the chymné bysyde,   1030
And there he drawes hym on dryghe and derely hym thonkkes
Of the wynne worschip that he hym wayved hade,
As to honour his hous on that hyghe tyde,
And enbelyse his burgh with his bele chere.
'Iwysse sir, quyl I leve, me worthes the better   1035
That Gawayn has ben my gest at Goddes awen fest.'
'Grant merci, sir,' quoth Gawayn, 'in god fayth hit is yowres,
Al the honour is your awen—the heghe kyng yow yelde!
And I am wyghe at your wylle to worch youre hest,
As I am halden therto, in hyghe and in lowe,   1040
    bi right.'
    The lorde fast can hym payne
    To holde lenger the knyght.
    To hym answares Gawayn,
    Bi non way that he myght.   1045

44(22)

Then frayned the freke ful fayre at himselven
Quat derve dede had hym dryven at that dere tyme
So kenly fro the kynges kourt to kayre al his one,
Er the halidayes holly were halet out of toun.
'For sothe, sir,' quoth the segge, 'ye sayn bot the trawthe,   1050
A heghe ernde and a hasty me hade fro tho wones,
For I am sumned myselfe to sech to a place,
I ne wot in worlde whederwarde to wende hit to fynde.
I nolde bot if I hit negh myght on Nw Yeres morne
For alle the londe inwyth Logres, so me oure lorde help!   1055
Forthy, sir, this enquest I require yow here,
That ye me telle with trawthe if ever ye tale herde
Of the grene chapel, quere hit on grounde stondes,
And of the knyght that hit kepes, of colour of grene.
Ther was stabled bi statut a steven uus bytwene   1060
To mete that mon at that mere, yif I myght last;
And of that ilk Nw Yere bot neked now wontes,
And I wolde loke on that lede, if God me let wolde,
Gladloker, bi Goddes sun, then any god welde!
Forthi, iwysse, bi yowre wylle, wende me bihoves,   1065
Naf I now to busy bot bare thre dayes,
And me als fayn to falle feye as fayly of myyn ernde.
Thenne laghande quoth the lorde, 'Now leng the byhoves,

1029 *latches, catches*

1031 *holds/backs* (l. 724)
1032 *shown*

1034 *embellish*
1035 *Indeed/live/become* (l. 678)

1039 *behest*

1042 *did/urge, take pains*

1047 *bold* (l. 1000)
1048 *ride* (l. 43)
1049 *wholly/gone*

1051 *dwelling*
1052 *summoned*
1053 *whither*
1054 *"I only wish I might be near it . . ."*

1056 *question/inquire*

1060 *established/appointment*
1061 *landmark*
1062 *little*

1064 *Gladlier/goods/wield, possess*

1066 *Have* + neg./*to* (be) *busy*
1067 *fay, fated to death/fail*
1068 *linger*

For I schal teche yow to that terme bi the tymes ende,
The grene chapayle upon grounde, greve yow no more;   1070
Bot ye schal be in yowre bed, burne, at thyn ese,
Quyle forth dayes, and ferk on the fyrst of the yere,
And cum to that merk at mydmorn, to make quat yow likes
   in spenne.
    Dowelles whyle New Yeres daye,   1075
    And rys, and raykes thenne,
    Mon schal yow sette in waye,
    Hit is not two myle henne.'

45(23)

Thenne was Gawan ful glad, and gomenly he laghed:
'Now I thonk yow thryvandely thurgh alle other thynge,   1080
Now acheved is my chaunce, I schal at your wylle
Dowelle, and elles do quat ye demen.'
Thenne sesed hym the syre and set hym bysyde,
Let the ladies be fette to lyke hem the better.
Ther was seme solace by hemself stille;   1085
The lorde let for luf lotes so myry,
As wygh that wolde of his wyte, ne wyst quat he myght.
Thenne he carped to the knyght, criande loude,
'Ye han demed to do the dede that I bidde;
Wyl ye halde this hes here at thys ones?'   1090
'Ye, sir, for sothe,' sayd the segge trwe,
'Whyl I byde in yowre borghe, be bayn to yowre hest.'
'For ye haf travayled,' quoth the tulk, 'towen fro ferre,
And sythen waked me wyth, ye arn not wel waryst
Nauther of sostnaunce ne of slepe, sothly I knowe;   1095
Ye schal lenge in your lofte, and lyghe in your ese
To-morn quyle the messequyle, and to mete wende
When ye wyl, wyth my wyf, that wyth yow schal sitte
And comfort yow with compayny, til I to cort torne;
   ye lende,   1100
    And I schal erly ryse,
    On huntyng wyl I wende.'
    Gauayn grantes alle thyse,
    Hym heldande, as the hende.

46(24)

'Yet firre,' quoth the freke, 'a forwarde we make: 1105
Quat-so-ever I wynne in the wod hit worthes to youres,

1069 *meeting place*

1071 *ease*
1072 *Until late in the day/ride*

1074 *in that place*
1075 *Dwell/until*
1076 *wander*

1078 *hence*

1079 *delightedly*
1080 *thrivingly*

1082 *deem*

1084 *fetched/please*
1085 *seemly*
1086 *let (out), said/words (l. 988)*
1087 *(right) mind/know not/was doing*

1090 *behest/at once*

1092 *obedient*
1093 *come/far*
1094 *kept awake/recovered*

1097 *until (l. 1072)/masstime*

1099 *return*
1100 *stay*

1104 *bowed (l. 972)*

1105 *further/pact (l. 409)*

And quat chek so ye acheve chaunge me therforne.
Swete, swap we so, sware with trawthe,
Quether, leude, so lymp lere other better.'
'Bi God,' quoth Gawayn the gode, 'I graunt thertylle,   1110
And that yow lyst for to layke, lef hit me thynkes.'
'Who brynges uus this beverage, this bargayn is maked':
So sayde the lorde of that lede; thay laghed uchone,
Thay dronken and daylyeden and dalten untyghtel,
Thise lordes and ladyes, quyle that hem lyked;   1115
And sythen with frenkysch fare and fele fayre lotes
Thay stoden and stemed and stylly speken,
Kysten ful comlyly and kaghten her leve.
With mony leude ful lyght and lemande torches
Uche burne to his bed was broght at the laste,   1120
    ful softe.
  To bed yet er thay yede,
  Recorded covenauntes ofte;
  The olde lorde of that leude
  Cowthe wel halde layk alofte.   1125

1107 *gain/exchange/therefore*

1109 *"for better or worse"*
1110 *thereto*
1111 *to play* (cf. l. 1023)/*dear*

1114 *dallied/dealt/unrestraint*, i.e., *"with abandon"*

1116 *French, fashionable/many*
1117 *stopped/stilly, quietly*

1119 *gleaming* (l. 591)

1122 *went*

1125 *Could, knew how*

PART III

47(1)

Ful erly bifore the day the folk uprysen,
Gestes that go wolde hor gromes thay calden,
And thay busken up bilyve blonkkes to sadel
Tyffen her takles, trussen her males,
Richen hem the rychest, to ryde alle arayde,   1130
Lepen up lyghtly, lachen her brydeles,
Uche wyghe on his way ther hym wel lyked.
The leve lorde of the londe was not the last
Arayed for the rydyng, with renkkes ful mony;
Ete a sop hastyly, when he hade herde masse,   1135
With bugle to bent-felde he buskes bylyve.
By that any daylyght lemed upon erthe,
He with his hatheles on hyghe horsses weren.
Thenne thise cacheres that couthe cowpled hor houndes,
Unclosed the kenel dore and calde hem theroute,   1140
Blwe bygly in bugles thre bare mote;
Braches bayed therfore and breme noyse maked;
And thay chastysed and charred on chasyng that went,
A hundreth of hunteres, as I haf herde telle,
    of the best.   1145
  To trystors vewters yod,
  Couples huntes of kest;
  Ther ros for blastes gode
  Gret rurd in that forest.

48(2)

At the fyrst quethe of the quest quaked the wylde;   1150
Der drof in the dale, doted for drede,
Highed to the hyghe, bot heterly thay were
Restayed with the stablye, that stoutly ascryed.
Thay let the herttes haf the gate, with the hyghe hedes,
The breme bukkes also with hor brode paumes;   1155
For the fre lorde hade defende in fermysoun tyme
That ther schulde no mon meve to the male dere.
The hindes were halden in with hay! and war!
The does dryven with gret dyn to the depe slades;
Ther myght mon se, as thay slypte, slentyng of arwes—   1160

1127 *grooms*
1128 *bustled/briskly/horses* (l. 785)
1129 *Readied/gear/bags*
1130 *Dressed*

1136 *grass-field* (l. 353)/*hurries/quickly*
1137 *By* (*the time*) *that*

1139 *kennelmen/coupled*

1141 *single notes*
1142 *Brachets, hounds/fierce* (l. 781)
1143 *turned back* (l. 850)

1146 *waiting places/dogkeepers/went*
1147 *hunters/cast off*

1149 *din*

1150 *notice* (cf. *quoth*)/*wild* (*beings*)
1151 *stunned* (cf. N.E. *dotty, dotage*)
1152 *Hied/high* (*ground*)/*fiercely*
1153 *Stayed/circle of beaters/cried*

1155 *palms, palm-like horn parts*
1156 *close season*
1157 *move, bother*

1159 *glades*
1160 *slipped/slanting/arrows*

At uche wende under wande wapped a flone—
That bigly bote on the broun with ful brode hedes.
What! thay brayen and bleden, bi bonkkes thay deyen,
And ay rachches in a res radly hem folwes,
Hunteres wyth hyghe horne hasted hem after   1165
Wyth such a crakkande kry as klyffes haden brusten.
What wylde so atwaped wyghes that schotten
Was al toraced and rent at the resayt,
Bi thay were tened at the hyghe and taysed to the wattres;
The ledes were so lerned at the lowe trysteres,   1170
And the grehoundes so grete, that geten hem bylyve
And hem tofylched, as fast as frekes myght loke,
        ther ryght.
    The lorde for blys abloy
    Ful oft con launce and lyght,   1175
    And drof that day wyth joy
    Thus to the derk nyght.

49(3)

Thus laykes this lorde by lynde-wodes eves,
And Gawayn the god mon in gay bed lyges,
Lurkkes quyl the daylyght lemed on the wowes,   1180
Under covertour ful clere, cortyned aboute;
And as in slomeryng he slode, sleghly he herde
A littel dyn at his dor, and derfly upon;
And he heves up his hed out of the clothes,
A corner of the cortyn he caght up a lyttel,   1185
And waytes warly thiderwarde quat hit be myght.
Hit was the ladi, loflyest to beholde,
That drogh the dor after hir ful dernly and stylle,
And bowed towarde the bed, and the burne schamed,
And layde hym doun lystyly, and let as he slepte;   1190
And ho stepped stilly and stel to his bedde,
Kest up the cortyn and creped withinne,
And set hir ful softly on the bed-syde,
And lenged there selly longe to loke quen he wakened.
The lede lay lurked a ful longe quyle,   1195
Compast in his concience to quat that cace myght
Meve other amount—to mervayle hym thoght,
Bot yet he sayde in hymself, 'More semly hit were
To aspye wyth my spelle in space quat ho wolde.'
Then he wakenede, and wroth, and to hir warde torned,   1200

1161 *turn/wood/arrow*
1162 *bit/brown (hide)/heads*
1163 *die*
1164 *rachets, hounds/rush/quickly* (l. 367)

1166 *"as if cliffs had burst"*
1167 *Whatever/wild (things)/escaped*
1168 *completely razed, torn down/receipt*
1169 *tormented/teased*
1170 *waiting places* (l. 1146)
1171 *quickly* (l. 1136)
1172 *pulled apart*

1174 *transported*

1178 *sports* (cf. l. 1125)/*eaves, edges*
1179 *lies*
1180 *walls* (l. 858)

1182 *slid/slyly* (l. 893)
1183 *boldly* (l. 1000)/*open*

1188 *stealthily* (l. 183)
1189 *ashamed, embarrassed*
1190 *artfully/pretended*

1194 *wondrously* (l. 963)

1196 *Turned over/case, occasion*
1197 *Move (on to)/or/amount (to)*

1199 *discover/speech* (l. 209)/*would, wishes*
1200 *writhed/toward her*

And unlouked his yghe-lyddes, and let as hym wondered,
And sayned hym, as bi his saye the saver to worthe,
   with hande.
Wyth chynne and cheke ful swete,
Bothe quit and red in blande,   1205
Ful lufly con ho lete,
Wyth lyppes smal laghande.

50(4)

'God moroun, Sir Gawayn,' sayde that gay lady,
'Ye ar a sleper unslyghe, that mon may slyde hider;
Now ar ye tan astyt! Bot true uus may schape,   1210
I schal bynde yow in your bedde, that be ye trayst';
Al laghande the lady lance tho bourdes.
'Goud moroun, gay,' quoth Gawayn the blythe,
'Me schal worthe at your wille, and that me wel lykes,
For I yelde me yederly and yeye after grace,   1215
And that is the best, be my dome, for me byhoves nede':
And thus he bourded agayn with mony a blythe laghter.
'Bot wolde ye, lady lovely, then leve me grante,
And deprece your prysoun and pray hym to ryse,
I wolde bowe of this bed and busk me better,   1220
I schulde kever the more comfort to karp yow wyth.'
'Nay for sothe, beau sir,' sayd that swete,
'Ye schal not rise of your bedde, I rych yow better,
I schal happe yow here that other half als,
And sythen karp wyth my knyght that I kaght have;   1225
For I wene wel, iwysse, Sir Wowen ye are,
That alle the worlde worchipes quere-so ye ride;
Your honour, your hendelayk is hendely praysed
With lordes, wyth ladyes, with alle that lyf bere.
And now ye ar here, iwysse, and we bot oure one;   1230
My lorde and his ledes ar on lenthe faren,
Other burnes in her bedde, and my burdes als,
The dor drawen and dit with a derf haspe;
And sythen I have in this hous hym that al lykes,
I schal ware my whyle wel, quyl hit lastes   1235
   with tale.
   Ye ar welcum to my cors,
   Yowre awen won to wale,
   Me behoves of fyne force
   Your servaunt be, and schale.'   1240

1202 *signed, crossed/saying/safer/become*

1205 *white/blend*
1206 *did she behave* (l. 1201)

1208 *Good morning*
1209 *"You must be . . . if"*
1210 *taken/at once/truce*
1211 *sure, trust*
1212 *lanced, threw/jests*

1215 *promptly* (l. 453)/*cry* (l. 67)
1216 *by/judgment/of need*

1219 *release/prisoner*
1220 *off/dress*
1221 *cover, obtain/talk (to)* (l. 1088)

1223 *direct*
1224 *hold* (l. 864)
1225 *afterward* (l. 791)
1226 *think* (l. 669)

1228 *hende-ness, courtesy*

1231 *length/gone*

1233 *locked/stout* (l. 1183)
1234 *since* (l. 1094)
1235 *use* (l. 402)

1237 *corpse, body*
1238 *own/course/choose* (l. 398)

51(5)

'In god fayth,' quoth Gawayn, 'gayn hit me thynkkes,
Thagh I be not now he that ye of speken;
To reche to such reverence as ye reherce here
I am wyghe unworthy, I wot wel myselven.
Bi God, I were glad, and yow god thoght,   1245
At sawe other at servyce that I sette myght
To the plesaunce of your prys—hit were a pure ioye.'
'In god fayth, Sir Gawayn,' quoth the gay lady,
'The prys and the prowes that pleses al other,
If I hit lakked other set at lyght, hit were littel daynté;   1250
Bot hit ar ladyes innoghe that lever wer nowthe
Haf the, hende, in hor holde, as I the habbe here,
To daly with derely your daynté wordes,
Kever hem comfort and colen her cares
Then much of the garysoun other golde that thay haven.   1255
Bot I louue that ilke lorde that the lyfte haldes,
I haf hit holly in my honde that al desyres,
        Thurghe grace.'
Scho made hym so gret chere,
That was so fayr of face,   1260
The knyght with speches skere
Answered to uche a cace.

52(6)

'Madame,' quoth the myry mon, 'Mary yow yelde,
For I haf founden, in god fayth, yowre fraunchis nobele;
And other ful much of other folk fongen hor dedes,   1265
Bot the daynté that thay delen for my disert nysen,
Hit is the worchyp of yourself, that noght bot wel connes.'
'Bi Mary,' quoth the menskful, 'me thynk hit an other;
For were I worth al the wone of wymmen alyve,
And al the wele of the worlde were in my honde,   1270
And I schulde chepen and chose to cheve me a lorde,
For the costes that I haf knowen upon the, knyght, here,
Of bewté and debonerté and blythe semblaunt,
And that I haf er herkkened and halde hit here trwee,
Ther schulde no freke upon folde bifore yow be chosen.'   1275
'Iwysse, worthy,' quoth the wyghe, 'ye haf waled wel better,
Bot I am proude of the prys that ye put on me,

1246 *"In words or deeds . . ."*

1250 *held/lightly/courtesy*
1251 *liefer/now*

1254 *Cover, obtain* (l. 1221)/*cool*
1255 *treasure*
1256 *praise/very* (l. 819)/*heaven* (cf. N.G. *Luft*, N.E. *loft*)
1257 *wholly* (l. 1049)

1261 *pure*
1262 *every/item*

1263 *repay* (l. 1038), or oath, as in Shks. usage
1264 *generosity* (l. 652)
1265 *from/(have) taken* (l. 919)/*customs*
1266 *courtesy* (l. 1250)/*attribute to/merit/is not (so)*
1267 *good/knows*

1269 *company*

1271 *barter* (cf. N.E. *cheap*)/*get*

1273 *bearing*
1274 *true*

1276 *chosen* (l. 1238)

And, soberly your servaunt, my soverayn I holde yow,
And yowre knyght I becom, and Kryst yow foryelde.'
Thus thay meled of muchquat til mydmorn paste,   1280
And ay the lady let lyk as hym loved mych;
The freke ferde with defence, and feted ful fayre.
'Thagh I were burde bryghtest,' the burde in mynde hade,
'The lasse luf in his lode'—for lur that he soght
        boute hone,   1285
    The dunte that schulde hym deve,
    And nedes hit most be done.
    The lady thenn spek of leve,
    He granted hir ful sone.

53(7)

Thenne ho gef hym god day, and wyth a glent laghed.   1290
And as ho stod, ho stonyed hym wyth ful stor wordes:
'Now he that spedes uche spech this disport yelde yow!
Bot that ye be Gawan, hit gos in mynde.'
'Querfore?' quoth the freke and freschly he askes,
Ferde lest he hade fayled in fourme of his castes;   1295
Bot the burde hym blessed and bi this skyl sayde:
'So god as Gawayn gaynly is halden,
And cortaysye is closed so clene in hymselven,
Couth not lyghtly haf lenged so long wyth a lady,
Bot he had craved a cosse, bi his courtaysye,   1300
Bi sum towch of summe tryfle at sum tales ende.'
Then quoth Wowen, 'Iwysse, worthe as yow lykes;
I schal kysse at your comaundement, as a knyght falles,
And fire, lest he displese yow, so plede hit no more.'
Ho comes nerre with that and caches hym in armes,   1305
Loutes luflych adoun and the leude kysses.
Thay comly bykennen to Kryst ayther other;
Ho dos hir forth at the dore withouten dyn more;
And he ryches hym to ryse and rapes hym sone,
Clepes to his chamberlayn, choses his wede,   1310
Bowes forth, quen he was boun, blythely to masse;
And thenne he meved to his mete that menskly hym keped,
And made myry al day, til the mone rysed,
        with game.
    Was never freke fayrer fonge   1315
    Bitwene two so dyngne dame,

1280 *talked* (l. 974)/*much*
1281 *acted as if* (l. 1201)

1283 *thought*
1284 *less/leading/loss*
1285 *but, without/delay*
1286 *dint/fell*
1287 *must*
1288 *leaving*

1290 *glance*
1291 *astonished/strong*

1293 *goes* (l. 375)

1295 *speeches* (l. 249)

1300 *kiss*
1301 *touch, hint*
1302 *let* (*it*) *be*

1304 *further*

1306 *Bends* (l. 418)
1307 *commend/each*
1308 *goes*
1309 *prepares* (l. 1223)/*hurries*
1310 *Calls*
1311 *ready* (l. 852)
1312 *worthily* (l. 914)/*waited*

1315 *received* (l. 919)
1316 *worthy*

The alder and the yonge;
Much solace set thay same.

54(8)

And ay the lorde of the londe is lent on his gamnes,
To hunt in holtes and hethe at hyndes barayne;   1320
Such a sowme he ther slowe bi that the sunne heldet,
Of dos and of other dere, to deme were wonder.
Thenne fersly thay flokked in folk at the laste,
And quykly of the quelled dere a querré thay maked.
The best bowed therto with burnes innoghe,   1325
Gedered the grattest of gres that ther were,
And didden hem derely undo as the dede askes;
Serched hem at the asay summe that ther were,
Two fyngeres thay fonde of the fowlest of alle.
Sythen thay slyt the slot, sesed the erber,   1330
Schaved wyth a scharp knyf and the schyre knitten,
Sythen rytte thay the foure lymmes and rent of the hyde,
Then brek thay the balé, the boweles out token,
Lystily forlaucyng the lere of the knot;
Thay gryped to the gargulun, and graythely departed,   1335
The wesaunt fro the wynt-hole and walt out the guttes;
Then scher thay out the schulderes with her scharp knyves,
Haled hem by a lyttel hole to have hole sydes.
Sithen britned thay the brest and brayden hit in twynne,
And eft at the gargulun bigynes on thenne,   1340
Ryves hit up radly ryght to the byght,
Voydes out the avanters and verayly therafter,
Alle the rymes by the rybbes radly thay lance;
So ryde thay of by resoun bi the rygge bones,
Evenden to the haunche, that henged alle samen,   1345
And heven hit up al hole, and hwen hit of there,
And that thay neme for the noumbles bi nome, as I trowe,
    bi kynde;
  Bi the byght al of the thyghes
  The lappes thay lance bihynde;   1350
  To hewe hit in two thay hyghes,
  Bi the bakbon to unbynde.

55(9)

Bothe the hede and the hals thay hwen of thenne,
And sythen sunder thay the sydes swyft fro the chyne,

1319 *occupied*
1320 *barren, without young*
1321 *sum/slew/sank* (l. 972)
1322 *deem, judge*
1323 *proudly/group*
1324 *quarry*

1326 *fat* (l. 425)
1327 *had/undone, cut up/requires*

1329 *Two fingers' (thickness of fat)*
1330 *indenture at throat base/gullet*
1331 *fair, white (flesh)/tied*
1332 *cut*
1333 *belly*
1334 *Skilfully* (l. 1190)*/(without) loosening/ligature*
1335 *throat* (cf. N.E. *gargle*)*/parted*
1336 *esophagus/wind-/threw*

1338 *Drew/whole*
1339 *broke* (l. 2)*/pulled* (l. 621)

1341 *Rips/crotch*
1342 *edible entrails of deer, found in neck* (cf. N.Fr. *avant*)
1343 *membranes*
1344 *rid/reasonably/ridge, back*
1345 *Evened*
1346 *heaved/hewed*
1347 *name/offal/name*

1350 *(skin) flaps*

1352 *backbone*

1353 *neck* (l. 621)
1354 *backbone*

And the corbeles fee thay kest in a greve;   1355
Thenn thurled thay ayther thik side thurgh by the rybbe,
And henged thenne ayther bi hoghes of the fourches,
Uche freke for his fee, as falles for to have.
Upon a felle of the fayre best fede thay thayr houndes
Wyth the lyver and the lyghtes, the lether of the paunches,   1360
And bred bathed in blod blende ther-amonges.
Baldely thay blw prys, bayed thayr rachches,
Sythen fonge thay her flesche, folden to home,
Strakande ful stoutly mony stiff motes.
Bi that the daylyght was done the douthe was al wonen   1365
Into the comly castel, ther the knyght bides
      ful stille,
   Wyth blys and bryght fyr bette.
   The lorde is comen thertylle;
   When Gawayn wyth hym mette,   1370
   Ther was bot wele at wylle.

                    56(10)

Thenne comaunded the lorde in that sale to samen alle the meny,
Bothe the ladyes on loghe to lyght with her burdes
Bifore alle the folk on the flette, frekes he beddes
Verayly his venysoun to fech hym byforne,   1375
And al godly in gomen Gawayn he called,
Teches hym to the tayles of ful tayt bestes,
Schewes hym the schyree grece schorne upon rybbes.
'How payes yow this play? Haf I prys wonnen?
Have I thryvandely thonk thurgh my craft served?'   1380
'Ye iwysse,' quoth that other wyghe, 'here is wayth fayrest
That I segh this seven yere in sesoun of wynter.'
'And al I gif yow, Gawayn,' quoth the gome thenne,
'For by acorde of covenaunt ye crave hit as your awen.'
'This is soth,' quoth the segge, 'I say yow that ilke: 1385
That I haf worthyly wonnen this wones wythinne,
Iwysse with as god wylle hit worthes to youres.'
He hasppes his fayre hals his armes wythinne,
And kysses hym as comlyly as he couthe awyse:
'Tas yow there my chévicaunce, I cheved no more;   1390
I wowche hit saf fynly, thagh feler hit were.'
'Hit is god,' quoth the god mon, 'graunt mercy therfore.
Hit may be such, hit is the better, and ye me breve wolde
Where ye wan this ilk wele bi wytte of yorselven.'

1355 *ravens/cast/grove*
1356 *pierced*
1357 *hocks/forks*

1359 *skin* (l. 943)/*beast*

1361 *bread/blood*
1362 *blew, announced/(the) take*
1363 *turned* (l. 499)
1364 *Sounding/single notes* (l. 1141)
1365 *company/won, come*

1368 *fire/kindled*

1372 *company* (l. 101)
1373 *"to alight below, down to the hall"*
1374 *bids*

1377 *Shows/tails/robust* (l. 988)

1380 *deserved*
1381 *game, meat*

1389 *devise*
1390 *Take/gain/achieved* (l. 1271)
1391 *vouch/completely/more* (cf. l. 890)

1393 *declare, brief*
1394 *won*

'That was not forward,' quoth he, 'frayst me no more,   1395
For ye haf tan that yow tydes, trawe ye non other
        ye mowe.'
Thay laghed, and made hem blythe
Wyth lotes that were to lowe;
To soper thay yede as-swythe,   1400
Wyth dayntés nwe innowe.

57(11)

And sythen by the chymné in chamber thay seten,
Wyghes the walle wyn weghed to hem oft,
And efte in her bourdyng thay baythen in the morn
To fylle the same forwardes that thay byfore maden;   1405
Wat chaunce so bytydes hor chevysaunce to chaunge,
What nwes so thay nome, at naght quen thay metten.
Thay acorded of the covenauntes byfore the court alle;
The beverage was broght forth in bourde at that tyme,
Thenne thay lovelych leghten leve at the last,   1410
Uche burne to his bedde busked bylyve.
Bi that the coke hade crowen and cakled bot thryse,
The lorde was lopen of his bedde, the leudes uch one;
So that the mete and the masse was metely delyvered,
The douthe dressed to the wod, er any day sprenged,   1415
        to chace;
    Hegh with hunte and hornes
    Thurgh playnes thay passe in space,
    Uncoupled among tho thornes
    Raches that ran on race.   1420

58(12)

Sone thay calle of a quest in a ker syde,
The hunt rehayted the houndes that hit fyrst mynged,
Wylde wordes hym warp wyth a wrast noyce;
The howndes that hit herde hastid thider swythe,
And fellen as fast to the fuyt, fourty at ones;   1425
Thenne such a glaver ande glam of gedered rachches
Ros that the rocheres rungen aboute;
Hunteres hem hardened with horne and wyth muthe.
Then al in a semblé sweyed togeder
Bitwene a flosche in that fryth and a foo cragge;   1430
In a knot bi a clyffe, at the kerre syde,
Ther as the rogh rocher unrydely was fallen,

1395 *agreed, the arrangement/ask* (ll. 391, 455, etc.)
1396 *taken* (l. 1210)/*betides/expect*
1397 *may*

1399 *praise* (l. 1256)
1400 *supper/went* (l. 1122)/*quickly*

1403 *choice* (l. 1010) *wine/brought*
1404 *joking* (cf. l. 1212)/*agreed*

1406 *exchange*
1407 *new* (*things*)/*took/night*

1410 *took, leave*

1412 *cock*
1413 *leaped*
1414 *duly*
1415 *company* (l. 1365)/*turned* (l. 445)/*sprang*
1416 *chase, hunt*
1417 *hunters* (l. 1147)

1420 *hounds* (l. 1362)

1421 *marsh*
1422 *exhorted* (l. 895)/*attracted*
1423 *cast* (l. 224)/*loud*

1425 *trail*
1426 *racket/din*
1427 *rocky hills*
1428 *urged on*
1429 *assembly*
1430 *pool/wood/fearsome*

1432 *as* (*if*)/*rough/in disorder*

Thay ferden to the fyndyng and frekes hem after,
Thay umbekesten the knarre and the knot bothe,
Wyghes, whyl thay wysten wel wythinne hem hit were,   1435
The best that ther breved was wyth the blodhoundes.
Thenne thay beten on the buskes and bede hym upryse,
And he unsoundyly out soght segges overthwert;
On the sellokest swyn swenged out there,
Long sythen fro the sounder that wight for olde.   1440
For he was breme, bor alther grattest,
Fulgrymme quen he gronyed, thenne greved mony,
For thre at the fyrst thrast he thryght to the erthe,
And sparred forth good sped boute spyt more.
Thise other halowed hyghe! ful hyghe, and hay! hay! cryed,   1445
Haden hornes to mouthe, heterly rechated;
Mony was the myry mouthe of men and of houndes
That buskkes after this bor with bost and wyth noyse
        to quelle.
    Ful ofte he bydes the baye,   1450
    And maymes the mute inn melle;
    He hurtes of the houndes, and thay
    Ful yomerly yaule and yelle.

59(13)

Schalkes to schote at hym schowen to thenne,
Haled to hym of her arewes, hitten hym oft;   1455
Bot the poyntes payred at the pyth that pyght in his scheldes,
And the barbes of his browe bite non wolde,
Thagh the schaven schaft schyndered in peces;
The hede hypped agayn were-so-ever hit hitte.
Bot quen the dyntes hym dered of her dryghe strokes,   1460
Then braynwod for bate, on burnes he rases,
Hurtes hem ful heterly ther he forth hyghes,
And mony arghed therat and on lyte drogen.
Bot the lorde on a lyght horce launces hym after
As burne bolde upon bent his bugle he blowes,   1465
He rechated and rode thurgh rones ful thyk,
Suande this wylde swyn til the sunne schafted.
This day wyth this ilk dede thay dryven on this wyse,
Whyle oure luflych lede lys in his bedde,
Gawayn graythely at home, in geres ful ryche   1470
        of hewe.
    The lady noght forgate

1433 *fared, went* (l. 1282)
1434 *cast around, searched/crag* (l. 721)
1435 *knew* (l. 461)
1436 *announced, briefed* (l. 1393)/*by*
1437 *bushes*
1438 *unwisely/through* (*a path of*)
1439 *One* (*of*)/*sellyest, most wondrous* (l. 475)/*swine, wild boars*
1440 *herd/because of/old age*
1441 *fierce* (l. 1155)/*boar/of all*
1442 *groaned, grunted*
1443 *thrust/pushed*
1444 *without/causing damage*

1446 *fiercely* (l. 1152)/*recall sounded*

1451 *maims/pack/in the midst*

1453 *painfully/yowl*

1454 *Men/shove*

1456 *are impaired/pitched/shields*

1459 *hopped/again/where-*
1460 *harmed/constant* (l. 724)
1461 *brain-wroth, crazy/because of/debate, battle*

1463 *recoiled* (cf. l. 241)/*drew back*

1465 *grass, field* (l. 353)
1466 *blew recall* (l. 1446)/*bushes*
1467 *Pursuing/slanted*

1472 *forgot*

Com to hym to salue;
Ful erly ho was hym ate,
His mode for to remwe.   1475

60(14)

Ho commes to the cortyn, and at the knyght totes.
Sir Wawen her welcumed worthy on fyrst,
And ho hym yeldes ayayn ful yerne of hir wordes,
Settes hir sofly by his syde, and swythely ho laghes,
And wyth a luflych loke ho layde hym thyse wordes   1480
'Sir, yif ye be Wawen, wonder me thynkkes,
Wyghe that is so wel wrast alway to god,
And connes not of compaynye the costes undertake,
And if mon kennes yow hom to knowe, ye kest hom of your mynde;
Thou has foryeten yederly that yisterday I taghtte   1485
Bi alder-truest token of talk that I cowthe.'
'What is that?' quoth the wyghe, 'Iwysse I wot never;
If hit be sothe that ye breve, the blame is myn awen.'
'Yet I kende yow of kyssyng,' quoth the clere thenne,
'Quere-so countenaunce is couthe, quikly to clayme,   1490
That bicumes uche a knyght that cortaysy uses.'
'Do way,' quoth that derf mon, 'my dere, that speche,
For that durst I not do, lest I devayed were;
If I were werned, I were wrang, iwysse, yif I profered.'
'Ma fay,' quoth the meré wyf, 'ye may not be werned,   1495
Ye ar stif innoghe to constrayne wyth strenkthe, yif yow likes,
Yif any were so vilanous that yow devaye wolde.'
'Ye, be God,' quoth Gawayn, 'good is your speche,
Bot threte is unthryvande in thede ther I lende,
And uche gift that is geven not with goud wylle.   1500
I am at your comaundement, to kysse quen yow lykes,
Ye may lach quen yow lyst, and leve quen yow thynkkes,
      in space.'
      The lady loutes adoun,
      And comlyly kysses his face,   1505
      Much speche thay ther expoun
      Of druryes greme and grace.

61(15)

'I woled wyt at yow, wyghe,' that worthy ther sayde,
'And yow wrathed not therwyth, what were the skylle,
That so yong and so yepe as ye at this tyme,   1510

1473 *salute*
1474 *at*
1475 *mood/change*

1476 *peeps*

1478 *eagerly*

1482 *wrested, turned/good*
1483 *knows/society/manners*
1484 *teaches*
1485 *forgotten/promptly* (l. 1215)
1486 *truest of all* (cf. l. 1441)

1489 *bright* (*one*)
1490 *favor/obvious*

1492 *bold* (l. 1000)
1493 *denied*
1494 *refused/wrong/offered*
1495 *My faith*

1499 *unthriving, unworthy/land/live*

1503 (*of time*)

1507 *love's/grief*

1508 *willed/* (*to*) *learn/from*
1509 *were wroth/reason*
1510 *bold* (l. 951)

So cortayse, so knyghtyly, as ye ar knowen oute—
And of alle chevalry to chose, the chef thyng alosed
Is the lel layk of luf, the lettrure of armes;
For to telle of this tevelyng of this trwe knyghtes,
Hit is the tytelet token and tyxt of her werkkes.   1515
How ledes for her lele luf hor lyves han auntered,
Endured for her drury dulful stoundes,
And after wenged with her walour and voyded her care,
And broght blysse into boure with bountees hor awen—
And ye ar knyght comlokest kyd of your elde,   1520
Your worde and your worchip walkes ayquere,
And I haf seten by yourself here sere twyes,
Yet herde I never of your hed helde no wordes
That ever longed to luf, lasse ne more;
And ye, that ar so cortays and coynt of your hetes,   1525
Oghe to a yonke thynk yern to schewe
And teche sum tokenes of trweluf craftes.
Why! ar ye lewed, that alle the los weldes?
Other elles ye demen me to dille your dalyaunce to herken?
    For schame!   1530
  I com hider sengel, and sitte
  To lerne at yow sum game;
  Dos, teches me of your wytte,
  Whil my lorde is fro hame.'

        62(16)

'In goud faythe,' quoth Gawayn, 'God yow foryelde!   1535
Gret is the gode gle and gomen to me huge,
That so worthy as ye wolde wynne hidere,
And pyne yow with so pouer a mon, as play wyth your knyght
With anyskynnes countenaunce, hit keveres me ese;
Bot to take the torvayle to myself to trwluf expoun,   1540
And towche the temes of tyxt and tales of armes
To yow that, I wot wel, weldes more slyght
Of that art, bi the half, or a hundreth of seche
As I am, other ever schal, in erde ther I leve,
Hit were a folé felefolde, my fre, by my trawthe.   1545
I wolde yowre wylnyng worche at my myght,
As I am hyghly bihalden, and evermore wylle
Be servaunt to yourselven, so save me dryghten!'
Thus hym frayned that fre, and fondet hym ofte,
For to haf wonnen hym to woghe, what-so scho thoght elles;   1550

1511 *outside (in the world)*
1512 *praised*
1513 *loyal* (l. 449)/*game* (l. 1125)/*learning*
1514 *tasks*
1515 *titled*
1516 *adventured* (l. 27)
1517 *love* (l. 1507)/*doleful/times*
1518 *(a)venged/valor*

1520 *known* (l. 775)/*age* (l. 844)

1522 *beside you/(at) separate (times)/twice*
1523 *come* (l. 1104)

1525 *quaint, polite* (cf. l. 999)/*promises* (cf. l. 448)
1526 *Ought, owe/young/thing*

1528 *unlearned/reputation*
1529 *empty-headed, silly*

1533 *Do*
1534 *home*

1539 *any kind of/gives* (cf. l. 1221)
1540 *travail*
1541 *themes*
1542 *skill* (l. 916)

1544 *or/shall (be)/earth/live*
1545 *manifold* (cf. l. 890)/*noble (one)* (l. 1156)
1546 *will*

1548 *Lord* (l. 996)
1549 *tested* (l. 986)
1550 *woo*

Bot he defended hym so fayr that no faut semed,
Ne non evel on nawther halve, nawther thay wysten
   bot blysse.
Thay laghed and layked longe;
At the last scho con hym kysse,   1555
Hir leve fayre con scho fonge
And went hir waye, iwysse.

63(17)

Then ruthes hym the renk and ryses to the masse,
And sithen hor diner was dyght and derely served
The lede with the ladyes layked alle day,   1560
Bot the lorde over the londes launced ful ofte,
Swes his uncely swyn, that swynges bi the bonkkes
And bote the best of his braches the bakkes in sunder
Ther he bode in his bay, tel bawemen hit breken,
And madee hym mawgref his hed for to mwe utter,   1565
So felle flones ther flete when the folk gedered.
Bot yet the styffest to start bi stoundes he made,
Til at the last he was so mat he myght no more renne,
Bot in the hast that he myght he to a hole wynnes
Of a rasse bi a rokk ther rennes the boerne.   1570
He gete the bonk at his bak, bigynes to scrape,
The frothe femed at his mouth unfayre bi the wykes,
Whettes his whyte tusches; with hym then irked
Alle the burnes so bolde that hym by stoden
To nye hym on-ferum, bot neghe hym non durst   1575
   for wothe;
He hade hurt so mony byforne
That al thught thenne ful lothe
Be more wyth his tusches torne,
That breme was and braynwod bothe,   1580

64(18)

Til the knyght com hymself, kachande his blonk
Sygh hym byde at the bay, his burnes bysyde;
He lyghtes luflych adoun, leves hir corsour,
Braydes out a bryght bront and bigly forth strydes,
Foundes fast thurgh the forth ther the felle bydes.   1585
The wylde was war of the wyghe with weppen in honde,
Hef hyghly the here, so hetterly he fnast
That fele ferde for the freke, lest felle hym the worre.

1552 *knew* (l. 1435)

1558 *rouses*
1559 *set* (l. 678)

1562 *Pursues* (l. 1467)/*unlucky*
1563 *bit* (l. 1162)/*asunder*
1564 *till/bowmen/broke*
1565 *despite* (Fr. *maugré*)/*move/out* (*of cover*)
1566 *arrows* (l. 1161)
1567 *Even/flinch/at times* (l. 1517)
1568 *exhausted* (l. 336)/*run*

1570 *ledge/stream*

1572 *foamed/corners*
1573 *tusks*

1575 *annoy/*(*from*) *afar*
1576 *danger* (l. 488)

1580 *brain-wroth, mad* (l. 1461)

1581 *horse*
1582 *Sees*

1585 *Goes/fierce* (*one*) (l. 717)

1587 *Heaved/hair/snorted*
1588 *befell/worst*

The swyn settes hym out on the segge even,
That the burne and the bor were bothe upon hepes   1590
In the wyghtest of the water; the worre hade that other,
For the mon merkkes hym wel, as thay mette fyrst,
Set sadly the scharp in the slot even,
Hit hym up to the hult, that the hert schyndered,
And he yarrande hym yelde, and yedoun the water,   1595
    ful tyt.
  A hundreth houndes hym hent,
  That bremely con hym bite,
  Burnes him broght to bent,
  And dogges to dethe endite.   1600

65(19)

There was blawyng of prys in mony breme horne,
Heghe halowing on highe with hatheles that myght;
Brachetes bayed that best, as bidden the maysteres
Of that chargeaunt chace that were chef huntes.
Thenne a wyghe that was wys upon wodcraftes   1605
To unlace this bor lufly bigynnes.
Fyrst he hewes of his hed and on highe settes,
And sythen rendes him al roghe bi the rygge after,
Braydes out the boweles, brennes hom on glede,
With bred blent therwith his braches rewardes.   1610
Sythen he britnes out the brawen in bryght brode cheldes,
And has out the hastlettes, as hightly bisemes;
And yet hem halches al hole the halves togeder,
And sythen on a stif stange stoutly hem henges.
Now with this ilk swyn thay swengen to home;   1615
The bores hed was borne bifore the burnes selven
That him forferde in the forthe thurgh forse of his honde
    so stronge.
  Til he segh Sir Gawayne
  In halle hym thoght ful longe;   1620
  He calde and he com gayn
  His fees ther for to fonge.

66(20)

The lorde ful lowde with lote—and laghed myry
When he seghe Sir Gawayn—with solace he spekes;
The goude ladyes were geten, and gedered the meyny,   1625

1590 *in heaps, fallen*
1591 *fiercest*

1593 *firmly* (l. 437)/*sharp* (*blade*)/*throat hollow* (l. 1330)
1594 *hilt*
1595 *snarling/yielded* (*to*)/*went* (l. 1400) *downstream*
1596 *fast* (l. 299)

1600 *did, brought* (*him*)

1604 *difficult/hunters* (l. 1428)

1609 *coals* (l. 891)

1611 *breaks, cuts* (l. 1339)/*brawn, flesh/shields, slabs* (cf. 1456)
1612 *haslet, edible viscera/fitly*
1613 *fastens* (l. 939)
1614 *pole*

1617 *killed/ford*

1621 *promptly* (l. 1241)

1623 *word(s), speech* (l. 1399)

1625 *household* (l. 1372)

He schewes hem the scheldes and schapes hem the tale
Of the largesse and the lenthe, the lithernes alse
Of the were of the wylde swyn in wod ther he fled.
That other knyght ful comly comended his dedes,
And praysed hit as gret prys that he proved hade,   1630
For suche a brawne of a best, the bolde burne sayde,
Ne such sydes of a swyn segh he never are.
Thenne handeled thay the hoge hed, the hende mon hit praysed,
And let lodly therat the lorde for to here.
'Now, Gawayn,' quoth the god mon, 'this gomen is your awen   1635
Bi fyn forwarde and faste, faythely ye knowe.'
'Hit is sothe,' quoth the segge, 'and as siker trwe
Alle my get I schal yow gif agayn, bi my trawthe.'
He hent the hathel aboute the halse, and hendely hym kysses,
And eftersones of the same he served hym there.   1640
'Now ar we even,' quoth the hathel, 'in this eventide
Of alle the covenauntes that we knyt, sythen I com hider,
        bi lawe.'
    The lorde sayde, 'Bi saynt Gile,
    Ye ar the best that I knowe!   1645
    Ye ben ryche in a whyle,
    Such chaffer and ye drowe.

67(21)

Thenne thay teldet tables trestes alofte,
Kesten clothes upon; clere lyght thenne
Wakned bi wowes, waxen torches;   1650
Segges sette and served in sale al aboute;
Much glam and gle glent up therinne
Aboute the fyre upon flet, and on fele wyse
At the soper and after, mony athel songes,
As coundutes of Krystmasse and caroles newe   1655
With al the manerly merthe that mon may of telle,
And ever oure luflych knyght the lady bisyde.
Such semblaunt to that segge semly ho made
Wyth stille stollen countenaunce, that stalworth to plese,
That al forwondered was the wyghe, and wroth with hymselven   1660
Bot he nolde not for his nurture nurne hir ayaynes,
Bot dalt with hir al in daynté, how-se-ever the dede turned,
        towrast.
    Quen thay hade played in halle
    As longe as hor wylle hom last,   1665

1627 *ferocity/also*
1628 *fighting* (l. 726)

1632 *ere* (l. 239)

1634 *acted/loathly, awed*

1638 *take,* n.

1640 *soon after*

1647 *trade/if/carry on*

1648 *set up* (l. 884)*/trestles* (l. 884)

1650 *Shone/on/walls*

1652 *noise* (l. 1426)

1654 *noble* (l. 904)
1655 *part songs*

1659 *stolen, stealthy/stalwart* (*one*)
1660 *amazed*
1661 *wouldn't/upbringing/refuse*
1662 *dealt*
1663 *completely twisted* (cf. l. 1482)

To chambre he con hym calle,
And to the chemné thay past.

68(22)

Ande ther thay dronken and dalten, and demed eft nwe
To norne on the same note on Nwe Yeres even;
Bot the knyght craved leve to kayre on the morn,   1670
For hit was negh at the terme that he to schulde.
The lorde hym letted of that, to lenge hym resteyed,
And sayde, 'As I am trwe segge, I siker my trawthe
Thou schal cheve to the grene chapel thy charres to make,
Leude, on Nw Yeres lyght, longe bifore pryme.   1675
Forthy thow lye in thy loft and lach thyn ese,
And I schal hunt in this holt, and halde the towches,
Chaunge wyth the chevisaunce, bi that I charre hider;
For I haf fraysted the twys, and faythful I fynde the.
Now 'thrid tyme throwe best' thenk on the morne,   1680
Make we mery quyl we may and mynne upon joye,
For the lur may mon lach when-so mon lykes.'
This was graythely graunted, and Gawayn is lenged,
Blithe broght was hym drynk, and thay to bedde yeden
    with light.   1685
    Sir Gawayn lis and slepes
    Ful stille and softe al night;
    The lorde that his craftes kepes,
    Ful erly he was dight.

69(23)

After messe a morsel he and his men token;   1690
Miry was the mornyng, his mounture he askes.
Alle the hatheles that on horse schulde helden hym after
Were boun busked on hor blonkkes bifore the halle yates.
Ferly fayre was the folde, for the forst clenged;
In rede rudede upon rak rises the sunne,   1695
And ful clere costes the clowdes of the welkyn.
Hunteres unhardeled bi a holt syde,
Rocheres roungen bi rys for rurde of her hornes;
Summe fel in the fute ther the fox bade,
Trayles ofte a traveres bi traunt of her wyles   1700
A kenet kryes therof, the hunt on hym calles;
His felawes fallen hym to, that fnasted ful thike,
Runnen forth in a rabel in his ryght fare,

1669 *continue*
1670 *ride* (l. 1048)

1672 *dissuaded/linger/urged*
1673 *pledge* (l. 394)
1674 *achieve* (l. 1390)/*appointment*
1675 *first canonical offices of day*

1677 *agreement*
1678 *winnings* (l. 1406)/*return*
1679 *asked,* here *tested*

1681 *think* (l. 995)
1682 *loss* (l. 1284)
1683 *made to linger*

1690 *mass*
1691 *mount*
1692 *go* (l. 1523)
1693 *ready* (l. 1311)/*dressed/horses* (l. 1581)/*gates*
1694 *Wondrously* (l. 741)/*earth* (l. 1275)/*frost/clung*
1695 *ruddy red/(cloud) rack*
1696 *coasts/heavens* (l. 525)
1697 *unleashed*
1698 *Rocks/woods/noise*
1699 *track* (l. 1425)
1700 *back and forth/practice*

1702 *panted* (l. 1587)

And he fyskes hem byfore; thay founden hym sone,
And quen thay seghe hym with syght thay sued hym fast,   1705
Wreyande hym ful weterly with a wroth noyse;
And he trantes and tornayees thurgh mony tene greve,
Havilounes, and herkenes bi hegges ful ofte.
At the last bi a littel dich he lepes over a spenne,
Steles out ful stilly bi a strothe rande,   1710
Went haf wylt of the wode with wyles fro the houndes;
Thenne was he went, er he wyst, to a wale tryster,
Ther thre thro at a thrich thrat hym at ones,
      al graye.
He blenched ayayn bilyve   1715
And stifly start on-stray,
With alle the wo on lyve
To the wod he went away.

                    70(24)

Thenne was hit lif upon list to lythen the houndes,
When alle the mute hade hym met, menged togeder: 1720
Such a sorwe at that syght thay sette on his hede
As alle the clamberande clyffes hade clatered on hepes;
Here he was halawed, when hatheles hym metten,
Loude he was yayned with yarande speche;
Ther he was threted and ofte thef called,   1725
And ay the titleres at his tayl, that tary he ne myght;
Ofte he was runnen at, when he out rayked,
And ofte reled in ayayn, so Reniarde was wylé.
And ye he lad hem bi lagmon, the lorde and his meyny,
On this maner bi the mountes quyle myd-over-under,   1730
Whyle the hende knyght at home holsumly slepes
Withinne the comly cortynes, on the cholde morne.
Bot the lady for luf let not to slepe,
Ne the purpose to payre that pyght in hir hert,
Bot ros hir up radly, rayked hir theder   1735
In a mery mantyle, mete to the erthe,
That was furred ful fyne with felles wel pured,
No hwes goud on hir hede bot the hagher stones
Trased aboute hir tressour be twenty in clusteres;
Hir thryven face and hir throte throwen al naked,   1740
Hir brest bare bifore, and bihinde eke.
Ho comes withinne the chambre dore, and closes hit hir after,
Wayves up a wyndow, and on the wyghe calles,

1704 *frisks*

1706 *Bewraying/clearly*
1707 *tricks* (cf. l. 1700)/*turns*
1708 *Redoubles/hedges*
1709 *spinny, copse*
1710 *thicket border*
1711 *(to) have/escaped*
1712 *choice* (l. 1403)/*waiting station* (l. 1170)
1713 *fierce (ones)/thrust/threatened*

1715 *changed his course*
1716 *astray, on new course*

1719 *alive/joy/to hear*
1720 *pack* (l. 1451)/*mingled*

1724 *met/reproachful* (l. 1595)

1726 *hounds kept at hunting stations*
1727 *broke away*

1729 *yea/led/lagmon*, obscure
1730 *hills/midafternoon*

1734 *impair* (l. 1456)/*(was) pitched, set* (l. 1456)
1735 *went* (l. 1727)
1736 *equal, extending*
1737 *skins* (l. 1359)/*trimmed* (l. 154)
1738 *wrought*
1739 *hair snood*
1740 *thriving/thrown (open)*
1741 *also* (l. 90)

And radly thus rehayted hym with hir riche wordes,
    with chere: 1745
    'A, mon, how may thou slepe?
    This morning is so clere!'
    He was in drowping depe
    Bot thenne he con hir here.

71(25)

In dregh droupyng of dreme draveled that noble,   1750
As mon that was in mornyng of mony thro thoghtes,
How that destiné schulde that day dele hym his wyrde
At the grene chapel, when he the gome metes,
And bihoves his buffet abide without debate more;
Bot quen that comly com he kevered his wyttes,   1755
Swenges out of the swevenes, and swares with hast.
The lady luflych com laghande swete,
Felle over his fayre face, and fetly hym kyssed;
He welcumes hir worthily with a wale chere.
He segh hir so glorious and gayly atyred,   1760
So fautles of hir fetures and of so fyne hewes,
Wight wallande joye warmed his hert.
With smothe smylyng and smolt thay smeten into merthe,
That al was blis and bonchef that breke hem bitwene,
    and wynne.   1765
    Thay lanced wordes gode,
    Much wele then was therinne;
    Gret perile bitwene hem stod,
    Nif Maré of hir knyght mynne.

72(26)

For that prynces of pris depresed hym so thikke,   1770
Nurned hym so neghe the thred that nede hym bihoved,
Other lach ther hir luf, other ladly refuse.
He cared for his cortaysye, lest crathayn he were,
And more for his meschef, yif he schulde make synne,
And be traytor to that tolke that that telde aght.   1775
'God schylde,' quoth the schalk, 'that schal not befalle!'
With luf-laghyng a lyt he layd hym bysyde
Alle the speches of specialté that sprange of her mouthe.
Quoth that burde to the burne, 'Blame ye disserve,
Yif ye luf not that lyf that ye lye nexte,   1780
Bifore alle the wyghes in the worlde wounded in hert,

1744 *rallied* (l. 1422)

1748 *fitful sleep*

1750 *heavy* (l. 1460)/*muttered*
1751 *intense* (l. 1713)
1752 *fate*
1753 *man*

1755 *comely* (*one*)/*recovered*
1756 *dreams/answers* (l. 1108)

1758 *nicely*

1762 *Vigorously* (l. 1591)/*welling*
1763 *gentle/*(*were*) *smitten*
1764 *happiness*
1765 *joy* (l. 15)

1769 *If* + neg. = *Unless/thought, remembered* (l. 1681)

1770 *pressed*
1771 *Urged* (l. 1669)/*limit*
1772 *Either* . . . *or/loathly* (l. 1634)
1773 *blackguard*

1775 *tulk, man* (l. 1093)/*house/owned*

1777 *little*

Bot if ye haf a lemman, a lever, that yow lykes better,
And folden fayth to that fre, festned so harde
That yow lausen ne lyst—and that I leve nouthe;
And that ye telle me that now trwly, I pray yow,   1785
For alle the lufes upon lyve layne not the sothe
        for gile.'
    The knyght sayde, 'Be sayn Jon,'
    And smethely con he smyle,
    'In fayth I welde right non,   1790
    Ne non wil welde the quile.

73(27)

'That is a worde,' quoth that wyght, 'that worst is of alle,
Bot I am swared for sothe, that sore me thinkkes.
Kysse me now comly, and I schal cach hethen,
I may bot mourne upon molde, as may that much lovyes.'   1795
Sykande ho sweye doun and semly hym kyssed,
And sithen ho severes hym fro, and says as ho stondes,
'Now, dere, at this departyng do me this ese,
Gif me sumquat of thy gifte, thi glove if hit were,
That I may mynne on the, mon, my mournyng to lassen.'   1800
'Now, iwysse,' quoth that wyghe, 'I wolde I hade here
The levest thing for thy luf that I in londe welde,
For ye haf deserved, for sothe, sellyly ofte,
More rewarde bi resoun then I reche myght;
Bot to dele yow for drurye, that dawed bot neked,   1805
Hit is not your honour to haf at this tyme
A glove for a garysoun of Gawaynes giftes,
And I am here an erande in erdes uncouthe,
And have no men wyth no males with menskful thinges;
That mislykes me, ladé, for luf as this tyme,   1810
Iche tolke mon do as he is tan, tas to non ille
        ne pine.'
    'Nay, hende of hyghe honours,'
    Quoth that lufsum under lyne,
    'Thagh I hade noght of youres,   1815
    Yet schulde ye have of myne.'

74(28)

Ho raght hym a riche rynk of red golde werkes,
Wyth a starande ston stondande alofte
That bere blusschande bemes as the bryght sunne;

1782 *lover/more beloved*
1783 *plighted*
1784 *loosen/wish* (l. 1582)/*believe/now*

1786 *hide*

1788 *St. John*
1789 *gently*
1790 *possess/none*

1794 *go/hence*
1795 *earth/woman*
1796 *Sighing* (l. 753)/*sinks*

1800 *lessen*

1802 *dearest* (l. 49)

1804 *give*
1805 *love* (l. 1517)/*would be worth/little* (l. 1062)

1807 *talisman* (l. 1255)
1808 *strange* (l. 93)
1809 *bags* (l. 1129)/*precious* (l. 555)
1810 *That*
1811 *Each/man/must/taken, given* (*to do*)/*take*

1814 *linen*

1816 (*something*) *of mine*

1817 *reached, gave/ring*
1818 *staring/standing*
1819 *bore/blushing, shining*

Wyt ye wel, hit was worth wele ful hoge.   1820
Bot the renk hit renayed, and redyly he sayde,
'I wil no giftes for gode, my gay, at this tyme;
I haf none yow to norne, ne noght wyl I take.'
Ho bede hit hym ful bysily, and he hir bode wernes,
And swere swyfte by his sothe that he hit sese nolde,   1825
And ho soré that he forsoke and sayde therafter,
'If ye renay my rynk, to ryche for hit semes,
Ye wolde not so hyghly halden be to me,
I schal gif yow my girdel, that gaynes yow lasse.'
Ho laght a lace lyghtly that leke umbe hir sydes,   1830
Knit upon hir kyrtel under the clere mantyle,
Gered hit was with grene sylke and with golde schaped,
Noght bot arounde brayden, beten with fyngres,
And that ho bede to the burne, and blythely bisoght,
Thagh hit unworthi were, that he hit take wolde.   1835
And he nay that he nolde neghe in no wyse
Nauther golde ne garysoun, er God hym grace sende
To acheve to the chaunce that he hade chosen there.
'And therfore, I pray yow, displese yow noght,
And lettes be your bisinesse, for I baythe hit yow never   1840
    to graunte;
    I am derely to yow biholde
    Bicause of your sembelaunt,
    And ever in hot and colde
    To be your trwe servaunt.'   1845

75(29)

'Now forsake ye this silke,' sayde the burde thenne,
'For hit is symple in hitself? And so hit wel semes.
Lo! so hit is littel, and lasse hit is worthy;
Bot who-so knew the costes that knit ar therinne,
He wolde hit prayse at more prys, paraventure;   1850
For quat gome so is gorde with this grene lace,
While he hit hade hemely halched aboute,
Ther is no hathel under heven tohewe hym that myght,
For he myght not be slayn for slyght upon erthe.'
Then kest the knyght, and hit come to his hert,   1855
Hit were a juel for the jopardé that hym jugged were,
When he acheved to the chapel his chek for to fech;
Myght he haf slypped to be unslayn, the sleght were noble.
Thenne he thulged with hir threpe and tholed hir to speke,

1820 *huge*
1821 *refused*

1823 *offer* (l. 1771)
1824 *offer/refuses* (l. 1495)
1825 neg. + *would* = *wouldn't*

1828 *beholden*
1829 *less*
1830 *locked/around* (l. 589)
1831 *Knotted/mantle*
1832 *chaped, trimmed*
1833 *embroidered*

1836 *denied/(come) near*
1837 *treasure* (l. 1807)

1840 *let/consent* (l. 1404)

1843 *manner* (l. 1273)

1846 *refuse*

1849 *values*

1851 *girded*
1852 *duly/fastened* (l. 939)
1853 *hew (him) to pieces*
1854 *skill* (l. 1542)
1855 *cast (about)*
1856 *jewel/jeopardy/adjudged*
1857 *fate* (l. 1107)

1859 *acquiesced/coercion/suffered*

And ho bere on hym the belt and bede hit hym swythe—   1860
And he granted—and hym gafe with a goud wylle,
And bisoght hym, for hir sake, discever hit never,
Bot to lelly layne fro hir lorde; the leude hym acordes
That never wyghe schulde hit wyt, iwysse, bot thay twayne
    for noghte;   1865
    He thonkked hir oft ful swythe,
    Ful thro with hert and thoght.
    Bi that on thrynne sythe
    Ho has kyst the knyght so toght.

76(30)

Thenne lachches ho hir leve, and leves hym there,   1870
For more myrthe of that mon moght ho not gete.
When ho was gon, Sir Gawayn geres hym sone,
Rises and riches hym in araye noble,
Lays up the luf-lace the lady hym raght,
Hid hit ful holdely, ther he hit eft fonde.   1875
Sythen chevely to the chapel choses he the waye,
Prevély approched to a prest, and prayed hym there
That he wolde lyfte his lyf and lern hym better
How his sawle schulde be saved when he schuld seye hethen.
There he schrof hym schyrly and schewed his mysdedes,   1880
Of the more and the mynne, and merci beseches,
And of absolucioun he on the segge calles;
And he asoyled hym surely, and sette hym so clene
As domesday schulde haf ben dight on the morn.
And sythen he mace hym as mery among the fre ladyes,   1885
With comlych caroles and alle kynnes ioye,
As never he did bot that daye, to the derk nyght,
    with blys.
    Uche mon hade daynté thare
    Of hym, and sayde, 'Iwysse,   1890
    Thus myry he was never are,
    Syn he com hider, er this.'

77(31)

Now hym lenge in that lee, ther luf hym bityde!
Yet is the lorde on the launde ledande his gomnes.
He has forfaren this fox that he folwed longe;   1895
As he sprent over a spenne to spye the schrewe,
Ther as he herd the howndes that hasted hym swythe,

1861 *gave* (*in*)
1862 *uncover, disclose*
1863 *loyally* (l. 499)/*conceal* (l. 1786)

1867 *intensely* (l. 1713)
1868 *three/times* (l. 982)
1869 *tough* (cf. *taut*)

1873 *goes* (l. 8)
1874 *gave* (l. 1817)
1875 *carefully/(might) find*
1876 *chiefly, swiftly*

1879 *soul/go/hence*
1880 *shrove/clean*
1881 *less* (cf. N.E. *mini-*)
1882 *man,* here *priest*
1883 *absolved*
1884 *set* (l. 678)
1885 *makes*
1886 *joy*

1892 *Since*

1893 *sheltered place* (l. 849)
1894 *leading, pursuing/games*
1895 *obstructed* (*the path of*)
1896 *sprinted/spinny* (l. 1709)

Renaud com richchande thurgh a roghe greve,
And alle the rabel in a res ryght at his heles.
The wyghe was war of the wylde, and warly abides,   1900
And braydes out the bryght bronde, and at the best castes.
And he schunt for the scharp, and schulde haf arered;
A rach rapes hym to, ryght er he myght,
And ryght bifore the hors fete thay fel on hym alle,
And woried me this wyly wyth a wroth noyse.   1905
The lorde lyghtes bilyve, and laches hym sone,
Rased hym ful radly out of the rach mouthes,
Haldes heghe over his hede, halowes faste,
And ther bayen hym mony brath houndes.
Huntes hyghed hem theder with hornes ful mony,   1910
Ay rechatande aryght til thay the renk seghen.
Bi that was comen his compeyny noble,
Alle that ever ber bugle blowed at ones,
And ale thise other halowed that hade no hornes;
Hit was the myriest mute that ever men herde,   1915
The rich rurd that ther was raysed for Renaude saule
        with lote.
    How houndes thay ther rewarde,
    Her hedes thay fawne and frote,
    And sythen thay tan Reynarde,   1920
    And tyrven of his cote.

78(32)

And thenne thay helden to home, for hit was niegh nyght,
Strakande ful stoutly in hor store hornes.
The lorde is lyght at the laste at hys lef home,
Fyndes fire upon flet, the freke ther-byside,   1925
Sir Gawayn the gode, that glad was withalle,
Among the ladies for luf he ladde much ioye;
He were a bleaunt of blwe that bradde to the erthe,
His surkot semed hym wel that softe was forred,
And his hode of that ilke henged on his schulder,   1930
Blande al of blaunner were bothe al aboute.
He metes me this god mon inmyddes the flore,
And al with gomen he hym gret, and goudly he sayde,
'I schal fylle upon fyrst oure forwardes nouthe,
That we spedly han spoken, ther spared was no drynk.'   1935
Then acoles he the knyght and kysses hym thryes,
As saverly and sadly as he hem sette couthe.

1898 *dashing* (l. 1873)
1899 *rush* (l. 1164)
1900 *warily* (l. 1186)
1901 *beast*
1902 *shunted/retreated*
1903 *hound* (l. 1907)/*rushes* (l. 1309)

1906 *lights* (*down*), *dismounts* (l. 1583)

1909 *fierce*

1911 *blowing recall* (l. 1446, 1466)

1915 *pack* (l. 1720)
1916 *noise* (l. 1698)/*soul*

1919 *fondle/rub*
1920 *take* (l. 977)
1921 *strip*

1923 *Sounding/strong* (l. 1291)

1928 *rich robe* (l. 879)/*touched*
1929 *surcoat/beseemed, became/furred*

1931 *Adorned/fur* (l. 856)

1933 *playfully* (l. 1376)
1934 *fulfill/now* (l. 1784)
1935 *fortunately*
1936 *embraces*
1937 (*with as much*) *savor and vigor*

'Bi Kryst,' quoth that other knyght, 'Ye cach much sele
In chevisaunce of this chaffer, yif ye hade goud chepes.'
'Ye, of the chepe no charg,' quoth chefly that other,   1940
'As is pertly payed the chepes that I aghte.'
'Mary,' quoth that other mon, 'myn is bihynde,
For I haf hunted al this day, and noght haf I geten
Bot this foule fox felle—the fende haf the godes!—
And that is ful pore for to pay for suche prys thinges   1945
As ye haf thryght me here thro, suche thre cosses
    so gode.'
  'Innogh,' quoth Sir Gawayn,
  'I thonk yow, bi the rode,'
  And how the fox was slayn   1950
  He tolde hym as thay stode.

79(33)

With merthe and mynstralsye, wyth metes at hor wylle,
Thay maden as mery as any men moghten—
With laghyng of ladies, with lotes of bordes
Gawayn and the gode mon so glad were thay bothe—   1955
Bot if the douthe had doted, other dronken ben other.
Bothe the mon and the meyny maden mony iapes,
Til the sesoun was seghen that thay sever moste;
Burnes to hor bedde behoved at the laste.
Thenne loghly his leve at the lorde fyrst   1960
Fochches this fre mon, and fayre he hym thonkkes:
'Of such a selly soiorne as I haf hade here,
Your honour at this hyghe fest, the hyghe kyng yow yelde!
I yef yow me for on of youres, if yowreself lykes,
For I mut nedes, as ye wot, meve to-morne,   1965
And ye me take sum tolke to teche, as ye hyght,
The gate to the grene chapel, as God wyl me suffer
To dele on Nw Yeres day the dome of my wyrdes.'
'In god faythe,' quoth the god mon, 'wyth a goud wylle
Al that ever I yow hyght halde schal I redé.'   1970
Ther asyngnes he a servaunt to sett hym in the waye,
And coundue hym by the downes, that he no drechch had,
For to ferk thurgh the fryth and fare at the gaynest
    bi greve.
  The lorde Gawayn con thonk,   1975
  Such worchip he wolde hym weve;

1938 *good luck* (cf. N.E. *salacious,* etc., *Skoal!*)
1939 *gain* (l. 1678)/*trade* (l. 1647)/*bargains* (cf. l. 1271)

1941 *ought, owe* (l. 1775)

1944 *skin* (l. 1737)/*fiend, Devil*

1946 *thrust* (l. 1443)/*heavily* (l. 1751)/*kisses* (l. 1300)

1949 *rood, cross*

1953 *might*
1954 *sounds* (l. 1917)/*jokes* (l. 1409)

1956 *company* (l. 1415)/*grown dotty* (l. 1151)/*or . . . else*
1957 *jests* (l. 542)
1958 *must*

1960 *lowly, humbly* (l. 851)
1961 *Fetches*
1962 *wondrous* (l. 1803)/*sojourn*

1964 *give*
1965 *must*
1966 *promised* (l. 448)
1967 *way* (l. 930)
1968 *doom/fate* (l. 1752)

1972 *conduct/difficulty*
1973 *go, ride* (l. 1072)/*most advantageously*

Then at tho ladyes wlonk
The knyght has tan his leve.

80(34)

With care and wyth kyssynge he carppes hem tille,
And fele thryvande thonkkes he thrat hom to have,   1980
And thay yelden hym ayayn yeply that ilk;
Thay bikende hym to Kryst with ful colde sykynges.
Sythen fro the meyny he menskly departes;
Uche mon that he mette, he made hem a thonke
For his servyse and his solace and his sere pyne,   1985
That thay wyth busynes had ben aboute hym to serve;
And uche segge as soré to sever with hym there
As thay hade wonde worthyly with that wlonk ever.
Then with ledes and lyght he was ladde to his chambre
And blythely broght to his bedde to be at his rest.   1990
Yif he ne slepe soundyly, say ne dar I,
For he hade muche on the morn to mynne, yif he wolde,
    in thoght.
    Let hym lyghe there stille,
    He has nere that he soght;   1995
    And ye wyl a whyle be stylle
    I schal telle yow how thay wroght.

1977 *gracious* (l. 515)

1979 *speaks* (l. 1221)/*to*
1980 *many* (l. 1653)/*pressed*
1981 *promptly* (l. 1510)
1982 *commended* (l. 1307)/*sighs* (cf. l. 1796)
1983 *company* (l. 1957)/*courteously* (l. 1312)

1985 *kindness/constant, separate* (l. 1522)/*troubles* (l. 1812)

1988 *dwelled* (l. 814)
1989 *people* (l. 98)

1992 *remember* (l. 1800)

PART IV
81(1)

Now neghes the Nw Yere, and the nyght passes,
The day dryves to the derk, as dryghtyn biddes;
Bot wylde wederes of the worlde wakned theroute,   2000
Clowdes kesten kenly the colde to the erthe,
Wyth nyghe innoghe of the northe, the naked to tene;
The snawe snitered ful snart, that snayped the wylde;
The werbelande wynde wapped fro the hyghe,
And drof uche dale ful of dryftes ful grete.   2005
The leude lystened ful wel that legh in his bedde,
Thagh he lowkes his liddes, ful lyttel he slepes;
Bi uch kok that crue he knwe wel the steven.
Deliverly he dressed up, er the day sprenged,
For there was lyght of a laumpe that lemed in his chambre;   2010
He called to his chamberlayn, that cofly him swared,
And bede hym bryng hym his bruny and his blonk sadel;
That other ferkes hym up and feches hym his wedes,
And graythes me Sir Gawayn upon a grett wyse.
Fyrst he clad hym in his clothes the colde for to were,   2015
And sythen his other harnays, that holdely was keped,
Bothe his paunce and his plates, piked ful clene,
The rynges rokked of the roust of his riche bruny;
And al was fresch as upon fyrst, and he was fayn thenne
    to thonk;   2020
    He hadde upon uche pece,
    Wypped ful wel and wlonk;
    The gayest into Grece,
    The burne bede bryng his blonk.

82(2)

Whyle the wlonkest wedes he warp on hymselven—   2025
His cote wyth the conysaunce of the clere werkes
Ennurned upon velvet, vertuus stones
Aboute beten and bounden, enbrauded semes,
And fayre furred withinne wyth fayre pelures—
Yet laft he not the lace, the ladies gifte,   2030
That forgat not Gawayn for gode of hymselven.
Bi he hade belted the bronde upon his balge haunches,

1999 *(the) Lord* (l. 1548)

2002 *trouble* (l. 1169)
2003 *snow/shivered/harshly/bit* (*at*)
2004 *warbling, howling*

2006 *man* (Gawayn)

2008 *cock* (l. 1412)/*voice* (l. 242)
2009 *Quickly*

2011 *promptly/answered* (l. 1793)
2012 *mail shirt* (l. 861)/*horse* (l. 1693)

2015 *ward* (*off*)
2016 *gear/carefully*
2017 *pauncher, stomach armor/polished*
2018 *cleaned/rust*

2022 *Wiped*

2025 *cast* (l. 224)
2026 *cognizance, emblem*
2027 *adorned*

2029 *furs* (l. 154)
2030 *left*

2032 *bulging* (l. 967)

Then dressed he his drurye double hym aboute,
Swythe swethled umbe his swange swetely that knyght
The gordel of the grene silke, that gay wel bisemed,   2035
Upon that ryol red clothe that ryche was to schewe.
Bot wered not this ilk wyghe for wele this gordel,
For pryde of the pendauntes, thagh polyst thay were,
And thagh the glyterande golde glent upon endes,
Bot for to saven hymself, when suffer hym byhoved,   2040
To byde bale withoute dabate of bronde hym to were
      other knyffe.
   Bi that the bolde mon boun
   Wynnes theroute bilyve,
   Alle the meyny of renoun   2045
   He thonkkes ofte ful ryve.

      83(3)

Thenne was Gryngolet graythe, that gret was and huge,
And hade ben soiourned saverly and in a siker wyse,
Hym lyst prik for poynt, that proude hors thenne.
The wyghe wynnes hym to and wytes on his lyre,   2050
And sayde soberly hymself and by his soth sweres:
'Here is a meyny in this mote that on menske thenkkes,
The mon hem maynteines, ioy mot thay have;
The leve lady on lyve, luf hir bityde;
Yif thay for charyté cherysen a gest,   2055
And halden honour in her honde, the hathel hem yelde,
That haldes the heven upon hyghe, and also yow alle!
And yif I myght lyf upon londe, lede any quyle,
I schuld rech yow sum rewarde redyly, if I myght.'
Thenn steppes he into stirop and strydes alofte;   2060
His schalk schewed hym his schelde, on schulder he hit laght,
Gordes to Gryngolet with his gilt heles,
And he startes on the ston, stod he no lenger
      to praunce.
   His hathel on hors was thenne,   2065
   That bere his spere and launce.
   'This kastel to Kryst I kenne':
   He gef hit ay god chaunce.

      84(4)

The brygge was brayde doun, and the brode gates,
Unbarred and born open upon bothe halve.   2070

2033 *(token of) love* (l. 1805)
2034 *wrapped* (cf. N.E. *swaddle*)/*waist*

2036 *royal/see*
2037 *because of (its)/wealth*
2038 *polished* (l. 576)

2041 *debate, resistance/protect*

2043 *was ready* (l. 852)

2046 *rife, abundantly*

2048 *stabled/savorly, pleasantly* (l. 1937)
2049 *(to) gallop/condition*
2050 *looks/flesh* (l. 418)

2052 *moat = castle* (l. 910)/*courtesy* (l. 834)
2053 *maintains/may*
2054 *alive*
2055 *cherish/guest* (l. 1127)
2056 *hold/man = Lord/repay*

2061 *man* (l. 1776)
2062 *Spurs*

2067 *commend* (cf. l. 1982)

The burne blessed hym bilyve, and the bredes passed—
Prayses the porter bifore the prynce kneled,
Gef hym 'God and goud day,' that Gawayn he save—
And went on his way with his wyghe one,
That schulde teche hym to tourne to that tene place   2075
Ther the ruful race he schulde resayve.
Thay bowen bi bonkkes ther boghes ar bare,
Thay clomben bi clyffes ther clenges the colde.
The heven was up halt, bot ugly ther-under;
Mist muged on the mor, malt on the mountes,   2080
Uch hille hade a hatte, a myst-hakel huge.
Brokes byled and breke bi bonkkes aboute,
Schyre schaterande on schores, ther thay doun schowved.
Wela wylle was the way ther thay bi wod schulden,
Til hit was sone sesoun that the sunne ryses   2085
    that tyde.
    Thay were on a hille ful hyghe,
    The quyte snaw lay bisyde;
    The burne that rod hym by
    Bede his mayster abide.   2090

85(5)

'For I haf wonnen yow hider, wyghe, at this tyme,
And now nar ye not fer fro that note place
That ye han spied and spuryed so specially after;
Bot I schal say yow for sothe, sythen I yow knowe,
And ye ar a lede upon lyve that I wel lovy,   2095
Wolde ye worche bi my wytte, ye worthed the better.
The place that ye prece to ful perelous is halden;
Ther wones a wyghe in that waste, the worst upon erthe,
For he is stiffe and sturne, and to strike lovies,
And more is he then any mon upon myddelerde,   2100
And his body bigger then the best fowre
That ar in Arthures hous, hestor, other other.
He cheves that chaunce at the chapel grene,
Ther passes non bi that place so proude in his armes
That he ne dynges hym to dethe with dynt of his honde;   2105
For he is a mon methles, and mercy non uses,
For be hit chorle other chaplayn that bi the chapel rydes,
Monk other masseprest, other any mon elles,
Hym thynk as queme hym to quelle as quyk go hymselven.

2071 *crossed (himself)/planks*
2072 *(who) knelt before . . .*

2074 *only*

2076 *stroke/receive*
2077 *bend, turn/boughs*

2079 *uplifted*
2080 *(was) moist, damp* (cf. N.E. *muggy*)/*melted*
2081 *hat/mist-muffler* (cf. *dogs' hackles*)
2082 *Brooks/boiled*
2083 *shoved, pushed*
2084 *Well, very/wandering/should (go)*
2085 *time (of day)*
2086 *season (of year)*

2089 *"rode beside him"*

2091 *brought*
2092 neg. + *are/far/noted*
2093 *asked* (l. 901)

2095 *love*
2096 *"If . . . you would fare . . ."*
2097 *press/toward*

2100 *bigger/earth*
2101 *four*
2102 *"Hector, or others"*
2103 *"He runs the show . . ."*

2105 *strikes*
2106 *relentless*
2107 *churl*
2108 *mass-priest*
2109 *pleasant* (l. 578)/*"as to be alive himself"**

2109 Cf. *quick* 'alive' in "the quick and the dead."

Forthy I say the, as sothe as ye in sadel sitte,   2110
Com ye there, ye be kylled, may the, knyght, rede,
Trawe ye me that trewely, thagh ye had twenty lyves
    to spende.
He has wonyd here ful yore,
On bent much baret bende,   2115
Ayayn his dyntes sore
Ye may not yow defende.

86(6)

'Forthy, goude Sir Gawayn, let the gome one,
And gos away sum other gate, upon Goddes halve!
Cayres bi sum other kyth, ther Kryst mot yow spede,   2120
And I schal hygh me hom ayayn, and hete yow fyrre,
That I schal swere bi God and alle his gode halyes,
As help me God and the halydam, and othes innoghe,
That I schal lelly yow layne, and lance never tale
That ever ye fondet to fle for freke that I wyst.'   2125
'Grant merci,' quoth Gawayn, and gruchyng he sayde:
'Wel worth the, wyghe, that woldes my gode,
And that lelly me layne I leve wel thou woldes.
Bot helde thou hit never so holde, and I here passed,
Founded for ferde for to fle, in fourme that thou telles,   2130
I were a knyght kowarde, I myght not be excused.
Bot I wyl to the chapel, for chaunce that may falle,
And talk wyth that ilk tulk the tale that me lyste,
Worthe hit wele other wo, as the wyrde lykes,
    hit hafe.   2135
Thaghe he be a sturn knape
To stightel, and stad with stave,
Ful wel con dryghtyn schape
His servauntes for to save.

87(7)

'Mary!' quoth that other mon, 'now thou so much spelles,   2140
That thou wylt thyn awen nye nyme to thyselven,
And the lyst lese thy lyf, the lette I ne kepe.
Haf here thi helme on thy hede, thi spere in thi honde,
And ryde me doun This ilk rake bi yon rokke syde,
Til thou be broght to the bothem of the brem valay;   2145
Thenne loke a littel on the launde, on thi lyfte honde,
And thou schal se in that slade the self chapel,

2111 *be advised* (l. 373)
2112 *Trust, believe*

2114 *come/long ago*
2115 *grass, field* (l. 353)/(on) *fighting* (l. 353)/*bent*

2119 *go*
2120 *Ride* (l. 1670)/*land* (l. 460)
2121 *promise* (l. 1970)/*further* (l. 1304)
2122 *holies, saints*

2124 *loyally* (l. 1863)/*protect* (l. 1786)/*tell* (l. 1212)
2125 *hastened* (l. 1585)/*because of*
2126 *grudgingly*
2127 *fare/wishes*
2128 *believe* (l. 1784)
2129 *loyally*
2130 *fear/form, fashion*

2132 *will* (go) *to*

2134 *Befalls* (l. 2127)/*fate* (l. 1968)

2136 *man*
2137 *deal with/standing*

2141 *harm* (l. 58)/*take* (l. 1407)
2142 *wish* (l. 1784)/*lose*/(to) *hinder/care*

2144 *path*
2145 *bottom/wild* (l. 1142)
2146 *left*
2147 *same, very*

And the borelych burne on bent that hit kepes.
Now fares wel, on Godes half, Gawayn the noble!
For alle the golde upon grounde I nolde go wyth the,   2150
Ne bere the felawschip thurgh this fryth on fote fyrre.'
Bi that the wyghe in the wod wendes his brydel,
Hit the hors with the heles as harde as he myght,
Lepes hym over the launde, and leves the knyght there
      al one.   2155
   'Bi Goddes self,' quoth Gawayn,
   'I wyl nauther grete ne grone;
   To Goddes wylle I am ful bayn,
   And to hym I haf me tone.'

                     88(8)

Thenne gyrdes he to Gryngolet, and gederes the rake,   2160
Schowves in bi a schore at a schawe syde,
Rides thurgh the roghe bonk ryght to the dale;
And thenne he wayted hym aboute, and wylde hit hym thoght,
And seghe no syngne of resette bisydes nowhere,
Bot hyghe bonkkes and brent upon bothe halve,   2165
And rughe knokled knarres with knorned stones;
The skwes of the scowtes skayned hym thoght.
Thenne he hoved, and wythhylde his hors at that tyde,
And ofte chaunged his cher the chapel to seche:
He segh non suche in no syde, and selly hym thoght,   2170
Sone, a lyttel on a launde, a lawe as hit were;
A balgh berg bi a bonke the brymme bysyde,
Bi a fors of a flode that ferked thare;
The borne blubred therinne as hit boyled hade.
The knyght kaches his caple and com to the lawe,   2175
Lightes doun luflyly, and at a lynde taches
The rayne and his riche with a roghe braunche.
Thenne he bowes to the berghe, aboute hit he walkes,
Debatande with hymself quat hit be myght.
Hit hade a hole on the ende and on ayther syde,   2180
And overgrowen with gresse in glodes aywhere,
And al was holw inwith, nobot an olde cave,
Or a crevisse of an olde cragge, he couthe hit noght deme
      with spelle.
   'We! Lorde,' quoth the gentyle knyght,   2185
   'Whether this be the grene chapelle?

2148 *burly* (l. 766)

2151 *further* (l. 2121)
2152 *turns* (l. 1102)

2155 *alone*

2157 *weep*
2158 *obedient*
2159 *taken*

2160 *path* (l. 2144)

2164 *sign/shelter*
2165 *steep*
2166 *knuckled/rocks/craggy*
2167 *clouds/jagged crags/grazed*
2168 *hove* (*to*) (l. 785)
2169 (*the direction of his*) *face*

2171 *mound* (l. 765)
2172 *hillock/*(*stream's*) *edge*
2173 *flowed* (l. 1973)
2174 *stream/as* (*if*) *it*
2175 *horse*
2176 *tree* (l. 1178)/*attaches*
2177 *splendid* (*horse*)

2181 *grass/glades, tufts*
2182 *hollow/within/nothing but*
2183 *deem, judge*
2184 *speech* (l. 1199)
2185 *Woe*
2186 *Might*

Here myght aboute mydnyght
The dele his matynnes telle!'

89(9)

'Now iwysse,' quoth Wowayn, 'wysty is here;
This oritore is ugly, with erbes overgrowen;   2190
Wel bisemes the wyghe wruxled in grene
Dele here his devocioun on the develes wyse.
Now I fele hit is the fende, in my fyve wyttes,
That has stoken me this steven to strye me here.
This is a chapel of meschaunce, that chekke hit bytyde!   2195
Hit is the corsedest kyrk that ever I com inne!'
With heghe helme on his hede, his launce in his honde,
He romes up to the roffe of tho rogh wones.
Thene herde he of that hyghe hil, in a harde roche
Biyonde the broke, in a bonk, a wonder breme noyse.   2200
Quat! hit clatered in the clyff, as hit cleve schulde,
As one upon a gryndelston hade grounden a sythe.
What! hit wharred and whette, as water at a mulne;
What! hit rusched and ronge, rawthe to here.
Thenne 'Bi Godde,' quoth Gawayn, 'that gere, as I trowe,   2205
Is ryched at the reverence me, renk, to mete
    bi rote.
  Let God worche! We loo,
  Hit helppes me not a mote.
  My lif thagh I forgoo,   2210
  Drede dos me no lote.'

90(10)

Thenne the knyght con calle ful hyghe,
'Who stightles in this sted me steven to holde?
For now is gode Gawayn goande ryght here.
If any wyghe oght wyl, wynne hider fast,   2215
Other now other never, his nedes to spede.'
'Abyde,' quoth on on the bonke above over his hede,
'And thou schal haf al in hast that I the hyght ones.'
Yet he rusched on that rurde rapely a throwe,
And wyth quettyng awharf, er he wolde lyght;   2220
And sythen he keveres bi a cragge, and comes of a hole,
Whyrlande out of a wro wyth a felle weppen,
A denes ax nwe dyght, the dynt with to yelde,
With a borelych bytte bende by the halme,

2188 *Devil/matins* (l. 756)

2189 *forsaken, desolate*
2190 *oratory*
2191 *(it) becomes* (l. 2135)/*wrapped*
2192 *(To) deal*
2193 *Fiend* (l. 1944)
2194 *stuck/tryst* (l. 1060)/*destroy*
2195 *misfortune* (l. 1857)

2198 *roof/dwelling* (l. 257)

2200 *brook*

2202 *grindstone/scythe*
2203 *whirred/whetted/mill*
2204 *raucous*

2206 *readied (for)*
2207 *custom*

2209 *bit*

2211 *"No noise will I dread"*

2213 *rules* (l. 2137)/*tryst* (l. 2194)
2214 *going*
2215 *anything/wishes*
2216 *Either . . . or . . .*
2217 *one*
2218 *promised* (l. 1970)
2219 *on (with)/noise* (l. 1916)/*quickly* (l. 1903)/*time*
2220 *whetting/turned*
2221 *proceeds*
2222 *nook*
2223 *Danish/made*
2224 *bent/shaft*

Fyled in a fylor, fowre fote large—   2225
Hit was no lasse bi that lace that lemed ful bryght—
And the gome in the grene gered as fyrst,
Bothe the lyre and the legges, lokkes and berde,
Save that fayre on his fote he foundes on the erthe,
Sette the stele to the stone and stalked bysyde.   2230
When he wan to the watter, ther he wade nolde,
He hypped over on hys ax, and orpedly strydes,
Bremly brothe on a bent that brode was aboute
    on snawe.
    Sir Gawayn the knyght con mete,   2235
    He ne lutte hym nothyng lowe;
    That other sayde, 'Now, sir swete,
    Of steven mon may the trowe.'

91(11)

'Gawayn,' quoth that grene gome, 'God the mot loke!
Iwysse thou art welcom, wyghe, to my place,   2240
And thou has tymed thi travayl as truee mon schulde.
And thou knowes the covenauntes kest uus bytwene:
At this tyme twelmonyth thou toke that the falled,
And I schulde at this Nwe Yere yeply the quyte.
And we ar in this valay verayly oure one;   2245
Here ar no renkes us to rydde, rele as uus likes.
Haf thy helme of thy hede, and haf here thy pay.
Busk no more debate then I the bede thenne
When thou wypped of my hede at a wap one.'
'Nay, bi God,' quoth Gawayn, 'that me gost lante,   2250
I schal gruch the no grwe for grem that falles.
Bot styghtel the upon on strok, and I schal stonde stylle
And warp the no wernyng to worch as the lykes,
    nowhare.'
    He lened with the nek, and lutte,   2255
    And schewed that schyre al bare,
    And lette as he noght dutte;
    For drede he wolde not dare.

92(12)

Then the gome in the grene graythed hym swythe,
Gederes up hys grymme tole Gawayn to smyte;   2260
With alle the bur in his body he ber hit on lofte,
Munt as maghtyly as marre hym he wolde;

2226 *less (in length than)/thong*

2228 *face* (l. 943)
2229 *feet/goes* (l. 2130)

2231 *came*
2232 *vigorously*
2233 *grim*

2236 *bowed* (l. 248)

2238 *tryst* (l. 1060)

2239 *may/look (out for)*

2243 *"what befell thee"*
2244 *requite*
2245 *alone*
2246 *separate/reel (about)*

2249 *". . . in one fell swoop"*
2250 *lent*
2251 *grudge/groat/grief*
2252 *"deal out but one stroke"* (l. 2137)

2256 *fair (flesh)*
2257 *let (on)/doubted, feared* (l. 784)

2261 *might/bore*
2262 *Aimed/mightily/(to) mar, destroy*

Hade hit dryven adoun as dregh as he atled,
Ther hade ben ded of his dynt that doghty was ever.
Bot Gawayn on that giserne glyfte hym bysyde,   2265
As hit com glydande adoun on glode hym to schende,
And schranke a lytel with the schulderes for the scharp yrne.
That other schalk wyth a schunt the schene wythhaldes,
And thenne repreved he the prynce with mony prowde wordes:
'Thou art not Gawayn,' quoth the gome, 'that is so goud halden, 2270
That never arghed for no here by hylle ne be vale,
And now thou fles for ferde er thou fele harmes!
Such cowardise of that knyght cowthe I never here.
Nawther fyked I ne flaghe, freke, quen thou myntest,
Ne kest no kavelacion in kynges hous Arthor.   2275
My hede flaw to my fote, and yet flagh I never;
And thou, er any harme hent, arghes in hert;
Wherfore the better burne me burde be called
    therfore.'
Quoth Gawayn, 'I schunt ones,   2280
And so wyl I no more;
Bot thagh my hede falle on the stones,
I con not hit restore.

93(13)

'Bot busk, burne, bi thi fayth, and bryng me to the poynt.
Dele to me my destiné, and do hit out of honde,   2285
For I schal stonde the a strok, and start no more
Til thyn ax have me hitte, haf here my trawthe.'
'Haf at the thenne!' quoth that other, and heves hit alofte,
And waytes as wrothely as he wode were.
He myntes at hym maghtyly, bot not the mon ryves,   2290
Withhelde heterly his honde, er hit hurt myght.
Gawayn graythely hit bydes, and glent with no membre,
Bot stode stylle as the ston, other a stubbe auther
That ratheled is in roché grounde with rotes a hundreth.
Then muryly efte con he mele, the mon in the grene,   2295
'So, now thou has thi hert holle, hitte me bihovs.
Halde the now the hyghe hode that Arthur the raght,
And kepe thy kanel at this kest, yif hit kever may.'
Gawayn ful gryndelly with greme thenne sayde,
'Wy! thresch on, thou thro mon, thou thretes to longe;   2300
I hope that thi hert arghe wyth thyn awen selven.'
'For sothe,' quoth that other freke, 'so felly thou spekes,

2263 *heavily* (l. 1750)/*meant* (l. 27)

2265 *battle-ax* (l. 375)/*glanced*
2266 *ground* (l. 2181)/*destroy*
2267 *iron* (l. 729)
2268 *shunt, flinch* (l. 1902)/*shiny* (*ax*)/*avoids*
2269 *reproved*

2271 *recoiled* (l. 1463)/*army*

2274 *flinched*

2277 *takes* (l. 1639)
2278 *deserve*

2289 *"as if he were mad"* (cf. l. 1580)
2290 *rips* (l. 1341)

2293 *stump/either*
2294 *planted*
2295 *say*
2296 (*to*) *hit*
2297 *reached, gave*
2298 *channel,* (*wind*)*pipe/recover*
2299 *stormily* (cf. l. 312)

2302 *fiercely* (l. 2222)

I wyl no lenger on lyte lette thin ernde
   right nowe.'
Thenne tas he hym strythe to stryke,   2305
And frounses bothe lyppe and browe;
No mervayle thagh hym myslyke
That hoped of no rescowe.

94(14)

He lyftes lyghtly his lome, and lette hit doun fayre
With the barbe of the bitte bi the bare nek;   2310
Thagh he homered heterly, hurt hym no more,
Bot snyrt hym on that on syde, that severed the hyde.
The scharp schrank to the flesche thurgh the schyre grece,
That the schene blod over his schulderes schot to the erthe;
And quen the burne segh the blode blenk on the snawe,   2315
He sprit forth spenne-fote more then a spere lenthe,
Hent heterly his helme, and on his hed cast,
Schot with his schulderes his fayre schelde under,
Braydes out a bryght sworde and bremely he spekes—
Never syn that he was burne borne of his moder   2320
Was he never in this worlde wyghe half so blythe—
'Blynne, burne, of thy bur, bede me no mo!
I haf a stroke in this sted withoute stryf hent,
And if thow reches me any mo, I redyly schal quyte,
And yelde yederly ayayn—and therto ye tryst—   2325
   and foo.
   Bot on stroke here me falles—
   The covenaunt schop ryght so,
   Fermed in Arthures halles—
   And therfore, hende, now hoo!'   2330

95(15)

The hathel heldet hym fro, and on his ax rested,
Sette the schaft upon schore, and to the scharp lened,
And loked to the leude that on the launde yede,
How that doghty, dredles, dervely ther stondes
Armed, ful aghles; in hert hit hym lykes.   2335
Thenn he meles muryly wyth a much steven,
And wyth a rynkande rurde he to the renk sayde,
'Bolde burne, on this bent be not so gryndel.
No mon here unmanerly the mysboden habbes,
Ne kyd, bot as covenaunde at kynges kort schaped.   2340

2303 *in/anticipation/leave, delay*

2305 *stance* (l. 846)
2306 *frowns*

2308 *rescue*

2309 *weapon*

2311 *hammered*
2312 *snicked*

2316 *sprang/"springing with his feet"*

2322 *Desist/blow* (l. 2261)

2326 *fearsomely* (l. 1430)

2328 *(was) shaped*

2330 *stop*

2331 *turned* (l. 1922)

2333 *went* (l. 1684)
2334 *stoutly* (cf. l. 1492)
2335 *fearless* (cf. l. 2301)
2336 *voice* (l. 242)
2337 *ringing/noise* (l. 2219)
2338 *grim*
2339 *mistreated*
2340 *acted*

I hyght the a strok and thou hit has, halde the wel payed;
I relece the of the remnaunt of ryghtes alle other.
Iif I deliver had bene, a boffet paraunter,
I couthe wrotheloker haf waret, to thee haf wroght anger.
Fyrst I mansed thee muryly with a mynt one,   2345
And rove the wyth no rof sore, with ryght I the profered
For the forwarde that we fest in the fyrst nyght,
And thou trystyly the trawthe and trwly me haldes,
Al the gayne thow me gef, as god mon schulde.
That other munt for the morne, mon, I the profered,   2350
Thou kyssedes my clere wyf—the cosses me raghtes.
For bothe two here I the bede bot two bare myntes
    boute scathe.
  Trwe mon trwe restore,
  Thenne thar mon drede no wathe,   2355
  At the thrid thou fayled thore,
  And therfor that tappe ta the.

96(16)

'For hit is my wede that thou weres, that ilke woven girdel,
Myn owen wyf hit weved, I wot wel for sothe.
Now know I wel thy cosses, and thy costes als,   2360
And the wowyng of my wyf; I wroght hit myselven.
I sende hir to asay the, and sothly me thynkkes
On the fautlest freke that ever on fote yede;
As perle bi the quite pese is of prys more,
So is Gawayn, in god fayth, bi other gay knyghtes.   2365
Bot here yow lakked a lyttel, sir, and lewté yow wonted;
Bot that was for no wylyde werke, ne wowyng nauther,
Bot for ye lufed your lyf; the lasse I yow blame.'
That other stif mon in study stod a gret whyle,
So agreved for greme he gryed withinne;   2370
Alle the blode of his brest blende in his face,
That al he schrank for schome that the schalk talked.
The forme worde upon folde that the freke meled,
'Corsed worth cowarddyse and covetyse bothe!
In yow is vylany and vyse that vertue disstryes.'   2375
Thenne he kaght to the knot, and the kest lawses,
Brayde brothely the belt to the burne selven:
'Lo! ther the falssyng, foule mot hit falle!
For care of thy knokke cowardyse me taght
To acorde me with covetyse, my kynde to forsake,   2380

2341 *promised* (l. 1966)

2343 *more alert* (l. 2009)
2344 *wrothlier/given* (l. 1235)
2345 *menaced*
2346 *ripped* (l. 1341)/*wound*
2347 *confirmed*

2351 *fair* (l. 1747)/*kisses*

2353 *without/injury*
2354 *must*
2355 *danger* (l. 1576)
2356 *there*

2364 "*As the pearl compared to the white pea . . .*"

2366 *loyalty*
2367 *wily*
2368 *less*

2370 *grief, shame* (ll. 2251, 2299)/*shook*

2373 *first/earth* (l. 1694)
2374 *be*
2375 *destroys*
2376 *cast, fastening/loosens*

2378 *deceitful object*

That is larges and lewté that longes to knyghtes.
Now I am fawty and falce, and ferde haf ben ever
Of trecherye and untrawthe: bothe bityde sorwe
   and care!
  I biknowe yow, knyght, here stylle,   2385
  Al fawty is my fare;
  Letes me overtake your wylle
  And efte I schal be ware.'

97(17)

Thenn loghe that other leude and luflyly sayde,
'I halde hit hardily hole, the harme that I hade.   2390
Thou art confessed so clene, beknowen of thy mysses,
And has the penaunce apert of the poynt of myn egge,
I halde the polysed of that plyght, and pured as clene
As thou hades never forfeted sythen thou was fyrst borne;
And I gif the, sir, the gurdel that is golde-hemmed,   2395
For hit is grene as my goune. Sir Gawayn, ye maye
Thenk upon this ilke threpe, ther thou forth thrynges
Among prynces of prys, and this a pure token
Of the chaunce of the grene chapel at chevalrous knyghtes.
And ye schal in this Nwe Yer ayayn to my wones,   2400
And we schyn revel the remnaunt of this ryche fest
   ful bene.'
  Ther lathed hym fast the lorde
  And sayde, 'With my wyf, I wene,
  We schal yow wel acorde,   2405
  That was your enmy kene.'

98(18)

'Nay, for sothe,' quoth the segge, and sesed hys helme,
And has hit of hendely, and the hathel thonkkes,
'I haf soiorned sadly; sele yow bytyde,
And he yelde hit yow yare that yarkkes al menskes!   2410
And comaundes me to that cortays, your comlych fere,
Bothe that on and that other, myn honoured ladyes,
That thus hor knyght wyth hor kest han koyntly bigyled.
Bot hit is no ferly thagh a fole madde,
And thurgh wyles of wymmen be wonen to sorwe,   2415
For so was Adam in erde with one bygyled,
And Salamon with fele sere, and Samson eftsones—

2381 *belongs*
2382 *faulty*

2385 *"I confess to you . . ."*

2389 *laughed*

2391 *mistakes*
2392 *edge (of ax)*
2393 *polished, cleaned*

2396 *gown*
2397 *encounter/go (l. 1021)*

2400 *(come) again/dwelling (l. 2198)*
2401 *shall*
2402 *well (cf. Fr. bien)*
2403 *invited*

2409 *sojourned (l. 2048)/good fortune (l. 1938)*
2410 *readily/controls/honors (l. 2052)*
2411 *companion (l. 695)*

2413 *cast, craft/slyly (l. 1525)*
2414 *marvel (l. 796)/fool/be mad*

2417 *many/separate (ones)*

Dalyda dalt hym hys wyrde—and Davyth therafter
Was blended with Barsabe, that much bale tholed.
Now these were wrathed wyth her wyles, hit were a wynne huge   2420
To luf hom wel, and leve hem not, a leude that couthe.
For thes wer forne the freest, that folwed alle the sele
Excellently of alle thyse other, under hevenryche
     that mused;
  And alle thay were biwyled   2425
  With wymmen that thay used.
  Thagh I be now bigyled,
  Me think me burde be excused.

99(19)

'Bot your gordel,' quoth Gawayn 'God yow foryelde!
That wyl I welde wyth guod wylle, not for the wynne golde,   2430
Ne the saynt, ne the sylk, ne the syde pendaundes,
For wele ne for worchyp, ne for the wlonk werkkes,
Bot in syngne of my surfet I schal se hit ofte,
When I ride in renoun, remorde to myselven
The faut and the fayntyse of the flesche crabbed,   2435
How tender hit is to entyse teches of fylthe;
And thus, quen pryde schal me pryk for prowes of armes,
The loke to this luf-lace schal lethe my hert.
Bot on I wolde yow pray, displeses yow never:
Syn ye be lorde of the yonder londe ther I haf lent inne   2440
Wyth yow wyth worschyp—the wyghe hit yow yelde
That uphaldes the heven and on hygh sittes—
How norne ye yowre ryght nome, and thenne no more?'
'That schal I telle the trwly,' quoth that other thenne,
'Bertilak de Hautdesert I hat in this londe.   2445
Thurgh myght of Morgne la Faye, that in my hous lenges,
And koyntyse of clergye, bi craftes wel lerned—
The maystrés of Merlyn mony ho has taken;
For ho has dalt drwry ful dere sumtyme
With that conable klerk, that knowes alle your knyghtes   2450
    at hame;
  Morgne the goddes
  Therfore hit is hir name:
  Weldes non so hyghe hawtesse
  That ho ne con make ful tame—   2455

2418 *Delilah/fate* (l. 2134)/*David*
2419 *deceived* (*by*)/*Bathsheba/endured*

2421 *believe*
2422 *formerly, of yore*
2423 *kingdom of heaven* (lit. *heaven's reich*)

2425 *deceived* (*with women's wiles*)

2428 *deserve/*(*to*) *be*

2429 *repay* (l. 1535)
2430 *wield, possess/winsome*
2431 *girdle* (l. 589)
2432 *elegant* (l. 2022)

2434 *recalling* (*remorsefully*)

2436 *stains* (cf. l. 917)

2438 *humble, temper*

2443 *call, name* (l. 1661)

2445 *am called* (l. 401)

2447 *skill/learning*
2448 *mysteries*
2449 *"For she has dealt in love . . ."* (l. 2033)
2450 *knowledgeable*
2451 *home*

2454 *pride* (O.Fr. *hautesse*)

100(20)

'Ho wayned me upon this wyse to your wynne halle
For to assay the surquidré, yif hit soth were
That rennes of the grete renoun of the Rounde Table;
Ho wayned me this wonder your wyttes to reve,
For to haf greved Gaynour and gart hir to dyghe   2460
With glopnyng of that ilke gome that gostlych speked
With his hede in his honde bifore the hyghe table.
That is ho that is at home, the auncian lady;
Ho is even thyn aunt, Arthures half-suster,
The duches doghter of Tyntagelle, that dere Uter after   2465
Hade Arthur upon, that athel is nowthe.
Therfore I ethe the, hathel, to com to thy naunt,
Make myry in my hous; my meny the lovies,
And I wol the as wel, wyghe, bi my faythe,
As any gome under God for thy grete trauthe.'   2470
And he nikked hym naye, he nolde bi no wayes.
Thay acolen and kyssen and kennen ayther other
To the prynce of paradise, and parten ryght there
        on coolde;
    Gawayn on blonk ful bene   2475
    To the kynges burgh buskes bolde,
    And the knyght in the enker grene
    Whiderwarde-so-ever he wolde.

101(21)

Wylde wayes in the worlde Wowen now rydes
On Gryngolet, that the grace hade geten of his lyve;   2480
Ofte he herbered in house and ofte al theroute,
And mony aventure in vale, and venquyst ofte,
That I ne tyght at this tyme in tale to remene.
The hurt was hole that he hade hent in his nek,
And the blykkande belt he bere theraboute   2485
Abelef as a bauderyk bounden bi his syde,
Loken under his lyfte arme, the lace, with a knot,
In tokenyng he was tane in tech of a faute.
And thus he commes to the court, knyght al in sounde.
Ther wakned wele in that wone when wyst the grete   2490
That gode Gawayn was commen; gayn hit hym thoght.
The kyng kysses the knyght, and the whene alce,
And sythen mony syker knyght that soght hym to haylce,

2456 *put* (l. 984)/*joyous* (l. 518)
2457 *pride* (l. 311)

2459 *deprive*
2460 *Guenivere/caused*
2461 *beholding*

2465 *Uther* (*Pendragon*)
2466 *noble/now*
2467 *ask* (l. 379)/*aunt*

2469 *will* (*it*), *wish* (*to have thee*)

2471 *nixed* (l. 706)/*wouldn't* (*would* + neg.)
2472 *hug* (l. 1936)/*commend*

2474 "*in the cold*"
2475 *horse/good* (l. 2402)

2477 *bright* (l. 159)
2478 *Whither*

2480 *that, who,* i.e., *Gawain*
2481 *harbored/outside*
2482 *vanquished* (*foes*)
2483 *intend/remember*
2484 *healed*
2485 *blinking, shining*
2486 *Diagonally*
2487 *left*
2488 *stain* (l. 2436)
2489 "*all safe and sound*"
2490 *knew*

2492 *queen/also*
2493 *sure/hail* (l. 972)

Of his fare that hym frayned; and ferlyly he telles,
Biknowes alle the costes of care that he hade,   2495
The chaunce of the chapel, the chere of the knyght,
The luf of the ladi, the lace at the last.
The nirt in the nek he naked hem schewed
That he laght for his unleuté at the leudes hondes
     for blame.   2500
     He tened quen he schulde telle,
     He groned for gref and grame;
     The blod in his face con melle,
     When he hit schulde schewe, for schame.

102(22)

'Lo! lorde,' quoth the leude, and the lace hondeled,   2505
'This is the bende of this blame I bere in my nek,
This is the lathe and the losse that I laght have,
Of couardise and covetyse that I haf caght thare;
This is the token of untrawthe that I am tan inne,
And I mot nedes hit were wyle I may last;   2510
For non may hyden his harme, bot unhap ne may hit,
For ther hit ones is tachched twynne wil hit never.'
The kyng comfortes the knyght, and alle the court als
Laghen loude therat, and luflyly acorden
That lordes and ladis that longed to the Table,   2515
Uche burne of the brotherhede, a bauderyk schulde have,
A bende abelef hym aboute of a bryght grene,
And that, for sake of that segge, in swete to were.
For that was acorded the renoun of the Rounde Table,
And he honoured that hit hade evermore after,   2520
As hit is breved in the best boke of romaunce.
This in Arthurus day this aunter bitidde,
The Brutus bokes therof beres wyttenesse;
Sythen Brutus, the bolde burne, bowed hider fyrst,
After the segge and the asaute was sesed at Troye,   2525
     iwysse,
     Mony aunteres here-biforne
     Haf fallen such er this.
     Now that bere the croun of thorne,
     He bryng uus to his blysse! AMEN   2530
          HONY SOYT QUI MAL PENCE.

2494 asked (l. 1549)/of wonders (l. 2414)
2495 Confesses (l. 2385)

2498 nick
2499 latched, received

2501 had difficulty (l. 2002)
2502 agony
2503 mingle

2506 band
2507 loathing

2509 untruth/taken
2510 wear
2511 unwrap
2512 attached/twin, separate

2515 belonged
2516 brotherhood
2517 slantwise (l. 2486)
2518 suite (l. 859)

2521 written (l. 1488)
2522 adventure (l. 27)

2525 siege/ceased (cf. l. 1)

2529 (he) who

SUPPLEMENTARY MATERIAL

1. Robert J. Blanch, ed., *Sir Gawain and Pearl: Critical Essays*, Bloomington, Ind., 1966.
2. Consideration of *Gawain* as cinematic material.
3. William Blades, ed., *The Boke of St. Albans*, London, 1901
(treatises on hunting, hawking, and heraldry).
4. F. J. Furnivall, ed., *Early English Meals and Manners*, EETS 32, London, 1868.
5. John Speirs, *Medieval English Poetry: The Non-Chaucerian Tradition*
(London, 1957), pp. 215-51.

PIERS PLOWMAN

Prologus, A-text

In a somer sesun   whon softe was the sonne,
I shop me into a schroud   a scheep as I were;
In habite as an hermite   unholy of werkes,
Wende I wydene in this world   wondres to here.
Bote in a Mayes morwnynge   on Malverne hulles   5
Me bifel a ferly   a feyrie me thouhte;
I was weori of wondringe   and wente me to reste
Undur a brod banke   bi a bourne syde
And as I lay and leonede   and lokede on the watres
I slumberde in a slepyng   hit sownede so murie.   10
Thenne gon I meeten   a mervelous swevene,
That I was in a wildernesse,   wuste I never where,
And as I beoheold into the est   anheigh to the sonne,
I sauh a tour on a toft   triyely imaket;
A deop dale bineothe   a dungun therinne,   15
With deop dich and derk   and dredful of siht.
A feir feld ful of folk   fond I ther bitwene,
Of alle maner of men,   the mene and the riche,
Worchinge and wondringe   as the world asketh.
Summe putten hem to the plough   and pleiden hem ful seldene, 20
In eringe and in sowynge   swonken ful harde,
That monie of theos wasturs   in glotonye distruen.
And summe putten hem to pruide   apparaylden hem therafter,
In cuntinaunce of clothinge   queinteliche degyset.
To preyere and to penaunce   putten heom monye,   25
For love of ur lord   liveden ful harde,
In hope for to have   heveneriche blisse;
As ancres and hermytes   that holdeth hem in heore celles,
Coveyte not in cuntré   to carien aboute,
For non likerous lyflode   heore licam to plese.   30
And summe chosen chaffare   to cheeven the bettre,
As hit semeth to ure siht   that suche men scholden,
And summe murthhes to maken   as munstrals cunne

2 *shaped, put/shroud, rustic garment/as (if)/shepherd*

4 *Went/wide*
5 *hills* (see map, Intro.)
6 *(To) me/marvel/of fairies*
7 *weary/wandering*
8 *brook's*
9 *leaned*
10 *sounded*
11 *dream*
12 *knew*
13 *on high*
14 *saw/tower/hillock* (cf. *tuft*)/*choicely/made*
15 *beneath*
16 *ditches/dark*
17 *fair/field*

19 *asks, requires*
20 *put/themselves/played/seldom*
21 *plowing* (O.E. *erian*)/*labored*
22 *wasters/gluttony/destroy*
23 *pride/appareled/accordingly*
24 *ostentation/quaintly/disguised*

26 *lived*
27 *(of the) kingdom of heaven*
28 *anchorites/keep (themselves)*
29 *Covet, yearn/"to roam around"*
30 *lecherous/livelihood/body*
31 *trade/achieve, prosper*
32 *should*
33 *mirth/minstrels/know how*

And gete gold with here gle   giltles, I trowe.
Bote iapers and iangelers,   Iudas children,   35
Founden hem fantasyes   and fooles hem maaden,
And habbeth wit at heor wille   to worchen yif hem luste.
That Poul precheth of hem,   I dar not preoven heere.
Qui loquitur turpiloquium,   hee is Luciferes hyne.
Bidders and beggers   faste aboute eoden,   40
Til heor bagges and heore balies   weren bratful icrommet;
Feyneden hem for heore foode,   foughten atte alle;
In glotonye, God wot,   gon heo to bedde,
And ryseth up with ribaudye   this Roberdes knaves.
Sleep and sleughthe   suweth hem evere.   45
Pilgrimes and palmers   plihten hem togederes
For to seche seint Ieme   and seintes at Roome;
Wenten forth in heore wey   with mony wyse tales,
And hedden leve to lyghen   al heore lyf aftir.
Ermytes on an hep   with hokide staves,   50
Wenten to Walsyngham   and here wenchis aftir;
Grete lobres and longe   that loth weore to swynke
Clotheden hem in copes   to beo knowen for bretheren;
And summe schopen hem to hermytes   heore ese to have.
I font there freres   all the foure ordres,   55
Prechinge the peple   for profyt of heore wombes,
Glosynge the gospel   as hem good liketh,
For covetyse of copes   construeth hit ille;
For monye of this maistres   mowen clothen hem at lyking,
For moneye and heore marchaundie   meeten ofte togedere.   60
Seththe charité hath be chapmon   and cheef to schriven lordes,
Mony ferlyes han bifalle   in a fewe yeres.
But holychirche biginne   holde bet togedere,
The moste mischeef on molde   mounteth up faste.
Ther prechede a pardoner   as he a prest were,   65
And brought up a bulle   with bisschopes seles,
And seide that himself mihte   asoylen hem alle
Of falsnesse and fastinge   and of vouwes ibroken.
The lewede men likede him wel   and leeveth his speche,
And comen up knelynge   and cusseden his bulle.   70
He bonchede hem with his brevet   and blered heore eighen,
And rauhte with his ragemon   ringes and broches.
Thus ye giveth oure gold   glotonye to helpen,
And leveth hit to losels   that lecherie haunten.
Weore the bisschop iblesset   and worth bothe his eres   75
Heo scholde not beo so hardi   to deceyve so the peple.

34 glee/guiltless/think
35 japers, jesters/janglers/Judas'
36 "Invent fantasies for themselves . . ."/made
37 But (nevertheless) have/wished
38 Paul/prove
39 "Who speaks slander"/servant
40 went
41 bellies/brimful/crammed
42 Feigned (hunger)/at the/ale(house)
43 knows/go/they
44 ribaldry/these/hoodlums
45 sloth/pursue
46 plighted, pledged
47 St. James

49 lie/"all the rest of their lives"
50 Hermits/heap, crowd/hooked

52 lubbers/tall/loath/labor
53 capes (of friars)/recognized/as
54 ease
55 found/friars
56 Preaching (to)/bellies
57 Glossing, expounding
58 illy
59 many/may/to their liking
60 merchandise
61 Since/tradesman
62 marvels (l. 6)/have
63 Unless/Holy Church (and the friars)/better
64 earth

66 (papal) bull
67 might/absolve
68 vows/broken
69 untaught/believed
70 kissed
71 banged/bleared/eyes, "hoodwinked them"
72 collected/assistant

74 rascals/practice
75 blessed
76 bold

Save hit nis not bi the bisschop   that the boye precheth,
Bote the parisch prest and he   departe the selver,
That have schulde the pore parisschens   yif that heo ne weore.
Persones and parisch prestes   playneth to heore bisschops,   80
That heore parisch hath ben pore   seththe the pestilence tyme,
And asketh leve and lycence   at Londun to dwelle
To singe ther for simonye   for selver is swete.
Ther hoveth an hundret   in hovves of selk
Seriauns hit semeth   to serven atte barre,   85
Pleden for pons   and poundes the lawe,
Not for love of ur lord   unloseth heore lippes ones.
Thow mihtest beter meten the myst   on Malverne hulles,
Then geten a mom of heore mouth   til moneye weore schewed.
I sauh ther bisschops bolde   and bachilers of divyn   90
Bicoome clerkes of acounte,   the kyng for to serven;
Erchedekenes and deknes   that dignité haven,
To preche the peple   and pore men to feede,
Beon lopen to londun   bi leve of heore bisschopes
To ben clerkes of the kynges benche   the cuntré to schende.   95
Barouns and burgeis   and bondemen also
I saugh in that semblé   as ye schul heren heraftur.
Bakers, bochers   and breusters monye,
Wollene websteris   and weveris of lynen,
Taillours, tanneris   and tokkeris bothe,   100
Masons, minours   and mony other craftes,
Dykers and delvers   that don heore dedes ille,
And driveth forth the longe day   with 'deu vous save, dam Emme!'
Cookes and heore knaves   cryen 'hote pies, hote!
Goode gees and grys!   gowe dyne, gowe!'   105
Taverners to hem   tolde the same tale
With good wyn of Gaskoyne   and wyn of Oseye,
To Ruyn and of Rochel   and rost to defye.
Al this I saugh slepynge   and seve sithes more.

THE SEVEN DEADLY SINS, *Passus V*, A-text

Thenne wakede I of my wink   me was wo with-alle
That I nedde sadloker islept   and iseghe more.
Er I a furlong hedde ifare   a feyntise me hente   *(5)
That forther mihti not afote   for defaute of sleep.

---

* Numbers in parentheses here and in the following selections correspond to
line designations in unabridged versions.

77 But/isn't (only)/by (leave of)/knave
78 divide/silver
79 "if it were not for them"
80 Parsons/complain

84 dwell/hoods/silk
85 Sergeants (of the law)/at the (l. 42)
86 (Who) plead/pence
87 loosen/once
88 measure
89 mumble
90 divinity

92 Archdeacons/deacons

94 Have/leaped, run
95 harm
96 burgesses/bondsmen
97 assembly
98 butchers/brewsters
99 '(Female) weavers of woolen cloth'
100 tanners/tuckers, fullers/also

102 Diggers
103 "God save you, Dame Emma"
104 hot
105 geese/pigs/Let's go/dine

107 Gascony/Alsace
108 Rhine/Rochelle/roast/digest
109 seven/times

1 When/nap/woeful
2 had not/more soundly/slept/seen
3 fared/faintness/seized
4 might I (go)/afoot

I sat softeliche adoun   and seide my beoleeve,   5
And so I blaberde on my beodes,   that brouhte me aslepe.
Then sauh I muche more   then I before tolde,
For I sauh the feld ful of folk   that ich of bifore schewede,   (10)
And Concience with a crois   com for to preche.
He preide the peple   have pité of hemselve,   10
And prevede that this pestilences   weore for puire synne
And this southwesterne wynt   on a Seterday at even
Was aperteliche for pruide   and for no poynt elles   (15)
Piries and plomtres   weore passchet to the grounde
In ensaumple to men   that we scholde do the bettre.   15
Beches and brode okes   weore blowen to the eorthe,
And turned upward the tayl   in toknyng of drede
That dedly synne or domesday   schulde fordon hem alle.   (20)
Of this matere I mihte   momele ful longe,
Bote I sigge as I sauh,   so me god helpe,   20
How Concience with a cros   comsede to preche.
He bad wastors go worche   what thei best couthe
And wynne that thei wasteden   with sum maner craft.   (25)
He preighede Pernel   hire porful to leve
And kepen hit in hire cofre   for catel at neode.   25
Thomas he taughte   to take twey staves,
And fette hom Felice   from wyvene pyne.
He warnede Watte   his wyf was to blame,
That hire hed was worth a mark   and his hod worth a grote.
He chargede chapmen   to chasten heore children   30
Let hem wonte non eighe   while that thei ben yonge.
He preyede preestes   and prelates togedere,
That thei prechen the peple   to preven hit in hemselven
'And libben as ye lereth us,   we wolen love ow the betere.'
And seththe he radde religioun   the rule for to holde   35
'Leste the kyng and his counseil   yor comunes apeire,
And beo stiward in oure stude   til ye be stouwet betere.
And ye that secheth seynt Iame   and seintes at Roome,
Secheth seint Treuthe,   for he may saven ow alle;
Qui cum patre et filio   feire mote you falle.'   40
Thenne ron Repentaunce   and rehersed this teeme,
And made William to weope   watur with his eghen.

SUPERBIA

Pernel Proudherte   platte hire to grounde
And lay longe ar heo lokede   and to ur ladi criede,

5 *down/belief, creed*
6 *mumbled/beads*

8 *I/spoke of*
9 *cross*
10 *prayed*
11 *pure, absolute*
12 *wind/evening*
13 *plainly/pride*
14 *Pears/pushed*
15 *example*

17 *tail/token*
18 *overcome*
19 *mumble*
20 *say*
21 *commenced*
22 *bade/knew how*

24 *prayed/Peronelle/decoration*
25 *coffer/property/need*
26 *two*
27 *fetch/home/women's pain, ?cucking stool*

29 *her/head(dress)*

31 *awe*

33 *prove, practice*
34 *live/teach/will/you*
35 *then/advised*
36 *provisions/confiscate*
37 *stead/established*

39 *Truth*
40 *"fare you well"*
41 *ran/theme*
42 *weep/eyes*

43 *flattened (cf. platter)*
44 *ere/Our Lady*

And beohighte to him   that us alle maade,   45
Heo wolde unsouwen hire smok   and setten ther an here
Forte fayten hire flesch   that frele was to synne,
'Schal never liht herte me hente   bote holde me lowe,
And suffre to beo misseid   and so dude I never.
And nou I con wel meke me   and merci beseche   50
Of al that ichave ihad   envye in myn herte.'

LUXURIA

Lechour seide 'allas!'   and to ur ladi criede
To maken him han merci   for his misdede,
Bitwene god almihti   and his pore soule,
With-that he schulde the Seterday   seven yer after   55
Drinken bote with the doke   and dynen but ones.

INVIDIA

Envye with hevi herte   asket aftur schrift,
And gretliche his gultus   biginneth to schewe.
As pale as a pelet   in a palesye he seemede,
Iclothed in a caurimauri   I couthe him not discreve;   60
A kertil and a courtepy,   a knyf be his side;
Of a freris frokke   were the foreslevys.
As a leek that hedde ileighen   longe in the sonne,
So loked he with lene chekes,   lourede he foule.
His bodi was bolled;   for wraththe he bot his lippes.   65
Wrothliche he wrong his fust,   he thoughte him awreke
With werkes or with wordes   whon he seigh his tyme.
'Venim or vernisch   or vinegre, I trouwe,
Walleth in my wombe   or waxeth, ich wene.
I ne mihte mony day don   as a mon ouhte,   70
Such wynt in my wombe   waxeth, er I dyne.
Ichave a neihghebor me neih   I have anuyghed him ofte,
Ablamed him behynde his bak   to bringe him in disclaundre,
And peired him bi my pouwer   ipunissched him ful ofte,
Bilowen him to lordes   to make him leose selver,   75
Idon his frendes ben his fon   with my false tonge;
His grase and his good hap   greveth me ful sore.
Bitwene him and his meyne   ichave imad wraththe,
Bothe his lyf and his leome   was lost thorw my tonge.
Whon I mette him in the market   that I most hate,   80
Ich heilede him as hendely   as I his frend weore.
He is doughtiore then I;   i dar non harm don him.

45 *behote, promised*
46 *unsew/hair (cloth)*
47 *For to/tame/frail*
48 *light*
49 *missaid, slandered/did*
50 *meeken, humble/beseech*
51 *all (for whom)/I have/had*

55 *Provided that/on*
56 *duck, i.e., water/dine*

57 *asked*
58 *greatly/guilts*
59 *pellet, pebble/palsy*
60 *rough garment/describe*
61 *short (pea)coat/by*
62 *frock/foresleeves*
63 *had/lain*
64 *lowered/foully*
65 *bowled, bent/bit*
66 *wrung/fist/(to) avenge*
67 *saw*
68 *varnish*
69 *Wells/belly (l. 56, Prol.)/I/think*
70 *do/ought*

72 *annoyed*
73 *slander*
74 *harmed (cf. l. 36)*
75 *(Be)lied/lose*
76 *Did, caused/foes*
77 *grace*
78 *household/made*
79 *limb/through*

81 *hailed/courteously*
82 *doughtier, hardier/than*

Bote hedde I maystrie and miht　I mortherde him for evere.
Whon I come to the churche　and knele bifore the roode,
And scholde preighe for the peple　as the prest us techeth,　　85
Thenne I crie uppon my knes　that Crist yive hem serwe
That hath ibore awei my bolle　and my brode schete.
From the auter I turne　myn eighe, and biholde
Hou Heyne hath a newe cote　and his wyf another;
Thenne I wussche hit weore myn　and al the web aftur.　　90
Of his leosinge I lauhwe;　hit liketh me in myn herte;
Ac for his wynnynge I wepe　and weile the tyme.
I deme men that don ille　and yit I do wel worse,
For I wolde that uch a wiht　in this world were mi knave,
And whoso hath more thanne I　that angrith myn herte.　　95
Thus I live loveles,　lyk a luther dogge,
That al my breste bolleth　for bitter of my galle;
May no suger so swete　aswangen hit unnethe,
Ne no _diopendion_　dryve hit from myn herte;
Yif schrift schulde hit thenne swopen out,　a gret wonder hit were.'　100
'Yus, rediliche,' quod Repentaunce　and radde him to goode,
'Serw for heore sunnes　saveth men ful monye.'
'Icham sori,' quod Envye　'I ne am but seldene other,
And that maketh me so mad　for I ne may me venge.'

AVARICIA*

Thenne com Covetyse　I couthe him not discreve,　　105
So hungri and so holewe　sire Hervi him loked.
He was bitel-brouwed　with twei blered eighen,
And lyk a letherne pors　lullede his chekes;
In a toren tabart　of twelve wynter age;
But yif a lous couthe lepe　I con hit not ileve　　110
Heo scholde wandre on that walk　hit was so thredbare.
'Ichave ben covetous,' quod this caityf　'I beknowe hit heere;
For sum tyme I servede　Simme atte noke,
And was his pliht prentys,　his profyt to loke.
Furst I leornede to lyghe　a lessun or tweyne,　　115
And wikkedliche for to weie　was myn other lessun.
To Winchestre and to Wych　ich wente to the feire
With mony maner marchaundise　as my mayster hinte;
Bote nedde the grace of gyle　igon among my ware,
Hit hedde ben unsold this seven yer,　so me god helpe!　　120
Thenne I drough me among this drapers　my donet to leorne,

---

* Ira, normally at this place in the seven sins, does not appear in the A-text.

83 *had/mastery/(would have) murdered*
84 *cross*
85 *pray*
86 *give/sorrow*
87 *borne/bowl/sheet*
88 *altar*

90 *wish/cloth*
91 *losing/laugh*
92 *But/wail*
93 *deem, judge*
94 *every/man*

96 *evil/dog*
97 *swells* (l. 65)/*bitterness*
98 *assuage/hardly*
99 *remedy*
100 *sweep*
101 *Yes/advised*
102 *Sorrow/sins*
103 *seldom*

106 *hollow/Sir Harvey* (name for a covetous man)
107 *beetle-browed/two*
108 *purse/lolled, flapped*
109 *torn/tabard*
110 *Unless/louse/leap/believe*
111 *walkway, cloth*
112 *wretch/admit*
113 *"Sim at the oak"*
114 *pledged/apprentice/look* (after)
115 *lie*
116 *wickedly/weigh*
117 *Weyhill/fair*
118 *bade*
119 *Unless/neg.* + *had/gone*
120 *had*
121 *drew/primer*

To drawe the lyste wel along   the lengore hit semede;
Among this riche rayes   lernde I a lessun,
Brochede hem with a pak-neelde   and pletede hem togedere,
Putte hem in a pressour   and pinnede hem therinne   125
Til ten yerdes other twelve   tolden out threttene.
And my wyf at Westmunstre   that wollene cloth made
Spak to the spinsters   for to spinne hit softe.
The pound that heo peysede by   peisede a quartun more
Then myn auncel dude   whon I weyede treuthe.   130
I bouhte hire barly;   heo breuh hit to sulle;
Peni-ale and piriwhit   heo pourede togedere
For laborers and louh folk   that liven be hemselven.
The beste in the bedchaumbre   lay bi the wowe;
Hose bummede therof   boughte hit therafter,   135
A galoun for a grote   got wot, no lasse,
Whon hit com in cuppemel,   such craftes me usede.
Rose the regratour   is hire rihte name;
Heo hath holden hoxterye   this ellevene wynter.
Bote I swere nou sothely   that sunne wol I lcte,   140
And nevere wikkedliche weye,   ne fals chaffare usen,
Bote weende to Walsyngham   and my wyf alse,
And bidde the rode of Bromholm   bringe me out of dette.'

GULA

Nou ginneth the Gloton   for to go to schrifte,
And carieth him to chircheward,   his schrift forte telle.   145
Thenne Betun the breustere   bad him gode morwe,
And seththen heo asked of him   'whoder that he wolde?'
'To holi chirche,' quod he   'for to here masse,
And seththen ichule ben ischriven   and sunge no more.'
'Ic have good ale, gossib,' quod heo,   'Gloton, woltou assaye?'   150
'Hastou ought i thi pors,' quod he   'eny hote spices?'
'Ye, Glotun, gossip,' quod heo   'god wot, ful goode;
I have peper and piane   and a pound of garlek,
A ferthing-worth of fenel seed   for this fastyng dayes.'
Thene geth Gloton in   and grete othus after;   155
Sesse, the souters wyf   sat on the benche,
Watte the warinar   and his wyf bothe,
Tomkyn the tinkere   and tweyne of his knaves,
Hikke the hakeney mon   and Hogge the neldere,
Clarisse of Cokkes lone   and the clerk of the churche,   160
Sire Pers of Pridye   and Pernel of Flaundres,

122 *selvage/longer*
123 *striped fabrics*
124 *Stitched/pack needle/pleated*
125 *press*
126 *or/thirteen*
127 *woolen*
128 *Spoke*
129 *weighed/quarter*
130 *balance, scale/did*
131 *her/brewed/sell*
132 *white perry*
133 *"by their own efforts"*
134 *best (ale)/wall*
135 *Whosoever/tippled*
136 *less*
137 *by cupfuls (cf. N.E. piecemeal)*
138 *retailer*
139 *huckstery*
140 *sin/let (go), leave*
141 *trade*
142 *go*
143 *pray/cross (l. 84)*

144 *begins/Glutton*
145 *goes/churchward/for to*
146 *female brewer*
147 *then/whither*

149 *I will/sin*
150 *gossip/will + you*
151 *anything/any*

153 *peonies*

155 *goes/oaths*
156 *Cis/shoemaker's*
157 *warrener*

159 *Hodge/needle-seller*
160 *Cock's Lane*
161 *Piers*

Dauwe the disschere   and a doseyn othere.
A ribibor, a ratoner,   a rakere of Chepe,
A ropere, a redyng-kyng,   and Rose the disschere,
Godfrei of Garlesschire   and Griffin the Walsche,   165
And of upholders an hep,   erly bi the morwe
Yive the Gloton with good wille   good ale to honsel.
Thenne Clement the cobelere   caste of his cloke,
And atte newe feire   he leyde hire to sulle;
And Hikke the ostiler   hutte his hod aftur,   170
And bad Bette the bocher   ben on his bisyde.
Ther weore chapmen ichose   the chaffare to preise;
Hose hedde the hod   schulde have amendes.
Thei risen up raply   and rouneden togedere,
And preiseden the peniworthus   and parteden bi hemselven;   175
Ther weoren othes an hep,   hose that hit herde.
Thei couthe not bi heore concience   acorde togedere,
Til Robyn the ropere   weore rad forte aryse,
And nempned for a noumpere   that no debat neore,
For he schulde preise the penyworthes   as hym good thought.   180
Thenne Hikke the ostiler   hedde the cloke,
In covenaunt that Clement   schulde the cuppe fulle,
And habbe Hikkes hod the ostiler   and hold him wel iservet;
And he that repenteth rathest   schulde arysen aftur,
And greten sir Gloten   with a galun of ale.   185
Ther was laughwhing and lotering   and 'let go the cuppe,'
Bargeyns and beverages   bigonne to aryse,
And seeten so til evensong   and songen sum while,
Til Gloten hedde igloupet   a galoun and a gille.
He pissede a potel   in a *paternoster* while,   190
And bleuh the ronde ruwet   atte ruggebones ende
That alle that herde the horn   heolden heore neose after,
And weschte that hit weore iwipet   with a wesp of firsen.
He hedde no strengthe to stonde   til he his staf hedde;
Thenne gon he for to go   lyk a gleomannes bicche,   195
Sum tyme asyde   and sum tyme arere,
As hose leith lynes   to lacche with foules.
Whon he drouh to the dore   then dimmede his eighen
He thrompelde atte thexwolde   and threuh to the grounde.
Clement the coblere   caughte Glotoun by the mydle,   200
And for to lyfte hym aloft   leide hym on his knees;
And glotoun was a gret cherl   and grym in the lyftynge,
And cowhede up a cawdel   in Clementis lappe,
That the hungriest hound   of Hertforde schire

162 *Daw/ditcher/dozen*
163 *rebeck-player/ratcatcher/raker/Cheapside*
164 *ropemaker/retainer/dish-seller*
165 *Garlickhithe/Welsh(man)*
166 *upholsterers/heap*
167 *Give/as a gift*
168 *off*
169 *New Fair/"laid it for bargaining"*
170 *hosteler/cast (down)/hood*
171 *butcher/side, "be his deputy"*
172 *chosen/merchandise/appraise*
173 *Whosoever/a dividend to make up value difference between cloak, hood*
174 *rapidly/whispered*
175 *pennyworths/apart*

178 *advised/for to*
179 *named/umpire/would be*

181 *had*

183 *hood/satisfied*
184 *reneged/first*
185 *greet*
186 *laughing/kibitzing*
187 *Bargains*

189 *guzzled/gill (¼ pt.)*
190 *pottle (2 qts.)/in (the time it takes to say) a*
191 *blew/bugle, sm. horn/spine's, ridge bone's*
192 *held/noses*
193 *wished/wiped/wisp/furze, briars*

195 *began/gleeman's/bitch*

197 *whoso/lays/lines, nets/latch, snare*
198 *drew*
199 *stumbled/threshold/threw (himself), fell*

202 *lifting*
203 *coughed/caudle*

Ne durst lape of that laveyne, so unloveli it smakith.   205
That with al the wo of this world his wyf and his wenche
Beeren him hom to his bed and brouhten him therinne.
And after al this surfet an accesse he hedde,
That he slepte Saturday and Sonenday til sonne wente to reste.
Thenne he wakede of his wynk, wypede his eighen;   210
The furste word that he spac was 'wher is the cuppe?'
His wyf warnede him tho of wikkednesse and of sinne.
Thenne was he aschomed, that schrewe, and schraped his eren,
And gon to grede grimliche and gret deol to make
For his wikkede lyf that he ilived hedde.   215
'For hungur other for furst I make myn avou,
Schal never fysch on Frydai defyen in my mawe,
Er Abstinence myn aunte have iyive me leve;
And yit ichave ihated hire al my lyftyme.'

SUPPLEMENTARY MATERIAL

1. Hieronymus Bosch's "The Seven Deadly Sins."
2. Chaucer's Parson's Tale in the *Canterbury Tales*.
3. "The Seven Deadly Sins" in the *Ancrene Riwle*.
4. Robert J. Blanch, ed., *Piers Plowman: Critical Essays*, Knoxville, Tenn.,
   1968.

205 *Dared not/lap up/leaving/smelled*
206 *daughter*
207 *Bore/brought*
208 *attack, sickness*
209 *sun*

212 *then*
213 *ashamed/rascal/rubbed*
214 *began/cry out/grimly/dolor*
215 *lived*
216 *thirst/vow*
217 *digest/belly*
218 *given*
219 *yet/I have/hated/her*

MANDEVILLE'S TRAVELS

CHAPTER XVIII

And fro that other cost of caldee toward the south
is Ethiope a gret contrée that streccheth to the ende
of Egypt; Ethiope is departed in ij parties princypall.
And that is in the Est partie and in the meridionall partie,
the which partie meridionall is clept Moretane.   5
And the folk of that contrée ben blake ynow and more
blake than in the tother partie and thei ben clept
mowres. In that partie is a well that in the day it
is so cold that no man may drynke there offe, and in
the nyght it is so hoot that no man may suffre hys   10
hond there in. And beyonde that partie toward the
south to passe by the See Occean is a gret lond and
a gret contrey. But men may not duell there, for the
fervent brennynge of the sonne, so is it passynge hoot
in that contrey. In Ethiope all the ryveres and all the 15
watres ben trouble and thei ben somdell salté for the
gret hete that is there. And the folk of that contree
ben lyghtly dronken and han but littill appetyt to mete
and thei han comounly the flux of the wombe and they
lyven not longe. In Ethiope ben many dyverse folk and 20
Ethiope is clept Cusis. In that contree ben folk that
han but o foot and thei gon so blyve that it is mervaylle
and the foot is so large that it schadeweth all the
body ayen the sonne whanne thei wole lye and reste hem.
In Ethiope whan the children ben yonge and lytill thei ben 25
all yalowe and whan that thei wexen of age that yalowness
turneth to ben all blak. In Ethiope is the cytée Of Saba
and the lond of the which on of the iij kynges that presented oure lord in Bethleem was kyng offe. Fro Ethiope
men gon into ynde be manye dyverse contreyes and men 30
clepen the high ynde Emlak. And ynde is devyded in iij
princypall parties: that is, the more, that is full hoot
contree, and the less, that is a full atempree contrey

1 *coast/Chaldea*

3 *divided/2/parts*
4 *meridionall,* here *southern*
5 *called/Mauritania*
6 *black/enough*
7 *other*
8 Moors

12 *Indian Ocean*
13 *dwell*
14 *burning/very, surpassing(ly)*
15 *rivers*
16 *muddy/somewhat*

18 *"become easily drunk"*
19 *dysentery*
20 *live*

22 *one/go (about)/quickly/marvel*
23 *shadows*
24 *against/will/themselves*

26 *yellow/grow*

28 *one/3*
29 *of*
30 *India/by*
31 *Evilak, Havilah*

33 *temperate*

that streccheth to the londe of Medé. And the iij part
toward the Septentrion is full cold so that for pure 35
cold and contynuell frost the water becometh Cristall.
And upon the roches of cristall growen the gode dyamandes
that ben of trouble colour; Yalow Cristall draweth colour
lyke oylle and thei ben so harde that noman may pollysch
hem and men clepen hem dyamandes in that contree and 40
Hamese in another contree. Othere dyamandes men fynden in
Arabye that ben not so gode and thei ben more broun and
more tendre. And other dyamandes also men fynden in the
Ile of Cipre that ben yit more tendre and hem men may wel
pollischen; and in the lond of Macedoyne men fynden dyamaundes 45
also, but the beste and the moste precyiouse ben in ynde.
And men fynden many tyme harde dyamaundes in a masse that
cometh out of gold whan men puren it and fynen it out of
the myne whan men breken that mass in smale peces. And
sum tyme it happeneth that men fynden summe as grete as a 50
pese and summe lasse and thei ben als harde as tho of
ynde. And all be it that men fynden gode dyamandes in
ynde, yit natheles men fynden hem more comounly upon the
roches in the see and upon hilles where the myne of
gold is. And thei growen many to gedre, on lytill, another 55
gret, and ther ben summe of the gretness of a bene and
summe als grete as an hasell note and thei ben square
and poynted of here owne kynde, bothe aboven and benethen,
withouten worchinge of mannes hond and thei growen togedre
male and femele and thei ben norysscht with the dew of 60
hevene and thei engendren comounly and bryngen forth
smale children that multiplyen and growen all the yeer.
I have often tymes assayed that yif a man kepe hem with
a lityll of the roche, and wete hem with may dew oftesythes
thei schull growe everyche yeer, and the smale wole wexen 65
grete. For right as the fyn perl congeleth and wexeth gret
of the dew of hevene, right so doth the verray dyamand,
and right as the perl of his owne kynde taketh roundness,
right so the dyamand be vertu of god taketh squareness.
And men schall bere the dyamaund on his left syde for it 70
is of grettere vertue thanne, than on the right syde;
for the strengthe of here growynge is toward the north,
that is the left syde of the world, and the left partie
of man is, whan he turneth his face toward the est. And
yif you lyke to knowe the vertues of the dyamand as men 75
may fynden in the lapidarye that many men knowen noght, I

34 *Media/third*
35 *North*

37 *rocks/diamonds*
38 *mottled/approaches (the) color*
39 *of oil/polish*

42 *brown*
43 *soft*
44 *Cyprus*
45 *Macedonia*

48 *purify/refine*

51 *pea/less/as/those*

53 *nevertheless*

55 *together/one*
56 *bean*
57 *as/hazel/nut*
58 *their/nature*
59 *working*
60 *nourished*

63 *tested, proved/"keep with him"*
64 *wet/oftentimes*
65 *shall/every/will*
66 *just*
67 *true*

69 *"by virtue of God"*

71 *then*

schall telle you as thei beyonde the see seyn and affermen,
of whom al science and all philosophie cometh from. He
that bereth the dyamand upon him, it yeveth him hardyness
and manhode and it kepeth the lemes of his body hole, it   80
yeveth him victorye of his enemyes in plee and in werre
yif his cause be rightfull, and it kepeth him that bereth
it in gode wytt. And it kepeth him fro strif and ryot,
fro evyll swevenes, from sorwes and from enchauntementes
and from fantasyes and illusiouns of wykked spirites.   85
And yif ony cursed wycche or enchauntour wolde bewycchen
him that bereth the dyamand, all that sorwe and mischance
schall turne to himself thorgh vertue of that ston and also
no wylde best dar assaylle the man that bereth it on him.
Also the dyamand scholde ben yoven frely withouten coveyt-   90
ynge and withouten byggynge and than it is of grettere
vertue. And it maketh a man more strong and more sad
ayenst his enemyes and it heleth him that is lunatyk
and hem that the fend pursueth or travayleth. And yif
venym or poysoun be brought in presence of the dyamand   95
anon it begynneth to wexe moyst and for to swete. There
ben also dyamandes in ynde that ben clept violastres,
for here colour is liche vyolet or more browne than
the violettes, that ben full harde and full precyous,
but yit sum men love not hem so wel as the othere, but   100
in soth to me I wolde loven hem als moche as the othere,
for I have seen hem assayed. Also there is a nother
maner of dyamandes that ben als white as cristall but
thei ben a lityll more trouble and thei ben gode and of
gret vertue and all thei ben square and poynted of here owne   105
kynde, and summe ben vj squared, summe iiij squared, and summe
iij, as nature schapeth hem and therfore whan grete lordes and
knyghtes gon to sechen worschipe in armes thei beren gladly the
dyamaund upon hem. I schal speke a litill more of the dyamandes
all though I tarye my matere for a tyme, to that ende that thei that   110
knowen hem not be not disceyved be gabberes that gon be the contree that sellen hem. For whoso wil bye the dyamand, it is nedfull
to him that he knowe hem be cause that men counterfeten hem often
of cristall that is yalow. And of Saphires of cytryne colour that
is yalow also, and of the Saphire loupe and of many other stones;   115
but I tell you theise contrefetes ben not so harde. And also the
poyntes wil breken lightly and men may esily pollisschen hem
but summe werkmen for malice wil not pollisschen hem, to that
entent to maken men beleve that thei may not ben pollisscht.

77 *say/affirm*

79 *gives*
80 *limbs*
81 *plea, suit/war*

83 *strife/riot*
84 *dreams/sorrows*

86 *any/witch*

89 *beast/dare*
90 *given*
91 *buying*
92 *grievous*
93 *against*
94 *fiend, devil*

96 *immediately/sweat*

98 *like*

101 *truth/much*

106 *6-sided/4-*

110 *tarry/subject matter*
111 *swindlers*

114 *citron*
115 *imperfect*

But men may assaye hem in this manere: first schere with hem   120
or write with hem in Saphires, in cristall or in other precious
stones. After that men taken the Ademand that is the schipmannes
ston that draweth the nedle to him. And men leyn the dyamand
upon the Ademand and leyn the nedle before the ademand and
yif the dyamand be gode and vertuous, the ademand draweth   125
not the nedle to him whils the dyamand is there present. And
this is the preef that thei beyonde the see maken. Natheles it
befalleth often tyme that the gode dyamand leseth his vertue
be synne and for Incontynence of him that bereth it and thanne
is it nedfull to make it to recoveren his vertue ayen or ell it   130
is of litill value.

FROM CHAPTERS XXX AND XXXI

From thens gon men be many iourneyes thorgh the lond of
Prestre Iohn, the grete Emperour of Ynde, and men clepen
his roialme the yle of Pentexoire. . . . Besyde the yle of Pentexoire
that is the lond of Prestre Iohn is a gret yle long and brode that   135
men clepen Milstorak and it is in the lordschipe of Prestre Iohn.
In that yle is a gret plentee of godes. There was dwellynge somtyme a riche man and it is not longe sithe and men clept him
Gatholonabes and he was full of cauteles and of sotyll disceytes.
And he hadde a full fair castell and a strong in a mountayne,   140
so strong and so noble that noman cowde devise a fairere ne a
strengere. And he had let muren all the mountayne aboute with
a strong wall and a fair and withinne tho walles he had the fairest gardyn that ony man myghte beholde and therein were trees
berynge all maner of frutes that ony man cowde devyse. And   145
therein were also all maner vertuous herbes of gode smell and
all other herbes also that beren faire floures. And he had also
in that gardyn many faire welles, and beside tho welles he had
lete make faire halles and faire chambres depeynted all with
gold and azure. And there weren jn that place many a dyverse   150
thinges and manye dyverse storyes. And of bestes and of
bryddes that songen full delectabely and meveden be craft,
that it semede that thei were quyke. And he had also in his
gardyn all maner of foules and of bestes that ony man myghte
thenke on for to have pley or desport to beholde hem. And   155
he had also in that place the faireste damyseles that myght
ben founde under the age of xv yeer and the faireste yonge
striplynges that men myghte gete of that same age; and all
thei weren clothed in clothes of gold full richely and he seyde
that tho weren aungeles. And he had also let make iij welles   160

120 *shear*

122 *lodestone*
123 *lay*

127 *proof/nevertheless*
128 *loses*
129 *by/sin*
130 *again/else*

133 *John/call*
134 *realm/isle*

138 *since*
139 *wiles/subtle/deceits*

142 *stronger/had enclosed*

144 *any*

149 *had made/painted*
150 *in*
151 *(painted) stories/beasts*
152 *birds/sang/moved*
153 *quick, alive*
154 *fowls*
155 *think of/play*
156 *damsels*

160 *angels*

faire and noble and all envyround with ston of jaspre, of
cristall, dyapred with gold and sett with precious stones
and grete orient perles. And he had made a conduyt under
erthe so that the iij welles, at his list, on scholde renne
mylk, another wyn and another hony; and that place he clept   165
paradys. And whan that ony gode knyght that was hardy
and noble cam to see this rialtee, he wolde lede him in to
his paradys and schewen him theise wonderfull thinges to
his desport and the merveyllous and delicious song of
dyverse briddes and the faire damyseles and the faire   170
welles of mylk, of wyn, and of hony, plenteuous rennynge.
And he wolde let make dyverse jnstrumentes of Musik
to sownen in an high tour so merily that it was ioye for
to here and noman scholde see the craft there of. And
tho he seyde weren aungeles of god and that place was   175
paradys that god had behight to his frendes seyenge:
Dabo vobis terram fluentem lacte et melle. And thanne
wolde he maken hem to drynken of a certeyn drynk wherof anon thei scholden be dronken, and thanne wolde hem
thinken gretter delyt than thei hadden before. And than   180
wolde he seye to hem that yif they wolde dyen for him and for
his love that after hire deth thei scholde come to his paradys
and thei scholden ben of the age of tho damyselles and thei
scholden pleyen with hem and yit ben maydenes. And after
that yit scholde he putten hem in fayrere paradys, there that   185
thei scholde see god of nature visibely in his magestee and in
his blisse. And than wolde he schewe hem his entent and seye
hem that yif they would go sle such a lord or such a man that
was his enemye or contrarious to his list, that thei scholde not
drede to don it and for to be slayn therfore hem self, for after   190
hire deth he wolde putten hem in another paradys, that was an
C fold fairere than ony of the tothere and there scholde thei
dwellen with the most fairest damyselles that myghte be and
pley with hem everemore. And thus wenten many dyverse
lusty Bacheleres for to sle grete lordes in dyverse contrees   195
that weren his enemyes and made hemself to ben slayn in hope
to have that paradys. And thus often tyme he was revenged of his
enemyes be his sotyll disceytes and false cawteles. And whan the
worthi men of the contree hadden perceyved this sotyll falshod
of this Gatholonabes, thei assembled hem with force, assayleden   200
his castell and slowen him and destroyeden all the faire places
and all the nobletees of that paradys. The place of the welles and
of the walles and of many other thinges ben yit apertly sene,

161 *environed, surrounded*
162 *diapered*
163 *conduit*
164 *desire/one/run*

167 *royalty*
168 *for*

173 *sound/tower*

175 *those*
176 *promised*
177 *"I will give you a land flowing with milk and honey"*

188 *slay*
189 *desire*

192 *hundredfold/others*

198 *wiles* (l. 139)

201 *slew*

203 *openly*

but the ricchesse is voyded clene. And it is not longes gon
sith that place was destroyed.   205

SUPPLEMENTARY MATERIAL

1. Edith Rickert, "Travel," *Chaucer's World*, ed. C. C. Olson and M. M. Crow, New York, 1948.
2. Compare the second Mandeville selection with *The Land of Cokaygne*, pp. 375–80.
3. Josephine W. Bennett, *The Rediscovery of Sir John Mandeville*, New York, 1954.
4. H. R. Patch, *The Other World, According to Descriptions in Medieval Literature*, Cambridge, Mass., 1950.

SECOND SHEPHERDS' PLAY

First Shepherd, Coll	*Mak's Wife, Gyll*
Second Shepherd, Gyb	*Angel*
Third Shepherd, Daw	*Mary*
Sheep Thief, Mak	*Christ Child*

I SHEP. Lord, what these weders ar cold,   *weathers/habited,*
   and I am yll happyd.   *dressed*
I am nerehande dold, so long have I nappyd.   *nearly/numb*
My legys thay fold, my fyngers ar chappyd.
It is not as I wold, for I am al lappyd   *wrapped*
In sorow.   5
In stormes and tempest
Now in the eest, now in the west,
Wo is hym has never rest
Mydday nor morow.

Bot we sely shephardes that walkys on the   10   *poor, miserable/walk*
   moore
In fayth we are nerehandys outt of the doore.
No wonder as it standys if we be poore
For the tylthe of oure landys lyys falow as   *tillable part*
   the floore
As ye ken.
We ar so hamyd   15   *hamstrung*
Fortaxed and ramyd,   *Overtaxed/rammed*
                                 (down)

We are mayde handtamyd   *tame*
With thyse gentlery men.

Thus thay refe us oure rest, oure lady theym   *deprive/Mary/curse*
    wary.
These men that ar lordfest, thay cause the   20 *lord-fast*
    ploghe tary.
That men say is for the best, we fynde it
    contrary.
Thus ar husbandys opprest, in ponte to   *point*
    myscary
On lyfe.   *Alive*
Thus hold thay us hunder,   *under*
Thus thay bryng us in blonder.   25 *blunder*
It were greatte wonder
And ever shuld we thryfe.

For may he gett a paynt slefe or a broche   *decorated sleeve (liv-*
    now on dayes,   *ery)/nowadays*
Wo is hym that hym grefe or onys agane   *grieve/once/gainsay*
    says.
Dar noman hym reprefe, what mastry he   30   *Dare/reprove/what-*
    mays,   *ever/employs*
And yit may noman lefe oone word that he   *believe*
    says,
No letter.
He can make purveance   *purveyance*
With boste and bragance,   *bragging*
And all is thrugh mantenance   35
Of men that ar gretter.

Ther shall com a swane as prowde as a po,   *swain, chap/peacock*
He must borow my wane, my ploghe also.   *wagon*
Then I am full fane to graunt or he go.   *ere*
Thus lyf we in payne, anger, and wo,   40
By nyght and day.
He must have, if he langyd   *longed, wanted*
If I shuld forgang it.   *"Even if I must forgo*
I were better be hangyd   *it"*
Then oones say hym nay.   45

It dos me good, as I walk thus by myn oone,   *alone*
Of this warld for to talk in a maner of mone.   *moan*

To my shepe wyll I stalk, and herkyn anone,
Ther abyde on a balk, or sytt on a stone   *untilled division strip*
Full soyne.   50   *in field*
For I trowe, perdé,   *soon*
Trew men if thay be   *swear/par dé 'by*
We gett more compané   *God'*
Or it be noyne.
(*exit*)   *Ere/noon*

II SHEP. Benste and Dominus, what may this   55   *Benedicite, bless us/*
    bemeyne?   *betoken*
Why fares this warld thus? Oft have we not   *seen (such as this)*
    sene.
Lord thyse weders ar spytus and the wyndys   *spiteful*
    full kene
And the frostys so hydus thay water myn   *hideous*
    eeyne,
No ly.
Now in dry, now in wete,   60
Now in snaw, now in slete,
Whan my shone freys to my fete   *shoes/freeze*
It is not all esy.

Bot as far as I ken, or yit as I go,   *know*
We sely wedmen dre mekyll wo   65   *wedded men/en-*
We have sorow then and then. It fallys oft   *dure/much*
    so.   *"again and again"*
Sely Copple, oure hen, both to and fro
She kakyls.   *cackles*
Bot begyn she to crok,
To groyne or to clok,   70   *cluck*
Wo is hym is oure cok   *Woeful*
For he is in the shakyls.

These men that ar wed have not all thare
    wyll.
When they ar full hard sted thay sygh full   *placed*
    styll.
God wayte thay ar led full hard and full yll.   75   *knows*
In bowere nor in bed thay say noght   *thereto*
    thertyll.

This tyde   *time*
My parte have I fun,   *found*
I know my lesson.
Wo is hym that is bun,   80   *bound*
For he must abyde.

Bot now late in oure lyfys, a mervell to me,   *lives/marvel*
That I thynk my hart ryfys sich wonders to   *breaks*
    see.
What that destany dryfys it shuld so be,   *drives*
Som men wyll have two wyfys and som men   85
    thre
In store.
Som ar wo that has any.
Bot so far can I:
Wo is hym that has many,   *know*
For he felys sore.   90   *feels*

Bot yong men of wowyng, for God that you   *wooing/who/re-*
    boght,   *deemed*
Be well war of wedyng and thynk in youre   *wary*
    thoght,
"Had I wyst" is a thyng that servys of noght.   *known*
Mekyll styll mowrnyng has wedyng hom   *Much (l. 65)/si-*
    broght   *lent/mourning*
And grefys,   95   *griefs*
With many a sharp showre.   *pain*
For thou may cach in an owre   *catch/hour*
That shall sow the full sowre   *sour*
As long as thou lyffys.   *live*

For as ever rede I pystyll, I have oone to my 100   *epistle/mate*
    fere
As sharp as thystyll, as rugh as a brere.   *thistle/rough/briar*
She is browyd lyke a brystyll with a sowre-   *browed/bristle/*
    loten chere.   *-looking/expression*
Had she oones wett hyr whystyll, she couth   *could*
    syng full clere
Hyr Paternoster.
She is as greatt as a whall,   105 *whale*
She has a galon of gall.
By hym that dyed for us all
I wald I had ryn to I had lost hir.   *would, wish/run/till*

I SHEP. God looke over the raw. Full defly ye
    stand.   *row, company/deafly*

II SHEP. Yee, the dewill in thi maw, so   110   *devil/belly/tarrying*
    tariand.   *(you are)*

Sagh thou awre of Daw?   *Saw/anything*

I SHEP.   Yee, on a ley-land   *lealand, fallow field*

Hard I hym blaw. He commys here at hand   *Heard/blow/comes*

Not far.

Stand styll.

II SHEP.   Qwhy?

I SHEP. For he commys, hope I.   115

II SHEP. He wyll make us both a ly   *tell*

Bot if we be war.   *Unless*

III SHEP. Crystys crosse me spede, and Sant   *Christ's*
    Nycholas.

Therof had I nede. It is wars then it was.   *worse*

Whoso wouthe take hede and lett the warld   120
    pas,

It is ever in drede and brekyll as glas,   *brittle*

And slythys.   *slithers*

This warld fowre never so   *fared*

With mervels mo and mo,

Now in weyll, now in wo,   125   *weal*

And all thyng wrythys.   *writhes, changes*

Was never syn Noë floode sich floodys seyn,   *since*

Wyndys and ranys so rude, and stormes so   *rains/keen*
    keyn.

Som stamerd, som stod in dowte, as I weyn.   *ween, think*

Now God turne all to good, I say as I mene,   130

For ponder.

These floodys so thay drowne,

Both in feyldys and in towne,   *fields*

And berys all downe,   *bears*

And that is a wonder.   135

We that walk on the nyghtys, oure catell to
    kepe,

We se sodan syghtys when othere men   *sudden/sights*
    slepe.

Yit me thynk my hart lyghtys. I se shrewys   *lightens/shrews, ras-*
   pepe.   *cals*
Ye ar two all-wyghtys. I wyll gyf my shepe   *monsters/give*
A turne.   140
Bot full yll have I ment.
As I walk on this bent   *field*
I may lyghtly repent   *do a light penance*
My toes if I spurne.   *stub*

A, syr, God you save and master myne.   145
A drynk fayn wold I have and somwhat to
   dyne.
I SHEP. Crystys curs, my knave, thou art a   *no-good/hind*
   ledyr hyne.
II SHEP. What, the boy lyst rave. Abyde unto   *wishes (to)/later*
   syne.
We have mayde it.
Yll thryft on thy pate.   150   *fortune*
Though the shrew cam late,
Yit is he in state
To dyne, if he had it.

III SHEP. Sich servandys as I that swettys and   *servants/sweats/toils*
   swynkys
Etys oure brede full dry and that me   155   *Eat/displeases*
   forthynkys.
We ar oft weytt and wery when master men   *wet/wink, sleep*
   wynkys.
Yit commys full lately both dyners and
   drynkys.
Bot nately   *thoroughly*
Both oure dame and oure syre
When we have ryn in the myre   160   *run*
Thay can nyp at oure hyre   *nip/hire, wages*
And pay us full lately.

Bot here my trouth master, for the fayr that   *troth/fare/give*
   ye make
I shall do therafter, wyrk as I take.   *according to how I*
     am paid

I shall do a lytyll syr and emang ever lake   165   *among, concur-*
     rently/always/
     play

For yit lay my soper never on my stomake   *supper*
In feyldys.
Therto shuld I threpe?   *quarrel*
With my staf can I lepe,
And men say, "Lyght chepe   170 *"A cheap bargain re-*
Letherly foryeldys."   *pays badly"*

I SHEP. Thou were an yll lad to ryde on
        wowyng
With a man that had bot lytyll of spendyng.
II SHEP. Peasse, boy, I bad. No more   *Peace/bade/jan-*
         ianglyng,   *gling, wrangling*
Or I shall make the full rad, by the hevens   175 *(thee) stop/quickly*
kyng.
With thy gawdys—   *tricks*
Wher ar oure shepe boy—we skorne.
III SHEP. Sir, this same day at morne
I thaym left in the corne
When thay rang lawdys.   180 *Lauds (canonical of-*
                                                     fice at dawn)

Thay have pasture good, thay can not go
     wrong.
I SHEP. That is right. By the roode, thyse   *cross*
        nyghtys ar long.
Yit I wold, or we yode, oone gaf us a song.   *wish/went*
II SHEP. So I thoght as I stode, to myrth us   *(make) mirth*
         emong.
III SHEP. I grauntt.   185
I SHEP. Lett me syng the tenory.
II SHEP. And I the tryble so hye.
III SHEP. Then the meyne fallys to me.   *mean*
Lett se how ye chauntt.

            (*Tunc intrat Mak in clamide se*   *"Then Mak enters*
            super togam vestitus.)   *with a cloak drawn*
                                                     over his tunic."

MAK. Now Lord, by the naymes vij, that   190 *seven/moon/stars*
     made both moyn and starnes
Well mo then I can neven, thi wyll, Lorde,   *name/lacks*
of me tharnys.

I am all unever; that moves oft my harnes.   *confused/brains*
Now wold God I were in heven, for ther   *babes*
   wepe no barnes
So styll.   *Continually*
I SHEP. Who is that pypys so poore?   195 *pipes*
MAK. Wold God ye wyst how I foore.   *fared*
Lo, a man that walkys on the moore,
And has not all his wyll.

II SHEP. Mak, where has thou gone? Tell us   *tidings*
   tythyng.
III SHEP. Is he commen? Then ylkon take   200 *everyone*
   hede to his thyng.
    (*Et accipit clamidem ab ipso.*)   *"He takes the cloak*
                                            from him."
MAK. What, ich be a yoman, I tell you, of   *I*
   the kyng,
The self and the some, sond from a greatt   *same/messenger*
   lordyng,
And sich.
Fy on you. Goyth hence   *Go*
Out of my presence.   205
I must have reverence.
Why, who be ich?

I SHEP. Why make ye it so qwaynt, Mak, ye   *strange/wrong*
   do wrang.
II SHEP. Bot, Mak, lyst ye saynt? I trow that   *wish/(act a) saint/*
   ye lang.   *long (to)*
III SHEP. I trow the shrew can paynt, the   210 *act, pretend*
   dewyll myght hym hang.
MAK. Ich shall make complaynt, and make   *be beaten*
   you all to thwang
At a worde,
And tell evyn how ye doth.   *do*
I SHEP. Bot, Mak, is that sothe?
Now take outt that Sothren tothe,   215 *Southern/tooth =*
And sett in a torde.   *speech*
                                         turd

II SHEP. Mak, the dewill in youre ee. A   *eye/lend*
   stroke wold I leyne you.

III SHEP. Mak, know ye not me? By God, I *harm*
    couthe teyn you.
MAK. God looke you all thre. Me thoght I *look (after)*
    had sene you.
Ye ar a fare compané.   220
I SHEP.   Can you now mene *remember/yourself*
    you?
II SHEP. Shrew, pepe.
Thus late as thou goys,   *go*
What wyll men suppos?
And thou has an yll noys   *noise, reputation*
Of stelyng of shepe.   225

MAK. And I am trew as steyll, all men waytt,   *steel/know*
Bot a sekenes I feyll that haldys me full   *sickness/feel/holds/*
    haytt.   hot
My belly farys not weyll, it is out of astate.   *fares/well/condition*
III SHEP. Seldom lyys the dewyll dede by
    the gate.
MAK. Therfor   230
Full sore am I and yll,
If I stande stone styll,   *May*
I ete not an nedyll   *(If) I/needle*
Thys moneth and more.   *month*

I SHEP. How farys thi wyff? By thi hoode,   235
    how farys sho?
MAK. Lyys walteryng, by the roode, by the   *wallowing/fire*
    fyere, lo.
And a howse full of brude. She drynkys   *brood, children*
    well, to.
Yll spede othere good that she wyll do.
Bot sho   *she*
Etys as fast as she can   240
And ilk yere that commys to man   *every*
She bryngys furth a lakan,   *baby*
And som yeres two.

Bot were I now more gracyus and rychere   *Unless*
    be far
I were eten outt of howse and of harbar.   245   *home*
Yit is she a fowll dowse, if ye com nar.   *foul/sweetheart*
                                (O.Fr. *douce*)

Ther is none that trowse nor knowys a war	*worse (one)*
Then ken I.	
Now wyll ye se what I profer?	
To gyf all in my cofer 250	
Tomorne at next to offer	*Tomorrow/latest*
Hyr hed-mas penny.	*"a mass for her soul"*

II SHEP. I wote so forwakyd is none in this	*know/worn out*
shyre.	
I wold slepe, if I takyd les to my hyere.	*took/hire*
III SHEP. I am cold and nakyd and wold have 255	
a fyere.	
I SHEP. I am wery, forrakyd and run in the	*footsore*
myre.	
Wake thou.	
II SHEP. Nay, I wyll lyg downe by	*lie/nearby*
For I must slepe, truly.	
III SHEP. As good a mans son was I 260	
As any of you.	

Bot Mak com heder. Betwene shall thou lyg	*hither/lie*
downe.	
MAK. Then myght I lett you bedene of that	*hinder/indeed/*
ye wold rowne,	*whisper*
No drede.	*Never fear*
Fro my top to my too, 265	*toe*
Manus tuas commendo,	*(a night spell, cor-*
Poncio Pilato.	*ruption of Luke*
Cryst crosse me spede.	*xxiii:46)*

(*Tunc surgit, pastoribus dormien-*	*"Then he rises up,*
tibus, et dicit:)	*the shepherds be-*
	ing asleep, and
	says:"
Now were tyme for a man that lakkys what	*lacks*
he wold	
To stalk prevely than unto a fold 270	*privily/then*
And neemly to wyrk than and be not to bold	*nimbly*
For he myght aby the bargan if it were told	*suffer for*
At the endyng.	
Now were tyme for to reyll,	*reel, hurry*

Bot he nedys good counsell   275   *needs*
That fayn wold fare weyll   *well*
And has bot lytyll spendyng.

Bot abowte you a serkyll, as rownde as a   *circle/round*
    moyn
To I have done that I wyll, tyll that it be   *Till/noon*
    noyn
That ye lyg stone styll to that I have doyne   280   *done*
And I shall say thertyll of good wordys a   *words/few*
    foyne,
On hight,
Over youre heydys, my hand I lyft.   *heads*
Outt go youre een. Fordo youre syght.   *eyes/Forgo*
Bot yit I must make better shyft   285   *means, efforts*
And it be right.   *(If) it/(is to) be*

Lord what thay slepe hard. That may ye all
    here.
Was I never a shepard, bot now wyll I lere.   *learn*
If the flok be skard, yit shall I nyp nere.   *nab, seize (a sheep)*
How, drawes hederward. Now mendys oure   290   *mends*
    chere
From sorow
A fatt shepe, I dar say,
A good flese, dar I lay.
Eft-whyte when I may,   *Pay again, repay*
Bot this wyll I borow.   295
        (*exit Mak, with sheep*)

How, Gyll, art thou in? Gett us som lyght.
GYLL. Who makys sich dyn this tyme of the
    nyght?
I am sett for to spyn. I hope not I myght   *do not think*
Ryse a penny to wyn, I shrew them on
    hight.
So farys   300
A huswyff that has bene
To be rasyd thus betwene.   *while working, con-*
Here may no note be sene   *stantly*
For sich small charys.   *work*
                                                     chores

MAK. Good wyff, open the hek. Seys thou   305   *(inner) door*
   not what I bryng?
GYLL. I may thole the dray the snek. A, com   *let/draw/latch*
   in, my swetyng.
MAK. Yee, thou thar not rek of my long   *took/reckoning/*
   standyng.   *standing (out-*
GYLL. By the nakyd nek art thou lyke for to   *doors)*
   hyng.   *hang*
MAK. Do way.
I am worthy my mete   310   *meat*
For in a strate can I gett   *strait*
More then thay that swynke and swette   *toil*
All the long day.

Thus it fell to my lott, Gyll. I had sich
   grace.
GYLL. It were a fowll blott to be hanged for 315
   the case.
MAK. I have skapyd, Ielott, oft as hard a   *escaped/Jelott/blow*
   glase.
GYLL. Bot so long goys the pott to the water,
   men says,
At last
Comys it home broken.
MAK. Well knowe I the token,   320   *meaning*
Bot let it never be spoken.
Bot com and help fast.

I wold he were flayn. I lyst well ete.   *skinned/wish/(to)*
This twelmothe was I not so fayn of oone   *eat*
   shepe mete.   *sheep's/meat*
GYLL. Com thay or he be slayn and here   325
   the shepe blete.
MAK. Then myght I be tane. That were a   *taken*
   cold swette.
Go spar   *fasten (with a spar,*
The gaytt doore.   *beam)*
GYLL.   Yis, Mak,
For and thay com at thy bak—   *if*
MAK. Then myght I by, for all the pak,   330   *buy, get/from*
The dewill of the war.   *worse*

GYLL. A good bowrde have I spied, syn thou   *jest/know*
    can none.
Here shall we hym hyde, to thay be gone,   *till*
In my credyll. Abyde. Lett me alone,   *cradle*
And I shall lyg besyde in chylbed and grone.   335
MAK. Thou red   *ready, prepare*
And I shall say thou was lyght   *delivered*
Of a knave childe this nyght.   *male*
GYLL. Now well is me day bright
    That ever was I bred.   340

This is a good gyse and a far cast,   *guise*
Yit a woman avyse helpys at the last.   *advice/helps*
I wote never who spyse. Agane go thou fast.   *know/spies/return*
MAK. Bot I com or thay ryse, els blawes a   *Unless/ere*
    cold blast.
        (*returns to field with shepherds*)
I wyll go slepe.   345
Yit slepys all this meneye,   *company*
And I shall go stalk prevely
As it had never bene I   *As (if)*
    That caryed thare shepe.

I SHEP. *Resurrex a mortruus.* Have hold my   350
    hand.
Iudas carnas dominus. I may not well stand.
My foytt sleepys, by Iesus, and I water   *foot/sleeps/fasting*
    fastand.
I thoght that we layd us full nere Yngland.
II SHEP. A, ye?
Lord, what I have slep weyll.   355   *well*
As fresh as an eyll,   *eel*
As lyght me feyll,   *feel*
    As leyfe on a tre.   *leaf*

III SHEP. *Benste* be herein. So me qwakys,   *Benedicite (l. 55)/*
My hart is outt of skyn, whatso it makys.   360   *quakes*
Who makys all this dyn. So my browes   *causes it*
    blakys,   *blackens, darkens*

To the dowore wyll I wyn. Harke, felows, *door/wake*
    wakys.
We were fowre— *four*
Se ye awre of Mak now? *"Did you see Mak*
I SHEP. We were up or thou.   365   *anywhere?" (cf. l.*
II SHEP. Man, I gyf God avowe   111)
Yit yede he nawre. *ere*
    went/nowhere (ne
    + awre, l. 364)
III SHEP. Me thoght he was lapt in a wolfe *wrapped*
    skyn.
I SHEP. So ar many hapt now, namely *dressed (l. 1)*
    within.
III SHEP. When we had long napt, me   370   *engine, contrivance,*
    thoght with a gyn   *trap*
A fatt shepe he trapt, bot he mayde no dyn.
II SHEP. Be styll.
Thi dreme makys the woode. *mad*
It is bot fantom, by the roode.
I SHEP. Now God turne all to good,   375
If it be his wyll.

II SHEP. Ryse, Mak, for shame. Thou lygs
    right lang.
MAK. Now Crystys holy name be us emang.
What is this. For Sant Iame, I may not well *St. James/go, walk*
    gang.
I trow I be the same. A, my nek has lygen   380
    wrang
Enoghe.
Mekill thank. Syn yister-even,
Now by Sant Stevyn,
I was flayd with a swevyn, *dream, nightmare*
My hart out of sloghe.   385   *slough, skin*

I thoght Gyll began to crok and travell full *labor*
    sad
Wel ner at the fyrst cok, of a yong lad
For to mend oure flok. Then be I never *amend, enlarge*
    glad.

I have tow on my rok more than ever I
    had. *"flax on my distaff" = more work*

A, my heede. 390 *head*
A house full of yong tharmes, *bellies*
The dewill knok outt thare harnes. *brains (l. 192)*
Wo is hym has many barnes, *children*
And therto lytyll brede. *bread*

I must go home, by your lefe, to Gyll, as I 395 *leave/thought (to do)*
    thoght.
I pray you looke my slefe, that I steyll *look (at), inspect/ sleeve*
    noght.
I am loth you to grefe, or from you take
    oght.
        (*leaves*)
III SHEP. Go furth, yll myght thou chefe. *achieve*
    Now wold I we soght
This morne,
That we had all oure store. 400
I SHEP. Bot I will go before.
Let us mete.
II SHEP.   Whore? *Where*
III SHEP. At the crokyd thorne. *crooked*

      (*outside Mak's cottage*)
MAK. Undo this doore. Who is here? How
    long shall I stand?
GYLL. Who makys sich a bere. Now walk 405 *noise/waning (un- lucky) moonlight*
    in the wenyand.
MAK. A, Gyll, what chere. It is I, Mak, youre
    husbande.
GYLL. Then may we se here the dewill in a *(neck)band, noose*
    bande,
Syr Gyle.
Lo, he commys with a lote, *noise*
As he were holden in the throte. 410 *As (if)/held*
I may not syt at my note *work (l. 303)*
A handlang while. *hand-long, short*

MAK. Wyll ye here what fare she makys to *fanfare/excuse*
    gett hir a glose?

And dos noght bot lakys and clowse hir toose.	*plays* (l. 65)/*claws*/ *toes*
GYLL. Why, who wanders, who wakys? 415 Who commys, who gose?	
Who brewys, who bakys? What makys me thus hose?	*hoarse*
And than	
It is rewthe to beholde,	
Now in hote, now in colde,	
Full wofull is the householde 420	
That wantys a woman.	*wants, lacks*

Bot what ende has thou mayde with the hyrdys, Mak?	(*shep*)*herds*
MAK. The last worde that thay sayde when I turnyd my bak,	
Thay wold looke that thay hade thare shepe, all the pak.	
I hope thay wyll nott be well payde when 425 thay thare shepe lak,	
Perdé.	
Bot how so the gam gose,	*game*
To me thay wyll suppose,	*suspect*
And make a fowll noyse,	
And cry outt apon me. 430	

Bot thou must do as thou hyght.	*promised*
GYLL. I accorde me thertyll.	*thereto*
I shall swedyll hym right in my credyll.	*swaddle/cradle*
If it were a gretter slyght, yit couthe I help tyll.	*trick/toward*
I wyll lyg downe stright. Com hap me.	*cover* (cf. l. 369)
MAK. I wyll.	
GYLL. Behynde. 435	
Com Coll and his maroo,	*mate*
Thay will nyp us full naroo.	*seize, nab* (l. 289)/ *narrow*
MAK. Bot I may cry 'out, haroo,'	
The shepe if thay fynde.	*harrow*

GYLL. Harken ay when thay call. Thay will 440 com onone.	*ever/anon, straight-away*

Com and make redy all, and syng by thyn   *own, self*
  oone.
Syng lullay thou shall, for I must grone,   *lullaby*
And cry outt by the wall on Mary and Iohn,   *John*
For sore.   *pain*
Syng lullay on fast   445
When thou heris at the last,
And bot I play a fals cast,   *unless/trick*
Trust me no more.

  (shepherds meet at the Crooked
    Thorn)
III SHEP. A, Coll, goode morne. Why slepys
  thou nott?
I SHEP. Alas, that ever was I borne. We have   450   *blot, disgrace*
  a fowll blott.
A fat wedir have we lorne.   *wether/lost (cf. N.E.*
                                                           forlorn)

III SHEP.   Mary, Godys forbott.   *forbid*
II SHEP. Who shuld do us that skorne. That
  were a fowll spott.
I SHEP. Som shrewe.
I have soght with my dogys   *dogs*
All Horbery shrogys,   455   *"All the thickets of*
And of xv hoygs   *Horbury" (4 mi.*
Fond I bot oone ewe.   *from Wakefield)*
                                                         hogs (young sheep)

III SHEP. Now trow me, if ye will—by Sant
  Thomas of Kent,
Ayther Mak or Gyll was at that assent.   *Either/"was mixed*
I SHEP. Peasse, man, be still. I sagh when he   460   *up in it"*
  went.
Thou sklanders hym yll. Thou aght to   *slander*
  repent
Goode speede.
II SHEP. Now as ever myght I the,   *thrive*
If I shuld evyn here de,   *die*
I wol say it were he   465
That dyd that same ded.   *deed*

III SHEP. Go we theder, I rede, and ryn on   *thither/advise/run*
  oure feete.

Shall I never ete brede, the sothe to I wytt.　　　*bread/"till I know*
ı shep. Nor drynk in my heede, with hym　　　　　*the truth"*
　　tyll I mete.　　　　　　　　　　　　　　*head/"till I meet*
ıı shep. I wyll rest in no stede tyll that I　　470　*with him"*
　　hym grete,
My brothere.
Oone I wyll hight:　　　　　　　　　　　　*One (thing)/prom-*
Tyll I se hym in sight,　　　　　　　　　　　*ise*
Shall I never slepe one nyght
Ther I do anothere.　　　　　　　　　　475　*Where*

　　　　(shepherds approach. Gyll
　　　　groans. Mak sings)
ııı shep. Will ye here how thay hak? Oure　　*trill/wishes/(to)*
　　syre lyst croyne.　　　　　　　　　　　*croon*
ı shep. Hard I never none crak so clere out　　*Heard/bawl/tune*
　　of toyne.
Call on hym.
ıı shep.　　　Mak, undo youre doore soyne.　　*soon*
mak. Who is that spak, as it were noyne,　　　*spoke/as (if)/noon*
On loft.　　　　　　　　　　　　　　480　*loudly*
Who is that, I say?
ııı shep. Goode felowse, were it day.　　　　*(if only) it were*
mak. As far as ye may,
Good, spekys soft　　　　　　　　　　　　*Good (ones)/speak*

Over a seke womans heede that is at mayl-　　485　*sick/head/malaise*
　　leasse.
I had lever be dede or she had any dyseasse.　　*liefer/ere*
gyll. Go to anothere stede. I may not well　　*wheeze, breathe*
　　sweasse.
Ich fote that ye trede goys thorow my nese　　*Each/goes/nose*
So hee.　　　　　　　　　　　　　　　*high*
ı shep. Tell us, Mak, if ye may,　　　　490
How fare ye, I say.
mak. Bot ar ye in this towne to-day?
Now how fare ye?

Ye have ryn in the myre, and ar weytt yit.　　*run/wet/yet, still*
I shall make you a fyre, if ye will sytt.　　495
A norse wold I hyre. Thynk ye on yit?　　　*nurse/"Remember*
　　　　　　　　　　　　　　　　　my dream?"

Well qwytt is my hyre, my dreme, this is itt;
    (*gestures to cradle*)
A seson.
I have barnes, if you knewe,   *children*
Well mo then enewe,   500 *more/enough*
Bot we must drynk as we brew,
And that is bot reson.

I wold ye dynyd or ye yode. Me thynk that *dined/ere/went/*
    ye swette.   *sweat*
II SHEP. Nay, nawther mendys oure mode *neither/amends/*
    drynke nor mette.   *mood*
MAK. Why, syr, alys you oght bot goode? 505 *ails/aught*
III SHEP.   Yee,   *tend*
    oure shepe that we gett
Ar stollyn as thay yode. Oure los is grette.
MAK. Syrs, drynkys.
Had I bene thore,   *there*
Som shuld have boght it fullsore.
I SHEP. Mary, som men trowes that ye wore, 510 *were*
And that us forthynkys.   *displeases* (l. 155)

II SHEP. Mak, som men trowys that it shuld
    be ye.
III SHEP. Ayther ye or youre spouse, so say
    we.
MAK. Now if ye have suspowse to Gill or to *suspicion*
    me,
Com and rype oure howse, and then may ye 515 *pull apart*
    se
Who had hir.   *stole*
If I any shepe fott,   *fetched*
Ayther cow or stott,   *heifer*
And Gyll, my wyfe, rose nott
Here syn she lade hir,   520

As I am true and lele, to God here I pray *loyal*
That this be the fyrst mele that I shall ete
    this day.
      (*points to cradle*)

I SHEP. Mak, as have I ceyll, avyse the, I say,   *prosperity*
He lernyd tymely to steyll that couth not say   *early/steal*
   nay.
GYLL. I swelt.   525 *faint, swoon*
Outt, thefys, fro my wonys.   *thieves/dwelling*
Ye com to rob us for the nonys.   *"on purpose"*
MAK. Here ye not how she gronys.
Youre hartys shuld melt.
   (*shepherds approach cradle*)

GYLL. Outt, thefys, fro my barne. Negh   530 *babe/(Come)   near/*
   hym not thor.   *there*
MAK. Wyst ye how she had farne, youre   *Knew/fared*
   hartys wold be sore.
Ye do wrang, I you warne, that thus commys
   before
To a woman that has farne—bot I say no
   more.
GYLL. A, my medyll.   *middle*
I pray to God so mylde,   535
If ever I you begyld
That I ete this chylde
That lygys in this credyll.   *lies*

MAK. Pesse, woman, for Godys payn, and
   cry not so.
Thou spylls thy brane and makys me full   540 *spills*
   wo.
II SHEP. I trow oure shepe be slayn. What
   fynde ye two.
III SHEP. All wyrk we in vayn. As well may
   we go.
Bot hatters!   (obscure interjec-
I can fynde no flesh   tion)
Hard nor nesh,   545 *soft*
Salt nor fresh,
Bot two tome platers.   *empty*

Whik catell bot this, tame nor wylde,   *Quick, living*
None, as have I blys, as lowde as he smylde.   *smelled*
GYLL. No, so God me blys, and gyf me ioy   550 *bless*
   of my chylde.

I SHEP. We have merkyd amys. I hold ys begyld.		*marked/us*
II SHEP. Syr, don.		*completely*
Syr, oure Lady hym save,		
Is your chyld a knave?		*boy*
MAK. Any lord myght hym have,	555	
This chyld, to his son.		
When he wakyns he kyppys, that ioy is to se.		*snatches*
III SHEP. In good tyme to hys hyppys and in celé.		*hips, i.e., "to him"/ happy (cf. l. 523) = a wish*
Bot who was his gossyppys so sone redé.		*godparents/ready*
MAK. So fare fall thare lyppys.	560	*"Good luck to them (also)"*
I SHEP. (aside) Hark now a le.		*lie*
MAK. So God thaym thank.		
Parkyn and Gybon Waller I say,		*(names of godparents)*
And gentill Iohn Horne, in good fay,		*faith*
He made all the garray,	565	*commotion*
With the greatt shank.		*leg(s)*
II SHEP. Mak, freyndys will we be, for we ar all oone.		*friends/one, agreed*
MAK. We? Now I hald for me, for mendys gett I none.		*hold (out)/amends*
Fare well all thre. All glad were ye gone. (aside)		*"were I if you were gone"*
III SHEP. Fare wordys may ther be, bot luf is ther none		*love*
This yere.	570	
(exeunt shepherds)		
I SHEP. Gaf ye the chyld any thyng?		
II SHEP. I trow not oone farthyng.		
III SHEP. Fast agane will I flyng.		*return*
Abyde ye me there. (returns)		
Mak, take it to no grefe if I come to thi barne.	575	*grief/baby*

MAK. Nay, thou dos me greatt reprefe and   *reproof/fared*
    fowll has thou farne.
III SHEP. The child will it not grefe, that   *daystar*
    lytyll day-starne.
Mak, with youre leyfe, let me gyf youre   *leave*
    barne
Bot vj pence.   *sixpence*
MAK. Nay, do way. He slepys.   580
III SHEP. Me thynk he pepys.
MAK. When he wakyns he wepys.
I pray you go hence.
    (*I and II Shepherds return*)

III SHEP. Gyf me lefe hym to kys and lyft up   *cloth*
    the clowtt.
What the dewill is this! He has a long   585
    snowte.
I SHEP. He is merkyd amys. We wate ill   *marked*
    abowte.
II SHEP. Ill-spon weft, iwys, ay commys foull   *spun/woof/cer-*
    owte.   *tainly/ever*
Ay, so.
He is lyke to oure shepe.
III SHEP. How, Gyb, may I pepe?   590
I SHEP. I trow kynde will crepe   *nature/creep*
Where it may not go.   *walk, i.e., "in one*
                                                  way or another"
II SHEP. This was a qwantt gawde and a far   *sly/trick/deceit* (l.
    cast.   176)
It was a hee frawde.   *high*
III SHEP.   Yee, syrs, wast.   *it was*
Lett bren this bawde and bynd hir fast.   595   *burn*
A fals skawde hang at the last.   *scold*
So shall thou.
Wyll ye se how thay swedyll   *swaddle*
His foure feytt in the medyll?   *feet/middle*
Sagh I never in a credyll   600 *Saw*
A hornyd lad or now.   *ere*

MAK. Peasse, byd I, what, lett be youre fare.   *din*
I am he that hym gatt, and yond woman   *begat/bore*
    hym bare.

I SHEP. What dewill shall he hatt, Mak. Lo,   *be called/Mak's/heir*
    God, Makys ayre.
II SHEP. Lett be all that. Now, God gyf hym   605
    care
I sagh.
GYLL. A pratty child is he   *pretty*
As syttys on a womans kne.   *sits*
A dyllydowne, perdé,
To gar a man laghe.   610 *make/laugh*

III SHEP. I know hym by the eere-marke.
    This is a good tokyn.
MAK. I tell you, syrs, hark. Hys noyse was   *nose*
    brokyn.
Sythen told me a clerk that he was for-   *Since/bewitched*
    spokyn.
I SHEP. This is a fals wark. I wold fayn be   *work/avenged*
    wrokyn.
Gett wepyn.   615 *weapon*
GYLL. He was takyn with an elfe,   *by*
I saw it myself,
When the clok stroke twelf
Was he forshapyn.   *misshapen, trans-*
                                                    formed

II SHEP. Ye two ar well feft sam in a stede.   620 *endowed/together*
I SHEP. Syn thay manteyn thare theft, let do   *maintain/put . . . to*
    thaym to dede.   *death*
MAK. If I trespas eft, gyrd of my heede.   *again/knock/off*
With you will I be left.   *"I leave my fate in*
III SHEP.   Syrs, do my reede.   *your hands"*
For this trespas   *follow/advice*
We will nawther ban ne flyte,   625   *curse/argue*
Fyght nor chyte,   *chide*
Bot have done as tyte   *immediately*
And cast hym in canvas.
        (*Mak is tossed in a canvas*)

I SHEP. Lord, what I am sore, in poynt for to   *burst*
    bryst.
In fayth, I may no more. Therfor wyll I   630   *rest*
    ryst.

II SHEP. As a shepe of vij skore he weyd in
    my fyst.   *7 score/weighed*

For to slepe aywhore me thynk that I lyst.   *anywhere/wish*

III SHEP. Now I pray you

Lyg downe on this grene.

I SHEP. On these thefys yit I mene.   635   *think*

III SHEP. Wherto shuld ye tene?   *grieve*

Do as I say you.

    (they bed down)
    (Angelus cantat 'Gloria in exelsis';   "*An angel sings 'Glo-*
    postea dicat:)   *ria in exelsis'; then*
                                                      let him say:"

ANGEL. Ryse, hyrd-men heynd, for now is   *herdsmen/gracious*
    he borne

That shall take fro the feynd that Adam had   *fiend, devil/lost*
    lorne,

That warloo to sheynd, this nyght is he   640   *warlock/ruin*
    borne.

God is made youre freynd now at this   *friend*
    morne,

He behestys.   *promises*

At Bedlem go se   *Bethlehem*

Ther lygys that fre   *lies/free, noble*

In a cryb full poorely,   645   *(one)*

Betwyx two bestys.

    (exit)

I SHEP. This was a qwant stevyn that ever   *strange/voice/heard*
    yit I hard.

It is a mervell to nevyn, thus to be skard.   *marvel/name, tell/*
                                                      scared

II SHEP. Of Godys son of hevyn he spak up-
    ward.

All the wod on a levyn me thoght that he   650   *woods/in light/*
    gard   *caused*

Appere.

III SHEP. He spake of a barne   *babe*

In Bedlem, I you warne.

I SHEP. That betokyns yond starne.   *star (l. 577)*

Let us seke hym there.   655

III SHEP. Say, what was his song? Hard ye   *sang*
    not how he crakyd it,

Thre brefes to a long.   *breves*
III SHEP.   Yee, Mary, he hakt it.   *trilled* (l. 476)
Was no crochett wrong, nor nothyng that   *crotchet/it lacked*
    lakt it.
I SHEP. For to syng us emong, right as he   *sang*
    knakt it,
I can.   660
II SHEP. Let se how ye croyne.   *croon*
Can ye bark at the mone?   *moon*
III SHEP. Hold youre tonges. Have done.
I SHEP. Hark after, than.
        (*sings*)

II SHEP. To Bedlem he bad that we shuld   665   *go*
    gang.
I am full fard that we tary to lang.   *afraid/too*
III SHEP. Be mery and not sad; of myrth is
    oure sang.
Everlastyng glad to mede may we fang,   *gladness/for reward/*
Wythoutt noyse.   *take*
I SHEP. Hy we theder forthy,   670   *Hie/thither/there-*
If we be wete and wery,   *fore*
To that chyld and that lady.
We have it not to lose.

II SHEP. We fynde by the prophecy—let be
    youre dyn—
Of David and Isay and mo then I myn,   675   *Isaiah/remember*
Thay prophecyed by clergy, that in a vyrgyn
Shuld he lyght and ly, to slokyn oure syn   *a light/lie/suppress*
And slake it,
Oure kynde, from wo,
For Isay sayd so: 680
Ecce virgo
Concipiet a chylde that is nakyd.   *"Behold, a virgin*
                                                           shall con-
                                                           ceive . . ."

III SHEP. Full glad may we be and abyde
    that day
That lufly to se, that all myghtys may.   *lovely* (*one*)/*mighty*
                                                           (*things*)/*may*
                                                           (*do*)

Lord, well were me for ones and for ay,   685   *"I would be happy*
Myght I knele on my kne, som word for to   *for once and al-*
    say   *ways"*
To that chylde.
Bot the angell sayd
In a cryb was he layde.
He was poorly arayd,   690
Both mener and mylde.   *more humble*

1 SHEP. Patryarkes that has bene, and proph-   *Patriarchs*
    etys beforne,
Thay desyryd to have sene this chylde that
    is borne.
Thay ar gone full clene. That have thay
    lorne.
We shall se hym, I weyn, or it be morne,   695
To tokyn.   *As a sign*
When I se hym and fele,   *feel*
Then wote I full weyll   *know/well*
It is a trye as steyll   *as true/steel*
That prophetys have spokyn.   700

To so poore as we ar that he wold appere,
Fyrst fynd, and declare by his messyngere.   *"Find us first"*
II SHEP. Go we now, let us fare. The place is
    us nere.
III SHEP. I am redy and yare. Go we in fere   *eager/company*
To that bright.   705   *bright (one)*
Lord, if thi wylles be,   *will*
We ar lewde all thre,   *unlearned*
Thou grauntt us somkyns gle   *some kind of*
To comforth thi wight.   *comfort/creature =*
                                                        Christ child

            (enter stable)
1 SHEP. Hayll, comly and clene. Hayll, yong   710   *Hail*
    child.
Hayll, maker, as I meyne, of a madyn so   *creator/mean/*
    mylde.   *(born) of*
Thou has waryd, I weyne, the warlo so   *cursed/think/war-*
    wylde.   *lock, devil (l.*
The fals gyler of teyn, now goys he be-   *640)*
    gylde.   *grief*

Lo, he merys,   *is merry*
Lo, he laghys, my swetyng.   715
A wel fare metyng.
I have holden my hetyng.   *promise*
Have a bob of cherys.   *bunch/cherries*

II SHEP. Hayll, sufferan, savyoure, for thou   *sovereign*
    has us soght.
Hayll, frely foyde and floure, that all thyng   720   *noble child (l. 644)*
    has wroght.
Hayll, full of favoure, that make all of
    noght.
Hayll, I kneyll and I cowre. A byrd have I
    broght
To my barne.
Hayll, lytyll tyné mop   *moppet*
Of oure crede thou art crop.   725   *creed, belief/head*
I wold drynk on thy cop,   *cup*
Lytyll day-starne.

III SHEP. Hayll, derlyng dere, full of God-
    hede.
I pray the be nere when that I have nede.
Hayll, swete is thy chere. My hart wold   730   *face*
    blede
To se the sytt here in so poore wede,   *clothes*
With no pennys.
Hayll. Put furth thy dall.   *hand*
I bryng the bot a ball.
Have and play the withall   735
And go to the tenys.   *tennis*

MARY. The fader of heven, God omnypotent,
That sett all on seven, his son has he sent.   *set (up), arranged/*
My name couth he neven, and lyght or he   *everything/(in)*
    went.   *seven (days)*
I conceyvyd hym full even thrugh myght, as   740   *name, call/alight/ere*
    he ment.   *(the) might (of*
And now is he borne.   *God)/meant*
He kepe you fro wo.
I shall pray hym so.
Tell furth as ye go,
And myn on this morne.   745   *remember*

I SHEP. Fare well, lady, so fare to beholde,
With thy childe on thi kne.

II SHEP.   Bot he lygys
    full cold.
Lord, well is me. Now we go, thou behold.

III SHEP. Forsothe, allredy it semys to be told
Full oft.   750

I SHEP. What grace we have fun.   *found*

II SHEP. Com furth. Now ar we won.   *redeemed*

III SHEP. To syng ar we bun.   *bound*
Let take on loft.   *Let's/high, loud*

      (*Explicit pagina Pastorum.*)

SUPPLEMENTARY MATERIAL

1. *The Play of Daniel,* New York Pro Musica, Noah Greenberg, Dir.
   Decca Records DL 9402.

2. *The Play of Herod,* New York Pro Musica, Noah Greenberg, Dir.
   Decca Records DL 10,095.

EVERYMAN

HERE BEGYNNETH A TRETYSE

HOW YE HYE FADER OF HEVEN

SENDETH DETHE TO SOMON EVERY CREATURE

TO COME AND GYVE ACOUNTE OF THEYR LYVES

IN THIS WORLDE AND IS IN MANER

OF A MORALL PLAYE

God

Messenger	*Knowledge*
Death	*Confession*
Everyman	*Beauty*
Fellowship	*Strength*
Kindred	*Discretion*
Cousin	*Five Wits*
Goods	*Angel*
Good Deeds	*Doctor*

MESSENGER. I pray you all gyve your au-
 dyence
And here this mater with reverence,
By a fygure a morall playe.   *in form*
The 'Somonynge of Everyman' called it is,
That of our lyves and endynge shewes   5
How transytory we be all daye.
This mater is wonderous precyous,
But the entent of it is more gracyous   *serious*

And swete to bere awaye.

The story sayth: man, in the begynnynge   10
Loke well, and take good heed to the
    endynge,
Be you never so gay.
Ye thynke synne in the begynnynge full
    swete,
Whiche in the ende causeth the soule to
    wepe
Whan the body lyeth in claye.   15
Here shall you se how Felawshyp and   *Jollity*
    Iolyté,
Bothe Strengthe, Pleasure and Beauté,
Wyll fade from the as floure in maye.
For ye shall here how our heven kynge
Calleth Everyman to a generall rekenynge.   20
Gyve audyence and here what he doth saye.

GOD. I perceyve here in my maiesté
How that all creatures be to me unkynde,
Lyvynge without drede in worldly pros-
    peryté.
Of ghostly syght the people be so blynde,   25   *spiritual*
Drowned in synne they know me not for
    theyr god.
In worldely ryches is all theyr mynde,
They fere not my ryghtwysnes the sharpe   *righteousness*
    rod.
My lowe that I shewed whan I for them   *law*
    dyed
They forgete clene and shedynge of my   30
    blode rede.
I hanged bytwene two, it can not be denyed.
To gete them lyfe I suffred to be deed.   *dead*
I heled theyr fete; with thornes hurt was my
    heed.
I coude do no more than I dyde truely,
And nowe I se the people do clene forsake   35
    me.
They use the seven deedly synnes dampna-
    ble,
As pryde, coveytyse, wrathe and lechery
Now in the worlde be made commendable,

And thus they leve of aungelles, ye hevenly
    company.
Every man lyveth so after his owne pleasure,   40
And yet of theyr lyfe they be nothynge sure.
I se the more that I them forbere
The worse they be fro yere to yere,
All that lyveth appayreth faste.   *worsens, impairs*
Therefore I wyll, in all the haste,   45
Have a rekenynge of every mannes persone,
For, and I leve the people thus alone   *and* = *if,* freq.
In theyr lyfe and wycked tempestes,
Veryly they wyll become moche worse than
    beestes,
For now one wolde by envy another up ete;   50
Charyté they do all clene forgete.
I hoped well that every man
In my glory shulde make his mansyon,
And thereto I had them all electe.
But now I se, lyke traytours deiecte   55   *dejected*
They thanke me not for ye pleasure that I
    to them ment,
Nor yet for theyr beynge that I them have
    lent.
I profered the people grete multytude of
    mercy
And fewe there be that asketh it hertly.   *heartily*
They be so combred with worldly ryches   60   *encumbered*
That nedes on them I must do iustyce   *necessarily*
On every man lyvynge without fere.
Where art thou deth, thou myghty mes-
    engere?
DETHE. Almyghty God I am here at your
    wyll,
Your commaundement to fulfyll.   65
GOD. Go thou to Everyman,
And shewe hym in my name,
A pylgrymage he must on hym take,
Which he in no wyse may escape,
And that he brynge with hym a sure   70
    rekenynge
Without delay or ony taryenge.
DETHE. Lorde, I wyll in the worlde go renne   *run*
    over all

And cruelly out serche bothe grete and
    small.
Every man wyll I beset that lyveth beestly
Out of Goddes lawes and dredeth not foly.   75
He that loveth rychesse I wyll stryke with
    my darte
His syght to blynde and fro heven to de-
    parte,
Except that almes be his good frende,
In hell for to dwell, worlde without ende.
Loo, yonder I se Everyman walkynge.   80
Full lytell he thynketh on my comynge,
His mynde is on flesshely lustes and his
    treasure,
And grete payne it shall cause hym to en-
    dure
Before the lorde, heven kynge.
Everyman, stande styll. Whyder arte thou   85   *Whither/going*
    goynge
Thus gayly? hast thou thy maker forgete?
EVERYMAN. Why asketh thou?
Woldest thou wete?   *know*
DETHE. Ye, syr, I wyll shewe you:
In grete hast I am sende to the   90
Fro God out of his magesté.
EVERYMAN. What, sente to me?
DETHE. Ye, certaynly.
Thoughe thou have forgete hym here
He thynketh on the in the hevenly spere,   95   *sphere*
As, or we departe, thou shalte knowe.   *ere*
EVERYMAN. What desyreth God of me?
DETHE. That shall I shewe the:
A rekenynge he wyll nedes have,
Without ony lenger respyte.   100   *any/longer*
EVERYMAN. To gyve a rekenynge longer   *leisure*
    layser I crave.
This blinde mater troubleth my wytte.
DETHE. On the thou must take a longe
    iourney,
Therfore thy boke of counte with the thou   *account*
    brynge,
For turne agayne thou can not by no waye.   105   *return*
And loke thou be sure of thy rekenynge,

For before God thou shalte answere and
   shewe
Thy many badde dedes and good but a fewe,
How thou hast spente thy lyfe and in what
   wyse
Before the chefe lorde of paradyse.   110
Have ado we were in that waye,   *Get ready (so that)/*
For, wete thou well, thou shalte make none   *on the way*
   attournay.   *no one/(your) attor-*
EVERYMAN. Full unredy I am suche reken-   *ney*
   ynge to gyve.
I know the not. What messenger arte thou?
DETHE. I am Dethe, that no man dredeth.   115   *"who dreads no man"*
For every man I rest and no man spareth,   *arrest*
For it is Goddes commaundement
That all to me sholde be obedyent.
EVERYMAN. O deth, thou comest whan I had
   thee leest in mynde!
In thy power it lyeth me to save,   120
Yet of my good wyl I gyve thee, yf thou wyl   *goods, possessions*
   be kynde.
Ye, a thousande pounde shalte thou have
And dyfferre this mater tyll another daye.   *defer*
DETHE. Everyman, it may not be by no waye.
I set not by golde, sylver, nor rychesse,   125
Ne by pope, emperour, kynge, duke ne
   prynces,
For and I wolde receyve gyftes grete
All the worlde I myght gete,
But my custom is clene contrary.
I gyve the no respyte, come hens and not   130
   tary.
EVERYMAN. Alas, shall I have no lenger
   respyte?
I may saye deth gyveth no warnynge.
To thynke on the it maketh my herte seke,   *sick*
For all unredy is my boke of rekenynge.
But xii yere and I myght have abydynge   135   *"If I could have a res-*
My countynge boke I wolde make so clere,   *pite of only 12*
That my rekenynge I sholde not nede to   *years."*
   fere.
Wherfore, deth, I praye the, for Goddes
   mercy,

Spare me tyll I be provyded of remedy.
DETHE. The avayleth not to crye, wepe and   140
    praye.
But hast the lyghtly that thou were gone   *haste/quickly*
    that iournaye,
And preve thy frendes yf thou can.   *prove*
For, wete thou well, the tyde abydeth no
    man,
And in the worlde eche lyvynge creature
For Adams synne must dye, of nature.   145   *(by its) nature*
EVERYMAN. Dethe, yf I sholde this pylgrym-
    age take,
And my rekenynge suerly make,   *surely*
Shewe me, for saynt charyté,   *St. Charity*
Sholde I not come agayne shortly?
DETHE. No, Everyman, and thou be ones   150
    there,
Thou mayst never more come here,
Trust me veryly.
EVERYMAN. O gracyous God, in the hye sete
    celestyall,
Have mercy on me in this moost nede.
Shall I have no company fro this vale teres- 155
    tryall
Of myne acqueynte, that way me to lede?   *acquaintance*
DETHE. Ye, yf ony be so hardy
That wolde go with the and bere the com-
    pany.
Hye the, that thou were gone to Goddes   *Hie, hasten*
    magnyfycence,
Thy rekenynge to gyve before his presence.   160
What, wenest thou thy lyve is gyven the   *think/life*
And thy worldely goodes also?
EVERYMAN. I had wende so verylé.   *thought*
DETHE. Nay, nay, it was but lende the,
For as sone as thou arte go   165   *gone*
Another a whyle shall have it and than go
    ther fro,
Even as thou hast done.
Everyman, thou art made! Thou hast thy   *mad*
    wyttes fyve
And here on erthe wyll not amende thy lyve.
For sodeynly I do come.   170   *suddenly*

EVERYMAN. O wretched caytyfe, wheder   *caitiff, rascal/whither*
   shall I flee,
That I myght scape this endles sorowe?   *escape*
Now gentyll deth spare me tyll to morowe,
That I may amende me
With good advysement.   175
DETHE. Naye, therto I wyll not consent,
Nor no man wyll I respyte,
But to the herte sodeynly I shall smyte
Without ony advysement.
And now out of thy syght I wyll me hy,   180
Se thou make the redy shortely,
For thou mayst saye this is the daye
That no man lyvynge may scape awaye.
EVERYMAN. Alas I may well wepe with
   syghes depe
Now have I no maner of company   185
To helpe me in my iourney and me to kepe,
And also my wrytynge is full unredy.
How shall I do now for to excuse me?
I wolde to God I had never be gete.   *been/begotten*
To my soule a full grete profyte it had be,   190
For now I fere paynes huge and grete.
The tyme passeth; Lorde helpe that all
   wrought.
For though I mourne it avayleth nought.
The day passeth and is almoost ago,   *gone*
I wote not well what for to do.   195
To whome were I best my complaynt to
   make?
What and I to Felawshyp therof spake,
And shewed hym of this sodeyne chaunce,   *turn of events*
For in hym is all myne affyaunce.   *trust*
We have in the worlde so many a daye   200
Be good frendes in sporte and playe.
I se hym yonder certaynely,
I trust that he wyll bere me company,
Therfore to hym wyll I speke to ese my
   sorowe.
Well mette, good Felawshyp, and good   205
   morowe.
FELAWSHYP. Everyman, good morowe by
   this daye.

Syr, why lokest thou so pyteously?
If ony thynge be amysse I praye the me saye,   *tell me*
That I may helpe to remedy.
EVERYMAN. Ye, good Felawshyp, ye,   210
I am in greate ieopardé.
FELAWSHYP. My true frende, shewe to me
    your mynde,
I wyll not forsake the to thy lyves ende,
In the way of good company.
EVERYMAN. That was well spoken and   215
    lovyngly.
FELAWSHYP. Syr, I must nedes knowe your
    hevynesse.
I have pyté to se you in ony dystresse.
If ony have you wronged, ye shall revenged
    be,
Thoughe I on the grounde be slayne for the,
Though that I knowe before that I sholde   220
    dye.
EVERYMAN. Veryly, Felawshyp, gramercy.
FELAWSHYP. Tusshe, by thy thankes I set
    not a strawe,
Shewe me your grefe and saye no more.
EVERYMAN. If I my herte sholde to you
    breke,
And than you to tourne your mynde fro me,   225
And wolde not me comforte whan ye here
    me speke,
Then wolde I ten tymes soryer be.
FELAWSHYP. Syr, I saye as I wyll do in dede.
EVERYMAN. Than be you a good frende at
    nede;
I have founde you true here before.   230
FELAWSHYP. And so ye shall evermore;
For, in fayth, and thou go to hell
I wyll not forsake the by the waye.
EVERYMAN. Ye speke lyke a good frende; I
    byleve you well,
I shall deserve it and I maye.   235
FELAWSHYP. I speke of no deservynge, by
    this daye,
For he that wyll saye and nothynge do
Is not worthy with good company to go.

Therfore shewe me the grefe of your mynde
As to your frende moost lovynge and kynde.   240
EVERYMAN. I shall shewe you how it is.
Commaunded I am to go a iournaye,
A longe waye, harde, and daungerous,
And gyve a strayte counte, without delaye,
Before the hye Iuge, Adonay.   245   *Judge/Adonai* =
Wherfore I pray you, bere me company,   Heb. 'God'
As ye have promysed, in this iournaye.
FELAWSHYP. That is mater in dede. Promyse   *reason*
    is duty
But and I sholde take suche vyage on me,   *voyage*
I knowe it well, it sholde be to my payne.   250
Also it makes me aferde, certayne.
But let us take counsell here, as well as we
    can,
For your wordes wolde fere a stronge man.
EVERYMAN. Why, ye sayd, yf I had nede,
Ye wolde me never forsake, quycke ne deed,   255   *quick, living*
Though it were to hell, truely.
FELAWSHYP. So I sayd certaynely,
But suche pleasure be set asyde, the sothe to
    saye,
And also, yf we toke suche a iournaye,
Whan sholde we come agayne?   260
EVERYMAN. Naye, never agayne, tyll the   *doom, judgment*
    daye of dome.
FELAWSHYP. In fayth, than wyll not I come
    there.
Who hath you these tydynges brought?
EVERYMAN. In dede, deth was with me here.
FELAWSHYP. Now, by God that all hathe   265   *redeemed*
    bought,
If deth were the messenger,
For no man that is lyvynge to daye
I wyll not go that lothe iournaye,   *loathly*
Not for the fader thar bygate me.
EVERYMAN. Ye promysed other wyse, pardé.   270
FELAWSHYP. I wote well I say so, truely,
And yet yf thou wylte ete and drynke and
    make good chere
Or haunt to women the lusty company,

I wolde not forsake you, whyle the day is
    clere,
Trust me veryly.   275
EVERYMAN. Ye, therto ye wolde be redy.
To go to myrthe, solas and playe
Your mynde wyll soner apply,
Than to bere me company in my longe
    iournaye.
FELAWSHYP. Now in good fayth, I wyll not   280   *will not (go)*
    that waye,
But and thou wyll murder, or ony man kyll,
In that I wyll helpe the with a good wyll.
EVERYMAN. O that is a symple advyse in
    dede.
Gentyll felawe, helpe me in my necessyté.
We have loved longe and now I nede,   285
And now, gentyll Felawshyp, remember me.
FELAWSHYP. Wheder ye have loved me or
    no,
By saynt Iohan I wyll not with the go.   *St. John*
EVERYMAN. Yet I pray the, take the labour
    and do so moche for me,
To brynge me forwarde, for saynt charyté,   290   *accompany me*
And comforte me tyll I come without the   *outside*
    towne.
FELAWSHYP. Nay, and thou wolde gyve me
    a newe gowne,
I wyll not a fote with the go,
But and thou had taryed I wolde not have
    lefte the so,
And, as now, God spede the in thy iournaye,   295
For from the I wyll departe as fast as I maye.
EVERYMAN. Wheder awaye, felawshyp?   *Whither*
    Wyll thou forsake me?
FELAWSHYP. Ye, by my faye. To God I be-   *faith/entrust*
    take the.
EVERYMAN. Farewell, good Fellawshyp. For
    the my herte is sore.
Adewe forever, I shall se the no more.   300   *Adieu*
FELAWSHYP. In fayth, Everyman, fare well
    now at the ende,
For you I wyll remember that partynge is
    mournynge.

EVERYMAN. Alacke, shall we thus departe
    in dede—
A, lady, helpe—without ony more comforte?
Lo, Felawshyp forsaketh me in my moost   305
    nede.
For helpe in this worlde wheder shall I re-
    sorte?
Felawshyp here before with me wolde mery
    make,
And nowe lytell sorowe for me dooth he
    take.
It is sayd 'in prosperyté men frendes may
    fynde
Whiche in adversyté be full unkynde.'   310
Nowe whither for socoure shall I flee,   *succor*
Syth that Felawshyp hath forsaken me?
To my kynnes men I wyll truely,
Prayenge them to helpe in my necessyté.
I byleve that they wyll do so   315
For 'kynde wyll crepe where it may not   *walk, i.e., "by one*
    go.'   *way or another"*
I wyll go saye, for yonder I se them go.   *assay, test*
Where be ye now, my frendes and kynnes-
    men?
KYNREDE. Here be we now at your com-
    maundement.
Cosyn I praye you shewe us your entent   320
In ony wyse and do not spare.
COSYN. Ye, Everyman, and to us declare
Yf ye be dysposed to go ony whyder.   *anywhere*
For, wete you well, we wyll lyve and dye
    togyder.
KYNREDE. In welth and wo we wyll with   325
    you holde,
For over his kynne a man may be bolde.
EVERYMAN. Gramercy, my frendes and kyn-
    nesmen kynde.
Now shall I shewe you the grefe of my
    mynde.
I was commaunded by a messenger
That is a hye kynges chefe offycer.   330
He bad me go a pylgrymage, to my payne,

And I knowe well I shall never come
    agayne.
Also I must gyve a rekenynge strayte,
For I have a grete enemy that hath me in   *is waiting for me*
    wayte,
Whiche entendeth me for to hynder.   335
KYNREDE. What accounte is that which ye
    must render?
That wolde I knowe.
EVERYMAN. Of all my workes I must shewe
How I have lyved, and my dayes spent.
Also of yll dedes that I have used   340
In my tyme syth lyfe was me lent,
And of all vertues that I have refused.
Therfore I praye you go thyder with me
To helpe to make myn accounte for saynt
    charyté.
COSYN. What? to go thydr? is that the mater?   345
Nay, Everyman, I had lever fast brede and   *liefer/fast (on)*
    water
All this fyve yere and more.   *"For the next five*
EVERYMAN. Alas, that ever I was bore,   *years"*
For now shall I never be mery   *born*
If that you forsake me.   350
KYNREDE. A, syr, what—ye be a mery man.
Take good herte to you and make no mone.   *moan, complaint*
But one thynge, I warne you, by saynt
    Anne,
As for me, ye shall go alone.
EVERYMAN. My cosyn, wyll you not with   355
    me go?
COSYN. No, by our lady. I have the crampe
    in my toe.
Trust not to me, for, so God me spede,
I wyll deceyve you in your moost nede.
KYNREDE. It avayleth not us to tyse.   *avails (you)/entice*
Ye shall have my mayde with all my herte.   360
She loveth to go to feestes there to be nyse   *nice = wanton, fool-*
And to daunce and abrode to sterte.   *ish*
        abroad/start, go
I wyll gyve her leve to helpe you in that
    iourney
If that you and she may agree.

EVERYMAN. Now, shewe me the very effecte   365
    of your mynde.
Wyll you go with me or abyde behynde?
KYNREDE. Abyde behynde? ye, that wyll I
    and I maye.
Therfore farewell tyll another daye.
EVERYMAN. Howe sholde I be mery or
    gladde?
For fayre promyses men to me make   370
But whan I have moost nede they me for-
    sake.
I am deceyved; that maketh me sadde.
COSYN. Cosyn Everyman, farewell now,
For veryly I wyll not go with you.
Also of myne owne lyfe an unredy rek-   375
    enynge
I have to accounte; therfore I make taryenge.   *tarrying*
Now God kepe the, for now I go.
EVERYMAN. A, Iesus, is all come hereto?
Lo, fayre wordes maketh fooles fayne;
They promyse and nothynge wyll do cer-   380
    tayne.
My kynnesmen promysed me faythfully
For to abyde with me stedfastly,
And now fast awaye do they flee.
Even so Felawshyp promysed me.
What frende were best me of to provyde?   385
I lose my tyme here longer to abyde,
Yet in my mynde a thynge there is:
All my lyfe I have loved ryches.
If that my Good now helpe me myght
He wolde make my herte full lyght.   390
I wyll speke to hym in this dystresse.
Where arte thou my Gooddes and ryches?
GOODS. Who calleth me—Everyman? What
    —hast thou haste?
I lye here in corners, trussed and pyled so
    hye,
And in chestes I am locked so fast,   395
Also sacked in bagges, thou mayst se with
    thyn eye,
I can not styre. In packes, lowe I lye.   *stir*
What wolde ye have, lyghtly me saye.

EVERYMAN. Come hyder, Good, in al the
    hast thou may,
For of counseyll I must desyre the.   400   *entreat*
GOODS. Syr, and ye in the worlde have sor-
    owe or adversyté,
That can I helpe you to remedy shortly.
EVERYMAN. It is another dysease that grev-
    eth me.
In this worlde it is not, I tell the so.
I am sent for an other way to go,   405
To gyve a strayte counte generall
Before the hyest Iupyter of all,   *Jupiter*
And all my lyfe I have had ioye and pleas-
    ure in the,
Therfore, I pray the, go with me,
For paraventure thou mayst before God al-   410
    myghty
My rekenynge helpe to clene and puryfye,   *purify*
For it is sayd ever amonge   *occasionally*
That 'money maketh all ryght that is
    wronge.'
GOODS. Nay, Everyman, I synge an other
    songe.
I folowe no man in suche vyages,   415 *voyages*
For, and I wente with the,
Thou sholdes fare much the worse for me,
For because on me thou dyd set thy mynde,
Thy rekenynge I have made blotted and
    blynde,
That thyne accounte thou can not make   420
    truly
And that hast thou for the love of me.
EVERYMAN. That wolde greve me full sore,
Whan I sholde come to that ferefull an-
    swere.
Up, let us go thyder to gyder.   *together*
GOODS. Nay, not so. I am to brytell; I may 425 *too/brittle, frail*
    not endure.
I wyll folowe no man one fote, be ye sure.
EVERYMAN. Alas, I have the loved and had
    grete pleasure
All my lyfe dayes on good and treasure.

GOODS. That is to thy dampnacyon, without *damnation/a lie*
lesynge,
For my love is contrary to the love ever-   430
lastynge,
But yf thou had me loved moderately   *during (life)*
durynge
As to the poore to gyve parte of me   *(So) as*
Than sholdest thou not in this dolour be,
Nor in this grete sorowe and care.
EVERYMAN. Lo, now was I deceyved or I was   435   *ere/aware*
ware,
And all, I may wyte, mysspendynge of   *blame/misspending*
tyme.
GOODS. What, wenest thou that I am thyne?
EVERYMAN. I had went so.   *thought*
GOODS. Naye, Everyman, I saye no.
As for a whyle I was lente the.   440
A season thou hast had me in prosperyté.
My condycyon is mannes soule to kyll.   *condition, nature*
Yf I save one, a thousande I do spyll.
Wenest thou that I wyll folowe the
From this worlde? nay, verylé.   445
EVERYMAN. I had wende otherwyse.   *thought*
GOODS. Therfore to thy soule Good is a thefe,
For whan thou arte deed, this is my gyse,   *guise, habit*
Another to deceyve in this same wyse
As I have done the and all to his soules   450   *reproach*
reprefe.
EVERYMAN. O false Good! cursed may thou
be,
Thou traytour to God, that hast deceyved
me
And caught me in thy snare.
GOODS. Mary, thou brought thy selfe in care,
Wherof I am right gladde.   455
I must nedes laught. I can not be sadde.
EVERYMAN. A, Good, thou hast had longe   *hearty*
my hertely love.
I gave the that which sholde be the Lordes
above.
But wylte thou not go with me indede?
I praye the trouth to saye.   460   *truth*
GOODS. No, so God me spede.

Therfore farewell and have good daye.

EVERYMAN. O, to whome shall I make my
    mone
For to go with me in that hevy iournaye?
Fyrst Felawshyp sayd he wolde with me   465
    gone;
His wordes were very plesaunte and gaye.
But afterwarde he lefte me alone.
Than spake I to my kynnesmen, all in de-
    spayre,
And also they gave me wordes fayre.
They lacked no fayre spekynge.   470
But all forsoke me in the endynge.
Than wente I to my Goodes, that I loved
    best,
In hope to have comforte, but there had I
    leest,
For my Goodes sharpely dyd me tell
That he bryngeth many into hell.   475
Than of my selfe I was ashamed,
And so I am worthy to be blamed.
Thus may I well my selfe hate.
Of whom shall I now counseyll take?
I thynke that I shall never spede   480
Tyll that I go to my Good Dede,
But, alas, she is so weke
That she can nother go nor speke.   *neither/walk*
Yet wyll I venter on her now.   *venture*
My Good Dedes, where be you?   485
GOOD DEDES. Here I lye, colde in the
    grounde,
Thy synnes hath me sore bounde
That I can nat stere.   *stir*
EVERYMAN. O Good Dedes, I stande in fere.
I must you pray of counseyll   490
For helpe now sholde come ryght well.
GOOD DEDES. Everyman I have understand-
    ynge
That ye be somoned accounte to make   *summoned*
Before Myssyas of Iherusalem kynge   *Messias/Jerusalem*
And you do by me that iournay with you   495
    wyll I take.

EVERYMAN. Therfore I come to you my *moan*
    moone to make.
I praye you that ye wyll go with me.
GOOD DEDES. I wolde full fayne but I can
    not stande, veryly.
EVERYMAN. Why is there ony thynge on you *fallen*
    fall?
GOOD DEDES. Ye, syr, I may thanke you of 500 *for*
    all.
Yf ye had parfytely chered me, *perfectly/cheered*
Your boke of counte full redy had be. *book/would have*
Loke, the bokes of your workes and dedes   *been*
    eke. *also*
Behold howe they lye under the fete,
To your soules hevynes. 505 *heaviness*
EVERYMAN. Our Lorde Iesus helpe me,
For one letter here I can not se.
GOOD DEDES. There is a blynde rekenynge in
    tyme of dystres.
EVERYMAN. Good Dedes, I praye you helpe
    me in this nede
Or elles I am for ever dampned indede. 510 *damned*
Therefore helpe me to make my rekenynge
Before the Redemer of all thynge
That kynge is and was and ever shall. *shall (be)*
GOOD DEDES. Everyman, I am sory of your
    fall,
And fayne wolde I helpe you and I were 515
    able.
EVERYMAN. Good Dedes, your counseyll I
    pray you gyve me.
GOOD DEDES. That shall I do veryly
Thoughe that on my fete I may not go.
I have a syster that shall with you also *(go) with*
Called Knowledge whiche shall with you 520
    abyde
To helpe you to make that dredefull rek-
    enynge.
KNOWLEGE. Everyman, I wyll go with the
    and be thy gyde
In thy moost nede to go by thy syde.
EVERYMAN. In good condycyon I am now in
    every thynge

And am holé content with this good thynge   525   *wholly*
Thanked be God my creature.   *creator*
GOOD DEDES. And whan he hath brought you
    there
Where thou shalte hele the of thy smarte
Than go you with your rekenynge and your
    Good Dedes togyder
For to make you ioyfull at herte   530
Before the blessyd Trynyté.
EVERYMAN. My Good Dedes, gramercy.
I am well content, certaynly,
With your wordes swete.
KNOWLEGE. Now go we togyder lovyngly   535
To Confessyon, that clensyng ryvere.   *river*
EVERYMAN. For ioy I wepe. I wolde we were
    there,
But I pray you gyve me cognycyon   *cognition*
Where dwelleth that holy man Confessyon?
KNOWLEGE. In the house of salvacyon.   540
We shall fynde hym in that place
That shall us comforte by Goddes grace.
Lo, this is Confessyon. Knele downe and
    aske mercy,
For he is in good conceyte with God al-   *esteem*
    myghty.
EVERYMAN. O gloryous foutayne that all un-   545   *fountain/unclean-*
    clennes doth claryfy,   *ness*
Wasshe fro me the spottes of vyce unclene,
That on me no synne may be sene.
I come with Knowlege for my redempcyon
Redempte with herte and full contrycyon,
For I am commaunded a pylgrymage to take   550
And grete accountes before God to make.
Now I praye you, shryfte, moder of sal-   *mother*
    vacyon,
Helpe my Good Dedes for my pyteous ex-
    clamacyon.
CONFESSYON. I knowe your sorowe well,
    Everyman,
Bycause with Knowlege ye come to me   555
I wyll you comforte as well as I can,
And a precyous iewell I wyll gyve the   *jewel*
Called penaunce, voyder of adversyté.

Therwith shall your body chastysed be

With abstynence and perseveraunce in   560
    Goddes servyce.

Here shall you receyve that scourge of me

Whiche is penaunce stronge that ye must
    endure

To remembre thy Savyour was scourged for
    the

With sharpe scourges and suffred it pa-   *patiently*
    cyently,

So must thou or thou scape that paynful   565
    pylgrymage.

Knowlege, kepe hym in this vyage

And by that tyme Good Dedes wyll be with
    the,

But in ony wyse be seker of mercy   *certain*

For your tyme draweth fast and ye wyll
    saved be.

Aske God mercy and he wyll graunte truely.   570

Whan with the scourge of penaunce man
    doth hym bynde,

The oyle of forgyvenes than shall he fynde.   *oil*

EVERYMAN. Thanked be God for his gra-
    cyous werke,

For now I wyll my penaunce begyn.

This hath reioysed and lyghted my herte   575   *rejoiced*

Though the knottes be paynfull and harde
    within.

KNOWLEGE. Everyman, loke your penaunce   *look*
    that ye fulfyll

What payne that ever it to you be,

And Knowlege shall gyve you counseyll at
    wyll

How your accounte ye shall make clerely.   580

EVERYMAN. O eternal God, O hevenly
    fygure.

O way of ryghtwysnes, O goodly vysyon,   *righteousness/vision*

Which descended downe in a vyrgyn pure

Because he wolde every man redeme

Whiche Adam forfayted by his dysobedy-   585   *forfeited*
    ence.

O blessyd Godheed, electe and hye devyne.

Forgyve me my grevous offence.

Here I crye the mercy in this presence.
O ghostly treasure, O raunsomer and re-   *ransomer*
   demer.
Of all the worlde hope and conduyter,   590   *conductor*
Myrrour of ioye, foundatour of mercy,   *founder*
Whiche enlumyneth heven and erth therby,   *enlumines*
Here my clamorous complaynt, though it
   late be;
Receyve my prayers, unworthy of thy be-   *benignity*
   nygnytye.
Though I be a synner moost abhomynable   595   *abominable*
Yet let my name be wryten in Moyses table.   *Moses'*
O Mary, praye to the maker of all thynge
Me for to helpe at my endynge
And save me fro the power of my enemy,
For Deth assayleth me strongly.   600
And lady, that I may by meane of thy
   prayer
Of your sones glory to be partynere   *partner*
By the meanes of his passyon I it crave.
I beseche you helpe my soule to save.
Knowlege, gyve me the scourge of penaunce.   605
My fleshe therwith shall gyve aquytaunce.   *acquittance*
I wyll now begyn if God gyve me grace.
KNOWLEGE. Everyman, God gyve you tyme
   and space.
Thus I bequeth you in ye handes of our
   Savyour.
Now may you make your rekenynge sure.   610
EVERYMAN. In the name of the Holy Try-
   nyte
My body sore punysshyd shall be:
Take this, body, for the synne of the flesshe.
Also thou delytest to go gay and fresshe,
And in the way of dampnacyon thou dyd me   615
   brynge,
Therfore suffre now strokes of punysshynge.
Now of penaunce I wyll wade the water
   clere
To save me from purgatory, that sharpe fyre.
GOOD DEDES. I thanke God, now I can walke
   and go
And am delyvered of my sykenesse and wo.   620

Therfore with Everyman I wyll go and not
   spare.
His good workes I wyll helpe hym to de-
   clare.
KNOWLEGE. Now, Everyman, be mery and
   glad.
Your Good Dedes cometh now, ye may not
   be sad.
Now is your Good Dedes hole and sounde,   625
Goynge upryght upon the grounde.
EVERYMAN. My herte is lyght and shalbe
   evermore.
Now wyll I smyte faster than I dyde before.
GOOD DEDES. Everyman, pylgryme, my spe-
   cyall frende,
Blessyd be thou without ende,   630
For the is preparate the eternall glorye   *prepared*
Ye have me made hole and sounde
Therfor I wyll byde by the in every stounde.   *instance*
EVERYMAN. Welcome my Good Dedes.
   Now I here thy voyce
I wepe for very swetenes of love.   635
KNOWLEGE. Be no more sad, but ever
   reioyce.
God seeth thy lyvynge in his trone above.   *throne*
Put on this garment to thy behove   *benefit*
Whiche is wette with your teres
Or elles before God you may it mysse   640
When ye to your iourneys ende come shall.
EVERYMAN. Gentyll Knowlege, what do you
   yt call?
KNOWLEGE. It is a garment of sorowe;
Fro payne it wyll you borowe.   *redeem*
Contrycyon it is   645
That getteth forgyvenes;
He pleaseth God passynge well.
GOOD DEDES. Everyman, wyll you were it for   *wear/healing*
   your hele?
EVERYMAN. Now blessyd be Iesu, Maryes
   sone,
For now have I on true contrycyon.   650
And lette us go now without taryenge.
Good Dedes, have we clere our rekenynge?

GOOD DEDES. Ye, in dede, I have here.

EVERYMAN. Than I trust we nede not fere.

Now, frendes, let us not parte in twayne.   655

KNOWLEGE. Nay, Everyman, that wyll we   *"certainly will not*
    nat certayne.   *(do)"*

GOOD DEDES. Yet must thou lead with the
Thre persones of grete myght.

EVERYMAN. Who sholde they be?

GOOD DEDES. Dyscrecyon and Strength they   660   *are called*
    hyght
And thy Beauté may not abyde behinde.

KNOWLEGE. Also ye must call to mynde
Your Fyve Wyttes, as for your counsey-
    lours.

GOOD DEDES. You must have them redy at all
    houres.

EVERYMAN. Howe shall I gette them hyder?   665   *hither*

KNOWLEGE. You must call them all togyder
And they wyll here you incontynent.   *straightaway*

EVERYMAN. My Frendes, come hyder and be
    present,
Discrecyon, Strengthe, my Fyve Wyttes and
    Beaute.

BEAUTE. Here at your wyll we be all redy.   670
What wyll ye that we shulde do?

GOOD DEDES. That ye wolde with Everyman
    go,
And helpe him in his pylgrymage.
Advyse you, wyll ye with him or not in that
    vyage?

STRENGTH. We wyll brynge hym all thyder   675
To his helpe and comforte, ye may byleve
    me.

DYSCRECYON. So wyll we go with hym all
    togyder.

EVERYMAN. Almyghty God, loved myght
    thou be.
I gyve the laude that I have hyder brought
Strength, Dyscrecyon, Beaute and Five   680
    Wyttes. Lacke I nought.
And my Good Dedes, with Knowlege clere,
All be in my company at my wyll here.
I desyre no more to my besynes.   *for/business*

STRENGTH. And I, Strength, wyll by you
    stande in dystres,
Though thou wolde in batayle fyght on the   685
    grounde.
FYVE WYTTES. And though it were thrugh
    the worlde rounde,
We wyll not departe for swete ne soure.
BEAUTE. No more wyll I, unto dethes houre   *until*
What so ever therof befall.
DYSCRECYON. Everyman, advyse you fyrst of   690
    all
Go with a good advysement and delybera-   *deliberation*
    cyon.
We all gyve you vertuous monycyon   *admonition*
That all shall be well.
EVERYMAN. My Frendes, harken what I
    wyll tell:
I praye God rewarde you in his hevenly   695 *sphere*
    spere.
Now herken all that be here,
For I wyll make my testament
Here before you all present.
In almes halfe my good I wyll gyve with my
    handes twayne
In the way of charyte with good entent,   700
And the other halfe styll shall remayne
In queth to be retourned there it ought to   *bequest*
    be.
This I do in despyte of the fende of hell,   *fiend*
To go quyte out of his perell   *quite*
Ever after and this daye.   705
KNOWLEGE. Everyman, herken what I saye,
Go to Presthode, I you advyse,
And receyve of hym in ony wyse,
The holy sacrament and oyntement togyder.
Than shortly se ye tourne agayne hyder.   710
We wyll all abyde you here.
FYVE WYTTES. Ye, Everyman, hye you that
    ye redy were.
There is no emperour, kinge, duke, ne
    baron,
That of God hath commycyon   *commission, power*
As hath the leest preest in the worlde beynge.   715 *existing*

For of the blessyd sacramentes pure and be-   *benign*
  nygne
He bereth the keyes and therof hath the
  cure
For mannes redempcyon, it is ever sure,
Whiche God for our soules medycyne
Gave us out of his herte with grete payne,   720
Here in this transytory lyfe for the and me.
The blessyd sacramentes seven there be—
Baptym, confyrmacyon, with preesthode   *Baptism*
  good,
And ye sacrament of Goddes precyous flesshe
  and blod,
Maryage, the holy extreme unccyon, and   725
  penaunce.
These seven be good to have in remem-
  braunce.
Gracyous sacramentes of hye devynyte.
EVERYMAN. Fayne wolde I receyve that holy
  body,
And mekely to my ghostly fader I wyll go.
FYVE WYTTES. Everyman, that is the best   730
  that ye can do.
God wyll you to salvacyon brynge,
For preesthode excedeth all other thynge.
To us holy scrypture they do teche,
And converteth man fro synne heven to
  reche.
God hath to them more power gyven   735
Than to ony aungell that is in heven.
With five wordes he may consecrate
Goddes body in flesshe and blode to make
And handeleth his maker bytwene his
  hande.
The preest byndeth and unbyndeth all   740
  bandes,
Both in erthe and in heven.
Thou mynystres all the sacramentes seven.   *administer*
Though we kyste thy fete, thou were   *kissed*
  worthy.
Thou arte surgyon that cureth synne deedly.   *deadly*
No remedy we fynde under God   745
But all onely preesthode.   *Except only*

Everyman, God gave preests that dygnyté
And setteth them in his stede amonge us to   *place*
   be.
Thus be they above aungelles in degree.
   (*exit Everyman to priest*)
KNOWLEGE. If preestes be good, it is so,   750   *surely*
   suerly.
But whan Iesu hanged on ye crosse with
   grete smarte,
There he gave out of his blessyd herte
The same sacrament in grete tourment.   *torment*
He solde them not to us, that lorde omnypo-
   tent,
Therefore saynt Peter the apostell dothe saye   755
That Iesus curse hath all they
Whiche God theyr Savyour do by or sell
Or they for ony money do take or tell.
Synfull preests gyveth the synners example
   bad.
Theyr chyldren sytteth by other mennes   760   *heard*
   fyres, I have harde,
And some haunteth womens company
With unclen lyfe, as lustes of lechery.
These be with synne made blynde.
FYVE WYTTES. I trust to God no suche may
   we fynde.
Therfore let us preesthode honour,   765
And folowe theyr doctryne for our soules   *succor*
   socoure.
We be theyr shepe, and they shepeherdes
   be,
By whome we all be kepte in suerté.   *surety*
Peas, for yonder I se Everyman come   *Peace*
Whiche hath made true satysfaccyon.   770
GOOD DEDES. Me thynke it is he indede.
EVERYMAN. Now Iesu be your alder spede.   *of you all/salvation*
I have receyved the sacrament for my re-
   dempcyon
And than myne extreme unccyon.
Blessyd be all they that counseyled me to   775
   take it,
And now frendes, let us go without longer
   respyte.

I thanke God that ye have taryed so longe.

Now set each of you on this rodde your   *rood, cross*
   honde

And shortely folowe me.

I go before there I wolde be. God be our   780
   gyde.

STRENGTHE. Everyman, we will nat fro you
   go

Tyll ye have gone this vyage longe.

DYSCRECYON. I, Dyscrecyon wyll byde by
   you also.

KNOWLEGE. And though this pylgrymage be   *ever so hard*
   never so stronge

I wyll never parte you fro.   785 *from you*

STRENGTH. Everyman, I will be as sure by   *remain/surely*
   the

As ever I was by Iudas Machabe.   *Judas Maccabee*

EVERYMAN. Alas, I am so faynt I may not
   stande,

My lymmes under me doth folde.

Frendes, let us nat tourne agayne to this   790
   lande,

Nat for all the worldes golde,

For into this cave must I crepe

And torne to erthe and there slepe.

BEAUTE. What, in to this grave, alas!

EVERYMAN. Ye, there shall ye consume,   795 *decay/all of you*
   more and lesse.

BEAUTE. And what, sholde I smoder here.   *smother*

EVERYMAN. Ye, by my fayth, and never
   more appere.

In this worlde lyve no more we shall

But in heven before the hyest lorde of all.

BEAUTE. I crosse out all this. Adewe by   800 *Adieu/St. John*
   saynt Iohan.

I take my cappe in my lappe and am   *"I grab my hat and*
   gone.   *rush off"**

EVERYMAN. What, Beaute, whyder wyll   *whither will you*
   ye?   *(go)*

BEAUTE. Peas. I am defe, I loke not behynde   *Peace/deaf*
   me.

---

801 Other readings of this line include *tappe* for *cappe* and "I doff my cap (to
you) as low as my lap."

Nat and thou woldest gyve me all the golde
   in thy chest.
EVERYMAN. Alas, wherto may I truste?   805
Beaute gothe fast awaye fro me.
She promysed with me to lyve and dye.
STRENGTH. Everyman I wyll the also forsake
   and denye.
The game lyketh me nat at all.
EVERYMAN. Why than ye wyll forsake me   810
   all.
Swete strength, tary a lytell space.
STRENGTH. Nay, syr, by the rode of grace,
I wyll hye me from the fast,
Though thou wepe tyll thy hert to-brast.   *completely burst*
EVERYMAN. Ye wolde ever byde by me, ye   815
   sayd.
STRENGTH. Ye, I have you ferre ynoughe   *far/enough*
   conveyde.
Ye be olde ynoughe, I understande,
Your pylgrymage to take on hande.
I repent me that I hyder came.
EVERYMAN. Strengthe, you to dysplease I   820   *for displeasing you*
   am to blame,
Yet promyse is dette, this ye well wot.   *debt/know*
STRENGTH. In fayth I care not.
Thou arte but a foole to complayne.
You spende your speche and wast your
   brayne.
Go thryst the into the grounde.   825   *thrust*
EVERYMAN. I had wende surer I sholde you   *thought, weened*
   have founde.
He that trusteth in his strength
She hym deceyveth at the length.
Bothe Strength and Beaute forsaketh me,
Yet they promysed me fayre and lovyngly.   830
DYSCRECYON. Everyman I wyll after
   Strengthe be gone.
As for me, I wyll leve you alone.
EVERYMAN. Why Dyscrecyon, wyll ye for-
   sake me?
DYSCRECYON. Ye, in good fayth, I wyll go fro
   the,
For whan Strength goth before   835

I folowe after ever more.

EVERYMAN. Yet I pray the for the love of the
    Trynyté,

Loke in my grave ones pyteously.

DYSCRECYON. Nay, so nye wyll I not come.

Fare well everychone.   840   *every one*

EVERYMAN. O all thynge fayleth save God
    alone,

Beaute, Strengthe and Dyscrecyon,

For whan Deth bloweth his blast

They all renne fro me full fast.

FYVE WYTTES. Everyman, my leve now of   845
    the I take.

I wyll folowe the other, for here I the for-
    sake.

EVERYMAN. Alas, then may I wayle and
    wepe,

For I toke you for my best frende.

FYVE WYTTES. I wyll no lenger the kepe,

Now farewell, and there an ende.   850

EVERYMAN. O Iesu, helpe, All hath for-
    saken me.

GOOD DEDES. Nay, Everyman, I wyll byde
    with the.

I wyll not forsake the in dede.

Thou shalte fynde me a good frende at nede.

EVERYMAN. Gramercy, Good Dedes, now   855
    may I true frendes se.

They have forsaken me, everychone.

I loved them better than my Good Dedes
    alone.

Knowlege, wyll ye forsake me also?

KNOWLEGE. Ye, Everyman, when ye to Deth
    shall go,

But not yet for no maner of daunger.   860

EVERYMAN. Gramercy, Knowlege, with all
    my herte.

KNOWLEGE. Nay, yet I wyll not from hens   *hence*
    departe,

Tyll I se where ye shall be come.

EVERYMAN. Me thynke, alas, that I must
    be gone

To make my rekenynge and my dettes paye,   865

For I se my tyme is nye spent awaye.

Take example all ye that this do here or se,
How they that I love best do forsake me,
Excepte my Good Dedes that bydeth truely.
GOOD DEDES. All erthly thynges is but vanyte, 870
Beaute, Strength and Dyscrecyon do man
  forsake,
Folysshe frendes and kynnes men that fayre
  spake,
All fleeth save Good Dedes, and that am I.
EVERYMAN. Have mercy on me, God moost
  myghty,
And stande by me, thou moder and mayde, 875
  holy Mary.
GOOD DEDES. Fere not, I wyll speke for the.
EVERYMAN. Here I crye, God mercy.
GOOD DEDES. Shorte our ende and mynyshe   *Shorten/diminish*
  our payne,
Let us go and never come agayne.
EVERYMAN. Into thy handes, lorde, my soule 880
  I commende.
Receyve it, lorde, that it be nat loste.
As thou me boughtest, so me defende,
And save me fro the fendes boost,   *fiend's/boast*
That I may appere with that blessyd hoost   *host*
That shall be saved at the day of dome. 885 *doom*
In manus tuas, of myghtes moost,   *"Into thy hands"/*
For ever *commendo spiritum meum.*   *most*
        (*they climb into the grave*)   *"I commend my*
KNOWLEGE. Nowe hath he suffred that we   *spirit"*
  all shall endure.   (*so*) *that*
The good dedes shall make all sure.
Now hath he made endynge,   890
Me thynketh that I here aungelles synge,
And make grete ioy and melody,
Where Everymannes soule receyved shall
  be.
AUNGELL. Come excellente electe spouse to
  Iesu.
Here above thou shalte go,   895
Bycause of thy synguler vertue.
Now the soule is taken the body fro
Thy rekenynge is crystall clere.
Now shalte thou into the hevenly spere,
Unto the whiche all ye shall come   900

That lyveth well before the daye of dome.

EPILOGUE

DOCTOUR. This morall men may have in
   mynde.
Ye herers take it of worth, olde and yonge,
And forsake Pryde, for he desceyveth you
   in the ende,
And remembre Beaute, Five Wyttes,   905
   Strength and Dyscrecyon;
They all at the last do Everyman forsake,
Save his Good Dedes there doth he take.
But beware and they be small,
Before God he hath no helpe at all.
None excuse may be there for Everyman.   910   *may there be*
Alas, howe shall he do than?
For after dethe amendes may no man make,
For than mercy and pyte doth hym forsake,
If his rekenynge be not clere when he doth
   come,
God wyll saye *Ite maledicti in ignem eter-* 915   *"Depart ye cursed*
   num.   *into everlasting*
And he that hath his accounte hole and   *fire"*
   sounde
Hye in heven he shall be crounde,   *crowned*
Unto whiche place God brynge us all thyder
That we may lyve body and soule togyder.
Therto helpe the Trynyte.   920
Amen, saye ye for saynt charyté.

FINIS

THUS ENDETH THIS MORALL PLAYE OF EVERY MAN

SUPPLEMENTARY MATERIAL

1. L. V. Ryan, "Doctrine and Dramatic Structure in 'Everyman,'" *Speculum*, XXXII (1957), 722–35.
2. T. F. Van Laan, "'Everyman': A Structural Analysis," *PMLA*, LXXVIII
(1963), 465–75.

PLAY OF NOAH

Noah	First Son, Shem	First Daughter-in-law
God	Second Son, Ham	Second Daughter-in-law
Noah's Wife	Third Son, Japheth	Third Daughter-in-law

NOE. Myghtfull God veray / Maker of all
    that is,   *true*

Thre persons withoutten nay / oone God in
    endles blis,   *undeniably*

Thou maide both nyght and day / beest,
    fowle and fysh.

All creatures that lif may / wroght thou at
    thi wish,   *live*

As thou wel myght.   5

The son, the moyne, verament,   *sun/moon/truly* (cf.

Thou maide; the firmament,   l. 1)

The sternes also full fervent,   *stars*

To shyne thou maide ful bright

Angels thou maide ful even / all orders that   10
    is,

To have the blis in heven / this did thou
    more and les;

Full mervelus to neven, / yit was ther un-   *name*
    kyndnes

More bi foldys seven / then I can well ex-   *sevenfold*
    pres;

For whi?

Of all angels in brightnes   15

God gaf Lucifer most lightnes.

Yit prowdly he flyt his des,   *flitted (from)/dais*
And set hym even hym by.

He thoght hymself as worthi / as hym that   (i.e., as God)
    hym made
In brightnes, in bewty. / Therfor he hym   20   *beauty/degraded*
    degrade,
Put hym in a low degre / soyn after in a   *soon/flash, hurry*
    brade
Hym and all his menye, / wher he may be   *company*
    unglad
For ever.
Shall thay never wyn away   *win, escape*
Hence unto domysday,   25   *doomsday*
Bot burn in bayle for ay.   *bale, misery/ever*
Shall thay never dyssever.   *leave*

Soyne after, that gracyous lord / to his liknes
    maide man,
That place to be restord / even as he began.
Of the trinité bi accord / Adam and Eve that   30
    woman
To multiplie without discord / in paradise
    put he thaym
And sithen to both   *afterward*
Gaf in commaundement
On the tre of life to lay no hend.   *hand*
Bot yit the fals feynd   35   *false/fiend, devil*
Made hym with man wroth,

Entysyd man to glotony / styrd him to syn   *Enticed/stirred*
    in pride.
Bot in paradise securly / myght no syn
    abide.
And therfor man full hastely / was put out   *time*
    in that tyde,
In wo and wandreth for to be / in paynes   40   *hard*
    full unrid
To knowe.
Fyrst in erth and sythen in hell
With feyndys for to dwell
Bot he his mercy mell   *tells*
To those that will hym trawe.   45   *believe*

Oyle of mercy he hus hight / as I have hard red,

To every lifyng wight / that wold luf hym and dred.

Bot now before his sight / every liffyng leyde,

Most party day and nyght / syn in word and dede

Full bold: 50

Som in pride, ire and envy,

Som in covetous and glotyny,

Som in sloth and lechery,

And other wise manyfold.

Therfor I drede lest God / on us will take   55
veniance,

For syn is now alod / without any repent-
ance.

Sex hundreth yeris and od / have I, without
distance,

In erth, as any sod, / liffyd with grete grev-
ance

Allway.

And now I wax old,   60

Seke, sory and cold,

As muk apon mold

I widder away.

Bot yit will I cry / for mercy and call,

Noë, thi servant, am I / lord over all.   65

Therfor me, and my fry / shal with me fall,

Save from velany / and bryng to thi hall

In heven,

And kepe me from syn

This warld within.   70

Comly kyng of mankyn,

I pray the here my stevyn.

GOD. Syn I have maide all thyng / that is
liffand,

Duke, emperour and kyng / with myne
awne hand

Oil/us/promised/ heard/tell

living/creature

man

part (of the)

vengeance

allowed

odd, more

Sick
muck on mold, earth (formulaic)
wither

offspring
villainy

voice

Since/living (here and fol., -and = -ing)
own

For to have thare likyng / by see and bi   75
    sand,
Every man to my bydyng / shuld be
    bowand
Full fervent,
That maide man sich a creatoure,   *such*
Farest of favoure.
Man must luf me paramoure   80   O.Fr. *par amour*
By reson and repent.   *'with (all his)*
                                           love'

Me thoght I shewed man luf / when I made
    hym to be
All angels abuf / like to the trynyté.
And now in grete reprufe / full low ligys he   *lies*
In erth hymself to stuf / with syn that dis-   85
    pleasse me
Most of all.
Veniance will I take
In erth for syn sake.
My grame thus will I wake   *anger*
Both of grete and small.   90

I repente full sore / that ever maide I man.
Bi me he settys no store / and I am his   *sovereign*
    soferan.
I will distroy therfor / both beest, man and
    woman.
All shall perish, les and more; / that bargan   *curse*
    may thay ban
That ill has done.   95
In erth I se right noght
Bot syn that is unsoght.   *unatoned (for)*
Of those that well has wroght
Fynd I bot a fone.   *few*

Therfor shall I fordo / all this medill-erd   100   *destroy, do in/world*
With floodys that shal flo / and ryn with   *run/sound*
    hidous rerd.
I have good cause therto / for me no man is   *afraid*
    ferd.
As I say shal I do / of veniance draw my
    swerd

And make end
Of all that beris life,
Sayf Noë and his wife,
For thay wold never stryfe
With me then me offend.

Hym to mekill wyn / hastly will I go

To Noë my servand or I blyn / to warn hym
of his wo.
In erth I se bot syn / reynand to and fro

Emang both more and myn / ichon other fo
With all thare entent.
All shall I fordo
With floodys that shall floo.
Wirk shall I thaym wo
That will not repent.

Noë, my freend, I the commaund / from
cares the to keyle,
A ship that thou ordand / of nayle and bord
ful wele.
Thou was alway well-wirkand / to me trew
as stele,
To my bydyng obediand. / Frendship shal
thou fele
To mede.
Of lennthe thi ship be
Thre hundreth cubettys warn I the.
Of heght even thirté.
Of fyfty als in brede.

Anoynt thi ship with pik and tar / without
and als within,
The water out to spar. / This is a noble
gyn.
Look no man the mar. / Thre chese chambres begyn.
Thou must spend many a spar / this wark or
thou wyn
To end fully.

105 bears, possesses
     Save, except

     nor offend me

     "With great benefit
        (win) to him"
110 servant/ere/cease

     reigning/every-
        where
     smaller, "high and
        low"/"each one a
        foe to the other"
115

     cool, keep

     ordain, contrive

120

     As reward

     300 cubits/advise
125
     also/breadth

     pitch/outside

     shut/engine, contriv-
        ance
     hinder/tiers (of),
        poss. rel. to chess
130 use/beam/work/
        ere/complete

Make in thi ship also
Parloures oone or two
And houses of offyce mo
For beestys that ther must be.   135

Oone cubite on hight / a wyndo shal thou
   make.
On the syde a doore, with slyght / beneyth   *sleight, skill*
   shal thou take.
With the shal no man fyght / nor do the no   *kind (of)/harm*
   kyn wrake.
When all is doyne thus right / thi wife, that   *done/mate*
   is thi make,
Take in to the.   140
Thi sonnes of good fame,
Sem, Iaphet, and Came,   *Shem/Japheth/*
Take in also thame,   *Ham*
Thare wifys also thre.

For all shal be fordone / that lif in land, bot   145
   ye,
With floodys that from abone / shal fall and   *above*
   that plenté.
It shall begyn full sone / to rayn unces-   *incessantly*
   santlé,
After dayes seven be done / and induyr   *endure*
   dayes fourty
Withoutten fayll.
Take to thi ship also   150
Of ich kynd beestys two   *each*
Mayll and femayll, bot no mo,
Or thou pull up thi sayll.   *Ere*

For thay may the avayll / when al this
   thyng is wroght.
Stuf thi ship with vitayll / for hungre that   155
   ye perish noght.
Of beestys, foull and catayll— / for thaym   *cattle/keep*
   have thou in thoght—
For thaym is my counsayll / that som socour   *succor*
   be soght
In hast.

Thay must have corn and hay
And oder mete alway.   160   *other*
Do now as I the say,
In the name of the holy gast.   *ghost*

NOË. A, *benedicite!* / What art thou that
    thus
Tellys afore that shall be? / Thou art full   *Tells*
    mervelus.
Tell me, for charité / thi name so gracius.   165
GOD. My name is of dignyté / and also full
    glorius
To knowe.
I am god most myghty,
Oone god in trynyty,
Made the and ich man to be,   170
To luf me well thou awe.   *ought*

NOE. I thank the, lord so dere / that wold
    vowchsayf
Thus low to appere / to a symple knafe.   *knave*
Blis us, Lord, here / for charite I hit crafe.   *crave*
The better may we stere / the ship that we   175
    shall hafe,
Certayn.
GOD. Noe, to the and to thi fry
My blyssyng graunt I.
Ye shall wax and multiply
And fill the erth agane   180

Whan all thise floodys ar past / and fully
    gone away.
NOE. Lord, homward will I hast / as fast as
    that I may.
My wife will I frast / what she will say   *ask*
And I am agast / that we get som fray   *afraid/affray*
Betwixt us both,   185
For she is full tethee,   *touchy*
For litill oft angré.
If any thyng wrang be
Soyne is she wroth.
    (*Tunc perget ad uxorem*)   *"Then he shall cross*
                                    over to his wife"

God spede, dere wife. / How fayre ye?   190

WIFE. Now as ever myght I thryfe / the   *thrive/worse (be-*
    wars I the see.   *cause)*

Do tell me belife / where has thou thus long   *quickly/been*
    be

To dede may we dryfe / or lif, for the,   *death/drive, rush/*
For want.   *"for all you care"*

When we swete or swynk,   195 *sweat/toil*
Thou dos what thou thynk,
Yit of mete and of drynk
Have we veray skant.

NOE. Wife, we ar hard sted / with tythyngys   *placed/tidings*
    new.

WIFE. Bot thou were worthi be cled / in   200 *clad/blue, poss.*
    Stafford blew,   *"beaten black and*
                                                            blue"

For thou art alway adred / be it fals or trew.   *a-dread*

Bot God knowes I am led / and that may I
    rew,
Full ill.

For I dar be thi borow,   *pledge, surety*
From even unto morow   205

Thou spekys ever of sorow.

God send the onys thi fill.   *once*

We women may wary / all ill husbandys.   *curse*

I have oone, bi mary / that lowsyd me of my   *loosed/from/bonds*
    bandys.   *(of pregnancy)*

If he teyn, I must tary / howsoever it   210 *grieves*
    standys,

With seymland full sory / wryngand both   *semblance, expres-*
    my handys   *sion*
For drede.

Bot yit otherwhile,

What with gam and with gyle,   *game/guile*

I shall smyte and smyle   215
And qwite hym his mede.   *requite/reward (l.*
                                                            122)

NOE. We! hold thi tong ram-skyt / or I shall   *ram-flux*
    the still.

WIFE. By my thryft if thou smyte / I shal   *unto, "turn on thee"*
    turne the untill.

NOE. We shall assy as tyte. / Have at the   *assay, test/immedi-*
   Gill.   *ately*
Apon the bone shal it byte. / (*strikes her*)   220
WIFE.   A, so, mary,   *smite*
   thou smytys ill.
Bot I suppose
I shal not in thi det
Flyt of this flett.   *off/floor*
Take the ther a langett   *lace*
To tye up thi hose.   (*strikes him*)   225

NOE. A, wilt thou so? / Mary, that is myne.
WIFE. Thou shal thre for two / I swere by   *suffering, here Pas-*
   Godys pyne.   *sion*
NOE. And I shall qwyte the tho / in fayth or
   syne.
WIFE. Out apon the, ho. /
NOE.   Thou can both
   byte and whyne,
With a rerd.   230   *sound* (l. 101)
For all if she stryke,
Yit fast will she skryke.   *shriek*
In fayth I hold none slyke   *such*
In all medill-erd.

Bot I will kepe charyté / for I have at do.   235   *"business to do"*
WIFE. Here shal no man tary the / I pray
   the go to.
Full well may we mys the / as ever have I   *peace*
   ro.
To spyn will I dres me. /
NOE.   We, fare well,
   lo.
Bot wife,
Pray for me beselé   240   *busily*
To eft I com unto the.   *Till again*
WIFE. Even as thou prays for me
As ever myght I thrife.

NOE. I tary full lang / fro my warke, I traw.
Now my gere will I fang / and thederward   245   *take/thitherward*
   draw.
I may full ill gang / the soth for to knaw,   *go, progress/know*

Bot if God help amang / I may sit downe
   daw   *fool (jackdaw)*

To ken.   *"To be known for"*

Now assay will I

How I can of wrightry,   250   *carpentry*

In nomine patris, et filii,   *"In the name of the*

Et spiritus sancti. Amen.   *father, and of the*
                                          son, and of the
                                          holy ghost.
                                          Amen."

To begyn of this tree / my bonys will I   *wood/bones*
   bend.

I traw from the trynyte / socoure will be
   send.

It fayres full fayre, thynk me / this wark to   255   *hands*
   my hend.

Now blissid be he / that this can amend.

Lo, here the lenght,

Thre hundreth cubettys evenly.

Of breed, lo, is it fyfty.

The heght is even thyrty   260

Cubettys full strenght.

Now my gowne will I cast / and wyrk in my   *cast (off)*
   cote.

Make will I the mast / or I flyt oone foote.

A, my bak, I traw will brast. / This is a sory   *burst, break*
   note.

Hit is wonder that I last / sich an old dote,   265   *dotard*

All dold,   *dulled*

To begyn sich a wark.

My bonys ar so stark.   *stiff*

No wonder if thay wark,   *ache*

For I am full old.   270

The top and the sayll / both will I make.

The helme and the castell / also will I take.

To drife ich a nayll / will I not forsake.   *every nail*

This gere may never fayll / that dar I undertake.

Onone.   275   *Anon, immediately*

This is a nobull gyn.   *contrivance (l. 128)*

Thise nayles so thay ryn · · · · · · · · · · · · · · · · · · · *run*
Thoro more and myn · · · · · · · · · · · · · · · · · · · *Through/all* (l. 112)
Thise bordys ichon. · · · · · · · · · · · · · · · · · · · *boards/each one*

Window and doore, / even as he saide. · · · · 280
Thre ches chambre, / thay ar well maide. · · · · · · *tiers (of) rooms* (l.
Pyk and tar full sure / therapon laide. · · · · · · · · · 129)
This will ever endure / therof am I paide, · · · · · · *Pitch* (l. 127)
Forwhy · *satisfied*
It is better wroght · · · · · · · · · · · · · · · 285 · · · *Because*
Then I coude haif thoght.
Hym that maide all of noght
I thank oonly.

Now will I hy me / and nothyng be leder, · · · · · · · *lazy*
My wife and my meneye / to bryng even · · · 290 · · *household/hither*
      heder.
Tent hedir tydely / wife and consider. · · · · · · · · · *Pay attention/*
Hens must us fle / all sam togeder · · · · · · · · · · · · · *quickly*
In hast. · *Hence/"all together"*
WIFE. Whi, syr, what alis you? · · · · · · · · · · · · · *ails*
Who is that asails you · · · · · · · · · · · · · 295
To fle it avalis you
And ye be agast.

NOE. Ther is garn on the reyll / other, my · · · · · · *"There is other yarn*
      dame. · *on the reel"* =
WIFE. Tell me that ich a deyll / els get ye · · · · · · *"other business on*
      blame. · *hand"*
NOE. He that cares may keill / blessid be his · · 300 · *every deal, every bit,*
      name, · *all*
He has behete, for oure seyll / to sheld us · · · · · · · *cool* (l. 118)
      fro shame · *promised/prosperity*
And sayd · (cf. N.E. *sala-*
All this warld aboute · · · · · · · · · · · · · · · · · · · *cious,* etc.)
With floodys so stoute,
That shall ryn on a route · · · · · · · · · · · · 305 · · · *run/in a body*
Shall be overlaide.

He saide all shall be slayn / bot oonely we,
Oure barnes that ar bayn / and thare wifys · · · · · · · *children/obedient*
      thre.

A ship he bad me ordayn / to safe us and
oure fee.

*construct (l. 119)/
goods*

Therfor with all oure mayn / thank we that   310
fre

power/noble (one)

Beytter of bayll.

Abater

Hy us fast, go we thedir.

WIFE. I wote never whedir.

I dase and I dedir

For ferd of that tayll.   315

*know/whither
"quake and quail"
(cf. N.E. daze,
dither)
fear/tale*

NOE. Be not aferd. Have done. / Trus sam
oure gere.

*Truss/together (l.
292)*

That we be ther or none / without more
dere.

ere/noon/harm

I SON. It shall be done full sone. / Brether,
help to bere.

II SON. Full long shall I not hoyne / to do
my devere.

*delay/duty (O.Fr.
deveir)*

Brether, sam.   320

together or ?Shem

III SON. Without any yelp,

boast

At my myght shall I help.

With

WIFE. Yit for drede of a skelp

blow

Help well thi dam.

NOE. Now ar we there / as we shuld be.   325

Do get in oure gere / oure catall and fe

Into this vessell here / my chylder fre.

WIFE. I was never bard ere / as ever myght I
the,

*barred, cooped up/
thrive*

In sich an oostre as this.

hostelry

In fath I can not fynd   330

Which is before, which is behynd.

Bot shall we here be pynd,

penned

Noe, as have thou blis?

NOE. Dame, as it is skill / here must us abide
grace.

reasonable/await

Therfor, wife, with good will / com into   335
this place.

WIFE. Sir, for Iak nor for Gill / will I turne
my face

*Jack, Jill, i.e., for no
one*

Till I have on this hill / spon a space   *spun*
On my rok.
Well were he myght get me.
Now will I downe set me.   340
Yit reede I no man let me   *advise/hinder* (l.
For drede of a knok.   226)

NOE. Behold to the heven. / The cateractes
    all,
Thai ar open full even / grete and small,
And the planettys seven / left has thare stall.   345
Thise thoners and levyn / downe gar fall   *thunders/lightning/*
Full stout   *make*
Both halles and bowers,
Castels and towres.
Full sharp ar thise showers   350
That renys aboute.   *rain*

Therfor, wife, have done. / Com into ship
    fast.
WIFE. Yei, Noe, go cloute thi shone. / The   *cobble/shoes*
    better will thai last.
I DAU. Good moder, com in sone / for all is
    overcast,
Both the son and the mone /   355 *sun/moon*
II DAU.   And many
    wynd blast
Full sharp.
Thise floodys so thay ryn.
Therfor, moder, com in.
WIFE. In fayth, yit will I spyn.
All in vayn ye carp.   360 *chatter*

III DAU. If ye like ye may spyn / moder, in
    the ship.
NOE. Now is this twyys com-in, / dame, on   *second*
    my frenship.
WIFE. Wheder I lose or I wyn / in fayth,
    thi felowship,
Set I not at a pyn. / This spyndill will I slip
Apon this hill   365
Or I styr oone fote.

NOE. Peter, I traw we dote.   *think/are dotty*
Without any more note,   *ado*
Com in if ye will.

WIFE. Yei, water nyghys so nere / that I sit   370   *Yea/nighs*
    not dry.
Into ship with a byr / therfor will I hy   *rush*
For drede that I drone here. /   *drown*
NOE.   Dame, se-   *certainly*
    curly,
It bees boght full dere / ye abode so long by   *is*
Out of ship.
WIFE. I will not, for thi bydyng,   375
Go from doore to mydyng.   *dunghill*
NOE. In fayth, and for youre long taryyng
Ye shal lik on the whyp.   *lick, taste/whip*

WIFE. Spare me not, I pray the / bot even as
    thou thynk.
Thise grete wordys shall not flay me. /   380
NOE.   Abide,
    dame and drynk
For betyn shall thou be / with this staf to   *beaten/till*
    thou stynk.
Ar strokys good? say me. /
WIFE.   What say ye,   *Walter Wince, nick-*
    Wat Wynk?   *name (cf. Mr.*
NOE. Speke.   *Milquetoast)*
Cry me mercy, I say.
WIFE. Therto say I nay.   385
NOE. Bot thou do bi this day
Thi hede shall I breke.

WIFE. Lord I were at ese / and hertely full   *whole*
    hoylle
Might I onys have a measse / of wedows   *mess/widows' cab-*
    coyll.   *bage (cf. N.G.*
For thi saull without lese / shuld I dele   390   *Kohl, N.E. cole-*
    penny doyll.   *(slaw)*
So wold mo no frese / that I se on this sole   *soul/lie/dole*
Of wifys that ar here   *doubtless/"in this*
For the life that thay leyd   *place"*
Wold thare husbandys were ded,   *lead*

For as ever ete I brede   395
So wold I oure syre were.

NOE. Yee men that has wifys / whyls thay ar
   yong
If ye luf youre lifys / chastice thare tong.
Me thynk my hert ryfys / both levyr and   *breaks/liver/lung*
   long
To se sich stryfys / wedmen emong.   400   *strife(s)/wedded*
Bot I   *men, people*
As have I blys,
Shall chastyse this.
WIFE. Yit may ye mys
Nicholl Nedy.   405   *Nicholas Needy,*
                                                   nickname
NOE. I shall make the still as stone / begyn-   *beginner*
   nar of blunder.
I shall bete the bak and bone / and breke all   *asunder*
   in sonder.
WIFE. Out alas I am gone. / Oute apon the,
   mans wonder.
NOE. Se how she can grone / and I lig un-   *lie*
   der.
Bot wife   410
In this hast let us ho   *halt*
For my bak is nere in two.
WIFE. And I am bet so blo   *beaten/blue*
That I may not thryfe.

I SON. A, whi fare ye thus, / fader and   415   *spiteful/peril*
   moder both?
II SON. Ye shuld not be so spitus / standyng
   in sich a woth.
III SON. Thise weders ar so hidus / with   *weathers/hideous/*
   many a cold coth.   *disease*
NOE. We will do as ye bid us. / We will no
   more be wroth
Dere barnes.   *children (l. 308)*
Now to the helme will I hent   420   *seize*
And to my ship tent.   *attend (l. 291)*
WIFE. I se on the firmament
Me thynk the seven starnes.   *stars (planets)*

NOE. This a grete flood, / wife, take hede.
WIFE. So me thoght as I stode. / We are in   425
    grete drede.
Thise wawghes ar so wode. /   *waves/wild*
NOE.   Help, God,
    in this nede.
As thou art stere-man good / and best, as I
    rede,
Of all.
Thou rewle us in this rase   *rule/race, course*
As thou me behete hase.   430   *promised (l. 301)*
WIFE. This is a perlous case.
Help, God, when we call.

NOE. Wife tent the stere-tre / and I shall   *steering-stick, tiller*
    asay
The depnes of the see / that we bere if I
    may.
WIFE. That shall I do ful wysely. / Now go   435
    thi way,
For apon this flood have we / flett many day   *floated*
With pyne.
NOE. Now the water will I sownd.
A, it is far to the grownd.
This travell I expownd   440
Had I to tyne.   *for nothing*

Above all hillys bedeyn / the water is rysen   *forthwith*
    late
Cubettys xv. / Bot in a higher state   *higher*
It may not be, I weyn, / for this well I wate.   *think/know*
This fourty dayes has rayn beyn. / It will   445   *been*
    therfor abate
Full lele.   *loyally*
This water in hast
Eft will I tast.   *After/test*
Now am I agast.
It is wanyd a grete dele.   450

Now ar the weders cest / and cateractes   *ceased*
    knyt
Both the most and the leest. /

WIFE.   Me   thynk
    bi my wit
The son shynes in the eest. / Lo is not yond
    it?
We shuld have a good feest / were thise
    floodys flyt
So spytys.   455
NOE. We have been here all we
CCC dayes and fyfty.   350 days
WIFE. Yei, now wanys the see.
Lord well is us.

NOE. The thryd tyme will I prufe / what   460   prove, test
    depnes we bere.
WIFE. How long shall thou hufe. / Lay in   heave (to), wait
    thy lyne there.
NOE. I may towch with my lufe / the   palm
    grownd evyn here.
WIFE. Then begynnys to grufe / to us mery   grow/countenance
    chere.
Bot husband
What grownd may this be?   465
NOE. The hyllys of Armonye.   Armenia
WIFE. Now blissid be he
That thus for us ordand.

NOE. I see toppys of hyllys he / many at a   tops of high hills
    syght.
Nothyng to let me, / the wedir is so bright.   470   hinder
WIFE. Thise ar of mercy / tokyns full right.
NOE. Dame, thi counsell me / what fowll
    best myght
And cowth,
With flight of wyng
Bryng without taryyng   475
Of mercy som tokynyng,
Ayther bi north or southe.

For this is the fyrst day / of the tent moyne.   tenth/moon
WIFE. The ravyn, durst I lay, / will com   lay (a bet)/return
    agane sone.
As fast as thou may, / cast hym furth. Have   480
    done.

He may happyn to day / com agane or none
With grath.   *promptness*
NOE. I will cast out also
Dowfys oone or two.   *Doves*
Go youre way, go.   485
God send you som wathe.   *(hunting) catch*

Now ar thise fowles flone / into seyr coun-   *different*
    tré.
Pray we fast ichon, / kneland on oure kne   *each one/kneeling*
To hym that is alone / worthiest of degré
That he wold send anone / oure fowles   490   *anon, at once/catch*
    som fee
To glad us.
WIFE. Thai may not fayll of land,
The water is so wanand.
NOE. Thank we God all-weldand,   *all-wielding, al-*
That Lord that made us.   495   *mighty*

It is a wonder thyng / me thynk sothlé   *truly*
Thai ar so long taryyng / the fowles that we
Cast out in the mornyng. /
WIFE.   Syr it may be
Thai tary to thay bryng. /   *till*
NOE.   The ravyn is a-
    hungrye
Allway.   500
He is without any reson,
And he fynd any caryon   *carrion*
As peraventure may be fon   *befall*
He will not away.

The dowfe is more gentill. / Her trust I   505 *dove/unto, in*
    untew
Like unto the turtill / for she is ay trew.   *turtledove/always*
WIFE. Hence bot a litill / she commys, lew,   *comes*
    lew.
She bryngys in her bill / som novels new.   *news*
Behald!
It is of an olif-tre   510 *olive tree*
A branch, thynkys me.
NOE. It is soth, perdé.   O.Fr. *par dé* 'by God'
Right so is it cald.   *called*

Doufe byrd full blist, / fayre myght the be-   *Dove/blessed*
    fall.
Thou art trew for to trist / as ston in the   515   *trust*
    wall.
Full well I it wist / thou wold com to thi
    hall.
WIFE. A trew tokyn ist / we shall be savyd   *is + it*
    all,
Forwhi   *Because*
The water, syn she com
Of depnes plom   520   *plumb, straight*
Is fallen a fathom   *(down)*
And more hardely.

I SON. Thise floodys ar gone, / fader, behold.
II SON. Ther is left right none / and that be   *(of) that/certain*
    ye bold.
III SON. As still as a stone / oure ship is stold.   525   *stalled*
NOE. Apon land here anone / that we were,
    fayn I wold.
My childer dere,
Sem, Iaphet and Cam,
With gle and with gam,   *game*
Com go we all sam.   530   *together (l. 320)*
We will no long abide here.

WIFE. Here have we beyn, / Noy, long   *been/Noah*
    enogh
With tray and with teyn / and dreed mekill   *misery/grief/great*
    wogh.
NOE. Behald on this greyn. / Nowder cart   *green/Neither*
    ne plogh
Is left, as I weyn, / nowder tre then bogh   535   *think/nor*
Ne other thyng,
Bot all is away.
Many castels I say
Grete townes of aray
Flitt has this flowyng.   540   *Removed (l. 454)*

WIFE. Thise floodys not afright / all this   *unfrightened, un-*
    warld so wide   *daunted*
Has mevid with myght / on se and bi side.   *moved/shore*

NOE. To dede ar thai dyght / prowdist of pryde   *death/done, put*

Everich a wight / that ever was spyde,   *Every/person/spied,*

With syn.   545   *found out*

All ar thai slayn

And put unto payn.

WIFE. From thens agayn

May thai never wyn?   *win, escape* (l. 24)

NOE. Wyn? No, iwis, / bot he that myght 550 *certainly/who has* hase   *might*

Wold myn of thare mys / and admytte   *remember/miss, loss* thaym to grace.

As he in bayll is blis, / I pray hym in this space

In heven hye with his / to purvaye us a   *provide* place

That we

With his santys in sight   555 *saints*

And his angels bright

May con to his light.

Amen for charité.

      (*explicit processus Noe.*)

SUPPLEMENTARY MATERIAL

M. D. Anderson, *Drama and Imagery in English Medieval Churches*, Cambridge, 1963.

SIR ORFEO

Orfeo was a king,
In Inglond an heighe lording,
A stalworth man and hardi bo,   *both*
Large and curteys he was also.   *large-hearted, gen-*
                                                 erous/courtly
His fader was comen of King Pluto,   5
And his moder of King Iuno,   *Queen Juno*
That sum time were as godes yhold,   *once/held*
For aventours that thai dede and told.   *adventures*
Orfeo most of ony thing
Lovede the gle of harpyng.   10
Syker was every gode harpoure   *Sure*
Of hym to have moche honoure.
Hymself loved for to harpe,
And layde theron his wittes scharpe.
He lernyd so, ther nothing was   15   *learned so (well)/*
                                                 there wasn't

A better harper in no plas.
In the world was never man born
That ones Orpheo sat byforn,
And he myght of his harpyng here,
He schulde thinke that he were   20
In one of the ioys of Paradys,
Such ioy and melody in his harpyng is.
    This king soiournd in Traciens,   *sojourned, dwelled*
That was a cité of noble defens,
For Winchester was cleped tho   25   *called/then*
Traciens withouten no.   *undeniably*
The king hadde a quen of priis,   *price, worth*
That was ycleped Dame Herodis,
The fairest levedi, for the nones,   *lady/certainly*
That might gon on bodi and bones,   30   *"Who might live"*

Ful of love and of godenisse;

Ac no man may telle hir fairnise.   *But/no (mere) mor-*
                                                    tal

  Bifel so in the comessing of May,   *commencing*

When miri and hot is the day,

And oway beth winter-schours,   35   *away/-showers*

And everi feld is ful of flours,

And blosme breme on everi bough   *bright*

Overal wexeth miri anough,   *waxes, grows/enough*

This ich quen, Dame Heurodis,   *same*

Tok to maidens of priis,   40   *two*

And went in an undrentide   *midmorning*

To play bi an orchard side,

To se the floures sprede and spring,

And to here the foules sing.

  Thai sett hem doun al thre   45

Under a fair ympe-tre,   *orchard tree*

And wel sone this fair quene

Fel on slepe opon the grene.

The maidens durst hir nought awake,

Bot lete hir ligge and rest take.   50   *lie*

So sche slepe til afternone,

That undertide was al ydone.   *done, finished*

Ac sone as sche gan awake,   *began*

Sche crid and lothli bere gan make,   *cried/loathly/cry-*
                                                    ing

Sche froted hir honden and hir fet,   55   *rubbed*

And crached hir visage, it bled wete;   *scratched/face/wet*

Hir riche robe hye al torett,   *she/rent to pieces*

And was reveysed out of hir witt.   *ravished, carried*
                                                    away

The two maidens hir biside

No durst with hir no leng abide,   60   *longer*

Bot ourn to the palays ful right   *ran/palace/straight-*
                                                    away

And told bothe squier and knight

That her quen awede wold,   *their/would go mad*

And bad hem go and hir athold.   *restrain*

Knightes urn and levedis also,   65   *ran/ladies*

Damisels sexti and mo,   *more than sixty*

In the orchard to the quen hye come,   *they*

And her up in her armes nome,   *their/took*

And brought hir to bed atte last,
And held hir there fine fast;   70
Ac ever sche held in o cri,

            held to one cry, went
              on in the same
              way

And wold up and owy.   *away*
  When Orfeo herd that tiding,
Never him nas wers for no thing.   *ne + was/worse*
He come with knightes tene   75   *ten*
To chaumber right bifor the quene,
And biheld, and seyd with grete pité
'O lef liif, what is te,

              beloved/life/"what is
              it with you"

That ever yete hast ben so stille,
And now gredest wonder schille?   80   *cries out/(with)*
              wondrous/shrill-
              ness

Thi bodi, that was so white ycore,   *choice, excellent*
With thine nailes is al totore.   *torn to pieces*
Allas! thi rode, that was so red,   *(fair) face*
Is al wan as thou were ded;
And also thine fingres smale   85
Beth al blodi and al pale.
Allas! thi lovesom eyghen to   *eyes/two*
Loketh so man doth on his fo.   *as/foe*
A! dame, ich biseche merci!   *I*
Lete ben al this reweful cri,   90   *Let be, stop*
And tel me what the is, and hou,
And what thing may the help now.'
  Tho lay sche stille atte last,   *Then*
And gan to wepe swithe fast,   *very*
And seyd thus the king to: 95
'Allas, mi lord, Sir Orfeo,
Sethen we first togider were,   *Since*
Ones wroth never we nere,   *ne + were*
Bot ever ich have yloved the
As mi liif, and so thou me.   100
Ac now we mot delen ato;   *must/part (in two)*
Do thi best, for y mot go.'   *I*
  'Allas,' quath he, 'forlorn icham.   *ich + am = I am*
Whider wiltow go, and to wham?   *Whither/wilt +*
              you/whom

Whider thou gost, ichil with the,   105   *goest/ich + will (go)*
And whider y go, thou schalt with me.'
'Nay, nay, sir, that nought nis;   *nothing/ne + is, can-*
                                                              not be

Ichil the telle al hou it is:
As ich lay this undertide,
And slepe under our orchard-side,   110
Ther come to me to fair knightes   *two*
Wele y-armed al to rightes,   *correctly*
And bad me comen an heighing,   *in haste*
And speke with her lord the king.   *their*
And ich answerd at wordes bold,   115   *with*
I no durst nought, no y nold.   *"I dared not, nor*
                                                              would I"

Thai priked ogain as thai might drive;   *rode, pricked (with*
                                                              spurs)/again/as
                                                              fast as they might
                                                              go
Tho com her king also blive,   *Then/quickly*
With an hundred knightes and mo,
And damisels an hundred also,   120
Al on snowe-white stedes;
As white as milke were her wedes.   *weeds, clothes*
Y no seighe never yete bifore   *saw*
So fair creatours ycore.   *Such/excellent (l.*
                                                              81)

The king hadde a croun on hed,   125
It nas of silver, no of gold red,   *wasn't/nor*
Ac it was of a precious ston,
As bright as the sonne it schon.
And as son as he to me cam,
Wold ich, nold ich, he me nam,   130   *Would I, wouldn't*
                                                              I/took

And made me with him ride
Opon a palfray, bi his side,
And brought me to his palays,
Wele atird in ich ways,   *attired/every*
And schewed me castels and tours,   135   *towers*
Rivers, forestes, frith with flours,   *woods*
And his riche stedes ichon;
And sethen me brought ogain hom   *afterward*
Into our owhen orchard,   *own*
And said to me thus afterward: 140

"Loke, dame, to-morwe thatow be   *that + you*
Right here under this ympe-tre,
And than thou schalt with ous go,   *us*
And live with ous evermo;
And yif thou makest ous ylet,   145   *resistance*
Whar thou be, thou worst yfet,   *Wherever/will be/*
           fetched

And totore thine limes al,   *torn to pieces/limbs*
That nothing help the no schal;
And thei thou best so totorn,   *though/are*
Yete thou worst with ous yborn." '   150   *borne (away)*
  When King Orfeo herd this cas,
'O we!' quath he, 'allas, allas!   *woe*
Lever me were to lete mi liif,   *Liefer/let (go)*
Than thus to lese the quen, mi wiif.'
He asked conseyl at ich man,   155   *counsel/of*
Ac no man him help no can.

  Amorwe the undertide is come,
And Orfeo hath his armes ynome,   *taken*
And wele ten hundred knightes with him
Ich y-armed stout and grim;   160
And with the quen wenten he
Right unto that ympe-tre.
Thai made scheltrom in ich a side,   *shield-room, enclo-*
           sure of armed men

And sayd thai wold there abide,
And dye ther everichon,   165   *every one*
Er the quen schuld from hem gon.   *Ere/them/go*
Ac yete amiddes hem ful right
The quen was oway ytuight,   *snatched*
With fairi forth ynome;   *supernatural power,*
           magic/taken

Men wist never wher sche was bicome.   170   *knew/gone*
  Tho was ther criing, wepe and wo.
The king into his chaumber is go,
And oft swoned opon the ston,   *stone (floor)*
And made swiche diol and swiche mon   *such/dole/moan*
That neighe his liif was yspent: 175   *nearly*
Ther was non amendement.   *remedy*
  He cleped togider his barouns,
Erls, lordes of renouns;
And when thai al ycomen were,
'Lordinges,' he said, 'bifor you here   180

Ich ordainy min heighe steward		*ordain*
To wite mi kingdom afterward.		*guard*
In mi stede ben he schal,		
To kepe mi londes over al.		
For, now ichave mi quen ylore,	185	*I + have/lost*
The fairest levedi that ever was bore,		*lady/born*
Never eft y nil no woman se.		*ne + will*
Into wilderness ichil te,		*go*
And live ther evermore		
With wilde bestes in holtes hore.	190	*woods/hoar*
And when ye understond that y be spent,		*dead*
Make you than a parlement,		
And chese you a newe king.		*choose*
Now doth your best with al mi thing.'		*affairs*
Tho was ther wepeing in the halle,	195	
And grete cri among hem alle;		
Unnethe might old or yong		*Hardly*
For wepeing speke a word with tong.		
Thai kneled adoun al yfere,		*together*
And praid him, yif his wille were,	200	
That he no schuld nought fram hem go.		
'Do way,' quath he, 'it schal be so.'		
Al his kingdom he forsoke;		
Bot a sclavin on him he toke,		*pilgrim's mantle*
He no hadde kirtel no hode,	205	*(neither) . . . nor*
Schert, ne no nother gode,		*"nor any other*
		goods"
Bot his harp he tok algate,		*always*
And dede him barfot out atte yate.		*went barefooted/gate*
No man most with him go.		*must*
O way! what ther was wepe and wo,	210	*woe*
When he, that hadde ben king with croun,		
Went so poverlich out of toun!		*poorly*
Thurch wode and over heth		*Through/heath*
Into the wildernes he geth.		*went*
Nothing he fint that him is ays,	215	*finds/ease*
Bot ever he liveth in gret malais.		
He that hadde ywerd the fowe and griis,		*worn/varicolored*
		and gray fur
And on bed the purper biis,		*purple/linen*
Now on hard hethe he lith,		
With leves and gresse he him writh.	220	*covers*
He that hadde had castels and tours,		*towers*

River, forest, frith with flours,   *woods (l. 136)*
Now, thei it comenci to snewe and frese,   *though/commences/*
                                            snow/freeze

This king mot make his bed in mese.   *must/moss*
He that had yhad knightes of priis   225
Bifor him kneland, and levedis,
Now seth he nothing that him liketh,   *pleases him*
Bot wilde wormes bi him striketh.   *snakes/glide*
He that had yhad plenté
Of mete and drink, of ich deynté,   230   *dainty*
Now may he al day digge and wrote   *root*
Er he finde his fille of rote.   *roots*
In somer he liveth bi wild frut
And berien bot gode lite;   *berries/of but little*
                            (value) good

In winter may he nothing finde   235
Bot rote, grasses, and the rinde.   *bark*
Al his bodi was oway duine   *dwindled*
For missays, and al tochine.   *misease (cf. ma-*
                            laise)/all scarred

Lord! who may telle the sore   *pain*
This king sufferd ten yere and more?   240
His here of his berd, blac and rowe,   *rough*
To his girdelstede was growe.   *girdle-place, waist*
His harp, whereon was al his gle,
He hidde in an holwe tre;   *hollow*
And, when the weder was clere and bright,   245
He toke his harp to him wel right,
And harped at his owhen wille.   *own*
Into alle the wode the soun gan schille,   *resound*
That alle the wilde bestes that ther beth
For ioie abouten him thai teth;   250   *joy/gathered (cf.*
                            N.E. tether)

And alle the foules that ther were
Come and sete on ich a brere,   *briar*
To here his harping afine,   *to the end (O.Fr. a*
                            fin)
So miche melody was therin;   *much*
And when he his harping lete wold,   255   *would let up*
No best bi him abide nold.   *beast/ne + would*
    He might se him bisides   *near*
Oft in hot undertides

The king o fairy with his rout		*company*
Com to hunt him al about,	260	
With dim cri and bloweing;		
And houndes also with him berking;		
Ac no best thai no nome,		*took*
No never he nist whider thai bicome.		*ne + wist 'knew'/* *went*
And other while he might him se	265	
As a gret ost bi him te		*host/draw, go* (l. 188)
Wele atourned ten hundred knightes,		*equipped*
Ich y-armed to his rightes,		*Each/correctly* (l. 112)
Of cuntenaunce stout and fers,		
With mani desplaid baners,	270	
And ich his swerd ydrawe hold,		*drawn*
Ac never he nist whider thai wold.		
And other while he seighe other thing:		*saw*
Knightes and levedis com daunceing		
In queynt atire, gisely,	275	*elegant/skillfully*
Quent pas and softly;		*step*
Tabours and trunpes yede hem bi,		*Tabors/trumpets/* *went*
And al maner menstraci.		*minstrelsy*
And on a day he seighe him biside		
Sexti levedis on hors ride,	280	
Gentil and iolif as brid on ris—		*jolly/bird/bough*
Nought o man amonges hem ther nis,		
And ich a faucoun on hond bere,		*falcon*
And riden on haukin bi o rivere.		*a-hawking*
Of game thai founde wel gode haunt,	285	*a great plenty*
Maulardes, hayroun, and cormeraunt;		*Mallards/heron*
The foules of the water ariseth,		
The faucouns hem wele deviseth;		*descry*
Ich faucoun his pray slough.		*slew*
That seighe Orfeo, and lough:	290	*laughed*
'Parfay!' quath he, 'ther is fair game,		
Thider ichil, bi Godes name!		*I will (go)*
Ich was ywon swiche werk to se.'		*accustomed/such*
He aros, and thider gan te.		*go* (l. 266)
To a levedi he was ycome,	295	
Biheld, and hath wele undernome,		*took in, recognized*
And seth bi al thing that it is		

His owhen quen, Dam Heurodis.
Yern he biheld hir, and sche him eke, *Eagerly/also*
Ac noither to other a word no speke. 300 *neither*
For messais that sche on him seighe, *misease, hardship (l. 238)*

That had ben so riche and so heighe,
The teres fel out of her eighe. *eye*
The other levedis this yseighe,
And maked hir oway to ride, 305
Sche most with him no lenger abide. *must*
'Allas!' quath he, 'now me is wo.
Whi nil deth now me slo? *slay*
Allas! wreche, that y no might
Dye now after this sight! 310
Allas! to long last mi liif,
When y no dar nought with mi wiif,
No hye to me, o word speke. *Nor/she/one*
Allas! whi nil min hert breke?
Parfay!' quath he, 'tide wat bitide, 315 *"come what may"*
Whider so this levedis ride, *these*
The selve way ichil streche *self, same/stretch, go*
Of liif no deth me no reche.' *nor/reckon*
His sclavain he dede on also spac, *pilgrim's mantle (l. 204)/quickly*

And henge his harp opon his bac, 320
And had wel gode wil to gon— *go*
He no spard noither stub no ston. *stump/"he hurried"*
In at a roche the levedis rideth, *rock*
And he after, and nought abideth.
When he was in the roche ygo 325 *gone*
Wele thre mile other mo, *or*
He com into a fair cuntray,
As bright so sonne on somers day *as*
Smothe and plain and al grene, *level*
Hille no dale nas ther non ysene. 330 *seen*
Amidde the lond a castel he sighe, *saw*
Riche and real, and wonder heighe. *royal/wondrously*
Al the utmast wal *outmost/wall*
Was clere and schine as cristal; *shiny*
An hundred tours ther were about, 335
Degiselich, and bataild stout; *Wonderful/embat-tled, with battle-ments*

The butras com out of the diche,   *buttress/ditch, moat*
Of rede gold y-arched riche;
The vousour was anowed al   *vaulting/orna-*
                                                      mented

Of ich maner divers aumal.   340   *enamel*
Within ther wer wide wones   *halls*
Al of precious stones.
The werst piler on to biholde
Was al of burnist gold.   *burnished*
Al that lond was ever light,   345
For when it schuld be therk and night,   *dark*
The riche stones light gonne,
As bright as doth at none the sonne.   *noon*
No man may telle, no thenche in thought,   *nor/think*
The riche werk that ther was wrought;   350
Bi al thing him think that it is
The proude court of Paradis.
   In this castel the levedis alight;
He wold in after, yif he might.
Orfeo knokketh atte gate;   355
The porter was redi therate,
And asked what he wold have ydo.   *done*
'Parfay!' quath he, 'icham a minstrel, lo!
To solas thi lord with mi gle,   *please*
Yif his swete wille be.'   360
The porter undede the yate anon,   *undid*
And lete him into the castel gon.
   Than he gan bihold about al,
And seighe liggeand within the wal   *lying*
Of folk that were thider ybrought,   365
And thought dede, and nare nought.   *dead/ne + are*
Sum stode withouten hade,   *head*
And sum non armes nade,   *ne + had*
And sum thurch the bodi hadde wounde,   *through*
And sum lay wode, ybounde,   370   *mad*
And sum armed on hors sete,
And sum astrangled as thai ete,   *ate*
And sum were in water adreynt,   *drowned*
And sum with fire al forschreynt;   *shrunken*
Wives ther lay on childbedde,   375
Sum ded, and sum awedde;   *mad (l. 63)*
And wonder fele ther lay bisides,   *many*

Right as thai slepe her undertides.

slept/their/noontide
sleeps

Eche was thus in this warld ynome,
With fairi thider ycome.   380
Ther he seighe his owhen wiif,
Dame Heurodis, his lef liif,
Slepe under an ympe-tre:
Bi her clothes he knewe that it was he.
   And when he hadde bihold this mervails   385
   alle,
He went into the kinges halle.
Than seighe he ther a semly sight,
A tabernacle blisseful and bright,
Therin her maister king sete,
And her quen fair and swete.   390
Her crounes, her clothes, schine so bright,
That unnethe bihold he hem might.
   When he hadde biholden al that thing,
He kneled adoun bifor the king.
'O lord,' he seyd, 'yif it thi wille were,   395
Mi menstraci thou schust yhere.'
The king answerd, 'What man artow,
That art hider ycomen now?
Ich, no non that is with me,
No sent never after the;   400
Sethen that ich here regni gan,
Y no fond never so folehardi man
That hider to ous durst wende,
Bot that ichim wald ofsende.'

'Lord,' quath he, 'trowe ful wel,   405
Y nam bot a pover menstrel;
And, sir, it is the maner of ous
To seche mani a lordes hous;
Thei we nought welcom no be,
Yete we mot proferi forth our gle.'   410
   Bifor the king he sat adoun,
And tok his harp so miri of soun,
And tempreth his harp, as he wele can,
And blisseful notes he ther gan,
That al that in the palays were   415
Com to him for to here,

taken

beloved/life (l. 78)

she
marvels

fair
canopied seat

hardly (l. 197)

hear
are you

nor/none

Since/reign
found/foolhardy
us/dared/come
I + him/would send
for

trust
ne + am/poor

seek
Though
must/proffer

tunes

And liggeth adoun to his fete,   *lieth/at*
Hem thenketh his melody so swete.   *(It) seemed to them*
The king herkneth and sitt ful stille,
To here his gle he hath gode wille;   420
Gode bourde he hadde of his gle,   *entertainment*
The riche quen also hadde he.   *she*
    When he hadde stint his harping,
Than seyd to him the king,
'Menstrel, me liketh wele thi gle.   425
Now aske of me what it be,   *whatever you wish*
Largelich ichil the pay.   *Generously*
Now speke, and tow might asay.'   *you/test (it)*
'Sir,' he seyd, 'ich biseche the
Thatow woldest yive me   430   *That you/give*
That ich levedi, bright on ble,   *complexion*
That slepeth under the ympe-tre.'
'Nay,' quath the king, 'that nought nere!'   *"that may not be"*
A sori couple of you it were,
For thou art lene, rowe, and blac,   435   *rough*
And sche is lovesum, withouten lac;   *lovely*
A lothlich thing it were forthi   *loathly/therefore*
To sen hir in thi compayni.'
    'O sir,' he seyd, 'gentil king,
Yete were it a wele fouler thing   440
To here a lesing of thi mouthe,   *lie*
So, sir, as ye seyd nouthe,   *just now*
What ich wold aski, have y schold,
And nedes thou most thi word hold.'   *must*
The king seyd, 'Sethen it is so,   445   *Since*
Take hir bi the hond, and go;
Of hir ichil thatow be blithe.'   *"that you have joy of
                                                    her"*

    He kneled adoun, and thonked him   *quickly*
        swithe;
His wif he tok bi the hond,
And dede him swithe out of that lond,   450
And went him out of that thede,   *country*
Right as he come the way he yede.   *went*
    So long he hath the way ynome,   *taken*
To Winchester he is ycome,
That was his owhen cité;   455
Ac no man knewe that it was he.

No forther than the tounes ende
For knoweleche he no durst wende,   *(fear of)* recognition
Bot with a begger y-bilt ful narwe,   *lodged/poorly*
Ther he tok his herbarwe,   460 *refuge*
To him and to his owhen wiif,
As a minstrel of pover liif,   *poor*
And asked tidinges of that lond,
And who the kingdom held in hond.
The pover begger in his cote   465 *cottage*
Told him everich a grot: *every bit (of news)*
Hou her quen was stole owy   *away*
Ten yer gon with fairy;
And hou her king en exile yede,   *went*
Bot no man nist in wiche thede;   470 *knew (neg.; cf. wist*
                                                     'knew')

And hou the steward the lond gan hold;
And other mani thinges him told.
    Amorwe, oyain nonetide,   *against, toward*
He maked his wiif ther abide;
The beggers clothes he borwed anon,   475 *borrowed*
And heng his harp his rigge opon,   *"on his back (ridge)"*
And went him into that cité,
That men might him bihold and se.
Erls and barouns bold,
Buriays and levedis him gun bihold.   480 *Burgesses*
'Lo,' thai seyd, 'swiche a man!   *such*
Hou long the here hongeth him opan!   *"the hair hangs on*
                                                     him"

Lo, hou his berd hongeth to his kne!
He is yclongen also a tre!'   *withered/as*
    And as he yede in the strete,   485 *went*
With his steward he gan mete,
And loude he sett on him a crie:
'Sir steward,' he seyd, 'merci!
Icham an harpour of hethenisse;   *heathendom*
Help me now in this destresse!'   490
The steward seyd, 'Com with me, come;
Of that ichave thou schalt have some.   *"Of what I have"*
Everich gode harpour is welcom me to,
For mi lordes love Sir Orfeo.'
    In the castel the steward sat atte mete,   495
And mani lording was bi him sete.

Ther were trompours and tabourers,
Harpours fele, and crouders.   *many/fiddlers*
Miche melody thai maked alle,   *Much*
And Orfeo sat stille in the halle,   500
And herkneth. When thai ben al stille,
He toke his harp and tempred schille,   *tuned (it) (l. 413)/*
                                                             shrilly

The blissefulest notes he harped there
That ever ani man yherd with ere;
Ich man liked wele his gle.   505
   The steward biheld and gan yse,   *see*
And knewe the harp als blive;   *at once*
'Menstrel,' he seyd, 'so mot thou thrive,
Where hadestow this harp and hou?   *had you*
Y pray that thou me telle now.'   510
'Lord,' quath he, 'in uncouthe thede,   *unknown, strange/*
                                                             country

Thurch a wildernes as y yede,   *went*
Ther y founde in a dale
With lyouns a man totorn smale,   *lions/torn to pieces*
And wolves him frete with teth so scharp.   515   *ate*
Bi him y fond this ich harp;   *very*
Wele ten yere it is ygo.'   *ago*
'O,' quath the steward, 'now me is wo!
That was mi lord Sir Orfeo.
Allas! wreche, what schal y do,   520
That have swiche a lord ylore?   *lost*
A way! that ich was ybore!   *born*
That him was so hard grace y-yarked,   *(a) fate/decreed*
And so vile deth ymarked!'
Adoun he fel aswon to grounde.   525
His barouns him tok up in that stounde,   *moment*
And telleth him hou it geth—   *goeth*
It nis no bot of manes deth.   *"There is no balm*
                                                             for man's death"

   King Orfeo knewe wele bi than
His steward was a trewe man   530
And loved him as he aught to do,
And stont up and seyt thus: 'Lo,
Steward, herkne now this thing:
Yif ich were Orfeo the king,
And hadde ysuffred ful yore,   535   *long*

In wildernisse miche sore.   *much/sorrow*
And hadde ywon mi quen owy
Out of the lond of fairy,
And hadde ybrought the levedi hende   *gracious*
Right here to the tounes ende,   540
And with a begger her in ynome,   *taken*
And were miself hider ycome
Poverlich to the, thus stille,
For to asay thi gode wille,   *test (l. 428)*
And ich founde the thus trewe,   545
Thou no schust it never rewe.
Sikerlich, for love or ay,   *Certainly/fear, awe*
Thou schust be king after mi day.
And yif thou of mi deth hadest ben blithe,
Thou schust have voided also swithe.'   550   *been turned out/im-
                                                                     mediately*

    Tho al tho that therin sete   *Then/those*
That it was King Orfeo underyete,   *understood*
And the steward him wele knewe;
Over and over the bord he threw,   *board, table*
And fel adoun to his fet;   555
So dede everich lord that ther sete,
And al thai seyd at o criing,   *in one voice*
'Ye beth our lord, sir, and our king!'
Glad thai were of his live.
To chaumber thai ladde him als bilive,   560   *led/at once*
And bathed him and schaved his berd,
And tired him as a king apert.   *attired/to be seen*
And sethen with gret processioun   *afterward*
Thai brought the quen into the toun,
With al maner menstraci.   565
Lord! ther was grete melody!
For ioie thai wepe with her eighe   *joy/eye*
That hem so sounde ycomen seighe.   *(they) saw*
    Now King Orfeo newe coround is,   *crowned*
And his quen Dame Heurodis,   570
And lived long afterward;
And sethen was king the steward.
    Harpours in Bretaine after than
Herd hou this mervaile bigan,
And made herof a lay of gode likeing,   575
And nempned it after the king;   *named*

That lay 'Orfeo' is yhote,   *called*
Gode is the lay, swete is the note.
   Thus com Sir Orfeo out of his care.
God graunt ous alle wele to fare.   580

SUPPLEMENTARY MATERIAL

1. Ovid's *Metamorphoses*, X.
2. O.E. "Orpheus and Eurydice" in Alfred's *Boethius*.
3. Child ballad no. 19.

THE OWL AND THE NIGHTINGALE

(a)

Ich wes in one sumer dale,
In one swithe dyele hale,
Iherde ich holde grete tale
An ule and one nyhtegale.
That playd wes stif and starc and strong 5
Sum hwile softe and lud among;
And eyther ayeyn other swal,
And let that uvele mod ut al.
And eyther seyde of otheres custe
That alre-wurste that hi ywyste: 10
And hure and hure of othres songe
Hi holde playding swithe stronge.
 The Nihtegale bigon tho speke,
In one hurne of one beche,
And sat up one vayre bowe, 15
That were abute blostme ynowe,
In ore vaste thikke hegge
Imeynd myd spire and grene segge.
He wes the gladder vor the ryse,
And song a veole cunne wyse: 20
Bet thuhte the drem that he were
Of harpe and pipe than he nere:
But thuhte that heo were ishote
Of harpe and pipe than of throte.
 Tho stod on old stok thar byside, 25
Thar the ule song hire tyde,
And wes myd ivi al bigrowe;
Hit wes thare ule erdingstowe.
 The Nihtegale hi iseyh,
And hi bihold and overseyh, 30
And thuhte wel ful of thare ule,

1 I/(?)*summer* or *certain*/*valley*
2 *very*/*secluded*/*corner*
3 *Heard*/*argument*
4 *owl*/*nightingale*
5 *plea, debate*/*severe*
6 *Sometimes*/*loud*/*alternately*
7 *either, each*/*against*/*raged*
8 *evil*/*mood*/*out*
9 *character*
10 *worst* of *all*/*she*/*knew*
11 *particularly*
12 *pleading, debating*

14 *protected spot*/*beech tree*
15 *fair**/*bough*
16 *blossoms*/*enough*
17 *a*/*hedge*
18 *mixed*/*with**/*reeds*/*sedge*
19 *because of, for*/*twig, branch*
20 *many*/*kinds* (*of*)/*ways, tunes*
21 *Better, rather*/*seemed*/*sound*/(*it*) *might be*
22 *ne* + *were*
23 *shot, produced*

25 *Then*/*stock, stump*
26 *owl*/*times,* (*canonical*) *hours*
27 "*all overgrown with ivy*"
28 *the*/*owl's*/*dwelling place*
29 *she*/*saw*
30 *looked at* (*with derision*)
31 *foul*

---

15 Here and following, *v* = *f* freq.
18 Throughout the poem a distinction between *mid, myd* 'with' and *wyth* 'against' is maintained.

For me hi halt lodlich and fule.
"Unwyht," heo seyde, "awey thu fleo!
Me is the wurs that ich the iseo.
Iwis for thine vule lete   35
Wele ofte ich my song furlete;
Min heorte atflyhth and falt my tunge,
Hwenne thu art to me ithrunge.
Me luste bet speten thane singe
Of thine fule howelynge."   40
    Theos ule abod for hit wes eve,
Heo ne myhte no leng bileve,
Vor hire heortewes so gret
That wel neyh hire fnast atset,
And warp a word thar-after longe;   45
"Hw thynk the nu bi mine songe?
Wenestu that ich ne kunne singe,
The ich ne cunne of wrytelinge?
Ilome thu dest me grome,
And seist me bothe teone and schome.   50
If ich the heolde on myne vote,
(So hit bitide that ich mote!)
And thu were ut of thine ryse,
Thu scholdest singe on other wise."
    The Nihtegale yaf onsware: 55
"If ich me loki with the bare,
And me schilde wit the blete,
Ne recche ich nouht of thine threte.
If ich me holde in myne hegge,
Ne recche ich never hwat thu segge.   60
Ich wot that thu art unmilde,
With heom that ne muwe from the schilde;
And thu tukest wrothe and uvele,
Hwar thu myht over smale vowele.
Vorthi thu art loth al fowel-cunne,   65
And alle heo the dryveth heonne,
And the viscrycheth and bigredeth,
And wel narewe the byledeth;
And ek forthe the sulve mose,
Hire thonkes, wolde the totose.   70
Thu art lodlich to biholde,
And thu art loth in monye volde:
Thi body is scort, thi swere is smal,
Gretture is thin heved ne thu al;

32 *men/her/hold (to be)/loathly/foul*
33 *Un-man, monster/fly*
34 *(For) me/thee, you/see*
35 *Certainly/foul/appearance*
36 *for-let, neglected*
37 *flees, escapes (from me)/falters*
38 *pressed*
39 *pleases/(to) spit*
40 *howling*
41 *This/until*
42 *longer/remain (silent)*
43 *For*
44 *nearly/breath/vanished*
45 *threw, cast (lit. warped)*
46 *How/now/concerning*
47 *Think you/know how (to)*
48 *Though/know/trilling (of the nightingale)*
49 *Often/injury*
50 *say/reproach/shame*
51 *foot/"If I held thee in my power"*
52 *might*
53 *out/branch (l. 19)*
54 *another way*
55 *gave/answer*
56 *protect/against (l. 18n.)/bare (spaces), open*
57 *shield/against/lack of cover*
58 *reckon, care*
59 *"If I keep myself . . ."*
60 *(may) say*
61 *know*
62 *them/"may not from thee shield themselves"*
63 *treated/wrathfully/vilely*
64 *are able/fowl*
65 *Therefore/loathful (of)/fowl-kind*
66 *they/hence*
67 *beshriek/scold*
68 *narrow, closely/pursue*
69 *even/therefore/very/titmouse*
70 *Willingly/tear to pieces*

72 *many respects (cf. manifold)*
73 *short neck*
74 *Greater/head/than all the rest of you*

Thin eyen beoth colblake and brode,   75
Ryht so hi weren ipeynt myd wode;
Thu starest so thu wille abyten
Al that thu myht myd clyvre smyten;
Thi bile is stif and sarp and hoked,
Riht as on ewel that is croked;   80
Tharmyd thu clechest ever among,
And that is on of thine song.
Ac thu thretest to myne vleysse,
Mid thine clevres woldest me meysse.
The were icundere to one frogge   85
That sit at mulne under cogge;
Snayles, mus, and fule wihte,
Beoth thine cunde and thine rihte.
Thu sittest aday, and flyhst aniht,
Thu cuthest that thu art on unwiht.   90
Thu art lodlich and unclene,
Bi thine neste ich hit mene,
And ek bi thine fule brode,
Thu vedest on heom a wel ful vode
Wel wostu that hi doth thar-ynne,   95
Hi fuleth hit up the chynne;
Heo sytteth thar so hi beo bysne.
Hwarbi men seggeth a vorbysne—
"Dehaet habbe that ilke best
That fuleth his owe nest."   100
That other yer a faukun bredde;
His nest nowiht wel he ne bihedde;
Tharto thu stele in o day,
And leydest tharon thy fule ey.
Tho hit bycom that he hayhte,   105
And of his eyre briddes wrauhte;
Heo brouhte his briddes mete,
Biheold his nest, iseyh hi ete;
He iseyh bi one halve
His nest ifuled in the ut halve.   110
The faukun wes wroth with his bridde,
And lude yal and sturne chidde,
"Seggeth me hwo haveth this ido?
Eu nas never icunde therto;
Hit wes idon eu a lothe custe.   115
Seggeth me if ye hit wiste."
Tho queth that on and queth that other,

75 *eyes/are/coal-black/broad*
76 *Just as if/painted/woad*
77 *as if/bite*
78 *claws, talons/smite*
79 *bill/sharp*
80 *awl*
81 *Therewith/clack/constantly* (cf. l. 6)
82 *one, the sole content*
83 *But/threaten/flesh*
84 *claws* (l. 78)/*mash*
85 *(To) thee/more suitable*
86 *mill/cogwheel*
87 *mice/foul/creatures*
88 *Are/kind, natural/right (diet)*

90 *make known/monster* (l. 33)

93 *brood*
94 *feed (to)/them/foul/food*
95 *know you/what*
96 *befoul/(to) the chin*
97 *as if/blind*
98 *Whereby/say/proverb*
99 *Misfortune* (O.Fr. *deu hat* 'God's hate')/*same/beast*
100 *befouls/own*
101 *The other year, "once upon a time"/falcon*
102 *no whit, not at all/hid*

104 *egg*
105 *Then it happened/hatched*
106 *eggs/(young) birds/hatched*

108 *Watched/saw them eat*
109 *in one part*
110 *outside*

112 *loudly/yelled*
113 *Tell/who/done*
114 *You/natural; "It is against your nature"*
115 *"in loathly manner"*
116 *know*
117 *quoth/one*

"Iwis hit wes ure owe brother,
That yeonde that haveth that grete heved.
Way, that he nys tharof byreved!   120
Werp hit ut myd the vyrste
Thet his nekke him toberste!"
The faukun levede his ibridde,
And nom that fule brid amydde,
And warp hym of than wilde bowe,   125
That pie and crowe hit todrowe.
Therby men seggeth a byspel,
Theyh hit ne beo fulliche spel.
Al so hit is bi than ungode
That is icumen of fule brode   130
And is ymeynd with freo monne,
Ever he cuth that he com thenne,
That he com of than adel-eye
Theyh he a freo neste leye.
Theyh appel trendli from the treo,   135
Thar he and other myde grewe,
Theyh he beo thar-from bicume,
He cuth hwenene he is icume."
    Theos word ayaf the nihtegale,
And after thare longe tale   140
Heo song so lude and so scharpe,
Ryht so me grulde schille harpe.
Theos ule luste thider-ward
And heold hire eyen nether-ward
And sat toswolle and tobolewe   145
So heo hedde one frogge iswolwe;
For heo wel wiste and was iwar
That heo song hire a-bysemar.
And natheles heo yaf ondsware,
"Hwy neltu fleon in-to the bare,   150
And schewi hwether unker beo
Of brihter hewe, of fayrur bleo?"
"No, thu havest scharpe clawe,
Ne kepe ich noht that thu me clawe.
Thu havest clyvres swithe stronge,   155
Thu twengest thar-mid so doth a tonge.
Thu thoutest, so doth thine ilyche,
Mid fayre worde me biswike.
Ich nolde don that thu me raddest,
Ich wiste wel that thu me misraddest.   160

118 *Certainly/our/own*
119 *yonder/head* (l. 74)
120 *Alas/isn't/bereft*
121 *Cast* (l. 45)/*worst* (*of all*)
122 *break to pieces*
123 *believed/*(*young*) *birds*
124 *took/by the middle*
125 *cast* (l. 45)/*off/wild* (*wood*)/*bough*
126 *magpies/drew asunder*
127 *say/parable* (cf. N.E. *gospel*)
128 *Though/"isn't the full story"*
129 *Just/concerning* (l. 8)/*this un-good, evil* (*one*)
130 *come/foul/brood*
131 *mingled/free, noble/men*
132 *makes known* (l. 90)/*"where he comes from"*
133 *addle egg*
134 *Though/*(*in*) *a/lay*
135 *trundle, roll/tree*
136 *Where/with*
137 *"Though he goes far away from it"*
138 *makes known/whence*
139 *gave* (*out*)

142 *"Just as if one plucked a shrill harp"*
143 *listened/thitherward*
144 *downward*
145 *swollen* (*with anger*)/*bellowed* (*out*)
146 *As if/had/swallowed*
147 *knew/aware*
148 *sang/*(*to*) *her/insultingly*
149 *nevertheless/gave/answer*
150 *Why/will you not/fly/open* (l. 56)
151 *show/which of the two of us*
152 *brighter/hue/fairer/color*

154 *wish*
155 *claws* (l. 84)/*very*
156 *twinge, pinch/as/*(*pair of*) *tongs*
157 *ilk, sort*
158 *to deceive*
159 *wouldn't/do/advised*
160 *know/*(*would*) *misadvise, advise poorly*

Schomye the vor thine unrede!
Unwryen is thy swikehede!
Schild thi swike-dom from the lyhte,
And hud that wowe among the ryhte.
Hwanne thu wilt unriht spene,   165
Loke that hit ne beo isene;
Vor swikedom haveth schome and hete,
If hit is ope and under-yete.
Ne spedestu nouht mid thin unwrenche,
For ich am war and can blenche.   170
Ne helpeth noht that thu bo to thriste;
Ich wolde vyhte bet myd liste
Than thu mid al thine strengthe.
Ich habbe, on brede and ek on lengthe,
Castel god on myne ryse;   175
"Wel fyht that wel flyhth," seyth the wise.
Ac lete we awey theos cheste,
For suche wordes beoth unwreste,
And fo we on myd rihtc domc
Mid fayre worde and myd some.   180
Theyh we ne beon at one acorde,
We mawe bet myd fayre worde,
Withute cheste, and bute vyhte,
Playde mid sothe and mid ryhte,
And may ur eyther hwat he wile   185
Mid rihte segge and myd skile."

(b) --

The wrenne, for heo cuthe singe,
Thar com in thare moreweninge
To helpe thare nyhtegale,
Vor theih heo hadde stefne smale,   1720
Heo hadde gode throte and schille,
And fale monne song a wille.
The wrenne wes wel wis iholde,
Vor theih heo nere ibred a-wolde,
Heo wes itowen among mankunne.   1725
And hire wisdom brouhte thenne.
Heo myhte speke hwar heo wolde,
Tofore the kinge thah heo scholde.
"Lusteth," heo queth, "leteth me speke.
Hwat! wille ye this pays tobreke,   1730
And do thanne kinge such schome?
Yet nys heo nouther ded ne lome.

161 *"Shame on you for your bad counsel"*
162 *Uncovered/treachery*
163 *treachery*
164 *hide/wrong*
165 *When/do*
166 *seen*
167 *For/hate*
168 *open/understood*
169 *succeed you/spiteful tricks*
170 *wary/escape*
171 *be/too/bold*
172 *fight/better/cunning*

174 *breadth/also*
175 *Castle, stronghold/branch* (l. 83)
176 *"He who flies well, fights well"*
177 *"But let us refrain from this dispute"*
178 *futile*
179 *begin/judgment* (cf. N.E. *deem*)
180 *reconciliation*

182 *may*
183 *dispute* (l. 177)/*without/fight*
184 *Plead, debate*
185 *either of us*
186 *say/skill*

1717 *wren/"because of her singing talent"*
1718 *morning*

1720 *though/voice*
1721 *shrill*
1722 *many/men/to the pleasure of*
1723 *quite/wise/held* (to be)
1724 *For/though/wasn't/bred/in the woods*
1725 *brought up/mankind*
1726 *thence*

1728 *Before/even if*
1729 *Listen*
1730 *peace/destroy completely*
1731 *the/shame*
1732 *he's neither/lame, weak*

Hunke schal ityde harm and schonde
If we doth grythbruche on his londe.
Leteth beo, and beoth isome,   1735
And fareth riht to eure dome,
And leteth dom this playd tobreke.
Al so hit wes erure bispeke."
    "Ich unne wel," queth the Nihtegale,
"Ah, wrenne, nouht for thine tale,   1740
Ac do myre lauhfulnesse.
Ic nolde that unrihtfulnesse
Me at then ende over-come;
Ic nam ofdred of none dome.
Bihote ic habbe, soth hit is,   1745
That Mayster Nichole, that is wis,
Bitwihen us deme schulle,
And yet ic wene that he wulle.
Ah war myhte we hine funde?"
The wrenne sat in hore lynde,   1750
"Hwat! nute ye," quath heo, "his hom?
Heo wuneth at Porteshom,
At one tune in Dorsete,
Bi thare see in ore utlete
Thar he demeth mony riht dom,   1755
And diht and wryt mony wisdom,
And thurh his muthe and thurh his honde
Hit is the betere into Scotlonde.
To seche hyne is lyhtlych thing;
He naveth buten o wunyng.   1760
That is biscopen muchel schame,
And alle than that of his nome
Habbeth iherd, and of his dede.
Hwi nulleth hi nymen heom to rede,
That he were myd heom ilome   1765
Vor teche heom of his wisdome,
And yeve him rente on vale stude,
That he myhte ilome heom beo myde?"
    "Certes," quath the ule, "that is soth;
Theos riche men muchel mysdoth,   1770
That leteth thane gode man,
That of so fele thinge can,
And yeveth rente wel mislyche,
And of him leteth wel lyhtliche.
With heore kunne heo beoth mildre,   1775

1733 (To) you two (cf. l. 151)/betide/disgrace
1734 a breach of the peace (O.E. griþ 'peace' + bryce 'breach')
1735 reconciled (l. 180)
1736 go, proceed/our/judgment (l. 179)
1737 judgment (l. 179)/debate/break completely
1738 As/earlier/agreed
1739 grant
1740 But/argument
1741 my/lawfulness

1744 am not/afraid
1745 Promised/true

1747 Between/deem, judge/shall
1748 think/is willing
1749 But/where/him/find
1750 her/lime tree
1751 know you not/home
1752 He/dwells
1753 a town
1754 the sea/an outlet
1755 judges/many/true, proper/judgments
1756 composes/writes/much
1757 mouth
1758 as far as
1759 seek/him/easy
1760 neg. + has/but/one/dwelling (cf. l. 1752)
1761 to bishops
1762 those/name
1763 heard/deeds
1764 Why/neg. + will/they/(not) take/(for) themselves/as (an) adviser
1765 (So) that/often
1766 For, in order to
1767 give/income/many/places

1769 Certainly

1771 neglect
1772 many/knows
1773 give/indiscriminately
1774 lightly, easily
1775 their/kin/milder

And yeveth rente lutle childre;
So heore wit hi demeth a-dwole,
That ever abit Mayster Nichole,
Ah ute we thah to hym fare,
For thar is unker dom al yare."   1780
    "Do we," the Nihtegale seyde,
"Ah hwo schal unker speche rede
And telle tovore unker deme?"
    "Tharof ic schal the wel iqueme,"
Queth the ule; "for al, ende of orde,   1785
Telle ic con, word after worde,
And if the thinkth that ic misrempe
Thu stond ayeyn and do me crempe."
Mid thisse worde forth hi ferden,
Al bute here and bute verde,   1790

To Portesham ther heo bicome.
Ah hw heo spedde of heore dome,
Ne can ic eu namore telle;
Her nys namore of thisse spelle.
Explicit.   1795

SUPPLEMENTARY MATERIAL

1. Chaucer's Nun's Priest's Tale in the *Canterbury Tales*.
2. T. H. White, *The Bestiary, A Book of Beasts*, New York, 1954.
3. "Holly and Ivy," p. 348.

1776 *give/(to) little/children*
1777 *intelligence/they judge/in error (foolish)*
1778 *still/abides, awaits (preferment)*
1779 *But/let us/though/go*
1780 *our/ready*
1781 *Let's (do that)*
1782 *suit/read, present*
1783 *before/judge, n.*
1784 *please*
1785 *all (of it)/"from the beginning to the end"*

1787 *may go astray*
1788 *object/stop (crimp)*
1789 *went*
1790 *Without/(invading) army or (defensive) army,* i.e., *"supporting contenders"*
1791 *until/arrived at*
1792 *how/succeeded*
1793 *you/no more*
1794 *There/tale* (l. 128)

PEARL

I

(1) Perle, plesaunte to prynces paye
    To clanly clos in golde so clere,
    Oute of oryent, I hardyly saye,
    Ne proved I never her precios pere.
    So rounde, so reken in uche araye,   5
    So smal, so smothe her sydes were
    Quere so ever I jugged gemmes gaye,
    I sette hyr sengeley in synglure.
    Allas! I leste hyr in on erbere;
    Thurgh gresse to grounde hit fro me yot.   10
    I dewyne, fordolked of luf-daungere
    Of that pryvy perle wythouten spot.

(2) Sythen in that spote hit fro me sprange,
    Ofte haf I wayted, wyschande that wele,
    That wont was whyle devoyde my wrange   15
    And heven my happe and al my hele.
    That dos bot thrych my hert thrange,
    My breste in bale bot bolne and bele;
    Yet thoght me never so swete a sange
    As stylle stounde let to me stele.   20
    For sothe ther fleten to me fele,
    To thenke hir color so clad in clot.
    O moul, thou marres a myry iuele,
    My privy perle wythouten spotte.

(3) That spot of spyses mot nedes sprede,   25
    Ther such ryches to rot is runne;
    Blomes blayke and blwe and rede
    Ther schynes ful schyr agayn the sunne.
    Flor and fryte may not be fede
    Ther hit doun drof in moldes dunne;   30
    For uch gresse mot grow of graynes dede;

1 *pleasure*
2 *chastely/enclose, set*
3 *Orient*
4 *established/peer*
5 *radiant/each, every*

7 *Wheresoever/judged*
8 *apart/"as unique"*
9 *lost/(herb) garden*
10 *grass/went*
11 *dwindle, languish/completely wounded/love injury*
12 *private, special*

13 *Since/sprang*
14 *wishing (for)/weal*
15 *a while/to void/wrongs, sorrows*
16 *heaved, lifted/happiness/well-being*
17 *does/pierce/constantly*
18 *sorrow (cf. baleful)/bulges, swells/burns*
19 *song*
20 *time*
21 *floated/many (songs)*
22 *clod, clay*
23 *earth, mold/mar/delightful, merry/jewel*

25 *with spices/must needs be*

27 *yellow/blue*
28 *fair/against*
29 *Flower/fruit/faded*
30 *Where/(pearl) drove into/dun(-colored)*
31 *(blade of) grass/must/(from) grains*

No whete were elles to wones wonne.
Of goud uche goude is ay bygonne;
So semly a sede moght fayly not,
That spryngande spyces up ne sponne   35
Of that precios perle wythouten spotte.

(4) To that spot that I in speche expoun
I entred in that erber grene,
In Auguste in a hygh seysoun,
Quen corne is corven wyth crokes kene.   40
On huyle ther perle hit trendeled doun
Schadowed this wortes ful schyre and schene,
Gilofre, gyngure and gromylyoun,
And pyonys powdered ay bytwene.
Yif hit was semly on to sene,   45
A fayr reflayr yet fro hit flot.
Ther wonys that worthyly, I wot and wene,
My precious perle wythouten spot.

(5) Bifore that spot my honde I spenned
For care ful colde that to me caght;   50
A devely dele in my hert denned,
Thagh resoun sette myselven saght.
I playned my perle that ther was spenned,
Wyth fyrte skylles that faste faght;
Thagh kynde of Kryst me comfort kenned,   55
My wreched wylle in wo ay wraghte.
I felle upon that floury flaght,
Suche odour to my hernes schot;
I slode upon a slepyng-slaghte
On that precios perle wythouten spot.   60

II
(6) Fro spot my spyryt ther sprang in space;
My body on balke ther bod in sweven.
My goste is gon in Godes grace
In aventure ther mervayles meven.
I ne wyste in this worlde quere that hit wace,   65
Bot I knew me keste ther klyfes cleven;
Towarde a foreste I bere the face,
Where rych rokkes wer to dyscreven.

32 *for dwellings, homes/won, harvested*
33 *good/always/begun*
34 *seed/might/fail*
35 *springing/(could not have) spun, grown*

39 *festival time,* poss. *Lammas*
40 *When*/carved, cut/crooks, sickles*
41 *hill/trundled, rolled*
42 *Shadowed, protected/plants* (N.G. *Wort*)
43 *Gillyflower/ginger/gromwell*
44 *peonies/scattered*
45 *If/see*
46 *odor/floated*
47 *dwells* (cf. l. 32)/*think and hope*

49 *wrung*
50 *Because of/caught*
51 *desolate/dole/dinned*
52 *"tried to reconcile me"*
53 *lamented/clasped, imprisoned*
54 *fierce/contentions/hard/fought*
55 *(the) nature/taught*
56 *ever* (l. 33)/*wrought*
57 *turf*
58 *senses*
59 *slid/into/-spell*

62 *earth/bode/dream*
63 *spirit*
64 *marvels/move*
65 *knew/was*
66 *But/knew myself/cast/cliffs/cleaved, rose*
67 *turned*
68 *were/descry*

---

40 Here and following, *qu-* = *wh-* frequently, as in *Gawain*.

The lyght of hem myght no mon leven,
The glemande glory that of hem glent;   70
For wern never webbes that wyghes weven
Of half so dere adubbemente.

(7) Dubbed wern alle tho downes sydes
Wyth crystal klyffes so cler of kynde.
Holtewodes bryght aboute hem bydes   75
Of bolles as blwe as ble of Ynde;
As bornyst sylver the lef onslydes,
That thike con trylle on uch a tynde.
Quen glem of glodes agayns hem glydes,
Wyth schymeryng schene ful schrylle thay schynde.   80
The gravayl that on grounde con grynde
Wern precious perles of oryente.
The sunnebemes bot blo and blynde
In respecte of that adubbement.

(8) The adubbemente of tho downes dere   85
Garten my goste al greffe forgete.
So frech flavores of frytes were,
As fode hit con me fayre refete.
Fowles ther flowen in fryth in fere,
Of flaumbande hwes, bothe smale and grete;   90
Bot sytole-stryng and gyternere
Her reken myrthe moght not retrete;
For quen those bryddes her wynges bete,
Thay songen wyth a swete asent.
So gracios gle couthe no mon gete   95
As here and se her adubbement.

(9) So al was dubbet on dere asyse
That fryth ther fortwne forth me feres.
The derthe therof for to devyse
Nis no wygh worthé that tonge beres.   100
I welke ay forth in wely wyse;
No bonk so byg that did me deres.
The fyrre in the fryth, the feirer con ryse
The playn, the plonttes, the spyse, the peres;
And rawes and randes and rych reveres,   105
As fyldor fyn her bonkes brent.
I wan to a water by schore that scheres—
Lorde, dere was hit adubbement!

69 *them/believe*
70 *gleaming*
71 *were/webs/humans/woven*
72 *adornment*

73 *Adorned/downs'*
74 *clear/by nature*
75 *Woods*
76 *boles, trunks/blue (l. 27)/hue of India, indigo*
77 *burnished/leaves/slide, quiver*
78 *thick/did trill, vibrate/tendril*
79 *gleam/glades/against*
80 *shimmering/brilliantly/shone*
81 *gravel/did grind (underfoot)*

83 *dark and dim*
84 *comparison to*

86 *Caused/grief/(to) forget*
87 *fresh/fragrance*
88 *food/refresh*
89 *flew/woods/in flocks, together*
90 *flaming/hues*
91 *citole string/cithern player*
92 *Their/ready/reproduce*
93 *birds*
94 *harmony*
95 *Such/could*
96 *(to) hear/(to) see*

97 *in dear fashion*
98 *where fortune leads me forth*
99 *splendor/describe*
100 *No man/tongue*
101 *walk/happy*
102 *bank/hinder*
103 *further/fairer*
104 *plants/spice/pears*
105 *(hedge)rows/borders/rivers*
106 O.Fr. *fil d'or 'thread of gold'/steep*
107 *came/sheers, winds*
108 *its*

(10) The dubbemente of tho derworth depe
    Wern bonkes bene of beryl bryght.   110
    Swangeande swete the water con swepe,
    Wyth a rownande rourde raykande aryght.
    In the founce ther stonden stones stepe,
    As glente thurgh glas that glowed and glyght,
    As stremande sternes, quen strothe-men slepe,   115
    Staren in welkyn in wynter nyght;
    For uche a pobbel in pole ther pyght
    Was emerad, saffer, other gemme gente,
    That alle the loghe lemed of lyght,
    So dere was hit adubbement.   120

III

(11) The dubbement dere of doun and dales,
    Of wod and water and wlonk playnes,
    Bylde in me blys, abated my bales,
    For didden my stresse, dystryed my paynes.
    Doun after a strem that dryghly hales   125
    I bowed in blys, bredful my braynes;
    The fyrre I folwed those floty vales,
    The more strenghthe of ioye myn herte straynes.
    As fortune fares ther as ho fraynes,
    Whether solace ho sende other elles sore,   130
    The wygh to wham her wylle ho waynes
    Hyttes to have ay more and more.

(12) More of wele was in that wyse,
    Then I cowthe telle thagh I tom hade,
    For urthely herte myght not suffyse   135
    To the tenthe dole of tho gladnes glade;
    Forthy I thoght that Paradyse
    Was ther over gayn tho bonkes brade.
    I hoped the water were a devyse
    Bytwene myrthes by meres made;   140

    Byyonde the broke, by slente other slade,
    I hoped that mote merked wore.
    Bot the water was depe, I dorst not wade,
    And ever me longed ay more and more.

(13) More and more, and yet wel mare,   145
    Me lyste to se the broke byyonde;

109 dear-worth, precious/depths
110 pleasing, fair
111 Swinging, swirling
112 whispering/sound/flowing
113 bottom
114 glinted, glanced/glinted
115 streaming/stars/earth-, mortal
116 Stare, shine/heavens
117 pebble/pool/pitched, placed
118 emerald/sapphire/or/gentle, noble
119 (So) that/pool/gleamed

122 splendid
123 Built, established
124 Dispelled/destroyed
125 Down along/continually
126 brimful
127 further/watery
128 greater/joy/strains my heart
129 she/questions, makes trial
130 or/sorrow
131 man/whom/sends
132 Tends

133 weal, joy/way
134 time
135 earthly
136 part/joyful
137 Therefore
138 against
139 device, division
140 "Made by pools between joys" (poss. those of heaven and those of earth)
141 brook/slant, slope/or
142 moat/marked/were

145 more
146 wished

For if hit was fayr ther I con fare,
Wel loveloker was the fyrre londe.
Abowte me con I stote and stare;
To fynde a forthe faste con I fonde.   150
Bot wothes mo iwysse ther ware,
The fyrre I stalked by the stronde.
And ever me thoght I schulde not wonde
For wo, ther weles so wynne wore.
Thenne nwe note me com on honde   155
That meved my mynde ay more and more.

(14) More mervayle con my dom adaunt:
I segh byyonde that myry mere
A crystal clyffe ful relusaunt
Mony ryal ray con fro hit rere,   160
At the fote therof ther sete a faunt,
A mayden of menske, ful debonere,
Blysnande whyt was hyr bleaunt.
I knew hyr wel, I hade sen hyr ere.
As glysnande golde that man con schere,   165
So schon that schene anunder shore.
On lenghe I loked to hyr there;
The lenger, I knew hyr more and more.

(15) The more I frayste hyr fayre face,
Her fygure fyn quen I had fonte   170
Suche gladande glory con to me glace
As lyttel byfore therto was wonte.
To calle hyr lyste con me enchace,
Bot baysment gef myn hert a brunt.
I segh hyr in so strange a place,   175
Such a burre myght make myn herte blunt.
Thenne veres ho up her fayre frount,
Hyr vysayge whyt as playn yvore:
That stonge myn hert, ful stray atount,
And ever the lenger, the more and more.   180

        IV
(16) More then me lyste my drede aros.
I stod ful stylle and dorste not calle;
Wyth yghen open and mouth ful clos
I stod as hende as hawk in halle.
I hoped that gostly was that porpose;   185

147 *"where I was then"*
148 *lovelier/further*
149 *(did I) stop*
150 *ford/try*
151 *dangers/certainly/were*
152 *strand, shore*
153 *hesitate*
154 *Because of woe, harm/where/joyous/were*
155 *new/notion/came*

157 *marvels/daunted my judgment*
158 *saw*
159 *relucent*
160 *royal/rear, rise*
161 *infant*
162 *courtesy/debonaire*
163 *Glistening/white/robe*

165 *shear*
166 *below the*

168 *longer*

169 *scanned* (lit. *questioned*, l. 129)
170 *fine/found, confirmed*
171 *glide*
172 *seldom*
173 *"Desire to call her did pursue me"*
174 *confusion/blow*

176 *blow/stunned*
177 *raises/forehead*
178 *visage/smooth/ivory*
179 *stung/in awe/astounded*

183 *eyes*
184 *gentle*
185 *spiritual/intent, meaning*

I dred onende quat schulde byfalle,
Lest ho me eschaped that I ther chos,
Er I at steven hir moght stalle.
That gracios gay wythouten galle,
So smothe, so smal, so seme slyght,   190
Ryses up in hir araye ryalle,
A precios pyece in perles pyght.

(17) Perles pyghte of ryal prys
      There moght mon by grace haf sene,
      Quen that frech as flor-de-lys   195
      Doun the bonke con bowe bydene.
      Al blysnande whyt was hir beau mys,
      Upon at sydes, and bounden bene
      Wyth the myryeste margarys, at my devyse,
      That ever I segh yet with myn yghen;   200
      Wyth lappes large, I wot and I wene,
      Dubbed with double perle and dyghte;
      Her cortel of self sutc schcnc,
      Wyth precios perles al umbepyghte.

(18) A pyght coroune yet wer that gyrle   205
      Of mariorys and non other ston,
      Highe pynakled of cler quyt perle,
      Wyth flurted flowres perfet upon.
      To hed hade ho non other werle.
      Her lere leke al hyr umbegon,   210
      Her semblaunt sade for doc other erle,
      Her ble more blaght then whalles bon.
      As schorne golde schyr her fax thenne schon,
      On schylderes that leghe unlapped lyghte.
      Her depe colour yet wonted non   215
      Of precios perle in porfyl pyghte.

(19) Pyght was poyned and uche a hemme
      At honde, at sydes, at overture,
      Wyth whyte perle and non other gemme,
      And bornyste quyte was hyr vesture.   220
      Bot a wonder perle wythouten wemme
      Inmyddes hyr breste was sette so sure;
      A mannes dom moght dryghly demme,
      Er mynde moght malte in hit mesure.
      I hope no tong moght endure,   225

186 *concerning*
187 *escaped*
188 *with voice, speech*
189 *That . . . (one)/spot*
190 *seemly*
191 *royal* (l. 160)
192 *creature/bedecked*

194 *have seen*
195 *that (one)/fresh* (l. 87)/*fleur-de-lys*
196 *turn, come/at once*
197 *robe*
198 *Open/bound/fairly* (l. 110)
199 *merriest/margeries* (lit. 'pearls')/*in my opinion*
200 *saw/eyes* (l. 183)
201 *folds/think and expect*, a tag, cf. l. 47
202 *bedight*
203 *kirtle/same suit/fair*
204 *umbe* 'around' + *pitched, set* (l. 193)

205 *crown/wore*
206 *marjories, pearls* (l. 199)
207 *pinnacled/white*
208 *figured/perfect*
209 *On head/swirl, circular covering*
210 *face/enclosed/around* (l. 204n.)
211 *expression/grave (enough)/duke/or*
212 *color/whiter/whale's bone*
213 *shorn/hair* (cf. l. 165)
214 *shoulders/lay/unbound*
215 *nothing*
216 *embroidered border*

217 *"The cuffs and every hem were trimmed"*
218 *opening*

220 *burnished*
221 *wondrous/flaw*
222 *In the middle*
223 *judgment/continually/(be) damned, condemned*
224 *Ere/melt/in measuring it*
225 *think/tongue*

No saverly saghe say of that syght,
So was hit clene and cler and pure,
That precios perle ther hit was pyght.

(20) Pyght in perle, that precios pyece
On wyther half water com doun the schore.   230
No gladder gome hethen into Grece
Then I, quen ho on brymme wore.
Ho was me nerre then aunte or nece;
My joy forthy was much the more.
Ho profered me speche, that special spece,   235
Enclynande lowe in wommon lore,
Caghte of her coroun of grete tresore
And haylsed me wyth a lote lyghte.
Wel was me that ever I was bore
To sware that swete in perles pyghte!   240

V
(21) 'O perle,' quod I, 'in perles pyght,
Art thou my perle that I haf playned,
Regretted by myn one on nyghte?
Much longeyng haf I for the layned,
Sythen into gresse thou me aglyghte.   245
Pensyf, payred, I am forpayned,
And thou in a lyf of lykyng lyghte,
In Paradys erde, of stryf unstrayned.
What wyrde has hyder my iuel vayned,
And don me in thys del and gret daunger?   250
Fro we, in twynne, wern towen and twayned,
I haf ben a joyles juelere.'

(22) That juel thenne in gemmes gente
Vered up her vyse wyth yghen graye,
Set on hyr coroun of perle orient,   255
And soberly after thenne con ho say:
'Sir, ye haf your tale mysetente,
To say your perle is al awaye,
That is in cofer so comly clente
As in this gardyn gracios gaye,   260
Hereinne to lenge for ever and play,
Ther mys nee mornyng com never nere.
Her were a forser for the, in faye,
If thou were a gentyl jueler.

226 *appropriate, sweet/praise/(to) tell*
227 *"(Because) it was so . . ."*

229 *being*
230 *opposite/sides (of the)*
231 *man/from here*
232 *(stream's) brim, edge/was*
233 *nearer*
234 *therefore (l. 137)*
235 *being*
236 *Inclining/manner*
237 *Took off*
238 *hailed, greeted/sound*
239 *born*
240 *answer/sweet (one)*

242 *mourned (l. 53)*
243 *alone*
244 *concealed*
245 *Since (l. 13)/grass/glittered away*
246 *Pensive/broken/completely pained*
247 *alighted*
248 *land*
249 *fate/hither/jewel/brought*
250 *did, put/dole, sorrow*
251 *From (the time that)/two/drawn/parted*

254 *Lifted (l. 177)/face/eyes*

257 *misattended, -construed*

259 *closed, fastened*

261 *linger*
262 *miss(ing) nor mourning*
263 *coffer/faith*

(23) 'Bot, jueler gente, if thou schal lose   265
     That ioy for a gemme that the was lef,
     Me thynk the put in a mad porpose,
     And busyes the aboute a raysoun bref;
     For that thou lestes was bot a rose
     That flowred and fayled as kynde hyt gef.   270
     Now thurgh kynde of the kyste that hyt con close
     To a perle of prys hit is put in pref.
     And thou has called thy wyrde a thef,
     That oght of noght was mad the cler;
     Thou blames the bote of thy meschef,   275
     Thou art no kynde jueler.'

(24) A juel to me then was thys geste,
     And iueles wern hyr gentyl sawes.
     'Iwyse,' quod I, 'my blysfol beste,
     My grete dystresse thou al todrawes.   280
     To be excused I make requeste;
     I trawed my perle don out of dawes.
     Now haf I fonde hyt, I schal ma feste,
     And wony wyth hyt in schyr wod-schawes,
     And love my Lorde and al his lawes   285
     That has me broght thys blys ner.
     Now were I at yow biyonde thise wawes,
     I were a ioyfol jueler.'

(25) 'Jueler,' sayde that gemme clene,
     'Wy borde ye men? So madde ye be!   290
     The wordes has thou spoken at ene:
     Unavysed, for sothe, wern alle thre.
     Thou ne woste in worlde quat on does mene;
     Thy worde byfore thy wytte con fle.
     Thou says thou trawes me in this dene,   295
     Bycawse thou may wyth yghen me se;
     Another thou says, in thys countré
     Thyself schal won wyth me ryght here;
     The thrydde, to passe thys water fre—
     That may no ioyfol jueler.   300

          VI
(26) 'I halde that iueler lyttel to prayse
     That leves wel that he ses wyth yghe,
     And much to blame and uncortayse

266 *(to) thee/beloved*

268 *busy (yourself)/reason/brief, small*
269 *lost*
270 *nature/gave, intended*
271 *chest/enclose*
272 *proof, to the test*
273 *fate* (l. 249)/*thief*
274 *aught from nought, something from nothing/made/clearly*
275 *boot, remedy/for/misfortune*
276 *natural*

277 *guest*
278 *sayings, words* (cf. N.E. "*old saws*")
279 *Certainly/blissful/best (one)*
280 *draw away*

282 *believed/deprived of days, life*
283 *make fest, rejoice*
284 *dwell* (l. 47)/*woods*

287 *with you/waves*

290 *jest, mock*
291 *at once*

293 *knew/one*

295 *believed* (l. 282)/*valley*
296 *eyes*
297 *Another (thing), secondly*
298 *dwell* (l. 284)
299 *third/noble*

302 *believes/sees*

That leves oure Lorde wolde make a lyghe,
That lelly hyghte your lyf to rayse,   305
Thagh fortune dyd your flesch to dyghe.
Ye setten hys wordes ful westernays
That leves nothynk bot ye hit syghe.
And that is a poynt o sorquydryghe,
That uche god mon may evel byseme,   310
To leve no tale be true to tryghe
Bot that hys one skyl may dem.

(27) 'Deme now thyself if thou can dayly,
As man to God wordes schulde heve.
Thou says thou schal won in this bayly;   315
Me thynk the burde fyrst aske leve,
And yet of graunt thou myghtes fayle.
Thou wylnegh over thys water to weve;
Er moste thou cever to other counsayl:
Thy corse in clot mot calder keve.   320
For hit was forgarte at Paradys greve:
Oure yorefader hit con mysseyeme.
Thurgh drwry deth bos uch ma dreve,
Er over thys dam hym Dryghtyn deme.'

(28) 'Demes thou me,' quod I, 'my swete,   325
To dol agayn, thenne I dowyne.
Now haf I fonte that I forlete,
Schal I efte forgo hit er ever I fyne?
Why schal I hit bothe mysse and mete?
My precios perle dos me gret pyne.   330
What serves tresor, bot gares men grete
When he hit schal efte wyth tenes tyne?
Now rech I never for to declyne,
Ne how fer of folde that man me fleme.
When I am partles of perle myne,   335
Bot durande doel, what may men deme?'

(29) 'Thow demes noght bot doel-dystresse,'
Thenne sayde that wyght. 'Why does thou so?
For dyne of doel of lures lesse
Ofte mony mon forgos the mo.   340
The oghte better thyselven blesse,
And love ay God, in wele and wo,
For anger gaynes the not a cresse.

304 *lie*
305 *loyally/promised*
306 *caused/die*
307 *reversed*
308 *nothing/unless/see*
309 *pride*
310 *ill, evilly/beseem*
311 *under trial, when put to the test*
312 *own/reason/deem, judge*

313 *did idly (speak)*
314 *heave, lift (up)*
315 *say/dwell/domain* (cf. O.Fr. *baillie*)
316 *it behooves thee/to ask leave*
317 *(a) grant, permission*
318 *wish/pass*
319 *First/must/attain*
320 *corpse/clod, earth/colder/sink*
321 *ruined, corrupted/grove, garden*
322 *forefather, Adam/misesteem, -use*
323 *dreary/must each man pass*
324 *stream/the Lord/dooms, judges*

325 *(If) you deem*
326 *dole, sorrow/dwindle (away)*, cf. l. 11
327 *found/lost*
328 *again/finish (my life)*
329 *miss, lose/meet, find*

331 *makes/weep*
332 *torments/lose*
333 *reckon, care/about declining*
334 *far/earth/(may) banish*
335 *apart, deprived*
336 *enduring/dole, sorrow*

338 *person*
339 *din, tumult/losses/lesser*

343 *cress* (as in *watercress*)

Who nedes schal thole, be not so thro.
For thogh thou daunce as any do,   345
Braundysch and bray thy brathes breme,
When thou no fyrre may, to ne fro,
Thou moste abyde that he schal deme.

(30) 'Deme Dryghtyn, ever hym adyte,
Of the way a fote ne wyl he wrythe,   350
Thy mendes mountes not a myte,
Thagh thou for sorwe be never blythe.
Stynt of thy strot and fyne to flyte,
And sech hys blythe ful swefte and swythe.
Thy prayer may hys pyté byte,   355
That mercy schal hyr craftes kythe.
Hys comforte may thy langour lythe
And thy lures of lyghtly leme;
For, marre other madde, morne and mythe,
Al lys in hym to dyght and deme.'   360

VII

(31) Thenne demed I to that damyselle,
'Ne worthe no wrathe unto my Lorde,
If rapely I rave, spornande in spelle,
My herte was al wyth mysse remorde,
As wallande water gos out of welle.   365
I do me ay in hys myserecorde.
Rebuke me never wyth wordes felle,
Thagh I for loyne, my dere endorde,
Bot kythes me kyndely your coumforde,
Pytosly thenkande upon thysse: 370
Of care and me ye made acorde,
That er was grounde of alle my blysse.

(32) 'My blysse, my bale, ye han ben bothe,
Bot much the bygger yet was my mon;
Fro thou was wroken fro uch a wothe,   375
I wyste never quere my perle was gon.
Now I hit se, now lethes my lothe.
And, quen we departed, we wern at on;
God forbede we be now wrothe,
We meten so selden by stok other ston.   380
Thagh cortaysly ye carp con,

344 *must endure/impatient, fierce*
345 *doe*
346 *Brandish, toss (about)/furies/fierce*
347 *further/may (go)/nor*

349 *(If you) judge the Lord/indict*
350 *From/one foot/turn (for you)*
351 *amends, profits*
352 *sorrow*
353 *Stop/contention/end (l. 328)/debate*
354 *seek/swiftly/quickly*

356 *reveal*
357 *assuage, soothe*
358 *losses (l. 339)/off/send*
359 *bemoan or rave (be mad)/escape, conceal (feelings)*

361 *damsel*
362 *Let there be*
363 *hastily/spurning/speech*
364 *loss (l. 262)/(filled with) remorse*
365 *welling*
366 *put (myself)/mercy*
367 *cruel*
368 *err/adored (one)*
369 *show (l. 356)/comfort*
370 *Piteously/thinking*

372 *once/(the) ground, basis*

374 *moan*
375 *Since/removed/every peril, i.e., life*
376 *knew/where*
377 *eases/woe*
378 *one*

380 *seldom*
381 *speak*

I am bot mol and maneres mysse.
Bot Crystes mersy and Mary and Jon,
Thise arn the grounde of alle my blisse,

(33) 'In blysse I se the blythely blent,   385
And I a man al mornyf mate;
Ye take theron ful lyttel tente,
Thagh I hente ofte harmes hate.
Bot now I am here in your presente,
I wolde bysech, wythouten debate,   390
Ye wolde me say in sobre asente
What lyf ye lede erly and late.
For I am ful fayn that your astate
Is worthen to worschyp and wele, iwysse;
Of alle my joy the hyghe gate,   395
Hit is in grounde of alle my blysse.'

(34) 'Now blysse, burne, mot the bytyde,'
Then sayde that lufsoum of lyth and lere,
'And welcum here to walk and byde,
For now thy speche is to me dere.   400
Maysterful mod and hyghe pryde,
I hete the, arn heterly hated here.
My Lorde ne loves not for to chyde,
For meke arn alle that wones hym nere;
And when in hys place thou schal apere,   405
Be dep devote in hol mekenesse.
My Lorde the Lamb loves ay such chere,
That is the grounde of alle my blysse.

(35) 'A blysful lyf thou says I lede;
Thou woldes knaw therof the stage.   410
Thow wost wel when thy perle con schede
I was ful yong and tender of age;
Bot my Lorde the Lombe thurgh hys godhede,
He toke myself to hys maryage,
Corounde me quene in blysse to brede   415
In lenghe of dayes that ever schal wage;
And sesed in alle hys herytage
Hys lef is. I am holy hysse:
Hys prese, hys prys, and hys parage
Is rote and grounde of alle my blysse.'   420

382 *dust* (1. 23)/*miss, lack*

384 *are*

385 *blended*
386 *mournful/dejected*
387 *attent, heed*
388 *took/griefs/hot, burning*
389 *presence*

394 *turned/honor*
395 *way*
396 *at the base* (1. 372)

397 *man/must*
398 *lovesome* (*one*)/*form/face*

401 *mood*
402 *promise, assure/fiercely*

404 *dwell*

406 *deeply/devout/whole, complete*
407 *expression*

410 *wish to know/rank* (*of advancement*)
411 *know/fall*

415 *Crowned/grow*
416 *last*
417 *possessed of*
418 *beloved/wholly his*
419 *praise/price, worth/lineage*
420 *root*

VIII

(36) 'Blysful,' quod I, 'may thys be trwe?
Dyspleses not if I speke errour.
Art thou the quene of hevenes blwe,
That al thys worlde schal do honour?
We leven on Marye that grace of grewe,   425
That ber a barne of vyrgyn flour;
The croune fro hyr quo moght remwe
Bot ho hir passed in sum favour?
Now, for synglerty o hyr dousour,
We calle hyr Fenyx of Arraby,   430
That freles fleghe of hyr fasor,
Lyk to the Quen of cortaysye.'

(37) 'Cortayse Quen,' thenne sayde that gaye,
Knelande to grounde, folde up hyr face,
'Makeles Moder and myryest May,   435
Blessed bygynner of uch a grace!'
Thenne ros ho up and con restay,
And speke me towarde in that space:
'Sir, fele here porchases and fonges pray,
Bot supplantores none wythinne thys place.   440
That emperise al hevens has,
And urthe and helle, in her bayly,
Of erytage yet non wyl ho chace,
For ho is Quen of cortaysye.

(38) 'The court of the kyndom of God alyve   445
Has a property in hytself beyng:
Alle that may therinne aryve
Of alle the reme is quen other kyng,
And never other yet schal depryve,
Bot uchon fayn of otheres hafyng,   450
And wolde her corounes wern worthe tho fyve,
If possyble were her mendyng.
Bot my Lady of quom Jesu con spryng,
Ho haldes the empyre over uus ful hyghe;
And that dyspleses non of oure gyng,   455
For ho is Quene of cortaysye.

(39) 'Of courtaysye, as says Saynt Poule,
Al arn we membres of Jesu Kryst:

421 *Blissful (one)/true*
422 *Be not displeased*
423 *blue*

425 *believe/grew of, from*
426 *bore/babe*
427 *who/remove*
428 *she (who)/surpassed*
429 *singularity/sweetness*

431 *flawless/flew/from her creator*

434 *Kneeling/enfolding*
435 *Mateless, matchless Mother/Maid*
436 *every*
437 *restrain*
438 *space (of time)*
439 *many/purchase, seek/take/prize*
440 *usurpers*
441 *empress/has all heaven*
442 *bailiwick (cf. l. 315)*
443 *(its) heritage*

446 *its own*

448 *realm/or*
449 *one another*
450 *each one/glad/having*
451 *their (the others')/crowns/were/five times more*
452 *amending, improvement*

455 *company (cf. N.E. gang)*

457 *St. Paul*

As heved and arme and legg and navle
Temen to hys body ful trwe and tryste,   460
Ryght so is uch a Krysten sawle
A longande lym to the Mayster of myste.
Thenne loke what hate other any gawle
Is tached other tyghed thy lymmes bytwyste.
Thy heved has nauther greme ne gryste,   465
On arme other fynger thagh thou ber byghe.
So fare we alle wyth luf and lyste
To kyng and quene by cortyasye.'

(40) 'Cortayse,' quod I, 'I leve,
And charyte grete, be yow among,   470
Bot my speche that yow ne greve,

· · · · · · · · · · · · · · · · ·

Thyself in heven over hygh thou heve,
To make the quen that was so yonge.
What more honour moghte he acheve   475
That hade endured in worlde stronge,
And lyved in penaunce hys lyves longe
Wyth bodyly bale hym blysse to byye?
What more worschyp moght he fonge
Then corounde be kyng by cortayse?   480

IX
(41) 'That cortayse is to fre of dede,
Yyf hyt be soth that thou cones saye.
Thou lyfed not two yer in oure thede;
Thou cowthes never God nauther plese ne pray,
Ne never nawther Pater ne Crede,   485
And quen mad on the fyrst day!
I may not traw, so God me spede,
That God wolde wrythe so wrange away.
Of countes, damysel, par my fay,
Wer fayr in heven to halde asstate,   490
Other elles a lady of lasse aray;
Bot a quene! Hit is to dere a date.'

(42) 'Ther is no date of hys godnesse,'
Then sayde to me that worthy wyghte,
'For al is trawthe that he con dresse,   495
And he may do nothynk bot ryght.
As Mathew meles in your messe

459 *head/navel*
460 *Belong/true/tried*
461 *every/Christian/soul*
462 *belonging/(spiritual) mysteries, might*
463 *whether/or/gall*
464 *attached/or/tied/betwixt*
465 *neither/wrath/resentment* (cf. N.E. *grist*['*grind*']*mill*)
466 *or/bear/ring*
467 *love/glee*

469 *believe*

471 *(should) not grieve you*
472 (line omitted in MS.)
473 *heave, raise*

477 *life's length, all his life*
478 *buy*
479 *receive* (l. 439)
480 "*Than to be crowned king . . .*"

481 *too/indeed*
482 *do (say)*
483 *land*
484 *could/please (God)/pray*
485 *(knew) neither/Lord's Prayer/Apostles' Creed*
486 *(a) queen/made*
487 *believe*
488 *turn* (l. 350)/*wrongly*
489 *(For a) countess/by my faith*
490 *estate*
491 *less/array*
492 *too/early*

493 *date* here = *end*
494 *being*
495 *ordain*
496 *nothing*
497 *says/mass*

In sothful gospel of God almyght,
In sample he can ful graythely gesse,
And lyknes hit to heven lyghte.   500
"My regne," he says, "is lyk on hyght
To a lorde that hade a vyne, I wate;
Of tyme of yere the terme was tyght,
To labor vyne was dere the date.

(43) "That date of yere wel knawe thys hyne.   505
The lorde ful erly up he ros
To hyre werkmen to hys vyne,
And fyndes ther summe to hys porpos.
Into acorde thay con declyne
For a pené on a day, and forth thay gos,   510
Wrythen and worchen and don gret pyne,
Kerven and caggen and man hit clos.
Aboute under the lorde to marked tos,
And ydel men stande he fyndes therate.
'Why stande ye ydel?' he sayde to thos.   515
'Ne knawe ye of this day no date?

(44) " 'Er date of daye hider arn we wonne,'
So was al samen her answar soght.
'We haf standen her syn ros the sunne.
And no mon byddes uus do ryght noght.'   520
'Gos into my vyne, dos that ye conne,'
So sayde the lorde, and made hit toght.
'What resonabele hyre be naght be runne
I yow pay in dede and thoghte.'
Thay wente into the vyne and wroghte,   525
And al day the lorde thus yede his gate,
And nw men to hys vyne he broghte
Welnegh wyl day was passed date.

(45) "At the day of date of evensonge,
On oure byfore the sonne go doun,   530
He segh ther ydel men ful stronge
And sade to hem wyth sobre soun,
'Wy stonde ye ydel thise dayes longe?'
Thay sayden her hyre was nawhere boun.
'Gos to my vyne, yemen yonge,   535
And wyrkes and dos that at ye moun.'
Sone the worlde bycom wel broun;

499 *example, parable/readier/illustrate*
500 *likens*
501 *kingdom/high*
502 *vineyard/know*
503 *season/arrived*
504 *work/time was precious*

505 *laborers*

508 *(suited) to*
509 *agreement/agree, settle*

511 *Twist/toil/endure/travail*
512 *Cut/bind/make/close*
513 *undertide, noon/market/goes*

517 *Before/sunrise/come*
518 *together/found*
519 *since*
520 *anything*
521 *Go/do/may*
522 *firm*
523 *might be run (up), accrued*
524 *(will) pay*

526 *went/way (l. 395)*
527 *new*
528 *Well nigh (until)/daytime was past*

529 *time*

531 *saw/idle*

533 *idle*
534 *bound*
535 *Go/yeomen*
536 *work/do/which you may*
537 *Soon/dark*

The sunne was doun and hit wex late;
To take her hyre he mad sumoun;
The day was al apassed date.   540

X

(46) "The date of the daye the lorde con knaw,
Called to the reve, 'Lede, pay the meyny.
Gyf hem the hyre that I hem owe,
And fyrre, that non me may reprene,
Set hem alle upon a rawe   545
And gyf uchon inlyche a peny.
Bygyn at the laste that standes lowe,
Tyl to the fyrste that thou atteny.'
And thenne the fyrst bygonne to pleny
And sayden that thay hade travayled sore: 550
'These bot on oure hem con streny;
Uus thynk uus oghe to take more.

(47) "'More haf we scrvcd, uus thynk so,
That suffred han the dayes hete,
Thenn thyse that wroght not houres two,   555
And thou dos hem uus to counterfete.'
Thenne sayde the lorde to on of tho,
'Frende, no waning I wyl the yete;
Take that is thyn owne, and go.
And I hyred the for a peny agrete,   560
Quy bygynnes thou now to threte?
Was not a pené thy covenaunt thore?
Fyrre then covenaunde is noght to plete.
Wy schalte thou thenne ask more?

(48) "'More, wether louyly is me my gyfte,   565
To do wyth myn quat-so me lykes?
Other elles thyn yghe to lyther is lyfte
For I am goude and non beswykes?'"
"Thus schal I," quod Kryste, "hit skyfte:
The laste schal be the fyrst that strykes,   570
And the fyrst the laste, be he never so swyft;
For mony ben called thagh fewe be mykes."
Thus pore men her part ay pykes,
Thagh thay com late and lyttel wore;
And thagh her sweng wyth lyttel atslykes,   575
The merci of God is much the more.

538 *waxed, grew*
539 *made summon, called (them)*

542 *reeve/man/company*

544 *further/reproach*
545 *row*
546 *each one/alike*
547 *low (in rank)*
548 *attain, arrive*
549 *began/complain*

551 *one/hour/strain, exert (themselves)*
552 *ought*

556 *equate, "you do equal them to us"*
557 *one/those*
558 *grant*

560 *If/aggregate, as a group*

562 *agreement/then (when I hired you)*
563 *Further/than/plead, claim*

565 *Moreover/isn't it lawful*
566 *my (own gift)/whatsoever*
567 *Or/eye/evil/lifted*
568 *good/deceive*
569 *shift, arrange*
570 *comes (for his reward)*

572 *(the) chosen, favorites*
573 *always/pick, attain*
574 *were*
575 *swing, stroke/glides away askew*

(49) 'More haf I of ioye and blysse hereinne,
 Of ladyschyp gret and lyves blom,
 Then alle the wyghes in the worlde myght wynne
 By the way of ryght to aske dome.   580
 Whether welnygh now I con bygynne—
 In eventyde into the vyne I come—
 Fyrst of my hyre my Lorde con mynne:
 I was payed anon of al and sum.
 Yet other ther werne that toke more tom,   585
 That swange and swat for long yore,
 That yet of hyre nothynk thay nom.
 Paraunter noght schal to-yere more.'

(50) Then more I meled and sayde apert,
 'Me thynk thy tale unresounable.   590
 Goddes ryght is redy and evermore rert,
 Other Holy Wryt is bot a fable.
 In Sauter is sayd a verce overte
 That spekes a poynt determynable:
 "Thou quytes uchon as hys desserte,   595
 Thou hyghe kyng ay pretermynable."
 Now he that stod the long day stable,
 And thou to payment com hym byfore,
 Thenne the lasse in werke to take more able,
 And ever the lenger the lasse, the more.'   600

XI

(51) 'Of more and lasse in Godes ryche,'
 That gentyl sayde, 'lys no jopardé,
 For ther is uch mon payed inlyche,
 Whether lyttel other much be hys rewarde;
 For the gentyl Cheventayn is no chyche,   605
 Quether-so-ever he dele nesch other harde.
 He laves hys gyftes as water of dyche,
 Other gotes of golf that never charde.
 Hys fraunchyse is large that ever dard
 To hym that mas in synne rescoghe;   610
 No blysse bes fro hem reparde,
 For the grace of God is gret inoghe.

(52) 'Bot now thou motes, me for to mate,
 That I my peny haf wrang tan here;
 Thou says that I that come to late   615
 Am not worthy so gret fere.

578 *life's bloom*
579 *beings*
580 *judgment*

583 *remember*
584 *immediately*
585 *spent/time*
586 *toiled/sweated*
587 *received*
588 *Perhaps/for still a long time*

589 *spoke* (l. *497*)/*plainly*

591 *raised up*

593 *Psalter*

595 *requite, repay/each one*
596 *predetermining*

599 *less*

601 *reich, kingdom*
602 *gentle (one)/jeopardy*
603 *each/alike*

605 *Chieftain/chinch, miser*
606 *soft*
607 *pours forth/ditch*
608 *Or/streams/gulf/cease*
609 *franchise, generosity/that ever is hidden*
610 *makes from/sin/a rescue, recovery*
611 *will be withheld from them* (those who rescue themselves from sin)
612 *enough, indeed*

613 *argue/shame*
614 *wrongly/taken*
615 *too*
616 *worthy (of)/fee*

Where wystes thou ever any bourne abate,
Ever so holy in hys prayere,
That he ne forfeted by sumkyn gate
The mede sumtyme of hevenes clere?   620
And ay the ofter, the alder thay were,
Thay laften ryght and wroghten woghe.
Mercy and grace moste hem then stere,
For the grace of God is gret innoghe.

(53) 'Bot innoghe of grace has innocent.   625
As sone as thay arn borne, by lyne
In the water of babtem thay dyssente;
Then arne thay boroght into the vyne.
Anon the day, wyth derk endente,
The niyght of deth dos to enclyne;   630
That wroght never wrang er thenne thay wente,
The gentyle Lorde thenne payes hys hyne.
Thay dyden hys heste; thay wern thereine.
Why schulde he not her labour alow,
Yys, and pay hem at the fyrst fyne?   635
For the grace of God is gret innoghe.

(54) 'Inoghe is knawen that mankyn grete
Fyrste was wroght to blysse parfyt;
Oure forme fader hit con forfete
Thurgh an apple that he upon con byte.   640
Al wer we dampned for that mete,
To dyghe in doel out of delyt
And sythen wende to helle hete,
Therinne to won wythoute respyt.
Bot theron com a bote astyt.   645
Ryche blod ran on rode so roghe,
And wynne water then at that plyt:
The grace of God wex gret innoghe.

(55) 'Innoghe ther wax out of that welle,
Blod and water of brode wounde.   650
The blod uus boght fro bale of helle
And delyvered uus of the deth secounde;
The water is baptem, the sothe to telle,
That folwed the glayve so grymly grounde,
That wasches away the gyltes felle   655

617 *knew/man/endure*
618 *However*
619 *some kind of/way*
620 *meed, reward/heaven's brightness*
621 *oftener/older*
622 *left/woe*
623 *must/steer*

625 *(the) innocent*
626 *lineage*
627 *baptism/descend*
628 *are/brought*
629 *Immediately/darkness/marked*
630 "*To, toward the night of death inclines*"
631 *Those (who)/thence*
632 *laborers* (l. 505)
633 *did/behest, commandment/therein* (in the vineyard)
634 *allow*
635 *Yes/end* (see l. 545f.)

637 *(As well) enough is known*
638 *perfect*
639 *first*

641 *meat, food*
642 *die/dole/without delight*
643 *afterward/go*
644 *dwell*
645 *boot, favor/immediately*
646 *rood, cross*
647 *blessed/plight*

650 *broad/wound*

653 *baptism* (l. 627)
654 *spear, lance*
655 *cruel* (l. 367)

That Adam wyth inne deth uus drounde.
Now is ther noght in the worlde rounde
Bytwene uus and blysse bot that he wythdrow,
And that is restored in sely stounde;
And the grace of God is gret innogh.   660

XII

(56) 'Grace innogh the mon may have
That synnes thenne new, yif him repente,
Bot wyth sorw and syt he mot hit crave,
And byde the payne therto is bent.
Bot resoun of ryght that con noght rave   665
Saves evermore the innossent;
Hit is a dom that never God gave,
That ever the gyltles schulde be schente.
The gyltyf may contryssyoun hente
And be thurgh mercy to grace thryght;   670
Bot he to gyle that never glente
At inoscente is saf and ryghte.

(57) 'Ryght thus I knaw wel in this cas
Two men to save is god by skylle:
The ryghtwys man schal se hys face,   675
The harmles hathel schal com hym tylle.
The Sauter hyt sas thus in a pace:
"Lorde, quo schal klymbe thy hygh hylle,
Other rest wythinne thy holy place?"
Hymself to onsware he is not dylle,   680
"Hondelynges harme that dyt not ille,
That is of hert bothe clene and lyght,
Ther schal hys step stable stylle";
The innosent is ay saf by ryght.

(58) 'The ryghtwys man also sertayn   685
Aproche he schal that proper pyle,
That takes not her lyf in vayne,
Ne glaveres her nieghbor wyth no gyle.
Of thys ryghtwys sas Salamon playn
How kyntly onore con aquyle;   690
By wayes ful streght he con hym strayn,
And scheued hym the rengne of God awhyle,
As quo says, "Lo, yon lovely yle!

658 *what/withdrew*
659 *blessed/time*

663 *sorrow/grief/must*
664 *pain (that)*
665 *err*

667 *judgment*
668 *grieved*
669 *guilty/contrition/seize*
670 *brought*
671 *at (guile)/glanced*
672 *With (the) innocent*

674 *?good/by reasoning or God's judgment, skill*
675 *righteous*
676 *innocent/man/come to him*
677 *Psalter/says/passage*

680 *answer/slow*
681 *"He who did not wrongfully harm with hands"*

683 *(be) stable*

685 *certainly*
686 *fair/stronghold*

688 *deceives*
689 *righteous (one)*
690 *fittingly/honor/acquire*
691 *constrain*
692 *realm*

Thou may hit wynne if thou be wyghte."
Bot, hardyly, wythoute peryle,   695
The innosent is ay save by ryghte.

(59) 'Anende ryghtwys men yet sas a gome,
David in Sauter, if ever ye segh hit:
"Lorde, thy servaunt draw never to dome,
For non lyvyande to the is justyfyet."   700
Forthy to corte quen thou schal com
Ther alle oure causes schal be tryed,
Alegge the ryght, thou may be innome,
By thys ilke spech I have asspyed;
Bot he on rode that blody dyed,   705
Delfully thurgh hondes thryght,
Gyve the to passe, when thou arte tryed,
By innocens and not by ryghte.

(60) 'Ryghtwysly quo con rede,
He loke on bok and be awayed   710
How Jesus hym welke in are thede,
And burnes her barnes unto hym brayde.
For happe and hele that fro hym yede
To touch her chylder thay fayr hym prayed.
His dessypeles wyth blame let be hem bede   715
And wyth her resounes ful fele restayed.
Jesus thenne hem swetely sayde,
"Do way, let chylder unto me tyght.
To suche is hevenryche arayed";
The innocent is ay saf by ryght.   720

XIII
(61) 'Iesus con calle to hym hys mylde,
And sayde hys ryche no wygh myght wynne
Bot he com thyder ryght as a chylde,
Other elles nevermore com therinne.
Harmles, trwe, and undefylde,   725
Wythouten mote other mascle of sulpande synne,
Quen such ther cnoken on the bylde,
Tyt schal hem men the yate unpynne.
Ther is the blys that con not blynne
That the jueler soghte thurgh perré pres,   730
And solde alle hys goud, bothe wolen and lynne,
To bye hym a perle was mascelles.

694 *valiant*

696 *saved*

697 *Concerning* (l. 186)/*says/man*
698 *see*

700 *no living* (*man*)/*before thee/justified*
701 *Therefore/court/when*

703 *Allege/taken in*
704 *same/espied, observed*
705 *rood, cross*
706 *Dolefully/pierced* (l. 670)

709 *Rightly/*(*he*) *who/read*
710 *informed*
711 *walked* (*with*)/*early/people*
712 *men/babes* (l. 426)/*brought*
713 *happiness/healing/passed, emanated*
714 *children*
715 *disciples/rebuke/bade them to leave him alone*
716 *many/restrained*

718 *come*
719 *kingdom of heaven*

721 *mild* (*ones*)
722 *kingdom/no one*

725 *Innocent* (l. 676)/*true*
726 *speck/spot/soiling*
727 *knock/dwelling*
728 *Promptly/gate/unpin, open*
729 *cease*
730 *gems/precious*
731 *goods/wool/linen*
732 *flawless* (l. 726)

(62) 'This makelles perle, that boght is dere,
      The joueler gef fore alle hys god,
      Is lyke the reme of hevenesse clere;   735
      So sayde the Fader of folde and flode,
      For hit is wemles, clene and clere,
      And endeles rounde, and blythe of mode,
      And commune to alle that ryghtwys were.
      Lo, even inmyddes my breste hit stode.   740
      My Lorde the lombe, that schede hys blode,
      He pyght hit there in token of pes.
      I rede the forsake the worlde wode
      And porchace thy perle maskelles.'

(63) 'O maskeles perle in perles pure,   745
      That beres,' quod I, 'the perle of prys,
      Quo formed the thy fayre fygure,
      That wroght thy wede, he was ful wys.
      Thy beauté com never of nature;
      Pymalyon paynted never thy vys.   750
      Ne Arystotel nawther by hys lettrure
      Of carpe the kynde these propertés.
      Thy colour passes the flour-de-lys;
      Thyn angel-havyng so clene cortes.
      Breve me, bryght, quat kyn offys   755
      Beres the perle so maskelles?'

(64) 'My makeles Lambe that al may bete,'
      Quod scho, 'my dere destyné,
      Me ches to hys make, althagh unmete
      Sumtyme semed that assemblé.   760
      When I wente fro yor worlde wete,
      He calde me to hys bonerté:
      "Cum hyder to me, my lemman swete,
      For mote ne spot is non in the."
      He gef me myght and als bewté;   765
      In hys blod he wesch my wede on dese,
      And coronde clene in vergynté,
      And pyght me in perles maskelles.'

(65) 'Why, maskelles bryd that bryght con flambe,
      That reiates has so ryche and ryf,   770
      Quat kyn thyng may be that Lambe
      That the wolde wedde unto hys vyf?

734 *gave for it/goods*
735 *realm/heaven's brightness* (l. 620)
736 *earth/sea*
737 *stainless* (l. 221)
738 *endlessly*

742 *placed/peace*
743 *advise/mad*

748 *clothes*

750 *Pygmalion/face* (l. 254)
751 *Nor/in/literature, writings*
752 *Speak of/nature*

754 *-manner/completely/courteous*
755 *Tell/bright* (one)/*what kind of office, rank*

757 *"who surpasses all"*

759 *chose* (as)/*mate/unmeet, unfitting*
760 *Once/union*
761 *your/wet, rainy*
762 (O.Fr. *boneurte* 'goodness') *blessedness*
763 *lover, beloved*
764 *stain*

766 *washed/clothes* (l. 748)/*dais*
767 *crowned* (me)
768 *adorned, set*

769 *bride/glow*
770 *royalty/rife*
771 *kind* (of)/*being*
772 *as/wife*

Over alle other so hygh thou clambe
To lede wyth hym so ladyly lyf.
So mony a comly onunder cambe   775
For Kryst han lyved in much stryf;
And thou con alle tho dere out dryf
And fro that maryag al other depres,
Al only thyself so stout and styf,
A makeles may and maskelles.'   780

XIV

(66) 'Maskelles,' quod that myry quene,
    'Unblemyst I am, wythouten blot,
    And that may I wyth mensk menteene;
    Bot "makeles quene" thenne sade I not.
    The Lambes vyves in blysse we bene,   785
    A hondred and forty fowre thowsande flot,
    As in the Apocalyppes hit is sene;
    Sant John hem sygh al in a knot.
    On the hyl of Syon, that semly clot,
    The apostel hem segh in gostly drem   790
    Arayed to the weddyng in that hyl-coppe,
    The nwe cyté o Jerusalem.

(67) 'Of Jerusalem I in speche spelle.
    If thou wyl knaw what kyn he be,
    My Lombe, my Lorde, my dere juelle,   795
    My ioy, my blys, my lemman fre,
    The profete Ysaye of hym con melle
    Pitously of hys debonerté:
    "That gloryous gyltles that mon con quelle
    Wythouten any sake of felonye,   800
    As a schep to the slaght ther lad was he;
    And, as lombe that clypper in hande nem,
    So closed he hys mouth fro uch query,
    Quen Jues hym iugged in Jerusalem."

(68) 'In Jerusalem was my lemman slayn   805
    And rent on rode wyth boyes bolde.
    Al oure bales to bere ful bayn,
    He toke on hymself oure cares colde.
    Wyth boffetes was hys face flayn
    That was so fayr on to byholde.   810
    For synne he set hymself in vayn,

773 *climbed*
774 *such* (a)/*ladylike*
775 *comely* (one)/*under, wearing*/*comb*
776 *has*/*strife, conflict*
777 *those*/*dear* (ones)
778 *marriage*/*deprive*
779 *strong*/*bold*
780 *matchless*/*maid* (1. 435)/*spotless* (1. 769)

782 *Unblemished*
783 *courtesy*/*maintain* (1. 162)

785 *wives*/*be*
786 *host*

788 *saw*/*throng*
789 *clod, plot* (of ground)
790 *saw*
791 *for*/*on*/*hilltop*
792 *new*/*city*

793 *speak* (out)

796 *joy*/*beloved* (1. 763)/*free* (one)
797 *Isaiah*/*speak*
798 *Pityingly*/*gentleness*
799 *guiltless* (one)
800 *cause,* (criminal) *charge*
801 *sheep*/*slaughter*/*led*
802 *shearer*/*seizes*

806 *rood, cross*/*knaves, thieves*
807 *ready*

809 *buffets*/*flayed*

811 *Because of*/*at nought*

That never hade non hymself to wolde.
For uus he lette hym flyghe and folde
And brede upon a bostwys bem;
As meke as lomp that no playnt tolde   815
For uus he swalt in Jerusalem.

(69) 'In Jerusalem, Jordan, and Galalye,
Ther as baptysed the goude Saynt Jon,
His wordes acorded to Ysaye.
When Jesus con to hym warde gon,   820
He sayde of hym thys professye,
"Lo, Godes Lombe as trwe as ston,
That dos away the synnes dryghe
That alle thys worlde has wroght upon.
Hymself ne wroght never yet non;   825
Whether on hymself he con al clem.
Hys generacyoun quo recen con,
That dyghed for uus in Jerusalem?"

(70) 'In Ierusalem thus my lemman swete
Twyes for lombe was taken thare,   830
By trw recorde of ayther prophete,
For mode so meke and al hys fare.
The thryde tyme is therto ful mete,
In Apokalypes wryten ful yare;
Inmydes the trone, there sayntes sete,   835
The apostel John hym sagh as bare,
Lesande the boke with leves sware
There seven syngnettes wern sette in seme;
And at that syght uche douth con dare
In helle, in erthe, and Jerusalem.   840

XV

(71) 'Thys Jerusalem Lombe hade never pechche
Of other huee bot quyt jolyf.
That mot ne masklle moght on streche,
For wolle quyte so ronk and ryf.
Forthy uche saule that hade never teche   845
Is to that Lombe a worthyly wyf;
And thagh uch day a store he feche,
Among uus commes nouther strot ne stryf;
Bot uchon enlé we wolde were fyf—

812 *possess, be guilty of*
813 *let (himself)/(be) flayed/bent*
814 *drawn, stretched/rough/beam*
815 *lamb/complaint*
816 *died*

819 *Isaiah (1. 797)*
820 *toward him go*
821 *prophecy*
822 *true*
823 *oppressive, heavy*
824 *practiced*

826 *Though/claim, accept*
827 *generation/who can reckon, recount*
828 *died*

830 *Twice/as (a) lamb*
831 *true/either, each*
832 *mood/meek/behavior*
833 *third/fully/fitting*
834 *plainly*
835 *In the midst (of)/throne*
836 *saw/clearly*
837 *Loosening/square*
838 *signets, seals/seam, border*
839 *each/creature/tremble*

841 *sin (O.Fr. peché), mark*
842 *white/jolly, fair*
843 *spot/speck/reach*
844 *wool/abundant/rife*
845 *Therefore/soul/stain*
846 *worthy*
847 *lot/(may) fetch*
848 *resentment*
849 *singly/five*

The mo the myryer, so God me blesse!   850
In compayny gret our luf con thryf
In honour more and never the lesse.

(72) 'Lasse of blysse may non uus bryng
      That beren thys perle upon oure bereste,
      For thay of mote couthe never mynge   855
      Of spotles perles that beren the creste.
      Althagh oure corses in clottes clynge,
      And ye remen for rauthe wythouten reste,
      We thurghoutly haven cnawyng;
      Of on dethe ful oure hope is drest.   860
      The Lombe uus glades, oure care is kest;
      He myrthes uus alle at uch a mes.
      Uchones blysse is breme and beste,
      And never ones honour yet never the les.

(73) 'Lest les thou leve my tale farande,   865
      In Appocalyppece is wryten in wro:
      "I seghe," says John, "the Lombe hym stande
      On the mount of Syon ful thryven and thro,
      And wyth hym maydennes an hundrethe thowsande,
      And fowre and forty thowsande mo.   870
      On alle her forhedes wryten I fande
      The Lombes nome, hys Faderes also.
      A hue from heven I herde thoo,
      Lyk flodes fele laden runnen on resse,
      And as thunder throwes in torres blo,   875
      That lote, I leve, was never the les.

(74) "Nautheles, thagh hit schowted scharpe,
      And ledden loude althagh hit were,
      A note ful nwe I herde hem warpe,
      To lysten that was ful lufly dere.   880
      As harpores harpen in her harpe,
      That nwe songe thay songen ful cler,
      In sounande notes a gentyl carpe;
      Ful fayre the modes thay fonge in fere.
      Ryght byfore Godes chayere   885
      And the fowre bestes that hym obes
      And the aldermen so sadde of chere,
      Her songe thay songen never the les.

851 *love/thrive*

853 *Less*

854 *breast*
855 *trifles/think*

857 *corpses* (l. 320)/*clods, earth*
858 *cry* (out)/*grief*
859 *throughout/have/knowing, consciousness*
860 *one/fully/addressed, set*
861 *gladdens/cast*
862 *every/meal*
863 *Each one's/intense* (l. 346)
864 *one's/any* (the less)

865 *believe/fitting*
866 *passage*

868 *vigorous/intense* (l. 344)

871 *found*
872 *name*
873 *then*
874 *sound of many floods/rush*
875 *rolls/dark hills*
876 *sound*

877 *Nevertheless/shouted, sounded*
878 *sound* (l. 874)
879 *cast* (out)

881 *on/harps*

883 *resounding/utterance*
884 *grasped/unison*
885 *chair*
886 *beasts/obey*
887 *elders/sober*

(75) "Nowthelese non was never so quoynt,
        For alle the craftes that ever thay knewe,   890
        That of that songe mygth synge a poynt,
        Bot that meyny the Lombe that swe;
        For thay arn boght fro the urthe aloynte
        As newe fryt to God ful due,
        And to the gentyl Lombe hit arn anioynt,   895
        As lyk to hymself of lote and hwe;
        For never lesyng ne tale untrwe
        Ne towched her tonge for no dysstresse.
        That moteles meyny may never remwe
        Fro that maskeles mayster, never the les." '   900

(76) 'Never the les let be my thonc,'
        Quod I, 'My perle, thagh I appose;
        I schulde not tempte thy wyt so wlonc,
        To Krystes chambre that art ichose.
        I am bot mokke and mul among,   905
        And thou so ryche a reken rose,
        And bydes here by thys blysful bonc
        Ther lyves lyste may never lose,
        Now, hynde, that sympelnesse cones enclose,
        I wolde the aske a thynge expresse,   910
        And thagh I be bustwys as a blose,
        Let my bone vayl neverthelese.

    XVI
(77) 'Neverthelese cler I yow bycalle,
        If ye con se hyt be to done;
        As thou art gloryous wythouten galle,   915
        Wythnay thou never my ruful bone.
        Haf ye no wones in castel-walle,
        Ne maner ther ye may mete and won?
        Thou telles me of Jerusalem the ryche ryalle,
        Ther David dere was dyght on trone,   920
        Bot by thyse holtes hit con not hone,
        Bot in Judee hit is, that noble note.
        As ye ar maskeles under mone,
        Your wones schulde be wythouten mote.

(78) 'Thys moteles meyny thou cones of mele,   925
        Of thousandes thrygth so gret a route,
        A gret ceté, for ye arn fele,

889 *skilled*

891 *note*
892 *company/pursue*
893 *purchased, redeemed/earth/afar*
894 *fruit*
895 *they are joined*
896 *sound* (l. 876)/*hue*
897 *lie/untrue*

899 *move*
900 *spotless/master*

901 *thanks*

903 *noble*
904 *chosen*
905 *muck and mold/(mingled) together*
906 *rare*
907 *bank*
908 *desire*
909 *gracious (one)/simplicity/embodies*

911 *rustic/yokel*
912 *boon/avail*

913 *clearly*
914 *Whether/that it be done*

916 *Deny, reject/boon*
917 *dwelling/within*
918 *manor/dwell*
919 *royal realm*
920 *set/throne*
921 *groves/be situated*
922 *Judea/place*
923 *moon*

925 *speak*
926 *thronged*
927 *many*

Yow byhod have, wythouten doute.
So cumly a pakke of joly juele
Wer evel don schulde lygh theroute,   930
And by thyse bonkes ther I con gele
I se no bygyng nawhere aboute.
I trowe alone ye lenge and loute
To loke on the glory of thys gracious gote.
If thou has other lygynges stoute,   935
Now tech me to that myry mote.'

(79) 'That mote thou menes in Judy londe,'
That specyal spyce then to me spakk,
'That is the cyté that the Lombe con fonde
To soffer inne sor for manes sake,   940
The olde Jerusalem, to understonde;
For there the olde gulte was don to slake.
Bot the nwe, that lyght of Godes sonde,
The apostel in Apocalyppce in theme con take.
The Lompe ther wythouten spottes blake   945
Has feryed thyder hys fayre flote;
And as hys flok is wythouten flake,
So is hys mote wythouten moote.

(80) 'Of motes two to carpe clene,
And Jerusalem hyght bothe nawtheles—   950
That nys to yow no more to mene
Bot "ceté of God," other "syght of pes."
In that on oure pes was mad at ene;
Wyth payne to suffer the Lombe hit chese;
In that other is noght bot pes to glene   955
That ay schal laste wythouten reles.
That is the borgh that we to pres
Fro that oure flesch be layd to rote,
Ther glory and blysse schal ever encres
To the meyny that is wythouten mote.'   960

(81) 'Moteles may so meke and mylde,'
Then sayde I to that lufly flor,
'Bryng me to that bygly bylde
And let me se thy blysful bor.'
That schene sayde, 'That God wyl schylde;   965
Thou may not enter wythinne hys tor,

928 *it behooved you to have*

930 *evilly/(they) lie*
931 *tarry*
932 *dwelling*
933 *linger/go*
934 *stream*
935 *lodgings*
936 *Direct/moat, (walled) city*

937 *Judea*
938 *being/spoke*
939 *seek*
940 *suffer/sorely*
941 *so to speak, that is*
942 *guilt/ended*
943 *sending*

945 *black*
946 *ferried, led/company*

948 *moat/mote, speck*

949 *speak*
950 *called/nevertheless*
951 neg. + *is/mean*
952 *or/peace*
953 *one/once made*
954 *chose*
955 *glean*
956 *surcease*
957 *city/press toward*
958 *From (the time)/rot*
959 *increase*
960 *company*

961 *maid*
962 *lovely/flower*
963 *delightful/dwelling*
964 *bower*
965 *fair (one)/shield*
966 *tower*

Bot of the Lombe I have the aquylde
For a syght therof thurgh gret favor.
Utwyth to se that clene cloystor
Thou may, bot inwyth not a fote;   970
To strech in the strete thou has no vygour,
Bot thou wer clene wythouten mote.

XVII
(82) 'If I this mote the schal unhyde,
Bow up towarde thys bornes heved,
And I anendes the on this syde   975
Schal sue, tyl thou to a hil be veved.'
Then wolde I no lenger byde,
Bot lurked by launces so lufly leved,
Tyl on a hyl that I asspyed
And blusched on the burghe, as I forth dreved,   980
Byyonde the brok fro me warde keved,
That schyrrer then sunne wyth schaftes schon.
In the Apokalypce is the fasoun preved,
As devyses hit the apostel Jhon.

(83) As John the apostel hit sygh wyth syght,   985
I syghe that cyty of gret renoun,
Jerusalem so nwe and ryally dyght,
As hit was lyght fro the heven adoun.
The borgh was al of brende golde bryght
As glemande glas burnist broun,   990
Wyth gentyl gemmes anunder pyght,
Wyth banteles twelve on basyng boun,
The foundementes twelve of riche tenoun;
Uch tabelment was a serlypes ston;
As derely devyses this ilk toun   995
In Apocalyppes the apostel John.

(84) As John thise stones in writ con nemme,
I knew the name after his tale:
Jasper hyght the fyrst gemme
That I on the fyrst basse con wale;   1000
He glente grene in the lowest hemme;
Saffer helde the secounde stale;
The calsydoyne thenne wythouten wemme
In the thryd table con purly pale;
The emerade the furthe so grene of scale;   1005

967 *(for) you/spoken, gotten permission*

969 *(From) without/cloister*
970 *within/foot*
971 *go into/power*

973 *place/unhide, reveal*
974 *Bow, turn/stream's head*
975 *opposite* (cf. ll. 186, 697)
976 *pursue/brought* (cf. N.E. *"weave one's way"*)

978 *slipped/boughs/leaved*

980 *glimpsed/went*
981 *brook/from me* (cf. constr. l. 820)/*sank*
982 *brighter/shafts/shone*
983 *fashion/proved*
984 *describes/John*

985 *saw*
986 *saw*
987 *new/royally/bedight*
988 *As (if)/alighted, descended*
989 *burnt*
990 *gleaming/burnished/deeply*
991 *below/set, adorned*
992 *bantel* (one of a series of foundation tiers)/*bases/bound, fixed*
993 *foundations/tenon, joining*
994 *"Each tier in separate stone"*
995 *same/town*

997 *name*

999 *is called*
1000 *perceive*
1001 *glinted/border*
1002 *Sapphire/position*
1003 *chalcedony/flaw*
1004 *third/purely/(shine) pale*
1005 *emerald/fourth*

The sardonyse the fyfthe ston;
The sexte the rybé he con hit wale
In the Apocalyppce, the apostel John.

(85) Yet joyned John the crysolyt
The seventhe gemme in fundament;   1010
The aghtthe the beryl cler and quyt;
The topasye twynne-how the nente endent;
The crysopase the tenthe is tyght;
The jacynght the enleventhe gent;
The twelfthe, the gentyleste in uch a plyt,   1015
The amatyst purpre wyth ynde blente;
The wal abof the bantels bent
O jasporye, as glas that glysnande schon;
I knew hit by his devysement
In the Apocalyppes, the apostel John.   1020

(86) As John devysed yet saw I thare:
Thise twelve degres wern brode and stayre;
The cyté stod abof ful sware,
As longe as brode as hyghe ful fayre;
The stretes of golde as glasse, al bare,   1025
The wal of jasper that glent as glayre;
The wones wythinne enurned ware
Wyth alle kynnes perré that moght repayre.
Thenne helde uch sware of this manayre
Twelve forlonge space, er ever hit fon,   1030
Of heght, of brede, of lenthe to cayre,
For meten hit sygh the apostel John.

        XVIII
(87) As John hym wrytes yet more I syghe:
Uch pane of that place had thre yates;
So twelve in poursent I con asspye,   1035
The portales pyked of rych plates,
And uch gate of a margyrye,
A parfyt perle that never fates.
Uchon in scrypture a name con plye
Of Israel barnes, folewande her dates,   1040
That is to say, as her byrth-whates;
The aldest ay fyrst theron was done.
Such lyght ther lemed in alle the strates
Hem nedde nawther sunne ne mone.

1006 *sardonyx/fifth*
1007 *ruby*

1009 *Then/chrysolite*

1011 *eighth/white*
1012 *topaz/twin-hued/ninth/inlaid*
1013 *chrysoprase/set*
1014 *jacinth/eleventh/gentle*
1015 *every state*
1016 *amethyst/purple/indigo (l. 76)/blended*
1017 *wall/above/extended*
1018 *jasper/glistening*
1019 *description*

1022 *were/steep*
1023 *square*

1026 *glair, (egg-white) glaze*
1027 *dwellings/adorned/were*
1028 *kinds of/precious gems/might come together*
1029 *square, section/manor, city*
1030 *finished, ended*
1031 *breadth/attain*
1032 *measured/saw*

1033 *saw*
1034 *part, side*
1035 *enclosure, succession*
1036 *adorned/metals*
1037 *margery, pearl (l. 206)*
1038 *perfect/fades*
1039 *express*
1040 *children/following*
1041 *birth fortunes*
1042 *oldest*
1043 *gleamed/streets*
1044 *needed/neither/moon*

(88) Of sunne ne mone had thay no nede;   1045
      The self God was her lombe-lyght,
      The Lombe her lantyrne, wythouten drede;
      Thurgh hym blysned the borgh al bryght.
      Thurgh woghe and won my lokyng yede,
      For sotyle cler noght lette no lyght.   1050
      The hyghe trone ther moght ye hede
      Wyth alle the apparaylmente umbepyghte,
      As John the appostel in termes tyghte;
      The hyghe Godes self hit set upone.
      A rever of the trone ther ran outryghte   1055
      Was bryghter then bothe the sunne and mone.

(89) Sunne ne mone schon never so swete
      As that foysoun flode out of that flet;
      Swythe hit swange thurgh uch a strete
      Wythouten fylthe other galle other glet.   1060
      Kyrk therinne was non yete,
      Chapel ne temple that ever was set;
      The Almyghty was her mynster mete,
      The Lombe the sakerfyse ther to refet.
      The yates stoken was never yet,   1065
      Bot evermore upen at uche a lone;
      Ther entres non to take reset
      That beres any spot anunder mone.

(90) The mone may therof acroche no myghte;
      To spotty ho is, of body to grym,   1070
      And also ther ne is never nyght.
      What schulde the mone ther compas clym
      And to even wyth that worthly lyght
      That schynes upon the brokes brym?
      The planetes arn in to pover a plyght,   1075
      And the self sunne ful fer to dym.
      Aboute that water arn tres ful schym,
      That twelve frytes of lyf con bere ful sone;
      Twelve sythes on yer thay beren ful frym.
      And renowles nwe in uche a mone.   1080

(91) Anunder mone so gret merwayle
      No fleschly hert ne myght endeure,
      As quen I blusched upon that bayle,
      So ferly therof was the fasure.

1046 *very/lamplight*
1047 *lantern*
1048 *blazed*
1049 *wall/dwelling/went*
1050 *subtly/obstructed*
1051 *throne/heed, perceive*
1052 *adornment/set around, adorned*
1053 *set forth*
1054 *himself*
1055 *river/from/throne/right out*

1058 *full/flood/floor*
1059 *Swiftly*
1060 *or . . . or/debris*
1061 *Church/yet*

1063 *minster*
1064 *sacrifice/refresh*
1065 *stuck (closed), shut*
1066 *open/lane*
1067 *refuge*
1068 *under/moon*

1069 *acquire*
1070 *Too/too grim, ugly*

1072 *Why/(a) circle*
1073 *And be even, vie/worthy*
1074 *brook's/brim, edge*
1075 *are/too/poor*
1076 *very/far/too/dim*
1077 *bright*
1078 *fruits/soon*
1079 *times/abundantly*
1080 *renew/anew, again*

1081 *marvel*

1083 *glimpsed/domain (l. 442)*
1084 *marvelous/fashion*

I stod as stylle as dased quayle   1085
For ferly of that freuch fygure,
That felde I nawther reste ne travayle,
So was I ravyste wyth glymme pure.
For I dar say wyth conciens sure,
Hade bodyly burne abiden that bone,   1090
Thagh alle clerkes hym hade in cure,
His lyf were loste anunder mone.

XIX

(92) Ryght as the maynful mone con rys
Er thenne the day-glem dryve al doun,
So sodanly on a wonder wyse   1095
I was war of a prosessyoun.
This noble cité of ryche enpryse
Was sodanly ful wythouten sommoun
Of such vergynes in the same gyse
That was my blysful anunder croun;   1100
And coronde wern alle of the samc fasoun,
Depaynt in perles and wedes qwyte;
In uchones breste was bounden boun
The blysful perle wyth gret delyt.

(93) Wyth gret delyt thay glod in fere   1105
On golden gates that glent as glasse;
Hundreth thowsandes I wot ther were,
And alle in sute her livrés wasse;
Tor to knaw the gladdest chere.
The Lombe byfore con proudly passe   1110
Wyth hornes seven of red golde cler;
As praysed perles his wedes wasse.
Towarde the throne thay trone a tras.
Thagh thay wern fele, no pres in plyt,
Bot mylde as maydenes seme at mas,   1115
So drow thay forth wyth gret delyt.

(94) Delyt that hys come encroched
To much hit were of for to melle
Thise aldermen, quen he aproched,
Grovelyng to his fete thay felle.   1120
Legyounes of aungeles togeder voched
Ther kesten ensens of swete smelle.
Then glory and gle was nwe abroched;

1085 *dazed/quail*
1086 *wonder/noble/form, scene*
1087 *felt*
1088 *raptured/glimmer, radiance*

1090 *earthly/being/boon*
1091 *care*

1093 *mighty/rise*

1095 *suddenly/wondrous/way*
1096 *aware/procession*
1097 *emprise*
1098 *summon(ing)*
1099 *virgins/guise*
1100 *blissful (one)*

1102 *Arrayed/white*
1103 *bound/fast*

1105 *glided/company*
1106 *In/ways, streets*
1107 *know*
1108 *alike/livery/was*
1109 *Difficult/face*

1112 *prized, precious*
1113 *went/way*
1114 *many/press/array*

1116 *drew*

1117 *coming/brought*
1118 *Too/tell (l. 797)*
1119 *elders*

1121 *Legions/angels/summoned*
1122 *cast/incense*
1123 *newly/expressed*

Al songe to love that gay juelle.
The steven moght stryke thurgh the urthe to helle   1125
That the vertues of heven of joye endyte.
To love the Lombe is meyny in melle
Iwysse I laght a gret delyt.

(95) Delit the Lombe for to devise
Wyth much mervayle in mynde went.   1130
Best was he, blythest, and moste to pryse,
That ever I herde of speche spent;
So worthyly whyt wern wedes hys,
His lokes symple, hymself so gent.
Bot a wounde ful wyde and weete con wyse   1135
Anende hys hert, thurgh hyde torente.
Of his quyte syde his blod outsprent.
Alas, thoght I, who did that spyt?
Ani breste for bale aght haf forbrent
Er he therto hade had delyt.   1140

(96) The Lombe delyt non lyste to wene.
Thagh he were hurt and wounde hade,
In his sembelaunt was never sene,
So wern his glentes gloryous glade.
I loked among his meyny schene   1145
How thay wyth lyf wern laste and lade;
Then saw I ther my lyttel quene
That I wende had standen by me in sclade.
Lorde, much of mirthe was that ho made
Among her feres that was so quyt!   1150
That syght me gart to thenk to wade
For luf-longyng in gret delyt.

XX
(97) Delyt me drof in yghe and ere,
My manes mynde to maddyng malte;
Quen I segh my frely, I wolde be there,   1155
Byyonde the water thagh ho were walte.
I thoght that nothyng myght me dere
To fech me bur and take me halte,
And to start in the strem schulde non me stere,
To swymme the remnaunt, thagh I ther swalte.   1160
Bot of that munt I was bitalt;

1124 *sang/praise*
1125 *sound*
1126 *emit*
1127 *amid his company* (cf. l. 1118)
1128 *Certainly/took*

1132 "(*On whom*) *I ever . . ."*

1135 *wet/appear*
1136 *Below/all torn*
1137 *spurted out*
1138 *spite*
1139 *ought* (*to*) *have burned*

1141 *wished/doubt*

1143 *semblance*
1144 *glances/glad*

1146 *loaded/laden*

1148 *thought/stood/valley*

1150 *companions*
1151 *caused* (l. 331)/*think, want*

1153 *eye*
1154 *madness/melted*
1155 *fair* (*one*)/*wanted* (*to*)
1156 *kept*
1157 *hinder*
1158 (*a*) *blow/halt*
1159 *restrain*
1160 *died*
1161 *intention/shaken*

When I schulde start in the strem astraye,
Out of that caste I was bycalt:
Hit was not at my Prynces paye.

(98) Hit payed hym not that I so flonc   1165
Over mervelous meres, so mad arayde.
Of raas thagh I were rasch and ronk,
Yet rapely therinne I was restayed.
For, ryght as I sparred unto the bonc,
That brathe out of my drem me brayde.   1170
Then wakned I in that erber wlonk;
My hede upon that hylle was layde
Ther as my perle to grounde strayd.
I raxled, and fel in gret affray,
And, sykyng, to myself I sayd,   1175
'Now al be to that Prynces paye.'

(99) Me payed ful ille to be outfleme
So sodenly of that fayre regioun,
Fro alle tho syghtes so quyke and queme.
A longeyng hevy me strok in swone,   1180
And rewfully thenne I con to reme:
'O perle,' quod I, 'of rych renoun,
So was hit me dere that thou con deme
In this veray avysyoun!
If hit be veray and soth sermoun   1185
That thou so stykes in garlande gay,
So wel is me in thys doel-doungoun
That thou art to that Prynses paye.'

(100) To that Prynces paye hade I ay bente,
And yerned no more then was me gyven,   1190
And halden me ther in trwe entent,
As the perle me prayed that was so thryven,
As helde, drawen to Goddes present,
To mo of his mysterys I hade ben dryven;
Bot ay wolde man of happe more hente   1195
Then moghte by ryght upon hem clyven.
Therfore my ioye was sone toriven,
And I kaste of kythes that lastes aye.
Lorde, mad hit arn that agayn the stryven,
Other proferen the oght agayn thy paye.   1200

1162 *astray*
1163 *purpose/called*
1164 *to/pleasure*

1165 *rushed*
1166 *intentioned*
1167 *In/rush/impetuous*
1168 *quickly/restrained*
1169 *rushed/bank*
1170 *brashness/roused*
1171 *fair*

1174 *roused/confusion*
1175 *sighing*

1177 *outcast*

1179 *lifelike/pleasant*

1181 *lament*

1183 *reveal*
1184 *true/vision*

1186 *are so set*
1187 *dole-dungeon*

1189 *bowed*
1190 *yearned (for)/than*

1194 *led*
1195 *joy/seize*
1196 *adhere*
1197 *joy/destroyed*
1198 *cast/from/realms*
1199 *they/who/against/strive*
1200 *Or/proffer/aught*

(101) To pay the Prince other sete saghte
       Hit is ful ethe to the god Krystyin;
       For I haf founden hym, bothe day and naghte,
       A God, a Lorde, a frende ful fyin.
       Over this hyul this lote I laghte,   1205
       For pyty of my perle, enclyin,
       And sythen to God I hit bytaghte
       In Krystes dere blessyng and myn,
       That in the forme of bred and wyn
       The preste uus schewes uch a daye.   1210
       He gef uus to be his homly hyne
       Ande precious perles unto his pay.   Amen.   Amen.

SUPPLEMENTARY MATERIAL

See p. 138.

1201 *please/or/reconcile*
1202 *easy*
1203 *night*

1205 *On/hill/destiny/received*
1206 *inclined*
1207 *then, afterward/gave up*

1211 *servants* (l. 632)

LYRICS

THE BLACKSMITHS

Swarte smekyd smethes smateryd wyth
   smoke,
Dryve me to deth wyth den of here dyntes.
Swech noys on nyghtes ne herd men never;
What knavene cry and clateryng of
   knockes!
The cammede kongons cryen after 'col,
   col!'
And blowen here bellewys that al here
   brayn brestes.
'Huf, puf!' seyth that on; 'haf, paf!' that
   other.
Thei spyttyn and spraulyn and spellyn
   many spelles,
They gnauen and gnacchen, thei gronys to-
   gydere,
And holdyn hem hote wyth here hard ham-
   ers.
Of a bole hyde ben here barm-fellys;
Here schankes ben schakeled for the fere-
   flunderys;

Hevy hamerys thei han that hard ben han-
   dled,
Stark strokes thei stryken on a stelyd stokke.
'Lus, bus! las, das!' rowtyn be rowe.
Sweche dolful a dreme the devyl it todryve.

The mayster longith a lityl and lascheth a
   lesse,

Black/smoked/
   smiths
din/their/blows
Such
knaves'

pug-nosed/change-
   lings
bellows/"so that their
   brains all burst"
one

spit/sprawl/tell/
   tales
gnaw/gnash/groan

10   *hold, keep/them-*
   selves/hot
bull/lap-skin, aprons
shackled, protected
   with greaves/fire-
   flinders, sparks
hammers/have

steeled stock, anvil
15   *(they) beat/by turn*
noise/(may) the
   devil/destroy
master (-smith)/
   elongates/little
   (piece)/hammers/
   lesser (piece)

Twyneth hem tweyn, and towchith a tre-
    ble.

> twines/two (to-
> gether)/touches
> (?with his ham-
> mer)/treble
> (note)

'Tik, tak! hic, hac! tiket, taket! tyk, tak!
Lus, bus! lus, das!' swych lyf thei ledyn,   20
Alle clothemerys, Cryst hem gyve sorwe!

> mare-clothers, armor-
> makers/sorrow

May no man for brenwaterys on nyght han
    hys rest!

> burn-waters*/have

SUMER IS ICUMEN IN

Sumer is icumen in,
Lhude sing cuccu!

> Loud/cuckoo

Groweth sed and bloweth med
And springth the wde nu.

> blossoms, vb./
> meadow

Sing cuccu!   5

> wood

Awe bleteth after lomb,

> Ewe

Lhouth after calve cu,

> Loweth/cow

Bulluc sterteth, bucke verteth.

> leaps/breaks wind

Murie sing cuccu!
Cuccu, cuccu,   10
Wel singes thu cuccu.
Ne swik thu naver nu!

> stop/never

Sing cuccu nu, Sing cuccu! ⎫
Sing cuccu, Sing cuccu nu! ⎭ *Pes*

I SYNG OF A MAYDEN

I syng of a mayden
That is makeles;

> matchless, mateless

Kyng of alle kynges
To here sone sche ches.

> "For her son she
> chose"

He cam also stylle   5

> came/as

Ther his moder was

> Where

As dew in aprylle,
That fallyt on the gras.

> falls

---

22 M.E.D.: "nickname for a blacksmith who plunges hot iron into water."

He cam also stylle
To his moderes bowr   10   *bower*
As dew in aprille,
That fallyt on the flour.

He cam also stylle
Ther his moder lay
As dew in aprille,   15
That fallyt on the spray.   *branch, twig*

Moder and mayden
Was never non but sche;
Wel may swych a lady   *such*
Godes moder be.   20

THE CORPUS CHRISTI CAROL

Lully, lulley, lully, lulley,
The faucon hath borne my make away.   *falcon/mate*

He bar him up, he bar him down,
He bar him into an orchard broun.

Lully, lulley, etc.

In that orchard ther was an halle
That was hanged wyth purpre and palle.   *purple/rich cloth*

And in that halle ther was a bed,   5
It was hanged wyth gold so red.

And in that bed ther lythe a knight,
His woundes bledyng day and nyght.

By the beddes side ther kneleth a may,   *maid*
And she wepeth bothe nyght and day.   10

And by that beddes side ther stondeth a ston,
Corpus Christi wreten theron.   *written*

OF A ROSE, A LOVELY ROSE

Of a rose, a lovely rose,
Of a rose I syng a song.

Lyth and lystyn, both old and ying,   *Listen, hearken/*
How the rose begane to spryng;   *everybody*
A fayrer rose to owr lekyng   *our/liking*
    Sprong ther never in kynges lond.

V branchis of that rose ther ben,   5   *Five*
The wych ben both feyer and chene;   *"Which were both*
Of a maydyn, Mary, hevyn quene,   *fair and shiny"*
  Ought of hyr bosum the branch sprong. *Out*

The first branch was of gret honour,
That blyssed Mary shuld ber the flour,   10
Ther cam an angell ought hevyn toure,   *"out of heaven's*
  To breke the develes bond.   *tower"*

The secund branch was gret of myght,
That sprong upon Cristmes nyght;
The sterre shone and lemed bryght,   15 *star/gleamed*
  That man schuld se it both day and
    nyght.

The third branch can spryng and spred;   *began (to)*
Iii kynges than to branch gan led   *then*
Tho to Owr Lady in hure chyldbed;
  Into Bethlem that branch sprong ryght. 20

The fourth branch, it sprong to hell,
The develes powr for to fell,
That no soule therin shuld dwell,
  The brannch so blessedfully sprong.

The fifth branch, it was so swote,   25 *sweet*
Yt sprong to hevyn, both croppe and rote, *top/root*
In every ball to ben owr bott,   *bale, difficulty/boot,*
  So blessedly yt sprong.   *cure*

THE MOURNING OF AN HARE

Bi a forest as I gan fare,
Walkyng al myselven alone,
I hard a mornyng of an hare,   *heard*
Roufully sche made here mone.   4 *her moan, lament*

Dereworth God, how schal I leve   *Dear/live*
And leyd my lyve in lond?   *lead*
Fro dale to doune I am idreve;   *driven*
I not where I may syt or stond.   8 *neg. + know*

I may nother rest nor slepe   *neither*
By no vallay that is so derne,   *secluded*
Nor no covert may me kepe,
But ever I rene fro herne to herne. 12 *run/corner*

Honteris will not heyre ther mase   *Hunters/hear/mass*
In hope of huntyng for to wend;   *go*
They cowpullyt ther howndes more and   *couple/less*
    lase,
And bryngyth theme to the feldys ende.   16

Anon as they commyth me behynde,
I loke and syt ful style and lowe;   *still*
The furst man that me doth fynde,
Anon he cryit, "So howe, so hoowe!"   20

At wynter in the depe snowe
Men wyll me seche for to trace,
And by steppes I am iknowe,   *known*
And followyt me fro place to place.   24

And yf I syt and crope the kole,   *crop the cabbage*
And the wyfe be in the waye,
Anon sche wyll swere, "by cokkes soule,
There is an hare in my haye!"   28

As sone as I can ren to the laye,   *open field*
Anon the greyhondys wyl me have;
My bowele beth ithrowe awaye,
And I ame bore home on a stave.   32   *staff*

ALAS, ALAS THE WYLE, THAT EVER I COWDE
DAUNCE

Ladd Y the daunce a myssomur day;   *Led/I/midsummer*
Y made smale trippus soth for to say.   *trips, steps*
Iak oure haly watur clerk com be the way,   *Jack/holy/by*
And he lokede me upon, he thout that Y
    was gay.
Thout yc on no gyle.   5   *Thought/I/guile*
    Alas, alas, the wyle!   *while*
    Thout Y on no gyle,
    So have Y god chaunce.   *(May) I have good*
    Alas, alas, the wyle,   *fortune*
    That ever I cowde daunce.

Iak, oure haly watur clerk, the yonge strip-
    pelyng,
For the chesone of me he com to the ryng,   *"Because (of me)"*

And he trippede on my to, and made a
    twynkelyng;   *toe/wink*
Ever he cam ner, he sparet for no thynge.   *near/spared*
Thout Y on no gyle.   10
Burden: Alas, alas, the wyle, etc.

Iak, ic wot, priyede in my fayre face.   *know/pried, stared*
He thout me ful worly, so have Y god grace.   *attractive*
As we turndun owre daunce in a narw   *turned/narrow*
    place,
Iak bed me the mouth—a cyssynge ther was.   *bid/kissing*
Thout Y on no gyle.   15
Burden

Iak tho began to rowne in my ere,   *whisper*
'Loke that thou be privey and grante that
    thou the bere
A peyre wyth glovus ic ha to thyn were.'   *pair/white/gloves/*
'Gremercy, Iacke,' that was myn answere.   *have/(for) wear-*
Thout Y on no gyle.   20   *ing*
Burden

Sone aftur evensong Iak me mette,
'Com hom aftur thy glovus that ic the   *promised*
    byhette.'
Wan ic to his chambur com, doun he me
    sette.
From hym mytte Y nat go wan we were   *might/when*
    mette.
Thout Y on no gyle.   25
Burden

Schetus and chalonus, ic wot, were   *Sheets/blanket**
    yspredde.
Foresothe tho Iak and ic wenten to bedde.
He prikede and he pransede, nolde he never   *"as if he would never*
    lynne.   *cease"*
Yt was the murgust nyt that ever I cam inne.   *merriest/night*
Thout Y on no gyle.   30
Burden

Wan Iak had don, tho he rong the belle.   *then/?spread the*
Al nyght ther he made me to dwelle.   *news*

---

26 M.E.D.: "a figured woolen material named for Chalons-sur-Marne."

Oft, Y trewe, we haddun yserved the   *Truly/ragged*
  reagged devel of helle;
Of othur smale burdus kep Y nout to telle.   *frivolities, jokes*
Thout Y on no gyle.   35
Burden

The other day at prime Y com hom, as ic   *first hour/suppose*
  wene.
Meth Y my dame, coppud and kene,   *Met/crabby/sharp*
'Sey thou stronge strumpeth ware hastu   *strumpet, harlot/*
  bene?   *have you*
Thy trippyng and thy dauncyng wel it wol
  be sene.'
Thout Y on no gyle.   40
Burden

Ever bi on and by on my damme reched me   *Continually/dealt/*
  clot.   *clout, blow*
Ever Y ber it privey wyle that Y mouth,   *might*
Tyl my gurdul aros; my wombe wax out.   *girdle/waxed, grew*
'Evel yspunne yern ever it wole out.'   *Evilly, badly/spun/*
Thout Y on no gyle.   45   *ravel out*
Burden

HOLLY AND IVY

Nay, Ivy, nay, / hyt shal not be, iwys;   *indeed*
Let Holy hafe the maystry, / as the   *have/mastery*
  maner ys.

Holy stond in the hall, / fayre to behold;
Ivy stond without the dore; / she ys ful sore   *outside*
  acold.

Holy and hys mery men, / they dawnsyn   *dance*
  and they syng;
Ivy and hur maydenys, / they wepyn and   *maidens/weep/suf-*
  they wryng.   *fer*

Ivy hath a kybe; / she kaght yt with the   5   *chilblain/caught*
  colde;
So mot they all haf ay, / that with Ivy hold.   *may/always*
Holy hat berys / as rede as any rose;   *has/berries*

The foster, the hunters / kepe hem fro the
  doos.   *forester/does*

Ivy hath berys / as blake as any slo;   *black*
Ther com the oule / and ete hym as she goo.   10   *owl/goes*

Holy hath byrdys, / a ful fayre flok,   *birds*
The nyghtyngale, the poppynguy, / the   *parrot/gentle/lark*
  gayntyl lavyrok.

Gode Ivy, / what byrdys ast thou?   *have*
Non but the howlat, / that kreye, 'How,   *owlet/cries*
  how!'

FOWELES IN THE FRITH

  Foweles in the frith,   *Fowls/wood*
  The fisses in the flod,   *fish/flood, sea*
  And I mon waxe wod.   *must/grow/mad*
  Mulch sorw I walke with   *Much/sorrow*
  For beste of bon and blod.   *(the) best/bone/*
                                                          blood

NOW SPRINGS THE SPRAY

  Nou sprinkes the sprai,   *Now/springs/spray,*
  Al for love icche am so seek   *twigs*
  That slepen I ne mai.   *I/sick*

  Als I me rode this endre dai   *"As I rode out the*
                                                          other day"

  O mi playinge,   *On*
  Seih I hwar a litel mai   *Saw/where/maid*
  Bigan to singe,
  'The clot him clinge!   5   *"May the clod, earth*
                                                          (of grave) . . ."
  Wai es him i love-longinge   *Woe/(to) him*
                                                          (who)/(is) in
  Sal libben ai!'   *Shall/ever*
  Refrain

  Son iche herde that mirie note,   *"As soon as I"*
  Thider I drogh.   *Thither/drew*
  I fonde hire in an herber swot   10   *arbor/sweet*
  Under a bogh,

With ioie inogh.   *joy/enough*
Son I asked, 'Thou mirie mai,
Hwi sinkestou ai?'   *Why/sing you*
Refrain

Than answerde that maiden swote   15
Midde wordes fewe,
'Mi lemman me haves bihot   *lover/promised*
Of love trewe;
He chaunges anewe.   *once again*
Yif I mai, it shal him rewe   20   *If/he'll rue it*
Bi this dai.'
Refrain

Ubi sunt qui ante nos fuerunt?
WHERE BETH THEY BIFOREN US WEREN?

Where beth they biforen us weren,   *they (who)/lived*
Houndes ladden and havekes beren   *(who) led hounds/*
                                                 bore, carried
                                                 hawks
And hadden feld and wode?   *owned/fields/woods*
The riche levedies in hoere bour,   *ladies/their/bower*
That wereden gold in hoere tressour   5   *wore/headdress*
With hoere brightte rode?   *face*

Eten and drounken and maden hem glad;   *(they) ate/drank/*
                                                 made merry
Hoere lif was al with gamen ilad;   *led, "conducted in*
                                                 pleasure"
Men keneleden hem biforen,   *knelt*
They beren hem wel swithe heye,   10   *themselves/very/*
And in a twincling of on eye   *high*
Hoere soules weren forloren.   *utterly lost*

Were is that lawing and that song,   *laughing*
That trayling and that proude yong,   *parading/going, gait*
Tho havekes and tho houndes?   15
Al that ioye is went away,   *joy*
That wele is comen to weylaway,   *woe*
To manie harde stoundes.   *times*

Hoere paradis hy nomen here,   *paradise/they/took*
And nou they lien in helle ifere, 20   *together*

The fuir hit brennes hevere. *fire/burns/ever*
Long is 'ay' and long is 'ho,' *alas/oh*
Long is 'wy' and long is 'wo.' *woe*
Thennes ne cometh they nevere. *Thence*

Drey here, man, thenne if thou wilt, 25 *Endure, suffer*
A luitel pine that me the bit, *little/pain/men/bid*
Withdrau thine eyses ofte, *eases, comforts*
They thi pine be ounrede; *Though/severe*
And thou thenke on thi mede *If/meed, reward*
Hit sal the thinken softe. 30 *It (pain)/shall/seem*
to you

If that fend, that foule thing, *fiend*
Thorou wikke roun, thorou fals egging, *Through/wicked/*
Nethere the haveth icast, *whisper/urging*
Oup and be god chaunpioun! *"Has cast you down"*
Stond, ne fal namore adoun 35 *Up/champion*
For a luytel blast.

Thou tak the rode to thi staf, *rood, cross*
And thenk on Him that thereonne yaf *gave*
His lif that wes so lef. *dear*
He hit yaf for the; thou yelde hit Him, 40 *"you repay him for*
it"
Ayein His fo that staf thou nim, *Against/foe/take*
(up)
And wrek Him of that thef. *wreck, avenge/thief*

Of rightte bileve, thou nim that sheld, *belief/shield*
The wiles that thou best in that feld *While/are/field*
Thin hond to strenkthen fonde, 45 *Your/try*
And kep thy fo with staves ord, *oppose/end*
And do that traytre seien that word. *make/say/word (of*
surrender)
Biget that murie londe. *Get, obtain*

Thereinne is day withouten night,
Withouten ende strenkthe and might, 50
And wreche of everich fo, *vengeance/every*
Mid God himselwen eche lif, *himself/eternal*
And pes and rest withoute strif,
Wele withouten wo.

Mayden moder, hevene quene, 55
Thou might and const and owest ot bene *can, are able/ought*

Oure sheld ayein the fende.

Help ous sunne for to flen,   *"Help us to flee sin"*

That we moten thi sone iseen   *may/son/see*

In ioye withouten hende.   60   *end* (cf. l. 21, *hevere*
                               'ever')

NOU GOTH SONNE UNDER WOD

Nou goth sonne under wod;   *sun/wood* (of the

Me reweth, Marie, thi faire rode.   *cross*)

Nou goth sonne under tre;   *rue, feel pity/face*

Me reweth, Marie, thi sone and the.

ERTHE TOC OF ERTHE

Erthe toc of erthe erthe wyth woh,   *Earth/took/woe*

Erthe other erthe to the erthe droh,   *drew*

Erthe leyde erthe in erthene throh;   *trough*

Tho hevede erthe of erthe erthe ynoh.   *Then/had/enough*

THE AGINCOURT CAROL

[On the occasion of Henry V's victory]   (with music)

   Deo gracias anglia,   *"Render thanks to
                              God,*

   Redde pro victoria.   *England, for victory"*

Owre kynge went forth to Normandy,

With grace and myght of chyvalry;

Ther God for hym wrought mervelusly,

Wherfore Englonde may calle and cry,

   Deo gracias!   5

He sette a sege, the sothe for to say,   *siege*

To Harflu toune with ryal aray;   *Harfleur* town/*royal*

That toune he wan and made afray,   *won*

That Fraunce shal rywe tyl domesday,   *rue*

   Deo gracias!   10

Than went our kynge with alle his oste   *host*

Thorwe Fraunce, for alle the Frenshe boste, *boast*

He spared no drede of lest ne moste,   *least*

Tyl he come to Agincourt coste,

   Deo gracias!   15

Than for soth that knyght comely,
In Agincourt feld he faught manly;
Thorw grace of God most myghty,
He had bothe the felde and the victory.
 Deo gracias!   20

There dukys and erlys, lorde and barone   *dukes/earls*
Were take and slayne, and that wel sone;   *soon*
And summe were ladde into Lundone,   *led/London*
With ioye and merthe and grete renone.   *joy/renown*
 Deo gracias!   25

Now gracious God, he save oure kynge,
His peple and alle his wel-wyllynge;   *well-wishers*
Yef hym gode lyfe and gode endynge,   *Give*
That we with merth nowe savely synge,   *may/safely*
 Deo gracias!   30

SUPPLEMENTARY MATERIAL

1. *Music of the Medieval Court and Countryside*, New York Pro Musica, Noah Greenberg, Dir. (Decca Records, DL 9400).
2. Comparison of ballads with medieval affinities such as "Kemp Owyne," "Lady Isabel and the Elf-Knight," and "Thomas Rymer."
3. See also the references on pp. 527–28.

BRUT

(A) THE APPORTIONING OF LEAR'S KINGDOM

Bladud hafde enne sunne. Leir wes ihaten.
Efter his fader daie, he heold this drihliche lond,
Somed an his live sixti winter.
He makede ane riche burh, thurh radfulle his crafte,
And he heo lette nemnen, efter him seolvan.   5
Kaer Leir hehte the burh—leof heo wes than kinge—
Tha we an ure leod-quide Leirchestre clepiath.
Yeare, a than holde dawen heo wes swithe athel burh,
And seoththen ther seh toward, swithe muchel seorwe,
That heo wes al forfaren, thurh there leodene uæl.   10
Sixti winter hefde Leir this lond al to welden.
The king hefde threo dohtren by his drihliche quen;
Nefde he nenne sune (ther fore he warth sari)
His manscipe to halden buten tha threo dohtren.
The ældeste dohter haihte Gornoille, tha other Ragau, tha thridde   15
    Cordoille.
Heo wes tha yungeste suster, a wliten alre vairest.
Heo wes hire fader al swa leof swa his aghene lif.
Tha ældede the king, and wakede an athelan,
And he hine bi thohte wet he don mahte
Of his kineriche æfter his deie.   20
He seide to himsulven that that uvel wes:
"Ic wlle mine riche todon allen minen dohtren
And yeven hem mine kinetheode and twemen mine bearnen.
Ac ærst ic wille fondien whulchere beo mi beste freond,
And heo scal habbe that beste del of mine drihlichen lond."   25
Thus the king thohte and ther æfter he worhte.
He clepede Gornoille, hes guthfulle dohter,
Ut of hire bure to hire fader deore,
And theus spac the alde king ther he on æthelen seat,
"Sei me, Gornoille, sothere worden.   30
Swithe dure theo eart me; hu leof æm ich the?

1 *had/a/son/called*
2 *noble*
3 *Together/in/life/sixty years*
4 *burgh/wise*
5 *"let it be named"*
6 *was called/beloved/(to) the*
7 *Then/our language/Leicester/called (it)*
8 *(Of) yore/in the old days/very/noble*
9 *after/came to it/very/sorrow*
10 *destroyed/slaughter (O.E. wæl) of the people*
11 *wield, control*
12 *three/daughters/noble (l. 2)*
13 *neg. + had/neg. + a/was/sorry*
14 *"to receive his power except . . ."*
15 *was called/Goneril/Regan/Cordelia*

16 *She/beauty/fairest of all*
17 *(to) her father/as dear as/own*
18 *grew old/weakened in power*
19 *"thought to himself what he might do"*
20 *Concerning/kingdom/day*
21 *"that which was evil"*
22 *I/will/reich/divide (among) all*
23 *give/them/kingdom/divide (among)/children*
24 *But/first/find (out)/which/is/friend*
25 *part (deal)*
26 *"and according he wrought"*
27 *called/good*
28 *Out/bower, chamber/dear*
29 *thus/spoke/old/where/sat in state*
30 *Speak (to) me/in true words*
31 *Very/dear/are (to)/how/beloved/(to) you*

Hu mochel worth leste thu me to walden kineriche?"
Gornoille was swithe wær, swa beoth wifmen wel ihwær,
And seide ane lesinge heore fædere thon king,
"Leofe fæder dure, swa bide ich godes are,   35
Swa helpe me Apollin (for min ilæfe is al on him),
That levere theo ært me æne thane this world al clane.
And yet ic the wlle speken wit, theou ært leovere thene mi lif,
And this ich sucge the to seothe, thu mith me wel ileve."
Leir the king ilefde his doster læisinge,   40
And thas ænsware yef that wæs the olde king,
"Ich the, Gornoille, seuge, leove dohter dure,
God scal beon thi meda for thira gretinge.
Ic eam for mire ældde swthe unbalded
And thou me levoste swthe, mare than is on live.   45
Ich wille mi dirhliche lond a throe al to-dalen.
Thin is tha beste deal. Thu ært mi dohter deore,
And scalt habben to laverd min alre beste thein
Theo ich mai vinden in mine kinne-londe."
Æfter spac the olde kinge wit his dohter,   50
"Leove dohter Regau, wæt seist tu me to ræide?
Seie thu bifore mire dughden heo dure ich am the an herten.
Tha answærde mid rætfulle worden,
"Al that is on live nis me swa dure
Swa me is thin an lime, forthe min aghene lif."   55
Ah heo ne seide nathing soth, no more thenne hiire suster.
Alle hire lisinge hire vader ilefede.
Tha answarede the king—hiis doghter him icwemde—
"Thea thridde del of mine londe ich bitake the an honde.
Thu scalt nime loverd ther the is alre leowost."   60
Tha yet nolde the leod-king his sothscipe bilæven.
He hehte cumen him biforen his dohter Gordoille.
Heo was alre yungest, of sothe yærr witelest,
And the king heo lovede more thanne ba tueie the othre.
Cordoille iherde tha lasinge the hire sustren seiden thon kinge. 65
Nom hire leaffulne huie, that heo lighen nolden,
Hire fader heo wolde suge seoth, were him lef, were him lath.
Theo queth the alde king—unrad him fulded—
"Theren ich wlle of the, Cordoille,
Sua the helpe Appollin, hu deore the beo lif min."   70
Tha answarede Cordoille, lude and no wiht stille,
Mid gomene and mid lehtre to hire fader leve,
"Theo art me leof al so mi fæder, and ich the al so thi dohter.
Ich habbe to the sohfaste love, for we buoth swithe isibbe,

32 *much/believe/wield, control (in)*
33 *wary/as are women/everywhere*
34 *told a lie (to)*
35 *pray/mercy*
36 *belief*
37 *dearer/(to) me/clean, completely*

39 *say/in truth/may/believe*
40 *daughter's/lie*
41 *answer/gave/(he) who*
42 *say, tell*
43 *Good/meed, reward/thy, your/greeting*
44 *because of/my old age/very/enfeebled*
45 *"you love me very (much)"/more/in life*
46 *"divide my land in three (parts)"*

48 *for (a) lord/"the best of all my thanes"*
49 *That/find/kingdom*
50 *"with his (second) daughter"*
51 *"what say you to me for advice"*
52 *Say/my people/how/(to) you*
53 *wise (l. 4.)*
54 *in life/neg. + is*
55 *"As one of your limbs is"/before/own*
56 *But/than/her*
57 *lie/father*
58 *pleased*
59 *The third part/give/in*
60 *take/(a) lord/where/most pleasing of all*
61 *"The king still wouldn't leave his foolishness"*
62 *ordered*
63 *very/(most) wise, gifted*
64 *both/two*
65 *heard the lies which*
66 *(She) took/faithful/oath/wouldn't lie*
67 *say/"whether it was dear or loathful to him"*
68 *quoth/old/he followed bad counsel*
69 *Hear*
70 *So help you/how/(to) you*
71 *loud/not (a) whit, bit*
72 *game/laughter*
73 *(dear) as . . . as*
74 *soothfast, true/are very close (cf. N.E. sibling)*

And swa ich ibide are, ich wille the suge mare: 75
Al swa muchel thu bist woruh, swa thu velden ært,
And al swa muchel swa thu havest, men the wllet luvien.
For sone heo bith ilaghed, the mon the lutel ah."
Thus seide the mæiden Cordoille, and seoththen set swthe stille.
Tha iwarthe the king wærth, for he nes theo noht iquemed,   80
And wende on is thonke that hit weren for untheawe
That he hire weore swa unwourth, that heo hine nolde iwurthi
Swa hire twa sustren, the ba somed læsinge speken.
The king Leir iwerthe swa blac swlch hit a blac cloth weoren;
Iwærth his hude and his heowe, for he was suthe ihærmed.   85
Mid thære wræththe he wes isweved, that he feol iswowen.
Late theo he up fusde; that mæiden wes afeared.
Tha hit alles up brac—hit wes uvel that he spac—
"Hærne, Cordoille! ich the telle wlle mine wille.
Of mine dohtren thu were me durest; nu thu eært me arle læthest.   90
Ne scalt thu næver halden dale of mine lande,
Ah mine dohtren ich wlle delen mine riche,
And thu scalt worthen warchen and wonien in wansithe.
For navere ich ne wende that thu me woldes thus scanden.
Thar fore thu scalt beon dæd, ich wene. Fligh ut of min eæh-sene.   95
Thine sustren sculen habben mi kinelond, and this me is iqueme.
The duc of Cornwaile scal habbe Gornoille,
And the Scottene king Regau that scone,
And ic hem yeve al tha winne the ich æm waldinge over.
And al the alde king dude swa he hafvede idemed.   100
Ofte wes then mæidene wa and nævre wors thenne tha.
Wa hire wes on mode for hire fader wærthe.
Heo wende into hire boure, thar heo ofte sætte sare
For heo nolde lighen hire fadder leove.

- -

Tha nom tha olde king æthele his meiden   105
Mid seolven hire clathes and lette heo forthe lithen
Ofer tha stremes—hire fader hire wes sturne.
Aganippus the Frennsce king under-feng this meiden child,
(Al hiis folc hit wes iqueme) and makeden heo to quene.

(B) ARTHUR'S LAST BATTLE

Arthur for to Cornwale mid unimete ferde.
Modred that iherde, and him toyeines heolde
Mid unimete folke; ther weore monie væie.
Uppen there Tambre heo tuhten to-gadere.

75 *expect/mercy* (l. 35)/*say/more*
76 "*You are worth as much as you possess*"
77 "*Men will love you according to how much you have*"
78 *soon/is loathed/who owns little*
79 *afterward/very*
80 *became/wroth/wasn't pleased* (l. 58)
81 *thought* (*to himself*)/*contempt*
82 (*to*) *her/unworthy/she/him/esteem*
83 *two/sisters/both of whom together*
84 *became as black as* (*if*)
85 *hide/hue/very/harmed, grieved*
86 *stupefied/*(*so*)*that/fell in* (*a*) *swoon*
87 *Later/then/rose*
88 *all/broke* (*forth*)/*evil*
89 *Hearken*
90 *dearest/are/loathest of all to me*
91 *hold* (*a*) *share* (l. 46)
92 *But* (*to*) *my* (*other*) *daughters/divide*
93 *become/wretched/live/misery*
94 *thought* (l. 81)/*shame*
95 *dead/think* ("*I will consider you to be dead*")/*Fly out/eyesight*
96 *kingdom/is pleasing*
97 *duke*
98 *fair* (cf. N.G. *schön*)
99 *give* (*them*)/*possessions/king* (*wielder*)
100 *did* (*all*)/*had deemed, decided*
101 *woe/then*
102 *in mind/wrath*
103 *went/bower/where/sorry*
104 *wouldn't lie* (*to*)/*beloved*

105 *took/noble*
106 *only/sail*

108 *received*
109 (*To*) *all/pleasing/made her* (*his*) *queen*

1 *went/unmeasurable/army*
2 *heard/against*
3 *many/fated* (*to die*)
4 (*On the banks of the*)/*Tamar/they/met*

The stude hatte Camelford, ever mare ilast that ilke weorde.   5
And at Camelforde wes isomned sixti thusend,
And ma thusend ther to; Modred wes heore ælder.
Tha thiderward gon ride Arthur the riche,
Mid unimete folke, væie thah hit weore.
Uppe there Tambre heo tuhte to-somne.   10
Heven here-marken, halden to-gadere,
Luken sweord longe, leiden o the helmen;
Fur ut sprengen, speren brastlien,
Sceldes gonnen scanen, scaftes to-breken.
Ther faht al to-somne folc unimete.   15
Tambre wes on flode mid unimete blode.
Mon i than fihte non ther ne mihte ikennen nenne kempe.
No wha dude wurse no wha bet, swa that withe wes imenged.
For ælc sloh adun-riht, weore he swein weore he cniht.
Ther wes Modred of-slaghe, and idon of lif-daghe,   20
And alle his cnihtes islaghe in that fihte.
Ther weoren of-slaghe alle tha snelle,
Arthures hered-men heghe and lowe,
And the Bruttes alle of Arthures borde,
And alle his fosterlinges of feole kineriches,   25
And Arthur forwunded mid wal-spere brade,
Fiftene he hafde feondliche wunden.
Mon mihte i thare laste twa gloven ithraste.
Tha nas ther no mare i than fehte to lave,
Of twa hundred thusend monnen, tha ther leien to-hauwen,   30
Buten Arthur the king ane and of his cnihtes tweien.
Arthur wes for-wunded wunder ane swithe.
Ther to him com a cnave the wes of his cunne;
He wes Cadores sune, the eorles of Cornwaile;
Constantin hehte the cnave; he wes than kinge deore.   35
Arthur him lokede on, ther he lai on folden,
And thas word seide mid sorhfulle heorte:
'Costæntin, thu art wilcume, thu weore Cadores sone.
Ich the bitache here mine kineriche,
And wite mine Bruttes a to thines lifes,   40
And hald heom alle tha laghen tha habbeoth istonden a mine
    daghen,
And alle tha laghen gode tha bi Utheres daghen stode.
And ich wulle varen to Avalun, to vairest alre maidene,
To Argante there quene, alven swithe sceone,
And heo scal mine wunden makien alle isunde,   45
Al hal me makien mid haleweighe drenchen.

5 *place/called/lasts/same/word, name*
6 *gathered*
7 *more/their leader (elder)*

9 *fated (l. 3)/though it (the folk) were*
10 *together*
11 *Heaved, raised/army markers, standards/met*
12 *Drew/laid on/helmets*
13 *Fire (sparks)/sprang out/spears/clashed*
14 *began/(to) break/broke completely*
15 *fought*
16 *in flood/blood*
17 *"One might not recognize any (specific) warrior in the battle"*
18 *"Nor who did worse"/better/conflict/mingled, confused*
19 *each/slew/fiercely/swain/knight*
20 *slain/done (out of), deprived/life*
21 *slain*
22 *swift, bold (ones)*
23 *retainers/high*
24 *Britons/board = Round Table*
25 *foster children/many/kingdoms*
26 *mortally wounded/slaughter- (l. 10a)/broad*
27 *fiendish/wounds*
28 *"in the least (of the wounds)"/thrust two gloves*
29 *neg. + was/to leave = remaining*
30 *men/lay/hewn to pieces*
31 *But, except/alone/two*
32 *very wonderfully*
33 *(knave) youth (who)/kin*
34 *"son of Cador, earl of . . ."*
35 *was called/(to) the king*
36 *looked on him/ground*
37 *sorrowful*

39 *(to) you/commit*
40 *protect/Britons/always/(even) with/your life*
41 *hold/laws/stood/in my days*

42 *in Uther's days*
43 *go (l. 1)/fairest/of all*
44 *(of) elves, fairies/fair (l. 98a)*
45 *sound, healed*
46 *whole/holy, sacred (cups of) potions, drinks*

And seothe ich cumen wulle to mine kineriche,
And wunien mid Brutten mid muchelere wunne.'
Æfne than worden ther com of se wenden,
That wes an sceort bat lithen, sceoven mid uthen,   50
And twa wimmen ther inne wunderliche idihte,
And heo nomen Arthur anan, and aneouste hine vereden,
And softe hine adun leiden, and forth gunnen hine lithen.
Tha wes hit iwurthen that Merlin seide whilen,
That weore unimete care of Arthures forth-fare.   55
Bruttes ileveth yete that he bon on live,
And wunnien in Avalun mid fairest alre alven,
And lokieth evere Bruttes yete whan Arthur cumen lithe.
Nis naver the mon iboren of naver nane burde icoren,
The cunne of than sothe of Arthure sugen mare.   60
Bute while wes an witeye, Mærlin ihate.
He bodede mid worde, his quithes weoren sothe,
That an Arthur sculde yete cum Anglen to fulste.

SUPPLEMENTARY MATERIAL

1. R. S. Loomis, *Arthurian Literature in the Middle Ages* (Oxford, 1959), pp. 104–11.
2. Layamon's selection *a* may be compared to Geoffrey of Monmouth's *History of the Kings of Britain* (Baltimore, 1966), p. 81f.
3. Compare selection *b* with Malory, p. 451f.
4. H. C. Wyld, "Layamon as an English Poet," *Review of English Studies,* VI (1930), 1–30.
(See also Supplementary Material following the Malory selections.)

47 *afterward*
48 *dwell/much/joy*
49 *Even (with)/from (the) sea/proceeding*
50 *short, little/boat/moving/shoved/waves*
51 *decked out, bedight*
52 *took/at once/quickly/bore him*
53 *softly/laid him down/began/to carry*
54 *done, accomplished/formerly*
55 *(there should) be/because (of)/going forth, death*
56 *believe/is/alive*
57 *dwells/of all/fairies* (l. 44)
58 *look (forward to the time)/(lithe* 'come,' pleonastic with *cumen)*
59 *"There never was"/born/chosen lady*
60 *"Who knows the truth"/to say more*
61 *for a time/prophet/called*
62 *boded, foretold/sayings*
63 *"to the help of the Angles"*

"LOVE IS LIFE THAT LASTS AY"

Luf es lyf that lastes ay, thar it in Criste es feste,
For wele ne wa it chaunge may, als wryten has men wyseste.
The nyght it tournes intil the day, thi travel intyll reste;
If thou wil luf thus as I say, thou may be wyth the beste.　　　　4

Lufe es thoght wyth grete desyre of a fayre lovyng;
Lufe I lyken til a fyre that sloken may na thyng;
Lufe us clenses of oure syn; luf us botc sall bryng;
Lufe the keynges hert may wyn; lufe of ioy may syng.　　　　8

The settel of lufe es lyft hee, for intil heven it ranne;
Me thynk in erth it es sle, that makes men pale and wanne.
The bede of blysse it gase ful nee, I tel the as I kanne;
Thof us thynk the way be dregh, luf copuls God and manne.　　　　12

Lufe es hatter then the cole; lufe may nane beswyke.
The flawme of lufe wha myght it thole, if it war ay ilyke.
Luf us comfortes and mase in qwart, and lyftes tyl hevenryke;
Luf ravysches Cryste intyl owr hert; I wate na lust it lyke.　　　　16

Lere to luf, if thou wyl lyfe when thou sall hethen fare.
All thi thoght til hym thou gyf that may the kepe fra kare.
Loke thi hert fra hym noght twyn, if thou in wandreth ware,
Sa thou may hym welde and wyn and luf hym evermare.　　　　20

Iesu that me lyfe hase lent, intil thi lufe me bryng;
Take til the al myne entent, that thow be my yhernyng.
Wa fra me away war went, and comne war my covaytyng,
If that my sawle had herd and hent the sang of thi lovyng.　　　　24

Thi lufe es ay lastand, fra that we may it fele;
Tharein make me byrnand, that na thyng gar it kele.
My thoght take into thi hand, and stabyl it ylk a dele,
That I be noght heldand to luf this worldes wele.　　　　28

1 *always/where/fastened*
2 *woe/as/wisest*
3 *into/travail*

5 *beloved*
6 *slake*
7 *boot, cure/shall*
8 *king's*

9 *seat, throne/lifted/high*
10 *sly, secret*
11 *bed/goes/nigh*
12 *Though/tedious/couples*

13 *hotter/coal/none/cheat*
14 *flame/who/endure/alike, the same*
15 *makes/health/heavenly kingdom*
16 *ravishes, carries (off)/know*

17 *Learn/live/hence/go*
18 *give*
19 *Look/twin, part/trouble*
20 *So/wield, possess*

21 *has*
22 *intent/yearning, what I desire*
23 *Woe/come/(object of) coveting*
24 *soul/grasped/song/praise*

25 *lasting*
26 *burning/(may) make/cool*
27 *(make) stable/every part, entirely*
28 *inclining*

If I lufe any erthly thyng that payes to my wyll,
And settes my ioy and my lykyng when it may comm me tyll,
I mai drede of partyng, that wyll be hate and yll,
For al my welth es bot wepyng when pyne mi saule sal spyll.   32

The ioy that men hase sene es lyckend tyl the haye,
That now es fayre and grene, and now wytes awaye.
Swylk es this worlde, I wene, and bees till domesdaye,
All in travel and tene, fle that no man it maye.   36

If thou luf in all thi thoght and hate the fylth of syn,
And gyf hym thi sawle that it boght, that he the dwell within,
Als Crist thi sawle hase soght and therof walde noght blyn,
Sa thou sal to blys be broght and heven won within.   40

The kynd of luf es this, thar it es trayst and trew,
To stand styll in stabylnes and chaunge it for na new.
The lyfe that lufe myght fynd or ever in hert it knew,
Fra kare it tornes that kyend and lendes in myrth and glew.   44

For now, lufe thow, I rede, Cryste, as I the tell,
And with aungels take thi stede—that ioy loke thou noght sell!
In erth thow hate, I rede, all that thi lufe may fell,
For luf es stalworth as the dede, luf es hard as hell.   48

Luf es a lyght byrthen; lufe gladdes yong and alde;
Lufe es withowten pyne, als lofers hase me talde;
Lufe es a gastly wyne that makes men bygge and balde;
Of lufe sal he na thyng tyne that hit in hert will halde.   52

Lufe es the swettest thyng that man in erth hase tane;
Lufe es goddes derlyng; lufe byndes blode and bane.
In lufe be owre lykyng, I ne wate na better wane,
For me and my lufyng lufe makes bath be ane.   56

Bot fleschly lufe sal fare as dose the flowre in May,
And lastand be na mare than ane houre of a day,
And sythen syghe ful sare thar lust, thar pryde, thar play,
When thai er casten in kare til pyne that lastes ay.   60

When thair bodys lyse in syn, thair sawls mai qwake and drede,
For up sal ryse al men and answer for thair dede.
If thai be fonden in syn, als now thair lyfe thai lede,
Thai sal sytt hel within and myrknes hafe to mede.   64

Riche men thair hend sal wryng, and wicked werkes sal by
In flawme of fyre, bath knyght and keyng, with sorow schamfully.

29 *is pleasing*

31 *hot, bitter/ill, evil*
32 *but/weeping/grief/waste*

33 *likened*
34 *fair/withers*
35 *Such/ween, think*
36 *travail/trouble*

38 *bought, redeem*
39 *would/stop*

41 *nature/faithful*
42 *still, always*
43 *living one, man/it = love*
44 *nature/lands/on/glee*

45 *advise*
46 *place*
47 *destroy*
48 *death*

49 *burden/gladdens/old*
50 *lovers*
51 *spiritual/bold*
52 *lose/hold*

53 *taken*
54 *God's darling/blood/bone*
55 *know/dwelling*
56 *beloved/both/one*

57 *does*
58 *(the) lasting*
59 *afterward/sigh/sorely*

61 *lie/quake/dread*
62 *deeds*

64 *"sit in hell"/murkiness/reward*

65 *hands/buy*
66 *flame/both/king*

If thou wil lufe, than may thou syng til Cryst in melody;
The lufe of hym overcoms al thyng, tharto thou traiste trewly.   68

I sygh and sob, bath day and nyght, for ane sa fayre of hew.
Thar es na thyng my hert mai light bot lufe that es ay new.
Wha sa had hym in his syght or in his hert hym knew,
His mournyng turned til ioy ful bryght, his sang intil glew.   72

In myrth he lyfes, nyght and day, that lufes that swete chylde;
It es Iesu, forsoth I say, of all mekest and mylde.
Wreth fra hym walde al away, thof he wer never sa wylde;
He that in hert lufed hym, that day fra evel he wil hym schylde.   76

Of Iesu mast lyst me speke, that al my bale may bete.
Me thynk my hert may al tobreke when I thynk on that swete.
In lufe lacyd he hase my thoght, that I sal never forgete.
Ful dere me thynk he hase me boght with blodi hende and fete.   80

For luf my hert es bowne to brest when I that faire behalde.
Lufe es fair thare it es fest, that never will be calde;
Lufe us reves the nyght rest, in grace it makes us balde;
Of al warkes luf es the best, als haly men me talde.   84

Na wonder gyf I syghand be and sithen in sorow be sette;
Iesu was nayled apon the tre and al blody forbette.
To thynk on hym es grete pyté—how tenderly he grette—
This hase he sufferde, man, for the, if that thou syn wyll lette.   88

Thare es na tonge in erth may tell of lufe the swetnesse;
That stedfastly in lufe kan dwell, his ioy es endlesse.
God schylde that he sulde til hell that lufes, and langand es,
Or ever his enmys sulde hym qwell, or make his luf be lesse.   92

Iesu es lufe that lastes ay, til hym es owre langyng;
Iesu the nyght turnes to the day, the dawyng intil spryng.
Iesu thynk on us, now and ay, for the we halde oure keyng;
Iesu gyf us grace, as thou wel may, to luf the withowten endyng.   96

68 *trust*

70 *lighten*
71 *Whosoever*
72 *glee*

75 *Wrath/(go) away/though/ever so wild, sinful*
76 *shield*

77 *most/I wish to/abate*
78 *utterly break/sweet (one)*
79 *laced, snared*

81 *bowed/fair (one)/behold*
82 *fastened/cold*
83 *deprives/bold*
84 *works/holy/told*

85 *if/sighing/after (therefore)*
86 *beaten completely*
87 *wept*
88 *leave*

91 *shield, protect/should/(go) to/longing*
92 *enemies*

93 *longing*
94 *dawning/spring (of day), sunrise*

THE FORM OF LIVING

CHAPTER XII

Twa lyves thar er that cristen men lyfes. Ane es called
Actyve lyfe, for it es in mare bodili warke. Another, con-
templatyve lyfe, for it es in mare swetnes gastely. Actife
lyfe es mykel owteward, and in mare travel and in mare
peryle, for the temptacions that er in the worlde. Contempla-   5
tyfe lyfe es mykel inwarde, and forthi it es lastandar, and
sykerar, restfuller, delitabiler, luflyer, and mare
meedful. For it hase ioy in goddes lufe, and savowre
in the lyf that lastes ay, in this present tyme, if it be
right ledde. And that felyng of ioy in the lufe of Iesu   10
passes al other merites in erth. For it es swa harde to
com to, for the freelté of oure flesch, and the many
temptacions that we er umsett with, that lettes us
nyght and day. Al other thynges er lyght at comm to,
in regarde tharof, for that may na man deserve, bot   15
anely it es gifen of goddes godenes, til tham that
verrayli gifes tham to contemplacion and til quiete
for Cristes luf.

Til men or wymen that takes tham til actife lyfe,
twa thynges falles. Ane, for to ordayne thair meyne   20
in drede and in the lufe of god and fynd tham thaire
necessaries, and thamself kepe enterely the comandementes
of god, doand til thar neghbur als thai wil that thai do til
tham. Another es, that thai do at thar power the seven
werkes of mercy, the whilk es: To fede the hungry. To   25
gyf the thristi a drynk. To cleth the naked. To herbar hym
that hase no howsyng. To viset the seke. To comforth
tham that er in prysoun. And to grave dede men. Al
that mai and hase cost, thai may noght be qwyt with ane
or twa of thir, bot tham behoves do tham al, if thai wil   30
have the benyson on domesday, that Iesu sal til al gyf
that dose tham. Or els may thai drede the malysoun that

1 *Two/Christian/live/One*
2 *more bodily work*
3 *spiritual sweetness*
4 *much/outward/travail, labor*
5 *peril*
6 *therefore/more lasting*
7 *more certain/more delightful*
8 *meedful, rewarding/God's/savor*

10 *rightly led/feeling*
11 *so*
12 *because of/frailty*
13 *beset/hinder*
14 *lightly come to*
15 *comparison thereto*
16 *only/given/to those who*
17 *give themselves*

20 *two/One/ordain, order/household*

23 *doing*
24 *according to*
25 *which are*
26 *thirsty/clothe/harbor*
27 *comfort*
28 *bury/dead*
29 *funds/quit/one*
30 *these/it behooves them to*
31 *blessing/Doomsday/give to all*
32 *curse*

al mon have that wil noght do tham, when thai had godes
to do tham wyth.

Contemplatife lyf hase twa partyes, a lower and a heer.   35
The lower party es meditacion of haly wrytyng, that es
goddes wordes, and in other gude thoghtes and swete
that men hase of the grace of god, abowt the lufe of Iesu
Criste; and also in lovyng of god in psalmes and ympnes,
or in prayers. The hegher party of contemplation es be-   40
haldyng and yernyng of the thynges of heven, and ioy in the
haly gaste, that men hase oft, and if it be swa that thai
be noght prayand with the mowth, bot anely thynkand of
god, and of the fairehede of aungels, and haly sawles,
than may I say that contemplacion es a wonderful ioy of   45
goddes luf, the whilk ioy es lovyng of god, that may noght
be talde, and that wonderful lovyng es in the saule, and
for abundance of ioy and swettenes it ascendes intil the
mouth, swa that the hert and the tonge acordes in ane, and
body and sawle ioyes in god lyvand.   50

A man or woman that es ordaynd til contemplatife lyfe,
first god enspires tham to forsake this worlde, and al the
vanité and the covayties and the vile luste tharof. Sythen
he ledes tham by thar ane, and spekes til thar hert, and
als the prophete says, he gifes tham at sowke the swetnes   55
of the begynnyng of lufe, and than he settes tham in will
to gyf tham haly to prayers and meditacions and teres.
Sithen, when thai have sufferd many temptacions, and the
foule noyes of thoghtes that er ydel, and of vanitees, the
whilk wil comber tham that can noght destroy tham, er   60
passand away, he gars tham geder til tham thair hert
and fest anely in hym and opens til the egh of thair
sawls the yates of heven, swa that the ilk egh lokes
in til heven; and than the fire of lufe verrali ligges in
thair hert, and byrnes tharin and makes it clene of al   65
erthly filth; and sithen forward thai er contemplatife men,
and ravyst in lufe. For contemplacion es a syght, and
thai se in til heven with thar gastly egh. Bot thou sal witt
that naman hase perfite syght of heven whils thai er
lifand bodili here. Bot als sone als thai dye, thai er   70
broght before god and sese hym face til face, and egh
til egh, and wones with hym withouten ende. For hym
thai soght, and hym thai covayted, and hym thai lufed
in al thar myght.

Loo, Margarete, I have schortly sayde the the   75

33 *must/goods*

35 *parts/higher*
36 *holy*
37 *God's/good*

39 *hymns*

42 *holy ghost/so*
43 *praying/only/thinking*
44 *fairhood, -ness/souls*

46 *which*
47 *told*
48 *sweetness*
49 *one*
50 *rejoice, living in God*

53 *covetousness/Afterward*
54 *by themselves, alone*
55 *as/to suck*
56 *in the will, desire*
57 *wholly*

59 *annoyances/idle*
60 *which/encumber*
61 *passing/makes/gather*
62 *fasten/only/eye*
63 *gates/same/looks*
64 *lies*
65 *burns*
66 *from that time forward*
67 *ravished*
68 *spiritual/know*
69 *no man/perfect/while*
70 *living*
71 *see*
72 *dwell*

forme of lyvyng, and how thou may comm til perfection,
and to lufe hym that thou hase taken the til. If it do the gude,
and profit til the, thank god and pray for me. The grace of
Iesu Criste be with the and kepe the.
Amen.   80

explicit forma vivendi.

SUPPLEMENTARY MATERIAL

1. Evelyn Underhill, *Mysticism*, 12th ed., London, 1957.
2. Dom David Knowles, *The English Mystics*, London, 1927.

THE LAND OF COKAYGNE

Fur in see bi west Spayngne *Far/sea/Spain*
Is a lond ihote Cokaygne. *called*
Ther nis lond under hevenriche *neg. + is/(kingdom of) heaven*

Of wel, of godnis, hit iliche. *wealth/like it*
Thogh Paradis be miri and bright 5
Cokaygn is of fairir sight.
What is ther in Paradis
Bot grasse and flure and grene ris? *flowers/branches*
Thogh ther be ioi and gret dute, *joy/pleasure*
Ther nis met bote frute. 10 *meat = food*
Ther nis halle, bure, no bench, *bower*
Bot watir, manis thurst to quench. *man's*
Beth ther no men bot two,
Hely and Enok also. *Elijah/Enoch*
Elinglich mai hi go 15 *Miserably/they*
Whar ther wonith men no mo. *dwell/more*
In Cokaigne is met and drink,
Withute care, how, and swink. *anxiety/toil*
The met is trie, the drink is clere, *excellent*
To none, russin, and sopper. 20 *For noon/a light meal between dinner and supper*

I sigge forsoth, boute were, *say/doubtlessly*
Ther nis lond on erthe is pere. *its peer*
Under heven nis lond, iwisse, *certainly*
Of so mochil ioi and blisse. *much*
Ther is mani swete sighte; 25
Al is dai, nis ther no nighte.
Ther nis baret nother strif, *conflict/nor*
Nis ther no deth, ac ever lif. *but*
Ther nis lac of met no cloth,
Ther nis man no womman wroth, 30
Ther nis serpent, wolf, no fox,

Hors no capil, kowe no ox,   *cart horse, gelding*
Ther nis schepe no swine no gote,
No horwgh, la, God it wote,   *dirt, filth/knows*
Nother harace, nother stode.   35   (M.E.D.: "a place
                                              where horses are
                                              bred or kept")/
                                              stud

The lond is ful of other gode.
Nis ther flei, fle, no lowse   *fly/flea*
In cloth, in toune, bed, no house.
Ther nis dunnir, slete, no hawle,   *thunder/hail*
No non vile worme, no snawile,   40   *snail*
No non storme, rein, no winde.
Ther nis man no womman blinde,
Ok al is game, joi, and gle.   *But*
Wel is him that ther mai be.
Ther beth rivers gret and fine   45
Of oile, melk, honi, and wine.
Watir servith ther to nothing   *look at/for washing*
Bot to sight and to waiissing.   *kinds of*
Ther is mani maner frute.   *pleasure/delight*
Al is solas and dedute.   50   *pleasure/delight*
                                              (l. 9)
    Ther is a wel fair abbei   *abbey*
Of white monkes and of grei.
Ther beth bowris and halles,   *bowers*
Al of pasteiis beth the walles,   *pasties*
Of fleis, of fisse, and rich met,   55   *flesh = meat (cf.*
                                              meat = food)/fish
The likfullist that man mai et.
Fluren cakes beth the schingles alle   *Flour*
Of cherch, cloister, boure, and halle.
The pinnes beth fat podinges,   *pins, pegs/puddings*
                                              (sausages)
Rich met to princes and kinges.   60
Man mai therof et inogh,   *eat/enough, i.e. "all*
                                              he wants"
Al with right and noght with wogh.   *woe*
Al is commune to yung and old,
To stoute and sterne, mek and bold.
Ther is a cloister, fair and light,   65
Brod and lang, of sembli sight.   *long/seemly*
The pilers of that cloister alle   *pillars*

Beth iturned of cristale,		*turned*
With har bas and capitale		*their*
Of grene jaspe and rede corale.	70	*jasper*
In the praer is a tre		*meadow*
Swithe likful forto se.		*Very*
The rote is gingeuir and galingale,		*root/ginger*
The siouns beth al sedwale,		*shoots/zedoary*
Trie maces beth the flure,	75	*Choice (l. 19)*
The rind canel of swet odur,		*cinnamon*
The frute gilofre of gode smakke.		*clove/flavor*
Of cucubes ther nis no lakke.		*cubebs*
Ther beth rosis of rede ble		*hue*
And lilie likful forto se.	80	
Thai faloweth never dai no night.		*fallow, wither*
This aght be a swet sight.		*ought (to)*
Ther beth .iiij. willis in the abbei		*4/wells*
Of triacle, and halwei,		*healing drink*
Of baum, and ek piement,	85	*balm/also/spiced wine*
Ever ernend to right rent.		*running/profit*
Of thai stremis al the molde		*those (wells)/overflows/ground*
Stonis preciuse, and golde.		
Ther is saphir and uniune,		*pearl*
Carbuncle and astiune,	90	*astrion*
Smaragde, lugre, and prassiune,		*Emerald/ligure/prasine*
Beril, onix, topasiune,		*topaz*
Ametist and crisolite,		
Calcedun and epetite.		*Chalcedony/hepatite*
Ther beth briddes mani and fale,	95	*birds/many, numerous*
Throstil, thruisse, and nightingale,		*Song thrush/thrush*
Chalandre, and wodwale,		*Calander/woodwall*
And other briddes without tale,		
That stinteth never bi har might		*"concerning their might"*
Miri to sing dai and night.	100	
Yite I do yow mo to witte—		*Yet/give/know*
The gees irostid on the spitte		*roasted*
Flees to that abbai, God hit wot,		*Fly/knows*
And gredith, 'Gees, al hote, al hot!'		*cry out*

Hi bringeth garlek, gret plenté,   105
The best idight that man mai se.   *dressed*
The leverokes, that beth cuth,   *larks/well-known*
Lightith adun to manis muth   *man's*
Idight in stu ful swithe wel,   *very well*
Pudrid with gilofre and canel.   110 *Powdered, sprin-*
                                                kled/clove/cinna-
                                                mon (ll. 76–77)

Nis no spech of no drink,
Ak take inogh withute swink.   *But/toil*
Whan the monkes gooth to masse,
Al the fenestres that beth of glasse   *windows*
Turneth into cristal bright   115
To give monkes more light.
Whan the masses beth iseiid   *said*
And the bokes up ileiid,   *books/laid*
The cristal turnith into glasse
In state that hit rather wasse.   120 *formerly*
The yung monkes euch dai   *each*
Aftir met goth to plai.
Nis ther hauk no fule so swifte   *hawk/fowl*
Bettir fleing bi the lifte   *air*
Than the monkes, heigh of mode,   125 *mind, spirit*
With har slevis and har hode.   *their/hoods*
Whan the abbot seeth ham flee,   *fly*
That he holt for moch glee.   *holds*
Ak natheles, al theramang,   *nevertheless/in the*
                                                middle of it
He biddith ham light to evesang.   130 *a light/for evensong*
The monkes lightith noght adun   *down*
Ac furre fleeth in o randun.   *further/hurriedly*
Whan the abbot him iseeth   *sees*
That is monkes fram him fleeth,   *his*
He taketh maidin of the route   135 *maiden, virgin/*
                                                group, crowd
And turnith up hir white toute,   *buttocks*
And betith the taburs with is hond   *tabors*
To make is monkes light to lond.
Whan is monkes that iseeth,
To the maid dun hi fleeth   140
And goth the wench al abute,
And thakketh al hir white toute,   *pat*

And sith aftir her swinke   *then/labor, toil* (l. 18)

Wendith meklich hom to drink,   *meekly*
And goth to har collacione   145   *collection, assembly*
A wel fair processione.
  Another abbei is therbi,
Forsoth, a gret fair nunnerie,
Up a river of swet milke,
Whar is gret plenté of silk.   150
Whan the someris dai is hote,
The yung nunnes takith a bote
And doth ham forth in that river,   *take themselves, go*
Bothe with oris and with stere.   *oars/rudder*
Whan hi beth fur fram the abbei,   155
Hi makith ham nakid forto plei,   *play*
And lepith dune into the brimme   *water*
And doth ham sleilich forto swimme.   *slyly*
The yung monkes that hi seeth,
Hi doth ham up and forth hi fleeth, 160   (cf. l. 153)
And commith to the nunnes anon
And euch monke him taketh on,   *one*
And snellich berith forth har prei   *quickly/prey*
To the mochil grei abbei,   *great*
And techith the nunnes an oreisun   165   *orison, prayer*
With iambleve up and dun.   (O.Fr. *jambe* 'leg' + *levée* 'raised') *a dance step/down*

The monke that wol be stalun gode   *stallion*
And kan set aright is hode,   *hood* (cf. "set his cap")

He schal hab withoute danger
xij. wives euch yere,   170   *12*
Al throgh right and noght throgh grace,   (cf. l. 62)/*grace (of God)*

Forto do himsilf solace,   *pleasure*
And thilk monke that slepith best,   *the + same*
And doth his likam al to rest,   *body*
Of him is hoppe, God hit wote,   175   *hope/knows*
To be sone vadir abbot.   *soon/father*
Whose wl com that lond to,   *Who + so/will*
Ful grete penance he mot do.   *must*
Seve yere in swineis dritte   *Seven/swine's dirt, dung*

He mote wade, wol ye iwitte,   180   *believe*
Al anon up to the chynne.   *right/chin*
So he schal the lond winne.   *attain*
  Lordinges gode and hend,   *courteous*
Mot ye never of world wend   *May/from*
Fort ye stond to yure cheance   185   *Until/chance*
And fulfille that penance,
That ye mote that lond ise   *see*
And nevermore turne aye,   *(back) again*
Prey we God so mote hit be.
Amen, pur seint charité.   190

SUPPLEMENTARY MATERIAL

H. R. Patch, *The Other World, According to Descriptions in Medieval Literature* (Cambridge, Mass., 1950), pp. 7–22, 134–74.

WYNNERE AND WASTOURE

HERE BEGYNNES A TRETYS

AND GOD SCHORTE REFREYTE

BY-TWIXE WYNNERE AND WASTOURE

PROLOGUE

Sythen that Bretayne was biggede, and Bruyttus it aughte,
Thurgh the takynge of Troye with tresone with-inn,
There hathe selcouthes bene sene in seere kynges tymes,
But never so many as nowe by the nynde dele.
For nowe alle es witt and wylle that we with delyn,   5
Wyli wordes and slee, and icheon wryeth othere.
Wyse wordes with-inn, that writen were never:
Dare never no westren wy, while this werlde lasteth,
Send his sone south-warde to see ne to here,
That he ne schall holden by-hynde when he hore eld es.   10
For-thi sayde was a sawe of Salomon the wyse—
It hyeghte harde appone honde, hope I no nother—
When wawes waxen schall wilde and walles bene doun
And hares appon herthe-stones schall hurcle in hire fourme,
And eke boyes of no blode with boste and with pryde   15
Schall wedde ladyes in londe and lede at hir will,
Thene dredfull domesdaye it draweth neghe aftir.
Bot who-so sadly will see and the sothe telle,
Say it newely will neghe or es neghe here.
Whylome were lordes in londe that loved in thaire hertis   20
To here makers of myrthes that matirs couthe fynde.
And now es no frenchipe in fere bot fayntnesse of hert
Ne redde in no romance that ever renke herde.
Bot now a childe appon chere, with-owtten chin-wedys
That never wroghte thurgh witt three wordes togedire,   25

good/debate

1   *Since/built/Brutus/owned*

3   *marvels, strange sights/sundry*
4   *ninth/part*
5   *deal*
6   *Wily/sly/each one/betrays*

8   *man*
9   *son*
10 *"Instead he shall stay"/hoary/old*
11 *Therefore/saying*
12 *hies/upon/"I expected no less"*
13 *waves*
14 *crouch/warrens*
15 *also/boast*
16 *lead/(them) at their*
17 *Doomsday/nigh*
18 *soberly/sooth, truth*
19 *"it is imminent"*
20 *At one time*
21 *hear/(the poetic matters), themes/invent*
22 *in company, together*
23 *read/man*
24 *in appearance/chin-weeds, beard*

Fro he can jangle als a jaye, and japes telle,
He schall be levede and lovede and lett of a while
Wele more than the man that makes hym-selven.
But never the lattere at the laste, when ledys bene knawen,
Werke witnesse will bere who wirche kane beste.   30

FITT I

Bot I schall tell yow a tale that me by-tyde ones,
Als I went in the weste, wandrynge myn one,
Bi a bonke of a bourne, bryghte was the sone,
Undir a worthiliche wodde, by a wale medewe.
Fele floures gan folde ther my fote steppede.   35
I layde myn hede one ane hill, ane hawthorne be-syde.
The throstills full throly they threpe to-gedire,
Hipped up heghwalles fro heselis tyll othire,
Bernacles with thayre billes one barkes thay roungen,
The jay janglede one heghe, jarmede the foles;   40
The bourne full bremly rane the bankes ty-twene.
So ruyde were the roughe stremys, and raughten so heghe,
That it was neghande nyghte or I nappe myghte,
For dyn of the depe watir, and dadillyng of fewllys.
Bot as I laye at the laste, than lowked my eghne,   45
And I was swythe in a sweven sweped be-lyve.
Me thoghte I was in the werlde, I ne wiste in whate ende,
One a loveliche lande that was ylike grene,
That laye loken by a lawe the lengthe of a myle.
In aythere holte was ane here in hawberkes full brighte,   50
Harde hattes appon hedes and helmys with crestys,
Brayden owte thaire baners, bown for to mete,
Showen owte of the schawes, in schiltrons thay felle;
And bot the lenghte of a launde thies ledes by-twene.
And als I prayed for the pese till the prynce come,   55
For he was worthiere in witt than any wy ells,
For to ridde and to rede and to rewlyn the wrothe
That aythere here appon hethe had un-till othere.
At the creste of a clyffe a caban was rerede,
Alle raylede with rede the rofe and the sydes,   60
With Ynglysse besantes full brighte, betyn of golde,
And ichone gayly umby-gone with garters of inde,
And iche a gartare of golde gerede full riche.
Then were thies wordes in the webbe werped of he,
Payntted of plunket, and poyntes by-twene,   65

26 From (the time that)/as/jokes
27 believed/honored
28 composes (songs)
29 nevertheless/men/recognized (for real accomplishment)

32 alone
33 bank of a brook/sun
34 lovely wood/choice meadow
35 Many/where
36 on a/beside a
37 intensely/contended
38 Hopped/woodpeckers/hazels/to
39 Wild geese/on/rang
40 on high/sang/fowls
41 noisily
42 boisterous/reached
43 nearing/ere
44 chattering/fowls
45 then/locked, shut/eyes
46 swiftly/dream/swept/quickly
47 knew not
48 On, in/lovely/all (alike)
49 locked, shut in/hill
50 either, each/wood/army

52 Drawn out, unfurled/ready
53 Shoved/thickets/troops
54 lawn, green/men
55 peace
56 man
57 settle/advise/rule/wrath
58 either/army/heath/unto, for
59 cabin, covering for shelter
60 decorated/red/roof
61 English/coin-like ornaments/beaten
62 each one/gone around = surrounded/indigo
63 each/geared, decorated
64 worked above them
65 blue

That were fourmed full fayre appon fresche lettres,
And alle was it one sawe, appon Ynglysse tonge,
"Hethyng have the hathell that any harme thynkes."

Now the kyng of this kythe, kepe hym oure Lorde!
Upon heghe one the holt ane hathell up stondes,   70
Wroghte als a wodwyse, alle in wrethyn lokkes,
With ane helme one his hede, ane hatte appon lofte,
And one heghe one the hatte ane hatefull beste,
A lighte lebarde and a longe, lokande full kene.
Yarked alle of yalowe golde in full yape wyse.   75
Bot that that hillede the helme by-hynde in the nekke,
Was casten full clenly in quarteres foure,
Two with flowres of Fraunce be-fore and be-hynde
And two other of Ynglonde with sex irous bestes,
Thre leberdes one lofte, and thre on-lowe undir.   80
At iche a cornere a knoppe of full clene perle,
Tasselde of tuly silke, tuttynge out fayre.
And by the cabane I knewe the knyghte that I see,
And thoghte to wiete, or I went, wondres ynewe.
And als I waytted with-inn I was warre sone   85
Of a comliche kynge crowned with golde.
Sett one a silken bynce, with septure in honde
One of the lovelyeste ledis, who-so loveth hym in hert,
That ever segge under sonn sawe with his eghne.
This kynge was comliche clade in kirtill and mantill,   90
Bery-brown as his berde, brouderde with fewlys,
Fawkons of fyne golde, flakerande with wynges,
And ichone bare in ble, blewe als me thoghte,
A grete gartare of ynde gerede ful riche.
Full gayly was that grete lorde girde in the myddis,   95
A brighte belte of ble, broudirde with fewlis,
With drakes and with dukkes, daderande tham semede,
For ferdnes of fawcons fete, lesse fawked thay were.
And ever I sayd to my-selfe, full selly me thynke
Bot if this renke to the revere ryde umbestounde.   100
The kyng biddith a beryn by hym that stondeth,
One of the ferlyeste frekes that faylede hym never:
Thynke I dubbede the knyghte with dynttis to dele!
Wende wightly thy waye my willes to kythe.
Go bidd thou yondere bolde batell that one the bent hoves,   105
That they never neghe nerre to-gedire;
For if thay strike one stroke, stynte thay ne thynken.

66 *in*
67 *a saying* (l. 11)/*in English*
68 *Dishonor/man/malice* (cf. last line, *Gawain*)

69 *land*

71 *satyr/wreathed, curled/locks*
72 *aloft*
73 *on . . . on/an insignia of/beast*
74 *leopard/looking*
75 *Worked/clever*
76 *concealed*

81 *every/nob, cluster/pure*
82 *tile-colored/jutting*
83 *saw*
84 *know/ere* (l. 43)/*enough*
85 *aware/soon*
86 *comely*
87 *bench*
88 *men*
89 *man/sun/eyes*

91 *embroidered/fowls*
92 *Falcons/flapping*
93 *each one/hue*
94 *indigo* (l. 62)/*decorated*
95 *middle*

97 *ducks/doddering, quaking*
98 *fear/feet/seized*
99 *marvelous*
100 *Unless/man/on occasion*
101 *man*
102 *most excellent/men*
103 *Remember/thee/to deal dints, blows*
104 *Go quickly/make known*
105 *combatants/on/field/remains*
106 *near, approach/nearer*

I serve, lorde, said the lede, while my life dures.
He dothe hym doun one the bonke and dwellys a while,
Whils he busked and bown was, one his beste wyse.   110
He laped his legges in yren to the lawe bones,
With pysayne and with pawnce polischede full clene,
With brases of broun stele brauden full thikke,
With plates buklede at the bakke the body to yeme,
With a jupown full juste, joynede by the sydes;   115
A brod chechun at the bakke; the breste had another;
Thre wynges in-with, wroghte in the kynde,
Umbygon with a gold wyre. When I that gome knewe,
What, he was yongeste of yeris, and yapeste of witt,
That any wy in this werlde wiste of his age!   120
He brake a braunche in his hande, and brawndeschet it swythe,
Trynes one a grete trotte, and takes his waye
There bothe thies ferdes folke in the flede hoves.

Sayd, loo, the kyng of this kyth, ther kepe hym oure Lorde!
Sendes bodworde by me, als hym beste lyketh,   125
That no beryn be so bolde, one bothe his two eghne,
Ones to strike one stroke, ne stirre none nerre,
To lede rowte in his rewme, so ryall to thynke
Pertly with powers his pese to disturbe.
For this es the usage here and ever schall worthe,   130
If any beryn be so bolde with banere for to ryde
With-inn the kydde kyngdome, bot the kynge one,
That he schall losse the londe and his lyfe aftir.
Bot sen ye knowe noghte this kythe ne the kynges rythe,
He will forgiffe yow this gilt of his grace one.   135
Full wyde hafe I walked thies wyes amonges,
Bot sawe I never siche a syghte, segges, with myn eghne;
For here es alle the folke of Fraunce ferdede be-syde,
Of Lorreyne, of Lumbardye, and of Lawe Spayne;
Wyes of Westwale, that in were duellen;   140
Of ynglonde, of Yrlonde, Estirlynges full many,
That are stuffede in stele, strokes to dele.
And yondere a banere of blake that one the bent hoves,
With thre bulles of ble white brouden with-inn,
And iche one hase of henppe hynged a corde,   145
Seled with a sade lede; I say als me thynkes,
That hede es of holy kirke, I hope he be there,
Alle ferse to the fighte with the folke that he ledis.
Another banere es up-brayde with a bende of grene,

108 *man/endures*
109 *lets himself/on/dwells*
110 *dressed/ready* (l. 52)/*in*
111 *lapped/iron/low*
112 *upper-body armor/lower-body armor*
113 *braces* (*arm armor*)/*woven*
114 *protect*
115 *jupon, tunic*
116 *escutcheon*
117 *within/realistically*
118 *Surrounded* (l. 62)/*man*
119 *cleverest*
120 *man/knew*
121 *brandished/boldly*
122 *Proceeds/in*
123 *armies'/wait* (l. 105)

124 *country*
125 *message*
126 *man/in/eyes*
127 "*nor to stir any nearer*"
128 (*a*) *route/realm/royal*

130 *be*

132 *renowned/alone*
133 *lose*
134 *country/right*
135 *alone*
136 *men*
137 *men/eyes*
138 *mustered*
139 *Low*
140 *Westphalia/war/dwell*
141 *England/Ireland/Easterlings* (*East Germans*)
142 *dressed*

144 *hue*
145 *each/hemp/hanged*
146 *heavy leaden seal*
147 *He who/head/church*

149 *updrawn, raised*

With thre hedis white-herede with howes one lofte,   150
Croked full craftyly, and kembid in the nekke:
Thies are ledis of this londe that schold oure lawes yeme,
That thynken to dele this daye with dynttis full many.
I holde hym bot a fole that fightis whils flyttynge may helpe,
When he hase founden his frende that fayled hym never.   155

The thirde banere one bent es of blee whitte,
With sexe galegs, I see, of sable with-inn,
And iche one has a brown brase with bokeles twayne.
Thies are Sayn Franceys folke, that sayen'alle schall fey worthe';
They aren so ferse and so fresche, thay feghtyn bot seldom.   160
I wote wele for wynnynge thay wentten fro home;
His purse weghethe full wele that wanne thaym all hedire.

The fourte banere one the bent es brayde appon lofte,
With bothe the brerdes of blake, a balle in the myddes,
Reghte siche as the sone es in the someris tyde,   165
When moste es the maze one Missomer Even.
Thynkes Domynyke this daye with dynttis to dele;
With many blesenande beryn his banere es stuffede.
And sythen the pope es so priste thies prechours to helpe,
And Frauceys with his folke es forced besyde,   170
And alle the ledis of the lande ledith thurgh witt,
There es no man appon molde to machen thaym agayne,
Ne gete no grace appon grounde, undir God hym-selven.

And yitt es the fyfte appon the folde the faireste of tham alle,
A brighte banere of blee whitte with three bore-hedis;   175
Be any crafte that I kan Carmes thaym semyth,
For thay are the ledes that loven oure Lady to serve.
If I scholde say the sothe, it semys no nothire
Bot that the freris with othere folke schall the felde wynn.

The sexte es of sendell, and so are thay alle,   180
Whitte als the whalles bone, who-so the sothe tellys,
With beltys of blake, bocled to-gedir,
The poyntes pared off rownde, the pendants awaye,
And alle the lethire appon lofte that one-lowe hengeth,
Schynethe for scharpynynge of the schavynge iren.   185
The ordire of the Austyns, for oughte that I wene,
For by the blussche of the belte the banere I knewe!
And othere synes I seghe sett appon lofte,
Some witnesse of wolle, and some of wyne tounnes,
And other of merchandes merkes, so many and so thikke   190

150 *white-haired/hoods*
151 *Crimped/combed*
152 *protect* (l. 114)

154 *fool/debating*

156 *hue* (l. 144)
157 *galoshes*
158 *brace/buckles/two*
159 *dead/become*
160 *fight*

162 *weighs/won/hither*

164 *borders*
165 *Right such, just as/summertime*
166 *madness*
167 *Dominic* (these are Dominicans)
168 *glistening*
169 *prompt* (cf. *presto*)
170 *Francis*

172 *earth/match/against*

174 *yet/fifth/earth,* here *field*

176 *know/Carmelites*

179 *friars*

180 *rich* (silk) *fabric*
181 *whale's*
182 *buckled*

184 *hangs below*
185 *Shines/sharpening/iron*
186 *Augustinians/aught/think*
187 *appearance*
188 *signs*
189 *wool/wine tuns*
190 *merchants' marks*

That I ne wote in my witt, for alle this werlde riche,
Whatt segge under the sonne can the sowme rekken.
And sekere one that other syde are sadde men of armes,
Bolde sqwyeres of blode, bowemen many,
That, if thay strike one stroke, stynt thay ne thynken   195
Till owthir here appon hethe be hewen to dethe.
For-thi I bid yow bothe that thaym hedir broghte,
That ye wend with me, are any wrake falle,
To oure comely kyng that this kythe owethe;
And, fro he wiete wittirly where the wronge ristyth,   200
Thare nowthir wy be wrothe to wirche als he demeth.
Of ayther rowte ther rode owte a renke, als me thoghte,
Knyghtis full comly one coursers attyred,
And sayden, 'Sir sandisman, sele the be-tyde!
Well knowe we the kyng; he clothes us bothe,   205
And hase us fosterde and fedde this fyve and twenty wyntere.
Now fare thou by-fore and we schall folowe aftire.'
And now are thaire brydells up-brayde, and bown one thaire wayes.
Thay lighten doun at the launde, and leven thaire stedis,
Kayren up at the clyffe, and one knees fallyn.   210
The kynge henttis by the handes, and hetys tham to ryse,
And sayde, welcome, heres, as hyne of oure house bothen.
The kynge waytted one wyde, and the wyne askede;
Beryns broghte it anone in bolles of silvere.
Me thoghte I sowpped so sadly it sowrede bothe myn eghne.   215
And he that wilnes of this werke to wete any forthire,
Full freschely and faste, for here a fitt endes.

FITT II

Bot than kerpede the kynge, sayd, kythe what ye hatten,
And whi the hates aren so hote youre hertis by-twene.
If I schall deme yow this day, dothe me to here.   220
'Now certys, lorde,' sayde that one, 'the sothe for to telle,
I hatt Wynnere, a wy that alle this werlde helpis,
For I ledes cane lere, thurgh ledyng of witt.
Thoo that spedfully will spare, and spende not to grete,
Lyve appon littill-whattes, I lufe hem the bettir;   225
Witt wiendes me with, and wysses me faire;
Aye when I gadir my gudes, than glades myn hert.
Bot this felle false thefe that by-fore yowe standes
Thynkes to strike or he styntt, and stroye me for ever.
Alle that I wynn thurgh witt he wastes thurgh pryde;   230

192 *man/sun/sum*
193 *sure/on/sober*

195 *stop*
196 *either/army*

197 *Therefore/hither*
198 *go/ere/disaster*
199 *land/owns*
200 *from (the time)/knows/definitely/rests*
201 *neither/man/work/deems*
202 *From/either/man*
203 *on*
204 *messenger/prosperity*

208 *go/on*
209 *leave*
210 *go/on*
211 *takes (them)/commands*
212 *gentles/retainers*

214 *Men/bowls*
215 *strongly/seared/eyes*
216 *wishes/know/further*
217 *Fill*

218 *carped, said/reveal/are called*

220 *judge/cause . . . hear*
221 *certainly*
222 *am called/man*
223 *men/can teach*
224 *Those/speedily/too*
225 *little*
226 *goes with me/directs*
227 *Always/gather/goods/gladdens*
228 *evil/thief*
229 *ere/destroy*

I gedir, I glene, and he lattys goo sone;
I pryke and I pryne, and he the purse opynes.
Why hase this cayteffe no care how men corne sellen?
His londes liggen alle ley, his lomes aren solde,
Downn bene his dowfehowses, drye bene his poles,   235
The devyll wounder one the wele he weldys at home,
Bot hungere and heghe horses and howndes full kene!
Safe a sparthe and a spere sparrede in ane hyrne,
A bronde at his bede-hede, biddes he no nother
Bot acuttede capill to cayre with to his frendes.   240
Then will he boste with his brande, and braundesche hym ofte,
This wikkede weryed thefe, that wastoure men calles,
That, if he life may longe, this lande will he stroye.
For-thi deme us this daye, for Drightyns love in heven,
To fighte furthe with oure folke to owthire fey worthe.'   245

'Yee, wynnere,' quod wastoure, 'thi wordes are hye;
Bot I schall tell the a tale that tene schall the better.
When thou haste waltered and went and wakede alle the nyghte,
And iche a wy in this werlde that wonnes the abowte,
And hase werpede thy wyde howses full of wolle sakkes—   250
The bemys benden at the rofe, siche bakone ther hynges,
Stuffed are sterlynges undere stelen bowndes—
What scholde worthe of that wele, if no waste come?
Some rote, some ruste, some ratones fede.
Let be thy cramynge of thi kystes, for Cristis lufe of heven!   255
Late the peple and the pore hafe parte of thi silvere;
For if thou wydwhare scholde walke, and waytten the sothe,
Thou scholdeste reme for rewthe, in siche ryfe bene the pore.
For, and thou lengare thus lyfe, leve thou no nother,
Thou schall be hanged in helle for that thou here spareste;   260
For siche a synn haste thou solde thi soule in-to helle,
And there es ever wellande woo, worlde with-owtten ende.'
'Late be thi worde, wastoure,' quod wynnere the riche.
'Thou melleste of a mater, thou madiste it thi-selven,
With thi sturte and thi stryffe thou stroyeste up my gudes;   265
In wraxlinge and in wakynge in wyntteres nyghttis,
In owttrage, in unthrifte, in angarte pryde.
There es no wele in this werlde to wasschen thyn handes
That ne es gyffen and grounden are thou it getyn have.
Thou ledis renkes in thy rowte wele rychely attyrede;   270
Some hafe girdills of golde, that more gude coste
Than alle the faire fre londe that ye be-fore haden.

231 *gather/lets go soon*
232 *pin/opens*
233 *caitiff, wretch*
234 *lie/fallow/tools*
235 *dovehouses/pools*
236 *wonder on/wealth/wields*

238 *Save/halberd/kept, hid/corner*
239 *brand, sword/bed's head/asks/nothing else*
240 *gelded/horse/ride*
241 *brandish*
242 *cursed*

244 *Therefore/let us deem/the Lord's*
245 *forth/till/either (of us)/fated/shall become*

247 *disturb*
248 *"tossed and turned"*
249 *every/man/dwells/about you*
250 *warped, stuffed/wool*
251 *beams/roof/such/bacon*
252 *steel/bands*
253 *become (l. 245)*
254 *(would) rot/rats*
255 *chests*
256 *Let*
257 *"far and wide"/look for*
258 *weep/so rife, plentiful*
259 *if/longer/believe*

262 *welling/woe*

264 *talk*
265 *"stir and strife"*
266 *wrestling/winters'*
267 *haughty*

269 *given/ere*
270 *lead/men*

Ye folowe noghte youre fadirs that fosterde yow alle
A kynde herveste to cache, and cornes to wynn,
For the colde wyntter and the kene with clengande frostes,   275
Sythen dropeles drye in the dede monethe.
And thou wolle to the taverne, by-fore the toune-hede,
Iche beryne redy with a bolle to blerren thyn eghne,
Hete the whatte thou have schalte, and whatt thyn hert lykes,
Wyfe, wedowe, or wenche, that wonnes there aboute.   280
Then es there bott 'fille in' and 'feche forthe,' Florence to schewe,
'Wee-hee,' and 'worthe up,' wordes ynewe.
Bot when this wele es a-waye, the wyne moste be payede fore:
Than lympis yowe weddis to laye, or youre londe selle.
For siche wikked werkes, wery the oure Lorde!   285
And for-thi God laughte that he lovede, and levede that other,
Iche freke one felde ogh the ferdere be to wirche.
Teche thy men for to tille and tynen thyn feldes;
Rayse up thi rent-howses, ryme up thi yerdes,
Owthere hafe as thou haste done, and hope aftir werse—   290
That es firste the faylynge of fode, and than the fire aftir,
To brene the alle at a birre, for thi bale dedis:
The more colde es to come, als me a clerke tolde.'

'Yee, wynnere,' quod wastoure, 'thi wordes are vayne;
With oure festes and oure fare we feden the pore;   295
It es plesynge to the Prynce that paradyse wroghte;
When Cristes peple hath parte hym payes alle the better
Then here ben hodirde and hidde and happede in cofers,
That it no sonn may see thurgh seven wyntter ones;
Owthir it freres feche, when thou fey worthes,   300
To payntten with thaire pelers, or pergett with thaire walles.
Thi sone and thi sektours, ichone sewes othere;
Maken dale aftir thi daye, for thou durste never
Mawngery ne myndale, ne never myrthe lovediste.
A dale aftir thi daye dose the no mare   305
Than a lighte lanterne late appone nyghte,
When it es borne at thi bakke, beryn, be my trouthe.
Now wolde God that it were als I wisse couthe,
That thou, wynnere, thou wriche, and wanhope, thi brothir,
And eke ymbryne dayes, and evenes of sayntes,   310
The Frydaye and his fere one the ferrere syde,
Were drownede in the depe see there never droghte come,
And dedly synn for thayre dede were endityde with twelve;
And thies beryns one the bynches, with biggins one lofte

275 *clinging*
276 *After/dropless/dryness, drought/months*
277 *will (go)/"at the end of town"*
278 *man/bowl/blear/eyes*
279 *Promise*
280 *dwells*
281 *"barmaid (F.) to bring to you"*
282 *enough*

284 *"it comes to pass"/pledges*
285 *curse*
286 *therefore/latched, took/left*
287 *Each/man/ought/more zealous*
288 *fence*
289 *open*
290 *Or*

292 *one swoop/deeds*

298 *concealed/hasped*
299 *sun/once*
300 *Or/friars/fetch/fated (to die)/are*
301 *paint/pillars (with it)/plaster*
302 *son/executors/each one/pursues*
303 *dole/dare*
304 *"(give a) feast or commemoration, wake"*
305 *dole/does/more (good)*
306 *lighted*
307 *man/by*
308 *could conduct*
309 *wretch/despair*
310 *also/ember/eves of saints' days*
311 *Good Friday/companion/on/further (Holy Saturday)*
312 *"where drought never comes"*
313 *deadly/deed/indicted by*
314 *men/high headdresses*

That bene knowen and kydde for clerkes of the beste,   315
Als gude als Arestotle, or Austyn the wyse,
That alle schent were those schalkes, and Scharshull itwiste,
That saide I prikkede with powere his pese to distourbe!
For-thi, comely kynge, that oure case heris,
Late us swythe with oure swerdes swyngen to-gedirs,   320
For now I se it es full sothe that sayde es full yore:
'The richere of ranke wele, the rathere will drede;
The more havande that he hathe, the more of hert feble.'

Bot than this wrechede wynnere full wrothely he lukes,
Sayse, 'this es spedles speche to speken thies wordes.'   325
Loo, thou weryed wastoure, that wyde-whare es knawenn,
Ne es nothir kaysser, ne kynge, ne knyghte that the folowes,
Barone, ne bachelere, ne beryn that thou loveste,
Bot foure felawes or fyve, that the fayth owes;
And thou schall dighte thaym to dyne with dayntethes so many   330
That iche a wy in this werlde may wepyn for sorowe.
The bores hede schall be broghte with bayes appon lofte,
Buk-tayles full brode in brothes there be-syde,
Venyson with the frumentes, and fesanttes full riche,
Baken mete ther-by one the burde sett,   335
Chewettes of choppede flesche, charbiande fewlis,
And iche a segge that I see has sexe mens doke.
If this were nedles note, anothir comes aftir,
Roste with the riche sewes, and the ryalle spyces,
Kiddes cleven by the rigge, quartered swannes,   340
Tartes of ten ynche, that tenys myn hert
To see the borde over-brade with blasande disches,
Als it were a rayled rode with rynges and stones.
The thirde mese to me were mervelle to rekken,
For alle es Martynmesse mete that I with moste dele,   345
Noghte bot worttes with the flesche, with-owt wilde fowle,
Save ane hene to hym that the howse owethe;
And ye will hafe birdes bownn one a broche riche,
Barnakes and buturs and many billed snyppes,
Larkes and lyngwhittes, lapped in sogoure,   350
Wodcokkes and wodwales, full wellande hote,
Teeles and titmoyses, to take what yowe lykes;
Caudels of conynges, and custadis swete,
Daryols and dische-metis, that ful dere coste,
Mawmene that men clepen, your mawes to fill,   355
Twelve mese at a merke, by-twen twa men,

315 *renowned* (l. 132)
316 *St. Augustine*
317 *shamed/men/*(a Chief Justice in 1333)*/betwixt*
318 *spurred/peace*

320 *Let/swiftly*
321 *long ago*
322 *wealth*
323 *having*

324 *looks*
325 *unprofitable*
326 *cursed* (l. 285)*/far and wide* (cf. l. 257)

329 (*to*) *thee*
330 *direct/dainties*
331 *every man*

334 (an accompanying wheat dish), *frumenty*
335 *Baked/on* . . . *board*
336 *Meat pies/grilled/fowls*
337 *every man/six men's serving*
338 (*As*) *if/business/another* (*course*)
339 *sauces/royal*
340 *ridge, spine*
341 *grieves*
342 *overspread/blazing*
343 *As* (*if*)*/decorated rood, cross*
344 *mess, dish*
345 *Martinmas/mostly*
346 *vegetables* (cf. N.G. *Wort*)
347 *hen/owns*
348 *prepared* (l. 110)*/on a spit/richly*
349 *Wild geese* (l. 39)*/bitterns/snipes*
350 *linnets/sugar*
351 *woodpeckers*
352 *titmice*
353 *Hot rabbit broth/custards*
354 *Pastries*
355 (?a rich dish)*/call* (*it*)*/stomachs*
356 *messes/time/two*

Thoghe bot brynneth for bale your bowells with-in.
Me tenyth at your trompers, thay tounen so heghe
That iche a gome in the gate goullyng may here;
Than wil thay say to tham-selfe, as thay samen ryden,   360
Ye hafe no myster of the helpe of the heven kyng.
Thus are ye scorned by skyll, and scathed theraftir,
That rechen for a repaste a rawnsom of silver.
Bot ones I herd in a haule of a herdmans tong:
Better were meles many than a mery nyghte.   365
And he that wilnes of this werke for to wete forther,
Full freschely and faste, for here a fit endes.

FITT III

'Yee, wynnere,' quod wastour, 'I wote well my-selven
What sall lympe of the lede, within a lite yeris.
Then the pure plenté of corne that the peple sowes,   370
That God will graunte of his grace to growe on the erthe,
Ay to appaire the pris, that it passe nott to hye,
Schal make the to waxe wod for wanhope in erthe,
To hope aftir an harde yere, to honge thi-selven.
Woldeste thou hafe lordis to lyfe as laddes on fote,   375
Prelates als prestes that the parischen yemes,
Prowde marchandes of pris, as pedders in towns?
Late lordes lyfe als tham liste, laddes as tham falles,
Thay the bacon and beefe, thay botours and swannes,
Thay the roughe of the rye, thay the rede whete,   380
Thay the grewell gray, and thay the gude sewes.
And then may the peple hafe parte in povert that standes,
Sum gud morsell of mete to mend with thair chere.
If fewlis flye schold forthe, and fongen be never,
And wild bestis in the wodde wone al thaire lyve,   385
And fisches flete in the flode, and ichone frete other,
Ane henne at ane halpeny by halfe yeris ende,
Schold not a ladde be in londe a lorde for to serve.
This wate thou full wele witterly thi-selven,
Who so wele schal wyn, a wastour moste he fynde,   390
For if it greves one gome, it gladdes another.'
'Now,' quod wynner to wastour, 'me wondirs in hert
Of thies poure penyles men that peloure will by,
Sadills of sendale, with sercles full riche.
Lesse that ye wrethe your wifes, thaire willes to folowe,   395
Ye sellyn wodd aftir wodde in a wale tyme,

357 *burns*
358 *"I am grieved"/toot, make tune*
359 *every man/way/squawking*
360 *together*
361 *need*
362 *"quite reasonably scorned"/shamed*
363 *reach/ransom*
364 *once/hall/tongue*

366 *wishes/know/further*
367 *Refill*

369 *shall/become/people/a little time*

372 *Ever/impair/price/too*
373 *mad/despair* (l. 309)

376 *as/parish/protects* (l. 152)
377 *merchants/peddlers*
378 *Let/pleases/befalls*

380 *red*
381 *gruel/sauces*
382 *"people who in poverty stand have part"*
383 *"to amend their dispositions with"*
384 *fowls/never be taken*
385 *dwell*
386 *float/each one/gobble*
387 *A hen/halfpenny*

389 *know/surely* (l. 200)
390 *Whosoever/must*
391 *man*

393 *furs*
394 *rich stuff* (l. 180)
395 *make wroth*
396 *wood . . . wood/short*

Bothe the oke and the assche and all that ther growes;
The spyres and the yonge sprynge ye spare to your children
And sayne God wil grant it his grace to grow at the laste,
For to schadewe your sones: bot the schame es your ownn.   400
Nedeles save ye the soyle, for sell it ye thynken.
Your forfadirs were fayne, when any frende come,
For to schake to the schawe, and schewe hym the estres,
In iche holt that thay had ane hare for to fynde,
Bryng to the brode lande bukkes ynewe,   405
To lache and to late goo, to lightten thaire hertis.
Now es it sett and solde, my sorowe es the more,
Wasted alle wilfully, your wyfes to paye.
That are had lordes in londe and ladyes riche,
Now are thay nysottes of the new gett, so nysely attyred,   410
With side slabbande sleves, sleght to the grounde,
Ourlede all umbetourne with ermyn aboute,
That as harde es, I hope, to handil in the derne,
Als a cely symple wenche that never silke wroghte.
Bot who-so lukes on hir, oure lady of heven,   415
How scho fled for ferd ferre out of hir kythe,
Appon ane amblande asse, with-owtten more pride,
Safe a barne in hir barme, and a broken heltre
That Joseph held in hys hande, that hend for to yeme.
All-thofe scho walt al this werlde, hir wedes wer pore;   420
For to gyf ensample of siche, for to schew other
For to leve pompe and pride, that poverte eschewes.'

Than this wastour wrothly werped up his eghne,
And said, 'thou wynnere, thou wriche, me wondirs in hert
What hafe oure clothes coste the, caytef, to by,   425
That thou schal birdes up-brayd of thaire bright wedis,
Sythen that we vouche-safe that the silver payen.
It lyes wele for a lede his leman to fynde,
Aftir hir faire chere to forthir hir herte.
Then will scho love hym lelely as hir lyfe one,   430
Make hym bolde and bown with brandes to smytte,
To schonn schenchipe and schame, ther schalkes ere gadird;
And if my peple ben prode, me payes alle the better
To see tham faire and free to-fore with myn eghne;
And ye negardes, appon nyghte, ye nappen so harde,   435
Raxillen at your routtyng, raysen your hurdies;
Bedene ye wayte one the wedir, then wery ye the while,
That ye hade hightilde up your houses, and your hyne arayed.

398 *saplings*
399 *say*
400 *shadow*

403 *hie/wood/place* (estate)

405 *enough*
406 *latch, catch/let go*

408 *please*
409 *Those* (who)/*ere, formerly*
410 *"followers of the new fad"/foolishly*
411 *"long flowing sleeves, falling . . ."*
412 *bordered/around*
413 *I think/darkness*
414 *silly*

416 *she/fear/far/country*
417 *ambling*
418 *Save, except/babe/lap/halter*
419 *holy* (one)/*protect* (l. 376)
420 *Although/wielded, ruled/clothes*
421 *example/such*

423 *cast/eyes*
424 *wretch*
425 *caitiff* (l. 233)/*buy*
426 *maidens*
427 *Since*
428 *man/lover/maintain*

430 *loyally/own*
431 *ready/brands, swords/smite*
432 *shun/ignominy/men are gathered*

434 *before*
435 *niggards/at night*
436 *Writhe/snoring/buttocks*
437 *Constantly/weather/curse* (l. 285)
438 *repaired/servants* (l. 212)

For-thi, wynnere, with wronge thou wastes thi tyme;
For gode day ne glade getys thou never.   440
The devyll at thi dede-day schal delyn thi gudis,
The thou woldest that it ware, wyn thay it never;
Thi skathill sectours schal sever tham aboute,
And thou hafe helle full hotte for that thou here saved.
Thou tast no tent one a tale that tolde was full yore: 445
'I hold hym madde that mournes his make for to wyn;
Hent hit that hit haf schal, and hold hit his while;
Take the coppe as it comes, the case as it falles;
For who-so lyfe may lengeste lympes to feche
Woodd that he waste schall, to warmen his helys,   450
Ferrere than his fadir dide by fyvetene myle.'
Now kan I carpe no more; bot, Sir Kyng, by thi trouthe,
Deme us where we duell schall; me thynke the day hyes.
Yit harde sore es myn herte, and harmes me more
Ever to see in my syghte that I in soule hate.'   455

The kynge lovely lokes on the ledis twayne,
Says, 'blynnes, beryns, of your brethe and of youre brothe wordes,
And I schal deme yow this day where ye duelle schall,
Aythere lede in a lond ther he es loved moste.
Wende, wynnere, thi waye over the wale stremys,   460
Passe forthe by Paris to the Pope of Rome;
The cardynalls ken the wele, will kepe the ful faire,
And make thi sydes in silken schetys to lygge,
And fede the and foster the and forthir thyn hert,
As leefe to worthen wode as the to wrethe ones.   465
Bot loke, lede, be thi lyfe, when I lettres sende,
That thou hy the to me home on horse or one fote;
And when I knowe thou will come, he schall cayre uttire,
And lenge with another lede, til thou thi lefe lache;
For thofe thou bide in this burgh to thi beryinge-day,   470
With hym falles the never a fote for to strecche.
And thou, wastoure, I will that thou wonne ther ever
Ther moste waste es of wele, and wynges untill.
Chese the forthe into the chepe, a chambre thou rere,
Loke thi wyndowe be wyde, and wayte the aboute,   475
Where any berande potener thurgh the burgh passe;
Teche hym to the tonne till he tayte worthe;
Doo hym drynk al nyghte that he dry be at morow;
Sythen ken hym to the crete to comforth his vaynes,
Brynge hym to Bred Strete, bikken thi fynger,   480

441 *death-/divide/goods*
442 *Those/guard, have*
443 *scatheful/executors* (l. 302)
444 *what*
445 *take no account of/long ago*
446 *frets*
447 *Grasp (it)/who/time*
448 *cup*
449 *may live longest/comes to fetch*
450 *heels*
451 *Further/fifteen*
452 *talk*
453 *Judge/dwell/hies, hastens*

456 *lovingly/men*
457 *stop/men/brawls/bold*

460 *Go/quick/streams*

462 *know*
463 *sheets/lie*

465 *lief/become mad/make wroth*

468 *ride out*
469 *linger/leave/latch, take*
470 *though/burying-*
471 *befalls*
472 *dwell*
473 *Where/flies/(there) unto*
474 *Choose/Cheapside/build*

476 *bearing/purse*
477 *tun/tight/becomes*
478 *Make*
479 *After/show/Cretan (wine)*
480 *beckon*

Schew hym of fatt chepe scholdirs ynewe,
Hotte for the hungry, a hen other twayne,
Sett hym softe one a sete, and sythen send after,
Bryng out of the burgh the best thou may fynde,
And luke thi knave hafe a knoke bot he the clothe spred;   485
Bot late hym paye or he passe, and pik hym so clene
That fynd a peny in his purse, and put owte his eghe.
When that es dronken and don, duell ther no longer,
Bot teche hym owt of the townn, to trotte aftir more.
Then passe to the Pultrie, the peple the knowes,   490
And ken wele thi katour to knawen thi fode,
The herons, the hasteletez, the hennes wele served,
The pertrikes, the plovers, the other pulled byrddes,
The albus, the osulles, the egretes dere;
The more wastis thi wele, the better the wynner lykes.   495
And wayte to me, thou wynnere, if thou wilt wele chese,
When I wende appon werre my wyes to lede;
For at the proude paleys of Parys the riche
I thynk to do it in ded, and dub the to knyghte,
And giff giftes full grete of golde and of silver,   500
To ledis of my legyance that lufen me in hert,
And sythen kayren as I come, with knyghtis that me foloen,
To the kirke of Colayne ther the kynges ligges . . .

SUPPLEMENTARY MATERIAL

1. John Speirs, *Medieval English Poetry, The Non-Chaucerian Tradition* (London, 1957), pp. 263–89.
2. John D. Peter, *Complaint and Satire in Early English Literature,* Oxford, 1956.
3. Rossell H. Robbins, "Middle English Poems of Protest," *Anglia,* LXXVIII (1960), 193–203.

481 *sheep*
482 *or two*

485 *look/knock, blow/unless, if*
486 *ere*
487 *eyes, i.e., "hoodwink him"*

489 *show/(the way) out*
490 *Poultry*
491 *teach/caterer*
492 *roasted joints*
493 *partridges*
494 *alpine bullfinches*

496 *choose*
497 *into war/men*
498 *palace/Paris*

501 *allegiance/love*
502 *after/go/came/follow*
503 *church/Cologne (where)/(three) kings/lie*

THE PARLEMENT OF THE THRE AGES

In the monethe of Maye when mirthes bene fele,
And the sesone of somere when softe bene the wedres,
Als I went to the wodde my werdes to dreghe,
In-to the schawes my-selfe a schotte me to gete
At ane hert or ane hynde, happen as it myghte, 5
And as Dryghtyn the day drove frome the heven,
Als I habade one a banke be a bryme syde,
There the gryse was grene, growen with floures—
The primrose, the pervynke, and piliole the riche—
The dewe appon dayses donkede full faire, 10
Burgons and blossoms and braunces full swete,
And the mery mystes full myldely gane falle.
The cukkowe, the cowschote, kene were thay bothen,
And the throstills full throly threpen in the bankes,
And iche foule in that frythe faynere than other 15
That the derke was done and the daye lightenede.
Hertys and hyndes one hillys thay goven,
The foxe and the filmarte thay flede to the erthe,
The hare hurkles by hawes and harde thedir dryves,
And ferkes faste to hir fourme and fatills hir to sitt. 20
Als I stode in that stede one stalkynge I thoghte;
Bothe my body and my bowe I buskede with leves,
And turnede to-wardes a tree and tariede ther a while;
And als I lokede to a launde a littill me be-syde,
I seghe ane hert with ane hede, ane heghe for the nones; 25
Alle unburneschede was the beme, full borely the mydle,
With iche feetur as thi fote, for-frayed in the greves,
With auntlers one aythere syde egheliche longe.
The ryalls full richely raughten frome the myddes,
With surryals full semely appon sydes twayne; 30
And he assommet and sett of vi and of fyve,
And ther-to borely and brode and of body grete,
And a coloppe for a kynge, cache hym who myghte.

1 *many*
2 *weather(s)*
3 *As/wood/luck to test*
4 *thickets*

6 *(the) Lord*
7 *lingered on/beside a stream*
8 *grass*
9 *periwinkle/wild thyme*
10 *daisies/was dank*
11 *Buds/branches*
12 *began (to)*
13 *cuckoo/pigeon*
14 *boldly/contest (on)*
15 *each, every/wood*
16 *dark*
17 *Harts/on hills/proceeded*
18 *polecat*
19 *cringes/hedges/thither*
20 *goes/lair/readies*

22 *clothed, concealed*

24 *lawn, field*
25 *saw/(antlered) head/high (one)/to be sure*
26 *unburnished/beam/burly*
27 *feature, tine/rubbed/grooves*
28 *antlers/on either/grimly*
29 *royals, first branches off main antlers/projected from the midst*
30 *tines branching off royals/two*
31 *(was) summed, full-grown/decked with/about 5 or 6*
32 *burly (l. 26)*
33 *tasty snack*

Bot there sewet hym a sowre that servet hym full yerne,
That woke and warned hym when the wynde faylede,   35
That none so sleghe in his slepe with sleghte scholde hym dere,
And went the wayes hym by-fore when any wothe tyde.
My lyame than full lightly lete I doun falle
And to the bole of a birche my berselett I cowchide.
I waited wiesly the wynde by waggynge of leves,   40
Stalkede full stilly, no stikkes to breke,
And crepite to a crabtre and coverede me ther-undere.
Than I bende up by bowe and bownede me to schote,
Tighte up my tylere and taysede at the hert.
Bot the sowre that hym sewet sett up the nese,   45
And wayttede wittyly abowte and wyndide full yerne.
Then I moste stonde als I stode and stirre no fote ferrere,
For had I myntid or movede or made any synys,
Alle my layke hade bene loste that I hade longe wayttede.
Bot gnattes gretely me grevede and gnewen myn eghne.   50
And he stotayde and stelkett and starede full brode.
Bot at the laste he loutted doun and laughte till his mete.
And I hallede to the hokes and the hert smote,
And happenyd that I hitt hym by-hynde the lefte scholdire,
That the blode braste owte appon bothe the sydes.   55
And he balkede and brayed and bruschede thurgh the greves,
As alle had hurlede one ane hepe that in the holte longede,
And sone the sowre that hym sewet resorte to his feris,
And thay, forfrayede of his fare, to the fellys thay hyen,
And I hyede to my hounde and hent hym up sone,   60
And louset my lyame and lete hym umbycaste.
The breris and the brakans were blody by-ronnen,
And he assentis to that sewte and seches hym aftire,
There he was crepyde in-to a krage and crouschede to the erthe.
Dede als a dore-nayle doun was he fallen,   65
And I hym hent by the hede and heryett hym uttire,
Turned his troches and tachede thaym in-to the erthe,
Kest up that keudart and kutt of his tonge,
Brayde owte his bewells my bereselet to fede.
And I slitte hym at the assaye to see how me semyde,   70
And he was floreschede full faire of two fyngere brede.
I chese to the chawylls chefe to be-gynn
And ritte doun at a rase reghte to the tayle,
And than the herbere anone aftir I makede,
I raughte the righte legge by-fore, ritt it ther-aftir,   75
And so fro legge to legge I lepe thaym aboute,

34 *pursued, accompanied/sorrel (buck)/readily*

36 *sly/sleight/harm*
37 *danger threatened*
38 *leash*
39 *hound/put, couched*

42 *crept/crab tree*
43 *prepared to shoot*
44 *Set/crossbow stock/took aim*
45 *nose*
46 *sniffed/diligently*
47 *must/as/further*
48 *aimed/signs*
49 *sport*
50 *gnats/gnawed/eyes*
51 *paused/stalked*
52 *bowed/latched (on)to*
53 *hauled/hooks (of the bow)*

55 *(So) that/blood burst out*
56 *groves*
57 *As (if)/belonged*
58 *returned/companions*
59 *afraid/behavior/hills/hied*
60 *seized*
61 *loosed/leash/cast around, search*
62 *briars/brakes/bloody, covered with blood*
63 *pursuit/seeks*
64 *crouched*

66 *dragged him out*
67 *end tines/attached, pushed*
68 *Cast, turned/rascal/off*
69 *Drew/bowels/hound*
70 *test (point)*
71 *fatted/the breadth of two fingers*
72 *chose/jowls*
73 *ripped/race, rush/right*
74 *first stomach*
75 *grasped*
76 *leaped*

And the felle fro the fete fayre I departede
And flewe it doun with my fiste faste to the rigge.
I tighte owte my trenchore and toke of the scholdirs,
Cuttede corbyns bone and keste it a-waye.   80
I slitte hym full sleghely and slyppede in my fyngere,
Lesse the poynte scholde perche the pawnche or the guttys.
I soughte owte my sewet and semblete it to-gedire
And pullede oute the pawnche and putt it in an hole.
I grippede owte the guttes and graythede thaym be-syde   85
And than the nombles anone name I there-aftire
Rent up fro the rygge reghte to the myddis.
And then the fourches full fayre I fonge fro the sydes
And chynede hym chefely and choppede of the nekke
And the hede and the haulse homelyde in sondree.   90
The fete of the fourche I feste thurgh the sydis
And the hevede alle in-to ane hole and hidde it with ferne,
With hethe and with horemosse hilde it about,
That no fostere of the fee scholde fynde it ther-aftir;
Hid the hornes and the hede in ane hologhe oke,   95
That no hunte scholde it hent ne have it in sighte.
I foundede faste ther-fro for ferde to be wryghede,
And sett me oute one a syde to see how it chevede,
To wayte it frome wylde swyne that wyse bene of nesse.
And als I satte in my sette the sone was so warme,   100
And I for slepeles was slome and slomerde a while.
And there me dremed, in that dowte, a full dreghe swevynn,
And whate I seghe in my saule the sothe I schall telle.

I

I seghe thre thro men threpden full yerne,
And moten of myche-whate and maden thaym full tale.   105
And ye will, ledys, me listen ane hande-while,
I schal reken thaire araye redely for-sothe,
And to yowe neven thaire names naytly there-aftire.
The firste was a ferse freke, fayrere than thies othire,
A bolde beryn one a blonke bownne for to ryde,   110
A hathelle on ane heghe horse with hauke appon honde.
He was balghe in the breste and brode in the scholdirs,
His axles and his armes were i-liche longe,
And in the medill als a mayden menskfully schapen.
Longe legges and large, and lele for to schewe.   115
He streghte hym in his sterapis and stode up-rightes.

77 *skin/parted*
78 *flayed/ridge, backbone*
79 *drew/knife*
80 *corbie's, raven's bone* (gristle at base of sternum)/*cast*

82 *Lest/pierce*
83 *suet/assembled*

85 *set . . . beside*
86 *numbles, entrails*

88 *forks, thighs/took from*
89 *cut along spine/off*
90 *neck* (cf. N.G. *Hals*, N.E. *halter*)/*cut/sundry, asunder*
91 *fastened*
92 *head*
93 *hid*
94 (*So*) *that/forester*
95 *hollow*
96 *hunter/seize*
97 *hurried/fear/found out*
98 *achieved, fared*
99 *protect/nose* (l. 45)
100 *seat/sun*
101 *sleeplessness/groggy/slumbered*
102 *doubt/long/dream*
103 *saw/soul*

104 *intense/argue/eagerly*
105 *spoke/much-what, a lot/bold*
106 *If/men/a short while*
107 *reckon, give account of/readily*
108 *name/precisely*
109 *fierce/man*
110 *man/on a horse/ready*
111 *man/high/hawk*
112 *bulging, rounded*
113 *shoulders/alike, likewise*
114 *middle/excellently*
115 *loyal, handsome/show*
116 *stretched/stirrups*

He ne hade no hode ne no hatte bot his here one,
A chaplet one his chefe-lere, chosen for the nones,
Raylede alle with rede rose, richeste of floures,
With trayfoyles and trewloves of full triede perles,   120
With a chefe charebocle chosen in the myddes.
He was gerede alle in grene, alle with golde by-wevede,
Embroddirde alle with besanttes and beralles full riche.
His colere with calsydoynnes clustrede full thikke,
With many dyamandes full dere dighte on his sleves.   125
The semys with saphirs sett were full many,
With emeraudes and amatistes appon iche syde,
With full riche rubyes raylede by the hemmes.
The price of that perry were worthe powndes full many.
His sadill was of sykamoure that he satt inn,   130
His bridell alle of brente golde with silke brayden raynes,
His trapoure was of tartaryne, that traylede to the erthe,
And he throly was threven of thritty yere of elde,
And ther-to yonge and yape, and Youthe was his name
And the semelyeste segge that I seghe ever.   135

II

The seconde segge in his sete satte at his ese,
A renke alle in rosette that rowmly was schapyn
In a golyone of graye girde in the myddes
And iche bagge in his bosome bettir than othere.
One his golde and his gude gretly he mousede,   140
His renttes and his reches rekened he full ofte,
Of mukkyng, of marlelyng, and mendynge of howses,
Of benes of his bondemen, of benefetis many,
Of presanttes of polayle, of purfilis als,
Of purches of ploughe-londes, of parkes full faire,   145
Of profettis of his pasturs, that his purse mendis,
Of stiewardes, of storrours, stirkes to bye,
Of clerkes, of countours, his courtes to holde,
And alle his witt in this werlde was one his wele one.
Hym semyde for to see to of sexty yere elde,   150
And ther-fore men in his marche Medill elde hym callede.

III

The thirde was a laythe lede lenyde one his syde,
A beryne bownn alle in blake, with bedis in his hande,
Croked and courbede, encrampeschett for elde,

117 *hood/hair*
118 *head/occasion*
119 *decorated*
120 *trefoils/trueloves/precious*
121 *carbuncle*
122 *interwoven*
123 *gold coin-like ornaments/beryls*
124 *collar/chalcedonies*
125 *diamonds/bedight*
126 *seams*
127 *emeralds/amethysts/each, every*

129 *possessions, gems*

131 *burnt*
132 *saddle blanket/silken fabric of Tartary*
133 *thriven/thirty/age*
134 *vigorous*
135 *man*

137 *man/russet/fully*
138 *tunic*
139 *(?money)bag, badge*
140 *On/goods/mused*
141 *riches*
142 *"fertilizing with muck and marl"*
143 *petitions*
144 *poultry/(purfilis* unknown)*/also*

147 *storekeepers/stirks, second-year bullocks or heifers*

149 *on/weal, wealth/only*

151 *district/Middle Age*

152 *loathly/man/leaning*
153 *man/dressed*
154 *curved, bent/encramped, crooked*

Alle disfygured was his face, and fadit his hewe   155
His berde and browes were blanchede full whitte,
And the hare one his hede hewede of the same.
He was ballede and blynde, and alle babirlippede
Totheles and tenefull, I tell yowe for sothe,
And ever he momelide and ment and mercy he askede   160
And cried kenely one Criste and his crede sayde
With sawtries full sere tymes, to sayntes in heven
Envyous and angrye and Elde was his name.
I helde hym be my hopynge a hundrethe yeris of age
And bot his cruche and his couche he carede for no more.   165
Now hafe I rekkende yow theire araye, redely the sothe,
And also namede yow thaire names naytly there-aftire,
And now thaire carpynge I sall kythe, knowe it if yowe liste.

IV

Now this gome alle in grene so gayly attyrede
This hathelle one this heghe horse with hauke one his fiste   170
He was yonge and yape and yernynge to armes
And pleynede hym one paramours and peteuosely syghede
He sett hym up in his sadill and seyde theis wordes,
'My lady, my leman, that I hafe luffede ever,
My wele and my wirchip, in werlde where thou duellys,   175
My playstere of paramours, my lady with pappis full swete,
Alle my hope and my hele, myn herte es thyn ownn!
I by-hete the a heste and heghely I a-vowe
There schall no hode ne no hatt one my hede sitt,
Till that I ioyntly with a gesserante iustede hafe onere   180
And done dedis for thi love, doghety in armes.'

V

Bot then this gome alle in graye greved with his wordes
And sayde, 'Felowe, be my faythe thou fonnes full yerne,
For alle fantome and foly that thou with faris.
Where es the londe and the lythe that thou arte lorde over?   185
For alle thy ryalle araye renttis hase thou none,
Ne for thi pompe and thi pride, penyes bot fewe,
For alle thi golde and thi gude gloes one thi clothes,
And thou hafe caughte thi kaple thou cares for no fothire.
Bye the stirkes with thi stede and stalles thaym make.   190
Thi brydell of brent golde wolde bullokes the gete.
The pryce of thi perrye wolde purches the londes;
And wonne, wy, in thi witt, for wele-neghe thou spilles.'

155 *faded*

158 *bald/thick-lipped*
159 *woeful*
160 *mumbled/moaned*

162 *psalteries/many*
163 *(Old) Age*
164 *by/reckoning*
165 *except for*

167 *precisely*
168 *talking/shall/relate/wish*

170 *man*

172 *complained/about/piteously/sighed*

174 *lover/loved*
175 *worship/dwell*
176 *panacea, balm/breasts*
177 *health*
178 *"make you a promise"*

180 *jointly/mail, armor/jousted/honorably*
181 *deeds*

183 *prattle*
184 *produce*
185 *people*
186 *royal*

188 *glows*
189 *horse/no more*
190 *stirks (l. 147)/(for) them*

192 *gems (l. 129)*
193 *dwell/man/by thy wit/spill your brains*

VI

Than the gome alle in grene greved full sore
And sayd, 'Sir, be my soule, thi consell es feble.   195
Bot thi golde and thi gude thou hase no god ells.
For, be the lorde and the laye that I leve inne,
And by the Gode that me gaffe goste and soule,
Me were levere one this launde lengen a while
Stoken in my stele-wede one my stede bakke,   200
Harde haspede in my helme and in my here-wedys
With a grym grownden glayfe graythely in my honde,
And see a kene knyghte come and cowpe with my-selven
That I myghte halde that I hafe highte and heghely avowede,
And parfourme my profers and proven my strengthes   205
Than alle the golde and the gude that thoue gatt ever,
Than alle the londe and the lythe that thoue arte lorde over
And ryde to a revere redily there-aftir
With haukes full hawtayne that heghe willen flye
And when the fewlis bene founden, fawkoneres hyenn   210
To lache oute thaire lessches and lowsen thaym sone
And keppyn of thaire caprons, and casten fro honde,
And than the hawteste in haste hyghes to the towre
With theire bellys so brighte blethely thay ryngen
And there they hoven appon heghte as it were heven angelles.   215
Then the fawkoners full fersely to floodes thay hyen,
To the revere with thaire roddes to rere up the fewles
Sowssches thaym full serely to serven thaire hawkes
Than tercellettes full tayttely telys doun stryken,
Laners and lanerettis lighten to thes endes,   220
Metyn with the maulerdes and many doun striken.
Fawkons thay founden freely to lighte
With *hoo* and *howghe* to the heron thay hitten hym full ofte,
Buffetyn hym, betyn hym, and brynges hym to sege
And saylen hym full serely, and sesyn hym there-aftire.   225
Then fawkoners full fersely founden tham aftire,
To helpen thaire hawkes thay hyen thaym full yerne,
For the bitt of his bill bitterly he strikes.
They knelyn doun one theire knees and krepyn full lowe
Wynnen to his wynges and wrythen thaym to-gedire,   230
Brosten the bones and brekyn thaym in sondire,
Puttis owte with a penn the maryo one his glove,
And quopes thaym to the querrye, that quelled hym to the dethe.

197 *law, faith/believe*
198 *gave/ghost, spirit*
199 *liefer/linger*
200 *Stuck/steel-weeds, clothes/steed's*
201 *war-clothes*
202 *sword/ready*
203 *coup, contest*
204 *hold/what/have promised*
205 *"perform (what I) proffer"*
206 *got*

208 *river*
209 *haughty, proud*
210 *fowls/hie*
211 *latch, take/leashes/loosen*
212 *take off/hoods*

214 *bells/blithely*
215 *(are) heaved/high/as (if)*
216 *streams*
217 *rods/rouse*
218 *Strike (up)*
219 *aptly/teals*
220 *Lanners/lannerets*
221 *Meet/mallards*

224 *siege*
225 *assail/seize*

228 *(heron's) bill*

230 *twist*
231 *Burst*
232 *Put/quill/marrow*
233 *whoops (the hawks)/quarry/(hym = heron)*

He quyrres thaym and quotes thaym, quyppeys full lowde,
Cheres thaym full chefely ecchekkes to leve,   235
Than henttis thaym one honde and hodes thaym ther-aftire
Cowples up theire cowers, thaire caprons to holde
Lowppes in thaire lesses thorowe vertwells of silvere,
Than he laches to his luyre and lokes to his horse
And lepis upe one the lefte syde als the laghe askes.   240
Portours full pristly putten upe the fowlis
And taryen for theire tercelettis that tenyn thaym full ofte.
For some chosen to the echecheke, thoghe some chese bettire,
Spanyells full spedily thay spryngen abowte,
Be-dagged for dowkynge when digges bene enewede,   245
And than kayre to the courte that I come fro,
With ladys full lovely to lappyn in myn armes
And clyp thaym and kysse thaym and comforthe myn hert,
And than with damesels dere to daunsen in thaire chambirs;
Riche Romance to rede and rekken the sothe   250
Of kempes and of conquerours, of kynges full noblee,
How thay wirchipe and welthe wanne in thaire lyves.
With renkes in ryotte to revelle in haulle
With coundythes and carolles and compaynyes sere
And chese me to the chesse that chefe es of gamnes   255
And this es life for to lede while I schalle lyfe here,
And thou with wandrynge and woo schalte wake for thi gudes,
And be thou dolven and dede thi dole schall be schorte
And he that thou leste luffes schall layke hym there-with,
And spend that thou haste longe sparede, the devyll spede hym ells!'   260
Than this renke alle in rosett rothelede thies wordes:
He sayde, 'Thryfte and thou have threpid this thirtene wynter.
I seghe wele samples bene sothe that sayde bene full yore:
"Fole es that with foles delys." Flyte we no lengare!'

VII

Than this beryn alle in blake bownnes hym to speke,   265
And sayde, 'Sirres, by my soule, sottes bene ye bothe.
Bot will ye hendely me herken ane hande-while,
And I schalle stynte your stryffe and stillen your threpe.
I sett ensample bi my-selfe and sekis it no forthire.
While I was yonge in my youthe and yape for my dedys,   270
I was als everrous in armes as outher of youre-selven
And as styffe in a stourre one my stede bake,
And as gaye in my gere als any gome ells,

234 *quarries/calls/whips*
235 *Cheers, encourages/checks, inferior birds*
236 *grasps/hoods*
237 *Couples/fasteners/hoods*
238 *Loops/leashes/(through) rings*
239 *lure*
240 *as/law*
241 *promptly*
242 *tease*
243 *choose/checks (l. 235)/chose*

245 *Bedraggled/ducking/ducks/forced into the water*
246 *ride*

248 *clasp*

251 *champions*
252 *won*
253 *men*
254 *conduits, dances/many, diverse*
255 *chose/games*

257 *woe*
258 *"when you are"/delved, buried/riches*
259 *least/loves/sport*

261 *man/russet/rattled on (in)*
262 *argued (l. 104)/thirteen years*
263 *examples/long ago*
264 *Fool/deals/Argue/longer*

265 *man/readies (l. 153)*
266 *sots, fools*
267 *"If you will but"/courteously/short time (l. 106)*
268 *stop/strife/contention*
269 *example/seek/further*
270 *active/deeds*
271 *ambitious/either*
272 *staunch/battle/steed's back*
273 *man*

And as lelly by-luffede with ladyes and maydens.
My likame was lovely, es lothe nowe to schewe,   275
And as myche wirchip I wane, i-wis, as ye bothen.
And aftir irkede me with this, and ese was me levere,
Als man in his medill elde, his makande wolde have.
Than I mukkede and marlede and made up my howses,
And purcheste me ploughe-londes and pastures full noble,   280
Gatte gude and golde full gaynly to honde,
Reches and renttes were ryfe to my-selven.
Bot Elde undire-yode me, are I laste wiste,
And alle disfegurede my face and fadide my hewe,
Bothe my browes and my berde blawnchede full whitte   285
And when he sotted my syghtes, than sowed myn hert,
Croked me, cowrbed me, encrampeschet myn hondes,
That I ne may hefe tham to my hede, ne noghte helpe my-selven,
Ne stale stonden one my fete bot I my staffe have.
Makes youre mirrours bi me, men bi youre trouthe,   290
This schadowe in my schewere schunte ye no while.
And now es dethe at my dore that I drede moste.
I ne wot wiche daye, ne when, ne whate tyme he comes,
Ne whedir-wardes, ne whare, ne whatte to do aftire.
Bot many modyere than I, men one this molde,   295
Hafe passed the pase that I schall passe sone.
And I schall neven yow the names of nyne of the beste
That ever wy in this werlde wiste appon erthe,
That were conquerours full kene and kiddeste of other.

VIII

The firste was Sir Ector, and aldeste of tyme   300
When Troygens of Troye were tried to fighte
With Menylawse, the mody kynge and men out of Grece,
That thaire cité assegede and sayled it full yerne,
For Elayne, his ownn quene, that there-inn was halden,
That Paresche, the proude knyghte paramours lovede.   305
Sir Ectore was everous als the storye telles,
And als clerkes in the cronycle cownten the sothe.
Nowmbron thaym to nynety and ix mo by tale
Of kynges with crounes he killede with his handes
And full fele other folke, als ferly were ellis.   310
Then Achilles his adversarye undide with his werkes,
With wyles and no wirchipe woundede hym to dethe
Als he tentid to a tulke that he tuke of were

274 *loyally/beloved*
275 *body/loathsome*
276 *much/won/certainly*
277 *later/"I was bored with this"/ease/dearer*
278 *middle age/relaxing*
279 (l. 142)

281 *Got/goods*
282 *Riches/rife, plenty*
283 *overtook/ere/least/knew*

286 *he = Old Age/dimmed my vision/pained*
287 Cf. l. 154: *crooked/curved/bent*
288 *heave, lift*
289 *"Stand unaided without a cane"*
290 *Make*
291 (lit. *shower*) *mirror/shunt, evade*

293 *know*

295 *"superior to me"/earth*

297 *name/(the Nine Worthies)*
298 *man/knew*
299 *best known*

300 *Hector/oldest*

302 *Menelaus/excellent* (l. 295)
303 *assailed/eagerly*
304 *Helen*
305 *Paris*
306 *ambitious* (l. 271)

308 *Number/9 more*

310 *many/as/marvelous/else*

313 *tended/man/took/war,* i.e., *prisoner*

And he was slayne for that slaughte sleghely ther-after
With the wyles of a woman as he had wroghte by-fore.   315
Than Menylawse the mody kynge hade myrthe at his hert,
That Ectore hys enymy siche auntoure hade fallen
And with the Gregeis of Grece he girde over the walles,
The prowde paleys dide he pulle doun to the erthe
That was rialeste of araye and rycheste undir the heven.   320
And then the Trogens of Troye teneden full sore
And semblen thaym full serely, and sadly thay foughten,
Bot the lure at the laste lighte appon Troye
For there Sir Priamus the prynce put was to dethe
And Pantasilia the quene paste hym by-fore.   325
Sir Troylus, a trewe knyghte that tristyly hade foghten,
Neptolemus, a noble knyghte at nede that wolde noghte fayle,
Palamedes, a prise knyghte, and preved in armes,
Ulixes and Ercules that full everrous were bothe,
And other fele of that ferde fared of the same   330
As Dittes and Dares demyn to-gedir.

IX

Aftir this Sir Alysaunder alle the worlde wanne
Bothe the see and the sonde and the sadde erthe,
The iles of the Oryent to Ercules boundes,
Ther Ely and Ennoke ever hafe bene sythen,   335
And to the come of Antecriste unclosede be thay never,
And conquered Calcas knyghtly ther-aftire,
Ther ientille Iazon the Grewe wane the flese of golde,
Then grathede he hym to Gadres the gates full righte,
And there Sir Gadyfere the gude the Gaderayns assemblet   340
And rode oute full ryally to rescowe the praye.
And than Emenyduse hym mete, and made hym full tame
And girdes Gadyfere to the grounde, gronande full sore,
And there that doughty was dede and mekill dole makede.
Then Alixander the Emperour that athell kyng hym-selven   345
Arayed hym for to ryde with the renkes that he hade.
Ther was the mody Meneduse, a mane of Artage;
He was Duke of that douth and a dussypere.
Sir Filot and Sir Florydase, full ferse men of armes,
Sir Clyton and Sir Caulus, knyghtis full noble,   350
And Sir Garsyene the gaye, a gude man of armes,
And Sir Lyncamoure thaym ledys with a lighte will.
And than Sir Cassamus thaym kepide, and the kyng prayede

314 *slaughter/slyly*

317 *adventure*
318 *Greeks*
319 *palace*
320 *most royal*
321 *grieved*

323 *loss*

325 *Penthesilea*

328 *proved*
329 *Ulysses/Hercules/ambitious*
330 *many/group*
331 *Dictys/deemed*

332 *won*
333 *firm (earth)*

335 *Elias/Enoch/since*
336 *coming*

338 *gentle/Jason/Greek/fleece*
339 *Gaza*
340 *Gadifer of Larris*
341 *royally/prey*
342 *Emenidus*
343 *groaning*
344 *doughty (one)/much/dole, sorrow*
345 *noble*
346 *men*
347 *Emenidus/(?)Arcadia*
348 *host/one of the* 12 *peers* (O.Fr. *douze pers*)
349 ll. 349–352, Alexander's knights; *Floridas*

351 *Garsene*
352 *leads*
353 (a brother of Gadifer, l. 340)/*kept, held*

To fare in-to Fesome his frendis to helpe,
For one Carrus the kynge was comen owte of Inde,   355
And hade Fozome affrayede and Fozayne asegede
For Dame Fozonase the faire that he of lufe by-soughte.
The kynge agreed hym to goo and graythed hym sone
In mendys of Amenyduse that he hade mys-done.
Then ferde he to-warde Facron and by the flode abydes,   360
And there he tighte up his tentis and tarried there a while.
There knyghtis full kenely caughten theire leve
To fare in-to Fozayne Dame Fozonase to see,
And Idores and Edease, alle by-dene,
And there Sir Porus and his prynces to the poo avowede.   365
Was never speche by-fore spoken sped bettir aftir
For als thay demden to doo thay deden full even.
For there Sir Porus the Prynce in-to the prese thrynges
And bare the batelle one bake and abaschede thaym swythe
And than the bolde Bawderayne bowes to the kyng   370
And brayde owte the brighte brande owt of the kynges hande,
And Florydase full freschely foundes hym aftir,
And hent the helme of his hede and the halse crakede.
Than Sir Gadefere the gude gripis his axe
And in-to the Indyans ofte auntirs hym sone.   375
And thaire stiffe standerte to stikkes he hewes
And than Sir Cassamus the kene, Carrus releves.
When he was fallen appon fote he fet hym his stede
And aftyr that Sir Cassamus Sir Carus he drepitt
And for that poynte Sir Porus perset hym to dethe.   380
And than the Indyans ofte uttire tham droghen,
And fledden faste of the felde and Alexandere suede.
When thay were skaterede and skayled and skyftede in sondere,
Alexandere, oure athell kyng, ames hym to lenge,
And fares in-to Fozayne, festes to make,   385
And weddis wy un-to wy that wilnede to-gedire.
Sir Porus the pryce knyghte, moste praysed of othere,
Fonge Fozonase to fere, and fayne were thay bothe
The bolde Bawderayne of Bade-rose, Sir Cassayle hym-selven,
Bele Edyas the faire birde, bade he no nother.   390
And Sir Betys, the beryne the beste of his tyme,
Idores his awnn lufe aughte he hym-selven
Then iche lede hade the love that he hade longe yernede.
Sir Alixander oure Emperour ames hym to ryde,
And bewes to-wardes Babyloyne with the beryns that were levede,   395
By-cause of Dame Candace that comforthed hym moste

354 *go/Epheson*
355 *Clarus*
356 *Fesonas* (daughter of Gad., l. 340)/*frightened/Epheson*
357 *Fesonas*
358 *prepared*
359 *amends/Emenidus*
360 *went/*(a river)/*water*
361 *set*

364 *Edias/together;* daughters of Antigone, nieces of Fesonas
365 (son of Clarus)/*peacock*

367 *did*
368 *press, crowd/throngs*
369 *bore/on* (his) *back/very much*
370 *Baudrain* (a prisoner along with Porrus)
371 *drew*
372 *hastens* (after)
373 *neck* (l. 90)

375 *ventures/soon*
376 *standard*

378 *fetched*
379 *slew*
380 *pierced*
381 *out/*(with)*drew*
382 *pursued*
383 *shifted/asunder*
384 *noble/aims/linger*
385 *festivals, fetes*
386 *person to person/wished* (to be)

388 *Took/as companion, wife*
389 (of) *Bauderis*
390 *Fair/Edias/lady*
391 *man*
392 *own/love/got*
393 *each/man*

395 *bows, turns/men/left*

And that cité he by-segede and assayllede it aftire
While hym the yatis were yete, and yolden the keyes,
And there that pereles prynce was puysonede to dede;
Thare he was dede of a drynke, as dole es to here,   400
That the curssede Cassander in a cowpe hym broghte.
He conquered with conqueste kyngdomes twelve,
And dalte thaym to his dussypers when he the dethe tholede
And thus the worthieste of this werlde went to his ende.

X

Thane Sir Sezere hym-selven, that Iulyus was hatten,   405
Alle Inglande he aughte at his awnn will
When the Bruyte in his booke Bretayne it callede.
The trewe toure of Londone in his tyme he makede
And craftely the condithe he compaste there-aftire,
And then he droghe hym to Dovire, and duellyde there a while   410
And closede ther a castelle with cornells full heghe,
Warnestorede it full wiesely, als witnesses the sothe
For there es hony in that holde holden sythen his tyme.
Than rode he in-to Romayne, and rawnsede it sone,
And Cassabalount the kynge conquerede there-aftire   415
Then graythede he hym in-to Grece and gete it be-lyve
That semely cité Alexaunder seside he ther-aftire.
Affrike and Arraby and Egipt the noble,
Surry and Sessoyne sessede he to-gedir,
With alle the iles of the see appon iche a syde   420
Thies thre were paynymes full priste, and passed alle othire.

XI

Of the Iewes full gentill iugge we aftir
In the Olde Testament as the storye tellis
In a booke of the Bible that breves of kynges
And renkes that rede kane Regum it callen.   425
The firste was gentill Iosue that was a Iewe noble
Was heryet for his holynes in-to heven-riche.
When Pharaoo had flayede the folkes of Israelle
They ranne in-to the Rede See for radde of hym-selven.
And than Iosue the Iewe, Ihesu he prayed   430
That the peple myghte passe unpereschede that tyme.
And than the see sett up appon sydes twayne
In a manere of a mode walle that made were with hondes
And thay soughten over the see, sownnde alle to-gedir

398 *gates/gotten, surrendered/yielded*
399 *poisoned/death*
400 *dolorous, sad*
401 *cup*

403 *dealt (out)/twelve peers (l. 348)/suffered*

405 *Caesar/Julius/called*
406 *owned, ruled/own*
407 *Brut*
408 *tower*
409 *conduit/composed, devised*
410 *drew/dwelled*

412 *Provisioned*
413 *honey/held/since*
414 (a province of Rome)/*ransomed*
415 *Cassivellaunus*
416 *readied, prepared (himself) to go/quickly*
417 *seized*

419 *Syria/Saxony*
420 *every*
421 *paynims, pagans/respected*

422 *Jews/judge*

424 *tells*
425 *men/can read/Kings*
426 *Joshua*
427 *carried off/kingdom of heaven*
428 *Pharaoh*
429 *"because of their fear"*

431 *unperished, unharmed*

433 *mud*
434 *sound, safe*

And Pharaoo full fersely folowede thaym aftire.   435
And efte Iosue the Iewe Ihesus he prayede
And the see sattillede agayne and sanke thaym there-inn,
A soppe for the Sathanas, unsele have theire bones!
And aftire Iosue the Iewe full gentilly hym bere,
And conquerede kynges and kyngdomes twelve   440
And was a conqueroure full kene and moste kyd in his tyme.

XII

Than David the doughty, thurghe Drightynes sonde
Was caughte from kepyng of schepe and kyng made.
The grete grym Golyas he to grounde broghte
And sloughe hym with his slynge and with no sleghte ells.   445
The stone thurghe his stele helme stongen in-to his brayne
And he was dede of that dynt: the devyll hafe that reche!
And than was David full dere to Drightyn hym-selven
And was a prophete of pryse, and praysed full ofte
Bot yit greved he his God gretely ther-aftire,   450
For Urye his awnn knyghte in aventure he wysede
There he was dede at that dede, as dole es to here,
For Bersabee his awnn birde was alle that bale rerede.

XIII

The gentill Iudas Machabee was a Iewe kene
And there-to worthy in were, and wyse of his dedis.   455
Antiochus and Appolyne aythere he drepide,
And Nychanore, another kynge, full naytly there-aftire.
And was a conquerour kydde, and knawen with the beste.
Thies thre were Iewes full ioly and iusters full noble
That full loughe have bene layde sythen gane full longe tyme.   460
Of siche doughety doers looke what es worthen.

XIV

Of the thre Cristen to carpe couthely there-aftir
That were conquerours full kene and kyngdomes wonnen,
Areste was Sir Arthure and eldeste of tyme
For alle Inglande he aughte at his awnn will   465
And was kynge of this kythe and the crowne hade.
His courte was at Carlele comonly holden,
With renkes full ryalle of his rownnde table,
That Merlyn with his maystries made in his tyme,

436 *afterward*
437 *settled*
438 *sop/Satan/bad luck*

441 *renowned*

442 *(the) Lord's grace*

444 *Goliath*
445 *slew/sleight, skill (l. 36)*
446 *stung*

451 *Uriah/own/sent*
452 *dead/deed*
453 *Bathsheba/lady/reared, started*

455 *war (l. 313)*
456 *Apollonius/either, both/slew (l. 379)*

458 *renowned/known*
459 *jolly, good/jousters*
460 *low/since, gone*
461 *such/become*

462 *speak/knowledgeably*

464 *First*
465 *controlled*
466 *country*
467 *Carlisle/held*
468 *men/royal*
469 *mysteries*

And sett the sege perilous so semely one highte.   470
There no segge scholde sitt bot hym, scholde schame tyde,
Owthir dethe with-inn the thirde daye demed to hym-selven,
Bot Sir Galade the gude that the gree wanne.
There was Sir Launcelot de Lake full lusty in armes,
And Sir Gawayne the gude, that never gome harmede   475
Sir Askanore, Sir Ewayne, Sir Errake fytz Lake,
And Sir Kay the kene and kyd of his dedis,
Sir Percevelle de Galeys that preved had bene ofte,
Mordrede and Bedwere, men of mekyll myghte,
And othere fele of that ferde, folke of the beste.   480
Then Roystone the riche kyng, full rakill of his werkes,
He made a blyot to his bride of the berdes of kynges
And aughtilde Sir Arthures berde one scholde be.
Bot Arthure oure athell kynge another he thynkes
And faughte with hym in the felde till he was fey worthen.   485
And than Sir Arthure oure kyng ames hym to ryde.
Uppon Sayn Michaells Mounte mervaylles he wroghte,
There a dragone he dreped, that drede was full sore.
And than he sayled over the see in-to sere londes,
Whils alle the beryns of Bretayne bewede hym to fote.   490
Gascoyne and Gyane gatt he there-aftir,
And conquered kyngdomes and contrees full fele.
Than ames he in-to Inglonde in-to his awnn kythe,
The gates to-wardes Glassthenbery full graythely he rydes
And ther Sir Mordrede hym mett by a more syde,   495
And faughte with hym in the felde to alle were fey worthen,
Bot Arthur oure athell kyng, and Wawayne his knyghte.
And when the felde was flowen and fey bot thaym-selven,
Than Arthure Sir Wawayne athes by his trouthe
That he swiftely his swerde scholde swynge in the mere   500
And whatt selcouthes he see the sothe scholde he telle.
And Sir Wawayne swith to the swerde and swange it in the mere,
And ane hande by the hiltys hastely it grippes
And brawndeschet that brighte swerde and bere it a-waye
And Wawayne wondres of this werke and wendes by-lyve   505
To his lorde, there he hym lefte, and lokes abowte,
And he ne wiste in alle this werlde where he was by-comen.
And then he hyghes hym in haste and hedis to the mere
And seghe a bote from the banke and beryns there-inn.
There-inn was Sir Arthure and othire of his ferys,   510
And also Morgn la Faye that myche couthe of sleghte.
And there ayther segge seghe othir laste, for sawe he hym no more.

470 (*Siege Perilous*, king's seat)/*on high*
471 *man/betide* (*him*)
472 *Or/judged for, brought on*
473 *Galahad/Holy Grail*

475 *man*
476 *Escanor/Ywain/Erec fitz Lake*
477 *renowned*

479 *Bedivere/much, great*
480 *many/company*
481 *audacious*
482 *rich fabric* (*made into bedspread or garment*)
483 *intended*
484 *noble*
485 *fated* (*to die*)

487 *St./marvels*
488 *killed* (l. 456)
489 *diverse*
490 *bowed at his feet*

492 *many*
493 *country* (l. 466)
494 *way to Glastonbury/readily*

496 *till* (l. 336)/*had become fated* (l. 485)
497 *Gawain*
498 (*body of*) *troops/flown, fled*
499 *swears* (*oaths*)
500 *swing, fling/lake*
501 *wonders, marvels*
502 *quickly* (*drew out*)
503 *hilt*
504 *brandished*
505 *quickly*

507 *knew/what had become of him*
508 *hies/heads*
509 *saw/boat/people*
510 *companions* (l. 58)
511 *knew much of sleight, skill*
512 "*each man saw the other for the last time*"

XV

Sir Godfraye de Bolenn siche grace of God hade
That alle Romanye he rode and rawnnsunte it sone.
The Amorelle of Antyoche aftire he drepit   515
That was called Corborant, kiluarde of dedis,
And aftir he was callede kynge and the crownn hade
Of Ierusalem and of the Iewes gentill to-gedir
And with the wirchipe of this werlde he went to his ende.

XVI

Than was Sir Cherlemayne chosen chefe kynge of Fraunce,   520
With his doghty doussypers, to do als hym lykede.
Sir Rowlande the riche and Duke Raynere of Iene,
Olyver and Aubrye and Ogere Deauneys
And Sir Naymes at the nede that never wolde fayle
Turpyn and Terry, two full tryed lordes,   525
And Sir Sampsone hym-selfe of the Mounte Ryalle,
Sir Berarde de Moundres, a bolde beryn in armes,
And gud Sir Gy de Burgoyne, full gracyous of dedis,
The katur fitz Emowntez were kydde knyghtes alle
And other moo than I may myne or any man elles.   530
And then Sir Cherlles the chefe ches for to ryde,
And paste to-wardes Polborne to proven his strenghte.
Salamadyne the Sowdane he sloghe with his handis
And that cité he by-segede and saylede it full ofte,
While hym his yernynge was yett and the yates opynede   535
And Witthyne thaire waryed kynge wolde nott abyde,
Bot soghte in-to Sessoyne socoure hym to gete
And Charlemayne, oure chefe kynge, cheses in-to the burgh,
And Dame Nioles anone he name to hym-selven,
And maried hir to Maundevyle that scho hade myche lovede.   540
And spedd hym in-to hethyn Spayne spedely there-aftire
And fittilled hym to Flagott faire for to loge.
There Olyver the everous aunterde hym-selven,
And faughte with Sir Ferambrace and fonge hym one were,
And than they fologhed hym in a fonte, and Florence hym callede.   545
And than moved he hym to Mawltryple Sir Balame to seche
And that Emperour at Egremorte aftir he takes
And wolde hafe made Sir Balame a man of oure faythe
And garte feche forthe a founte by-fore-with his eghne,
And he dispysede it and spitte and spournede it to the erthe,   550

513 *Godfrey/Bouillon/such*
514 *Roman Empire/ransomed*
515 *Emir/killed*
516 *treacherous*

521 *twelve peers, knights* (l. 348)
522 *Reiner de Gennes* (Oliver's father)
523 *Aubrey* (*of Burgogne*)/*Ogier the Dane*
524 *Naimes* (*of Bavaria*)

527 *Mondisdier*
528 *Guy/Burgundy*
529 *Four Sons of Aymon*
530 *recall*
531 *chose*
532 *Paderborn* (Saxony)
533 *Sultan/slew*

535 *gotten, granted/gates/opened*
536 *Wittekind/cursed*
537 *Saxony*
538 *went* (l. 255)/*city*
539 *took*
540 *she/much*

542 *readied/*(a river)*/lodge*
543 *ambitious* (l. 329)/*ventured*
544 *Ferumbras/took/in war*
545 *baptized*
546 *Mautrible/Balan* (Ferumbras' father)
547 *Aigremorte*

549 *had fetched/before/eyes*

And one swyftely with a swerde swapped of his hede.
And Dame Floripe the faire was cristened there-aftire
And kende thaym to the Corownne that Criste had one hede,
And the nayles, anone, nayttly there-aftire,
When he with passyoun and pyne was naylede one the rode.   555
And than those Relikes so riche redely he takes
And at Sayne Denys he thaym dide, and duellyd there for ever.
And than bodworde un-to Merchill full boldly he sendys
And bade hym Cristyne by-come and one Criste leve,
Or he scholde bette doun his borowes and brenn hym there-inn   560
And garte Genyone goo that erande that grevede thaym alle.
Thane rode he to Rowncyvale, that rewed hym aftire,
There Sir Rowlande the ryche Duke refte was his lyfe.
And Olyver, his awnn fere that ay had bene trewe
And Sir Turpyn the trewe, that full triste was at nede,   565
And full fele othir folke, als ferly were elles.
Then suede he the Sarazenes seven yere and more
And the Sowdane at Saragose full sothely he fyndis;
And there he bett downn the burghe and Sir Merchill he tuke,
And that daye he dide to the dethe als he had wele servede.   570
Bot by than his wyes were wery and woundede full many
And he fared in-to France to fongen thaire riste
And neghede to-warde Nerbone that noyede thaym full sore
And that cité he asseggede appone sere halfves.
While hym the yates were yette and yolden the keyes   575
And Emorye made Emperour, even at that tyme
To have and to holde it to hym and to his ayers.
And then they ferden in-to Fraunce to fongen thaire ese
And at Sayn Denys he dyede at his dayes tyme.
Now hafe I nevened yow the names of nyne of the beste   580
That ever were in this werlde wiste appon erthe,
And the doghtyeste of dedis in thaire dayes tyme.
Bot doghetynes when dede comes ne dare noghte habyde.

XVII

Of wyghes that were wyseste will ye now here,
And I schall schortly yow schewe and schutt me ful sone.   585
Arestotle he was arste in Alexander tyme,
And was a fyne philozophire and a fynour noble,
The grete Alexander to graythe and gete golde when hym liste
And multiplye metalles with mercurye watirs
And with his ewe ardaunt and arsneke pouders   590

551 *lopped, swiped (off)*
552 *Floripas* (sister of Ferumbras)
553 *led, showed/Crown*
554 *rightly*
555 *cross*
556 *readily*
557 *St./put/dwelled*
558 *sent word/Marsile*
559 *believe* (l. 147)
560 *beat/burgs, cities/burn*
561 *made* (l. 549)/*Ganelon* (Roland's stepfather)

563 *bereft*
564 *own/companion/always*
565 *trusty*
566 *many/wondrous* (l. 310)
567 *pursued*
568 *Saragossa*

570 *put* (Sir M.)/*deserved*
571 *men*
572 *take/rest*
573 *Narbonne/annoyed*
574 *"on every side"*
575 *gates/gotten, surrendered/yielded* (l. 535)
576 *Aymeri* (de Narbonne)

580 *named*
581 *man/knew*

583 *abide*

584 *men*
585 *stop*
586 *first* (l. 464)

588 *prepare/wished*

590 *alcohol* (O.Fr. *eau ardente*)

With salpetir and sal-ieme and siche many othire
And menge his metalles and make fyne silvere,
And was a blaunchere of the beste thurgh blaste of his fyre.
Then Virgill thurgh his vertus verrayle he maket
Bodyes of brighte brasse full boldely to speke,   595
To telle whate be-tyde had and whate be-tyde scholde,
When Dioclesyane was dighte to be dere Emperour
Of Rome and of Romanye the rygalte he hade.

XVIII

Than Sir Salomon hym-selfe sett hym by hym one
His Bookes in the Bible bothe bene to-gedirs   600
That one of wisdome and of witt wondirfully teches
His sampills and his sawes bene sett in the tother
And he was the wyseste in witt that ever wonnede in erthe
And his techynges will bene trowede whills the werlde standes
Bothe with kynges and knyghtis and kaysers ther-inn.   605

XIX

Merlyn was a mervayllous man and made many thynges
And naymely nygromancye nayttede he ofte
And graythed Galyan a boure to keep hyr ther-in
That no wy scholde hir wielde ne wynne from hym-selven.
Theis were the wyseste in the worlde of witt that ever yitt were, 610
Bot dethe wondes for no witt to wende were hym lykes.

XX

Now of the prowdeste in presse that paramoures loveden
I schalle titly yow telle, and tary yow no lengere.
Amadase and Edoyne, in erthe are thay bothe,
That in golde and in grene were gaye in thaire tyme   615
And Sir Sampsone hym-selfe, full savage of his dedys
And Dalyda his derelynge, now dethe has tham bothe.
Sir Ypomadonn de Poele, full priste in his armes,
The faire Fere de Calabre, now faren are they bothe,
Generides the gentill, full ioly in his tyme,   620
And Calrionas that was so clere, are bothe nowe bot erthe.
Sir Eglamour of Artas, full everous in armes,
And Cristabelle the clere maye es crept in hir grave,
And Sir Tristrem the trewe, full triste of hym-selven
And Ysoute his awnn lufe, in erthe are thay bothe.   625
Whare es now Dame Dido was qwene of Cartage?

591 *salt gem (rock salt)*
592 *mingle*
593 (alchemical metal whitener)
594 *virtues/verily*

596 (*in past . . . in future*)
597 *set* (l. 125)
598 *Roman Empire* (l. 514)/*rule*

599 *alone, apart*

602 *examples/sayings/other*
603 *dwelled* (*on*)
604 *believed/while*

607 *necromancy/used, employed*
608 *prepared/bower*
609 *man*

611 *waits*

612 (*the*) *press, crowd*
613 *quickly*
614 *Idoine*

617 *Delilah/darling*
618 *Apulia/quick* (l. 241)
619 *La Fière/Calabria*
620 *jolly, good*

622 *Artois/ambitious*
623 *maid*
624 *trusty*
625 *Iseult*
626 (*who*) *was*

Dame Candace the comly was called quene of Babyloyne?
Penelopie that was price and passed alle othere,
And Dame Gaynore the gaye, nowe graven are thay bothen
And othere moo than I may mene, or any man elles.　　　　　630

XXI

Sythen doughtynes when dede comes ne dare noghte habyde,
Ne dethe wondes for no witt to wende where hym lykes
And ther-to paramours and pride puttes he full lowe,
Ne there es reches ne rent may rawnsone your lyves,
Ne noghte es sekire to youre-selfe in certayne bot dethe,　　　635
And he es so uncertayne that sodaynly he comes,
Me thynke the wele of this werlde worthes to noghte.
Ecclesiastes the clerke declares in his booke
Vanitas vanitatum et omia vanitas,
That alle es vayne and vanytes and vanyte es alle.　　　　640
For-thi amendes youre mysse whills ye are men here,
Quia in inferno nulla est redempcio,
For in helle es no helpe, I hete yow for sothe;
Als God in his gospelle graythely yow teches,
Ite ostendite vos sacerdotibus,　　　　645
Go schryve yow full schirle, and schewe yow to prestis;
Et ecce omnia munda sunt vobis,
And ye that wronge wroghte schall worthen full clene.
Thou man in thi medill elde, hafe mynde whate I saye,
I am thi sire and thou my sone, the sothe for to telle,　　　650
And he the sone of thi-selfe, that sittis one the stede,
For Elde es sire of Midill Elde and Midill Elde of Youthe,
And haves gud daye for now I go; to grave moste me wende;
Dethe dynges one my dore, I dare no lengare byde.'
When I had lenged and layne a full longe while　　　　655
I herde a bogle one a bonke be blowen full lowde,
And I wakkened ther-with and waytted me umbe.
Than the sone was sett and syled full loughe
And I founded appon fote and ferkede to-warde townn.
And in the monethe of Maye thies mirthes me tydde　　　660
Als I schurtted me in a schelfe in the schawes faire,
And belde me in the birches with bewes full smale,
And lugede me in the leves that lighte were and grene
There dere Drightyne this daye dele us of thi blysse,
And Marie, that es mylde qwene, amende us of synn. Amen. Amen.　665
　　　Thus Endes the Thre Ages

628 (Ulysses' wife)/*precious/surpassed*
629 *Guenivere/graved, buried*
630 *tell*

631 *Since, after/death/abide*
632 *hesitates/go*

634 (*neither*) *riches/ransom*
635 *surer*

637 *weal/comes*

643 *pledge*
644 *readily*

646 *cleanly*

648 *be made*
649 *middle age*
650 *son*

653 *have/must*
654 *raps* (*on*)
655 *lingered*
656 *bugle*
657 *waited around*
658 *sun/slid/low*
659 *hastened/went*
660 *betided*
661 *waited/ledge/woods*
662 *built* (*a waiting place*)/*boughs*
663 *lodged*
664 *Lord*

SUPPLEMENTARY MATERIAL

John Speirs, *Medieval English Poetry, The Non-Chaucerian Tradition*
(London, 1957), pp. 289–301.
(See also references to *Wynnere and Wastoure.*)

ROBERT MANNYNG

HANDLYNG SYNNE

["The Churchyard Dancers of Colbek," ll. 8987–9252]

Karolles, wrastlynges, or somour games,		*Carols (dances)/ summer*
Whoso ever haunteth any swyche shames		*frequents, attends*
Yn cherche, other yn chercheyerd,		*or*
Of sacrylage he may be aferd;		
Of entyrludes, or syngynge,	5	*interludes*
Of tabure bete, or other pypynge,		*tabor beating/piping*
Alle swyche thyng forbodyn es		*forbidden*
Whyle the prest stondeth at messe.		*priest/mass*
Alle swyche to every gode preste ys lothe,		*such/loathsome*
And sunner wyl he make hym wroth	10	*sooner/himself*
Than he wyl, that hath no wyt,		*he = one*
Ne undyrstondeth nat Holy Wryt.		
And specyaly at hygh tymes		
Karolles to synge and rede rymys		*read/rimes*
Noght yn none holy stedes.	15	*places*
That myght dysturble the prestes bedes,		*disturb/beads*
Or yyf he were yn orysun		*if/orison*
Or any outher devocyun,		*other/devotion*
Sacrylage ys alle hyt tolde,		
Thys and many other folde.	20	*manifold other (things)*
But for to leve yn cherche for to daunce,		*in order to leave (off), avoid/ dancing*
Y shal yow telle a ful grete chaunce,		*I/happening*
And y trow the most that fel		*swear/befell*
Ys as soth as the gospel,		

And fyl thys chaunce yn thys londe,   25   *befell/event*
Yn Ingland, as y undyrstonde,
Yn a kynges tyme that hyght Edward   *was called*
Fyl thys chaunce that was so hard.
Hyt was uppon a Crystemesse nyght
That twelve folys a karolle dyght   30   *fools/set up*
Yn wodehed, as hyt were yn cuntek,   *madness/contest*
They come to a tounne men calle Colbek.
The cherche of the tounne that they to come
Ys of Seynt Magne, that suffred martyr-   *St. Magnus*
dome.
Of Seynt Bukcestre hyt ys also,   35   *St. Bukchester*
Seynt Magnes suster, that they come to.
Here names of alle thus fonde y wryte,   *Their/found*
And as y wote now shul ye wyte.   *know/know*
Here lodesman, that made hem glew,   *leader/glee*
Thus ys wryte, he hyghte Gerlew.   40
Twey maydens were yn here coveyne,   *company*
Mayden Merswynde and Wybessyne.
Alle these come thedyr for that enchesone   *thither/because (of)*
Of the prestes doghtyr of the tounne.   *daughter*
  The prest hyght Robert, as y kan ame.   45   *can guess*
Azone hyght hys sone by name.   *son*
Hys doghter, that these men wulde have,   *would, wished (to)*
Thus ys wryte, that she hyght Ave.
Echoune consented to o wyl   *Each one/one, i.e.,*
                                                                "they all agreed"
Who shuld go Ave oute to tyl,   50   *"to entice out"*
They graunted echone out to sende
Bothe Wybessyne and Merswynde.
  These wommen yede and tolled here oute   *went/enticed*
Wyth hem to karolle the cherche aboute.   *them*
Bevune ordeyned here karollyng.   55   *directed/their*
Gerlew endyted what they shuld syng.   *dictated, decided*
Thys ys the karolle that they sunge,
As telleth the Latyn tunge:
  'Equitabat Bevo per siluam frondosam,
  Ducebat secum Merswyndam formosam.   60
  Quid stamus? cur non imus?'
  'By the leved wode rode Bevolyne,   *leafy*
  Wyth hym he ledde feyre Merswyne.   *fair*
  Why stonde we? Why go we noght?'
Thys ys the karolle that Grysly wroght.   65   *Gerlew*

Thys songe sunge they yn the chercheyerd,
Of foly were they no thyng aferd, *folly*
Unto the matynes were alle done, *Until/matins*
And the messe shuld bygynne sone. *soon*
The preste hym revest to begynne messe, 70 *vested himself*
And they ne left therfore never the lesse,
But daunsed furthe as they bygan, *forth*
For alle the messe they ne blan. *stopped*
The preste, that stode at the autere, *altar*
And herd here noyse and here bere, 75 *din*
Fro the auter down he nam, *took (himself)*
And to the cherche porche he cam,
And seyd 'On Goddes behalve, y yow for-
bede
That ye no lenger do swych dede, *longer/such*
But cometh yn on feyre manere 80 *in a fair manner*
Goddes servyse for to here,
And doth at Crystyn mennys lawe. *act according to/men's*

Karolleth no more, for Crystys awe.
Wurschyppeth hym with alle youre myght
That of the vyrgyne was bore thys nyght.' 85 *born*
For alle hys byddyng lefte they noght,
But daunsed furth, as they thoght.
The preste tharefor was sore agreved.
He preyd God that he on belevyd, *"in whom he be-lieved"*
And for Seynt Magne, that he wulde so 90 *work*
werche,
In whos wurschyp sette was the cherche,
That swych a veniaunce were on hem sent, *vengeance*
Are they oute of that stede were went, *Ere*
That they myght ever ryght so wende *go, continue just as they were, i.e., dancing*

Unto that tyme twelvemonth ende. 95
Yn the Latyne that y fonde thore *found/there*
He seyeth nat twelvemonth but evermore.
He cursed hem there alsaume *altogether*
As they karoled on here gaume. *"in their game"*
As sone as the preste hadde so spoke 100
Every hand yn outher so fast was loke *locked*
That no man myght with no wundyr

That twelvemonthe parte hem asundyr.
The preste yede yn, whan thys was done,   *went*
And commaunded hys sone Azone   105
That he shulde go swythe aftyr Ave,   *swiftly*
Out of that karolle algate to have.   *by all ways*
But al to late that wurde was seyd,
For on hem alle was the veniaunce leyd.   *laid*
   Azone wende weyl for to spede.   110   *thought/well*
Unto the karolle as swythe he yede,
Hys systyr by the arme he hente,   *seized*
And the arme fro the body wente.
Men wundred alle that there wore,   *were*
And merveyle mowe ye here more.   115   *marvel/may*
For, sethen he had the arme yn hand,   *after*
The body yede furth karoland,   *went/forth/caroling*
And nother the body ne the arme   *neither*
Bledde never blode, colde ne warme,
But was as drye, with al the haunche,   120   *around/shoulder*
As of a stok were ryve a braunche.   *As (if)/torn*
   Azone to hys fadyr went,
And broght hym a sory present.
'Loke, fadyr,' he seyd, 'and have hyt here,
The arme of thy doghtyr dere,   125
That was myn owne syster Ave,
That y wende y myght a save.   *thought (l. 110)/*
                                               have

Thy cursyng now sene hyt ys
Wyth veniaunce on thy owne flessh.
Fellyche thou cursedest, and over sone.   130   *Terribly/overly*
Thou askedest veniaunce; thou hast thy   *boon*
    bone.'
   Yow thar nat aske yyf there was wo   *need/not*
Wyth the preste, and wyth many mo.
The prest, that cursed for that daunce,
On some of hys fyl harde chaunce.   135   *fell/fortune*
He toke hys doghtyr arme forlorn
And byryed hyt on the morn.   *buried*
The nexte day the arme of Ave
He fonde hyt lyggyng above the grave.   *lying*
He byryed hyt on anouther day   140
And eft above the grave hyt lay.   *afterward*
The thrydde tyme he byryed hyt,   *third*
And eft was hyt kast oute of the pyt.

The prest wulde byrye hyt no more,
He dredde the veniaunce ferly sore.   145   dreaded/won-
                                                                drously

Ynto the cherche he bare the arme,
For drede and doute of more harme,
He ordeyned hyt for to be
That every man myght with ye hyt se.   eye
    These men that yede so karolland,   150
Alle that yere, hand yn hand,
They never oute of that stede yede,
Ne none myght hem thenne lede.   thence
There the cursyng fyrst bygan,
Yn that place aboute they ran,   155
That never ne felte they no werynes   felt/weariness
As many bodyes for goyng dos,   going, walking/do
Ne mete ete, ne drank drynke,
Ne slepte onely alepy wynke.   single
Nyght ne day they wyst of none,   160   knew
Whan hyt was come, whan hyt was gone.
Frost ne snogh, hayle ne reyne,   snow
Of colde ne hete, felte they no peyne.
Heere ne nayles never grewe,   Hair
Ne solowed clothes, ne turned hewe.   165   soiled/hue, complex-
                                                                ion
Thundyr ne lyghtnyng dyd hem no dere,   harm
Goddys mercy ded hyt fro hem were.   ward (off)
But sungge that songge that the wo wroght,
'Why stonde we? Why go we noght?'
    What man shuld thyr be yn thys lyve   170   there/life
That ne wulde hyt see and thedyr dryve?   thither/go
The Emperoure Henry come fro Rome
For to see thys hard dome.   doom, judgment
When he hem say, he wepte sore   saw
For the myschefe that he sagh thore.   175   saw
He ded come wryghtes for to make   commanded
Coveryng over hem, for tempest sake.
But that they wroght hyt was yn veyn,   vain
For hyt come to no certeyn,   certain (thing),
                                                                nothing
For that they sette on oo day   180   what/in/one
On the touther downe hyt lay.   other, next
Ones, twyys, thryys, thus they wroght,
And alle here makyng was for noght.

Myght no coveryng hyle hem fro colde   *protect*
Tyl tyme of mercy that Cryst hyt wolde.   185
   Tyme of grace fyl thurgh Hys myght   *fell*
At the twelvemonth ende, on the yole nyght.   *Yule*
The same oure that the prest hem banned,   *hour*
The same oure atwynne they woned.   *a-twin, in two/went*
That houre that he cursed hem ynne,   190
The same oure they yede atwynne,   *went/apart*
And as yn twynkelyng of an ye   *eye*
Ynto the cherche gun they flye,   *began*
And on the pavement they fyl alle downe
As they had be dede, or fal yn a swone.   195   *As (if)/been/*
                                                              fallen/swoon

   Thre days styl they lay echone,   *still/each one*
That none steryd other flesshe or bone   *stirred/either*
And at the thre days ende
To lyfe God graunted hem to wende.   *go*
They sette hem upp and spak apert   200
To the parysshe prest, syre Robert,
'Thou art ensample and enchesun   *example/cause*
Of oure long confusyun.   *confusion*
Thou maker art of oure travayle,   *travail*
That ys to many grete mervayle,   205   *marvel*
And thy traveyle shalt thou sone ende
For to thy long home sone shalt thou
   wende.'
   Alle they ryse that yche tyde   *same time*
But Ave. She lay dede besyde.
Grete sorowe had here fadyr, here brother.   210
Merveyle and drede had alle outher.
Y trow no drede of soule ded,   *soul's death*
But with pyne was broght the body dede.   *suffering/"the body*
                                                              was broght to
                                                              death"

The fyrst man was the fadyr, the prest,
That deyd aftyr the doghtyr nest.   215   *died/next*
Thys yche arme that was of Ave,   *same*
That none myght leye yn grave,
The Emperoure dyd a vessel werche   *ordered (1. 176)*
To do hyt yn, and hange yn the cherche,
That alle men myght se hyt and knawe   220
And thenk on the chaunce when men hyt   *event*
   sawe.

These men that hadde go thus karolland   *gone*
Alle the yere, fast hand yn hand,
Thogh that they were than asunder
Yit alle the worlde spake of hem wunder.   225
That same hoppyng that they fyrst yede,   *went*
That daunce yede they thurgh land and   *country*
    lede,
And, as they ne myght fyrst be unbounde,
So efte togedyr myght they never be founde,
Ne myght they never come ayeyn   230   *again*
Togedyr to oo stede certeyn.   *one certain place*
    Foure yede to the courte of Rome
And ever hoppyng aboute they nome.   *took (their way), proceeded*

Wyth sundyr lepys come they thedyr   *leaps*
But they come never efte togedyr.   235
Here clothes ne roted, ne nayles grewe,   *rotted*
Ne heere ne wax, ne solowed hewe.   *hair/grew/soiled*
Ne never hadde they amendement   *cure*
That we herde, at any corseynt,   lit. 'holy body' = *shrine*

But at the vyrgyne Seynt Edyght,   240   *St. Edith (of Wilton)*

There was he botened, Seynt Teodryght,   *benefited/Theodric*
On oure Lady day, yn lenten tyde,
As he slepte here toumbe besyde.
There he had hys medycyne
At Seynt Edyght, the holy vyrgyne.   245
    Brunyng the bysshope of seynt Tolous   *Bruno*
Wrote thys tale so merveylous.
Seththe was hys name of more renoun,   *Afterward*
Men called hym the pope Leoun.
Thys at the court of Rome they wyte,   250   *knew*
And yn the kronykeles hyt ys wryte
Yn many stedys beyounde the see,   *places*
More than ys yn thys cuntré.
Tharfor men seye, an weyl ys trowed,   *well/thought*
'The nere the cherche, the fyrther fro God.'   255   *nearer/further*
    So fare men here by thys tale,
Some holde hyt but a trotevale,   *fable*
Yn other stedys hyt ys ful dere
And for grete merveyle they wyl hyt here.
A tale hyt ys of feyre shewyng,   260   *fair*

Ensample and drede ayens cursyng.   *Example/against*
Thys tale y tolde yow to make yow aferde
Yn cherche to karolle, or yn chercheyerde,
Namely ayens the prestys wylle:
Leveth whan he byddeth yow be stylle.   265   *Believe*

SUPPLEMENTARY MATERIAL

1. E. K. Chambers, *The Medieval Stage* (London, 1903), I, 90ff.
2. L. P. Kurtz, *The Dance of Death*, New York, 1934.
3. D. W. Robertson, "The Cultural Tradition of *Handlyng Synne*," *Speculum*, XXII (1947), 162–85.

THOMAS CHESTRE

SIR LAUNFAL

Be doughty Artours dawes   *In/days*
That held Engelond yn good lawes
Ther fell a wondyr cas   *wondrous event*
Of a ley that was ysette   *lay/set down*
That hyght Launval, and hatte yette.   *was called/is called*
Now herkeneth how hyt was.   6
  Doughty Artoure som whyle   *"once upon a time"*
Sojournede yn Kardevyle   *Carlisle*
Wyth joye and greet solas   *pleasure*
And knyghtes that wer profitable   *worthy*
Wyth Artour of the Rounde Table
Never noon better ther nas.   12   *none/neg. + was*
  Sere Persevall and Syr Gawayn,   *Sir Percival*
Syr Gyheryes and Syr Agrafrayn,   *Gaheris/Agravaine*
And Launcelet du Lake,
Syr Kay and Syr Ewayn,
That well couthe fyghte yn playn,   *"in the field"*
Bateles for to take.   18
  Kyng Banbooght and Kyng Bos,   *Ban (of Benwick)/*
       Bors
Of ham ther was a greet los;   *them/great/reputa-*
       tion
Men sawe tho nowher her make.   *then/their/match*
Syr Galafre and Syr Launfale,
Wherof a noble tale
Among us schall awake.   24
  With Artoure ther was a bacheler,   *(a young candidate*
       for knighthood)
And hadde ybe well many a yer.   *been*
Launfal forsoth he hyght;

He gaf gyftys largelyche,   *gifts/largely, expan-*
                                                                         sively

Gold and sylver, and clothes ryche
To squyer and to knyght.   30
    For hys largesse and hys bounté,   *generosity*
The kynges stuward made was he
Ten yer, Y you plyght,   *pledge*
Of alle the knyghtes of the Table Rounde,
So large ther nas noon yfounde,
Be dayes ne be nyght.   36
    So hyt befyll yn the tenthe yer
Marlyn was Artours counsalere;   *Merlin*
He radde hym for to wende   *advised/go*
To Kyng Ryon of Irlond ryght,   *Ryence*
And fette hym ther a lady bryght,
Gwennere, hys doughtyr hende.   42   *Guenivere/gracious*
    So he dede, and hom her brought,
But Syr Launfal lykede her noght,
Ne other knyghtes that wer hende;
For the lady bar los of swych word   *bore/reputation* (l.
                                                                     20)/*such*
That sche hadde lemannys under her lord,   *lovers/as well as, in*
                                                                     addition to
So fele ther nas noon ende.   48   *many*
    They wer ywedded, as Y you say,
Upon a Wytsonday,
Before princes of moch pryde.
No man ne may telle yn tale
What folk ther was at that bredale   *bridal ceremony*
Of countreys fer and wyde.   54   *far*
    No nother man was yn halle ysette   *other*
But he wer prelat other baronette.   *Unless/or*
In herte ys naght to hyde.
Yf they satte noght alle ylyke,   (*Even*) *if*
Har servyse was good and ryche,   *Their*
Certeyn yn ech a syde.   60
    And whan the lordes hadde ete yn the
        halle,
And the clothes wer drawen alle,   *tablecloths/all drawn*
                                                                    off
As ye mowe her and lythe,   *may/hear/listen*
The botelers sentyn wyn   *brought/wine*
To alle the lordes that wer theryn,

Wyth chere bothe glad and blythe.   66
The quene yaf gyftes for the nones,   *gave/occasion*
Gold and selver and precyous stonys,
Her curtasye to kythe.   *show*
Everych knyght sche yaf broche other ryng,   *Every/or*
But Syr Launfal sche yaf no thyng.
That grevede hym many a sythe.   72 *time*
And whan the bredale was at ende,
Launfal tok hys leve to wende
At Artour the kyng,   *From*
And seyde a lettere was to hym come   *said*
That deth hadde hys fadyr ynome.   *taken*
He most to hys berynge.   78 *must (go)*
Tho seyde Kyng Artour, that was hende,   *Then/who/gracious*
"Launfal, yf thou wylt fro me wende,
Tak wyth the greet spendyng;
And my suster sones two   *sister's sons*
Bothe they schull wyth the go,
At hom the for to bryng."   84
Launfal tok leve, wythoute fable,   *truly*
Wyth knyghtes of the Rounde Table,
And wente forth yn hys journé
Tyl he com to Karlyoun,
To the meyrys hous of the toune,   *mayor's*
Hys servaunt that hadde ybe.   90 *"Who had been*
                                                      Launfal's servant"

The meyr stod, as ye may here,   *mayor*
And sawe hym come ryde up anblere   *ambling*
Wyth two knyghtes and other mayné.   *company*
Agayns hym he hath wey ynome,   *Toward/taken the*
                                                      way

And seyde, "Syr, thou art wellcome.
How faryth our kyng, tel me?"   96
Launfal answerede and seyde than,
"He faryth as well as any man,
And elles greet ruthe hyt wore.   *sorrow/were*
But, Syr Meyr, wythout lesyng,   *lie*
I am departyd from the kyng,
And that rewyth me sore.   102 *grieves*
Nether thar no man, benethe ne above,   *need*
For the Kyng Artours love,
Onowre me nevermore.   *Honor*
But, Sir Meyr, Y pray the, par amour,

May Y take wyth the sojour?   *lodging*
Somtyme we knewe us yore."   108   *"We have known*
                                                                        one another since
                                                                        long ago"

The meyr stod and bethoghte him there
What myght be hys answere,
And to hym than gan he sayn,
"Syr, seven knyghtes han her har in ynome,   *have taken their lodg-*
                                                                               ing

And ever Y wayte whan they wyl come,
That arn of Lytyll Bretayne."   114   *Brittany*
     Launfal turnede hymself and lowgh,   *laughed*
Therof he hadde scorn inowgh,   *enough*
And seyde to hys knyghtes tweyne,
"Now may ye se, swych ys service   *such*
Under a lord of lytyll pryse—   *worth*
How he may therof be fayn!"   120
     Launfal awayward gan to ryde.
The meyr bad he schuld abyde
And seyde yn thys manere:
"Syr, yn a chamber by my orchard syde,
Ther may ye dwelle with joye and pryde,
Yyf hyt your wyll were."   126
     Launfal anoon ryghtes,   *immediately*
He and hys two knytes,
Sojournede ther yn fere.   *company*
So savagelych hys good he besette   *goods/spent*
That he ward yn greet dette,   *became*
Ryght yn the ferst yere.   132
     So hyt befell at Pentecost
Swych tyme as the Holy Gost
Among mankend gan lyght,   *began (to) alight*
That Syr Huwe and Sir Jon
Tok her leve fro to gon   *go*
At Syr Launfal the knyght.   138   *From*
     They seyd, "Syr, our robes beth torent,   *are torn to pieces*
And your tresour ys all yspent,
And we goth ewyll ydyght."   *evilly, poorly/*
                                                                        dressed

Thanne seyde Syr Launfal to the knyghtes   *noble*
     fre,
"Tellyth no man of my poverté,
For the love of God almyght!"   144

The knyghtes answerede and seyde tho
That they nolde hym wreye never mo,   neg. + would/betray
All thys world to wynne.
Wyth that word they wente hym fro
To Glastynbery, bothe two,
Ther Kyng Artour was inne.   150
The kyng sawe the knyghtes hende,
And agens ham he gan wende,   toward (them)
For they wer of hys kenne;   kin
Noon other robes they ne hadde
Than they owt with ham ladde,   out, away/led, took
                                                        (in the first place)

And tho were totore and thynne.   156   torn to pieces/thin
    Than seyde Quene Gwenore, that was   who/evil
    fel:
"How faryth the prowde knyght, Launfal?
May he hys armes welde?"   "Can he still wield
                                                        his arms?"

"Ye, madame," sayde the knytes than.
"He faryth as well as any man,
And ellys, God hyt schelde!"   162   else/shield, forbid
    Moche worchyp and greet honour   Much
To Gonnore the quene and Kyng Artour   Guenivere
Of Syr Launfal they telde,
And seyde, "He lovede us so
That he wold us evermo
At wyll have yhelde.   168   Willingly/held, kept
    But upon a rayny day hyt befel
An huntynge wente Syr Launfel,
To chasy yn holtes hore.   hunt/woods/old
In our old robes we yede that day,   went
And thus we beth ywent away
As we before hym wore."   174   "As we were formerly
                                                        dressed"

Glad was Artoure the kyng
That Launfal was yn good lykyng.
The quene hyt rew well sore,   standing, condition
For sche wold wyth all her myght
That he hadde be, bothe day and nyght,
In paynys more and more.   180   pains, difficulty
    Upon a day of the Trinité,
A feste of greet solempnité
In Carlyoun was holde.

Erles and barones of that countré,
Ladyes and boriaes of that cité,   *burghers*
Thyder come bothe yongh and olde.   186
But Launfal, for hys poverté,
Was not bede to that semblé.   *asked/assembly*
Lyte men of hym tolde.   *Little/spoke*
The meyr to the feste was ofsent;   *sent for*
The meyrys doughter to Launfal went
And axede yf he wolde   192   *asked*
   In halle dyne with here that day.   *her*
"Damesele," he sayde, "nay.
To dyne have Y no herte.
Thre days ther ben agon,
Mete ne drynke eet Y noon,
And all was for povert.   198   *poverty*
   Today to cherche Y wolde have gon,
But me fawtede hosyn and schon,   *faulted, lacked/*
                                         hose/shoes
Clenly brech and scherte,   *breeches*
And for defawte of clothynge
Ne myghte Y yn wyth the peple thrynge.   *throng*
Ne wonder though me smerte!   204
   But o thyng, damesele, Y pray the,   *one*
Sadel and brydel lene thou me   *lend*
A whyle for to ryde,
That Y myght confortede be
By a launde under thys cyté   *meadow (N.E.*
                                         lawn)/near
Al yn thys underntyde."   210   *morningtime*
   Launfal dyghte hys courser   *saddled*
Wythoute knave other squyer.   *or*
He rood wyth lytyll pryde;
Hys horse slod and fel yn the fen,   *slid/mire*
Wherefore hym scorned many men   *"many men scorned*
                                         him"
Abowte hym fer and wyde.   216   *far*
   Poverly the knyght to hors gan sprynge.   *Miserably*
For to dryve away lokynge   *(to) escape/looking,*
                                         staring
He rood toward the west.
The wether was hot, the underntyde;
He lyghte adoun and gan abyde,
Under a fayr forest.   222   *Near (l. 209)*

And for hete of the wedere,   *weather*
Hys mantell he feld togydere, *folded*
And sette hym doun to reste.
Thus sat the knyght yn symplyté
In the schadwe under a tre
Ther that hym lykede best. 228
 As he sat yn sorow and sore, *pain, misery*
He sawe come out of holtes hore
Gentyll maydenes two.
Har kerteles wer of Inde-sandel *Their/Indian-/rich*
           fabric, silk
Ilased smalle, jolyf, and well. *Laced*
Ther myght noon gayer go. 234
Har manteles wer of grene felwet, *velvet*
Ybordured wyth gold, ryght well ysette,
Ipelvred wyth grys and gro. *Furred/(two kinds*
           of) gray pelts
Har heddys wer dyght well wythalle: *heads/adorned*
Everych hadde oon a jolyf coronall *Each/crown-like*
           headdress
Wyth syxty gemmys and mo. 240
 Har faces wer whyt as snow on downe;
Har rode was red, her eyn wer browne. *complexion/rosy/*
           eyes
I sawe never non swyche! *such*
That oon bar of gold a basyn,
That other a towayle whyt and fyn, *towel*
Of selk that was good and ryche. 246 *silk*
 Har kercheves wer well schyre, *fair*
Arayd wyth ryche gold wyre. *thread*
Launfal began to syche. *sigh*
They com to hym over the hoth; *heath*
He was curteys and agens hem goth *courteous/toward*
And greette hem myldelyche. 252 *mildly, gently*
 "Damesels," he seyde, "God yow se!"
"Syr Knyght," they seyde, "well the be!
Our lady, Dame Tryamour,
Bad thou schuldest com speke wyth here *her*
Yyf hit were thy wylle, sere,
Wythoute more sojour." 258 *delay*
 Launfal hem grauntede curteyslyche,
And wente wyth hem myldelyche.
They wheryn whyt as flour. *were*

And when they come in the forest an hygh,
A pavyloun yteld he sygh,   *pavilion/set up/saw*
Wyth merthe and mochell honour.   264   *much*
   The pavyloun was wrouth, for sothe,   *wrought/certainly*
   ywys,
All of werk of Sarsynys.   *Saracens*
The pomelles of crystall;   *(poles') pommels*
Upon the toppe an ern ther stod   *eagle*
Of bournede gold, ryche and good,   *burnished*
Yflorysched wyth ryche amall.   270   *Decorated, flour-*
                                          ished/enamel

   Hys eyn wer carbonkeles bryght—   *eyes/carbuncles*
As the mone they schon anyght,
That spreteth out ovyr all.   *spreads*
Alysaundre the conquerour,
Ne Kyng Artoure, yn hys most honour,
Ne hadde noon scwych juell.   276
   Ne fond yn the pavyloun
The kynges doughter of Olyroun,
Dame Tryamour that hyghte.   *was called*
Her fadyr was kyng of fayrye,   *fairies*
Of occient, fer and nyghe,   *(the) Occident/far/*
                                          near

A man of mochell myghte.   282
   In the pavyloun he fond a bed of prys,   *worth*
Yheled wyth purpur bys,   *Covered/purple/*
                                          linen

That semylé was of syghte.   *seemly*
Therinne lay that lady gent
That after Syr Launfal hedde ysent,   *had*
That lefsom lemede bryght.   288   *lovely (one)/*
                                          gleamed

   For hete her clothes down sche dede   *did, put*
Almost to here gerdyl-stede,   *girdle-place, waist*
Than lay sche uncovert.
Sche was as whyt as lylye yn May
Or sno that sneweth yn wynterys day
He seygh never non so pert.   294   *saw*
   The rede rose, whan sche ys newe,
Agens her rode nes naught of hewe,   *Against, compared*
                                          (with)/complex-
                                        ion/neg. + is

I dar well say yn sert.   *certainty*

Here here schon as gold wyre;   *Her/hair*
May no man rede here atyre,   *reckon*
Ne naught well thenke yn hert.   300
   Sche seyde, "Launfal, my lemman swete,   *"my sweet beloved"*
Al my joye for the Y lete,   *let (go), abandon*
Swetyng paramour.
Ther nys no man yn Cristenté   neg. + *is/Christen-*
                          dom

That Y love so moche as the,
Kyng neyther empourer!"   306   *nor*
   Launfal beheld that swete wyghth—   *creature*
All hys love yn her was lyghth—   *had lighted*
And keste that swete flour,
And sat adoun her bysyde,
And seyde, "Swetyng, what so betyde,
I am to thyn honour."   312   *"at your service"*
   She seyde, "Syr knyght, gentyl and
    hende,
I wot thy stat, ord and ende.   *know/estate, condi-*
                         tion/beginning

Be naught aschamed of me.
Yf thou wylt truly to me take,
And alle wemen for me forsake,
Ryche I wyll make the.   318
   I wyll the geve an alner   *purse*
Ymad of sylk and of gold cler,
Wyth fayre images thre.
As oft thou puttest the hond therinne,
A mark of gold thou schalt wynne,
In wat place that thou be."   324   *whatever*
   Also sche seyde, "Syr Launfal,
I geve the Blaunchard, my stede lel,   *loyal*
And Gyfre, my owen knave.
And of my armes oo pensel,   *a, one/standard*
Wyth thre ermyns ypeynted well   *painted*
Also thou schalt have.   330
   In werre ne yn turnement   *war*
Ne schall the greve no knyghtes dent   *"No knight's blow*
                         shall grieve, harm
                         you"

So well I schall the save."
Than answerede the gantyl knyght,
And seyde, "Gramarcy, my swete wyght, *being*

No bettere kepte I have."   336   *received*
  The damesell gan her up sette,
And bad her maydenes her fette   *fetch*
To hyr hondys watyr clere.   *For/hands*
Hyt was ydo wythout lette.   *done/delay*
The cloth was spred, the bord was sette,
They wente to hare sopere.   342   *their/supper*
Mete and drynk they hadde afyn,   *without end*
Pyement, claré, and Reynysch wyn,   *Spiced wines and*
                                                                  Rhenish
And elles greet wondyr hyt wer.
Whan they had sowped, and the day was   *supped*
  gon,
They wente to bedde, and that anoon,   *at once*
Launfal and sche yn fere.   348   *together*
  For play lytyll they sclepte that nyght,
Tyll on morn hyt was daylyght.
She badd hym aryse anoon.
Hy seyde to hym, "Syr gantyl knyght,   *She/gentle*
And thou wylt speke wyth me any wyght,   *If/whit, time*
To a derne stede thou gon.   354   *secret*
  Well privyly I woll come to the—   *will*
No man alyve ne schall me se—
As stylle as any ston."
Tho was Launfal glad and blythe;   *Then*
He cowde no man hys joye kythe,   *reveal*
And keste her well good won.   360   *repeatedly*
  "But of o thyng, Syr Knyght, I warne the,
That thou make no bost of me
For no kennes mede.   *kind of/reward*
And yf thou doost, Y warny the before,
All my love thou hast forlore!"   *lost*
And thus to hym sche seyde.   366
  Launfal tok hys leve to wende.   *go*
Gyfre kedde that he was hende,   *showed/courteous*
And brought Launfal hys stede.
Launfal lepte ynto the arsoun   *saddle*
And rood hom to Karlyoun
In hys pover wede.   372   *poor/clothes*
  Tho was the knyght yn herte at wylle.   *at ease*
In hys chaunber he hyld hym stylle   *chamber/kept*
All that underntyde.
Than come ther thorwgh the cyté ten

Well yharneysyd men
Upon ten somers ryde. 378 *pack horses/riding*
  Some wyth sylver, some wyth golde,
All to Syr Launfal hyt schold. *should (go)*
  To presente hym wyth pryde
Wyth ryche clothes and armure bryght,
They axede after Launfal the knyght, *asked*
Whare he gan abyde. 384
  The yong men wer clothed yn ynde; *indigo*
Gyfre he rood all behynde
Up Blaunchard, whyt as flour. *Upon*
  Tho seyde a boy that yn the market stod,
"How fere schall all thys good? *far/(shall) go*
Tell us, par amour." 390
  Tho seyde Gyfre, "Hyt ys ysent
To Syr Launfal, yn present, *as (a)*
That hath leved yn greet dolour." *misery*
  Than seyde the boy, "Nys he but a wrecche! *"He's nothing but a wretch"*

What thar any man of hym recce? *need/reckon, take account*

At the meyrys hous he taketh sojour." 396 *mayor's/lodging*
  At the meyrys hous they gon alyght,
And presented the noble knyghte
Wyth swych good as hym was sent; *such/goods*
And whan the meyr seygh that rychesse, *saw*
And Syr Launfales noblenesse,
He held hymself foule yschent. 402 *shamed*
  Tho seyde the meyr, "Syr, par charyté,
In halle today that thou wylt ete wyth me.
Yesterday Y hadde yment
At the feste we wold han be yn same *have been together*
And yhadde solas and game, *pleasure*
And erst thou were ywent." 408 *But/at once/gone*
  "Syr Meyr, God foryelde the! *repay*
Whyles Y was yn my poverté,
Thou bede me never dyne.
Now Y have more gold and fe, *possessions*
That myne frendes han sent me,
Than thou and alle thyne!" 414
  The meyr fro schame away yede. *went*
Launfal yn purpure gan hym schrede, *purple/dress*
Ipelvred wyth whyt ermyne. *Furred*

All that Launfal had borwyd before,
Gyfre, be tayle and be score,   *tally*
Yald hyt well and fyne.   420   *Yielded, repaid*
   Launfal helde ryche festes.
Fyfty fedde povere gestes   *"To feed fifty poor*
                                                    guests"
That yn myschef wer.   *misfortune*
Fyfty boughte stronge stedes;
Fyfty yaf ryche wedes   *gave/clothes*
To knyghtes and squyere.   426
   Fyfty rewardede relygyons;
Fyfty delyverede povere prisouns   *prisoners*
And made ham quyt and schere;   *paid up/debtless*
Fyfty clothede gestours.   *jesters, minstrels*
To many men he dede honours
In countreys fere and nere.   432   *far*
   Alle the lordes of Karlyoun
Lette crye a turnement yn the toun   *had announced*
For love of Syr Launfal,
And for Blaunchard, hys good stede,
To wyte how hym wold spede   *know*
That was ymade so well.   438
   And whan the day was ycome
That the justes were yn ynome,   *jousts/on/taken*
They ryde out al so snell.   *quickly (cf. N.G.*
                                                    schnell)

Trompours gon har bemes blowe.   *Trumpeters/horns*
The lordes ryden out arowe   *in a row*
That were yn that castell.   444
   Ther began the turnement,
And ech knyght leyd on other good dent   *laid*
Wyth mases and wyth swerdes bothe.   *maces*
Me myghte yse some, therefore   *see*
Stedes ywonne and some ylore,   *won/lost*
And knyghtes wonder wroth.   450   *wondrously*
   Syth the Rounde Table was,   *Since*
A bettere turnement ther nas,   *never was (neg. +*
                                                    was)

I dar well say, for sothe.
Many a lorde of Karlyoun
That day were ybore adoun.
Certayn, wythouten othe.   456
   Of Karlyoun the ryche constable

Rod to Launfal, wythout fable;
He nolde no lengere abyde.   *would no longer*
He smot to Launfal and he to hym;   *smote*
Well sterne strokes and well grym
There wer yn eche a syde.   462   *"on every side"*
    Launfal was of hym yware.   *wary*
Out of hys sadell he hym bar
To grounde that ylke tyde.   *same/time*
And whan the constable was bore adoun,
Gyfre lepte ynto the arsoun   *saddle*
And awey he gan to ryde.   468
    The Erl of Chestre therof segh;   *saw*
For wrethe yn herte he was wod negh   *wrath/nearly mad*
And rood to Syr Launfale,
And smot hym yn the helm on hegh   *helmet*
That the crest adoun flegh,   *(So) that/flew*
Thus seyd the Frenssch tale.   474
    Launfal was mochel of myght.   *much*
Of hys stede he dede hym lyght   *Off/caused/light
                                                     down, fall*

And bar hym doun yn the dale.   *"on the ground"*
Than come ther Syr Launfal abowte
Of Walssche knyghtes a greet rowte,   *Welsh/company*
The number Y not how fale.   480   *many*
    Than myghte me se scheldes ryve,   *men/riven*
Speres tobreste and todryve,   *burst completely/
                                                     splintered*

Behynde and ek before.   *also*
Thorugh Launfal and hys stedes dent   *steed's blows, charges*
Many a knyght verement   *truly*
To ground was ibore.   486   *borne*
    So the prys of that turnay
Was delyvered to Launfal that day,
Wythout oath yswore.   *"Without (a need
                                                     of) sworn oaths,"
                                                     "without doubt"*

Launfal rod to Karlyoun
To the meyrys hous of the toun
And many a lorde hym before.   492
    And than the noble knyght Launfal
Held a feste, ryche and ryall,   *royal*
That leste fourtenyght.   *lasted*
Erles and barouns fale   *many*

Semely wer sette yn sale   *hall*
And ryaly were adyght.   498   *bedight*
    And every day Dame Triamour,
Sche com to Syr Launfal bour   *bower*
Aday whan hyt was nyght.   *Daily, at the same*
                                                                 time

Of all that ever wer ther tho,
Segh her non but they two,   *Saw*
Gyfre and Launfal the knyght.   504
    A knyght there was yn Lumbardye.
To Syr Launfal hadde he greet envye.
Syr Valentyne he hyghte.   *was called*
He herde speke of Syr Launfal
That he couth justy well   *joust*
And was a man of mochel myghte.   510
    Syr Valentyne was wonder strong.
Fyftene feet he was longe.
Hym thoughte he brente bryghte   *would burn up*
But he myghte wyth Launfal pleye   *Unless*
In the feld, betwene ham tweye,   *"the two of them"*
To justy, other to fyghte.   516
    Syr Valentyne sat yn hys halle.
Hys massengere he let ycalle,   *had called*
And seyde he moste wende   *must*
To Syr Launfal the noble knyght
That was yholde so mychel of myght.   *held/much*
To Bretayne he wolde hym sende.   522
    "And sey hym for the love of hys lemman,   *lover, ladylove*
Yf sche be any gantyle woman,
Courteys, fre, other hende,   *noble (l. 142)/or/*
                                                                 gracious

That he come wyth me to juste
To kepe hys harneys from the ruste,   *harness*
And elles hys manhod schende."   528   *disgrace*
    The messenger ys forth ywent
To do hys lordys commaundement.
He hadde wynde at wylle.   *wind*
When he was over the water ycome
The way to Syr Launfal he hath ynome
And grette hym wyth wordes stylle,   534
    And seyd, "Syr, my lord, Syr Valentyne,
A noble werrour, and queynte of gynne,   *warrio./shrewd/in-*
                                                                 vention, stratagem

Hath me sent the tylle,   *"to thee"*
And prayth the, for thy lemmanes sake,
Thou schuldest wyth hym justes take."
Tho lough Launfal full stylle.   540   *laughed/continually*
   And seyde, as he was gentyl knyght,
Thylke day a fourtenyght   *The very, same*
He wold wyth hym play.
He yaf the messenger, for that tydyng,   *gave/news*
A noble courser and a ryng,
And a robe of ray.   546   *striped fabric*
   Launfal tok leve at Triamour,
That was the bryght berde yn bour   *lady/bower*
And keste that swete may.   *maid*
Thanne seyde that swete wyght,   *creature*
"Dreed the nothyng, Syr gentyl knyght,
Thou schalt hym sle that day."   552   *slay*
   Launfal nolde nothyng wyth hym have
But Blaunchard hys stede and Gyfre hys
     knave
Of all hys fayr mayné.   *household, company*
He schypede and hadde wynd well good,   *shipped (over)*
And wente over the salte flod   *water*
Into Lumbardye.   558
   Whan he was over the water ycome,
Ther the justes schulde be nome,   *taken*
In the cité of Atalye,
Syr Valentyne hadde a greet ost,   *host*
And Syr Launfal abatede her bost   *their/boast*
Wyth lytyll companye.   564
   And whan Syr Launfal was ydyght   *decked out*
Upon Blaunchard, hys stede lyght,
Wyth helm and spere and schelde,
All that sawe hym yn armes bryght
Seyde they sawe never swych a knyght,
That hym wyth eyen beheld.   570   *eyes*
   Tho ryde togydere thes knyghtes two,   *Then/at one another*
That har schaftes tobroste bo,   *(So) that/burst com-*
    pletely/both
And toscyverede yn the felde.   *utterly shivered,*
    splintered
Another cours togedere they rod,   *bout, round*
That Syr Launfal helm of glod,   *glided off*
In tale as hyt ys telde.   576

Syr Valentyn logh and hadde good game.   *laughed*
Hadde Launfal never so moche schame
Beforhond yn no fyght.
Gyfre kedde he was good at nede   *showed*
And lepte upon hys maystrys stede—   *master's*
No man ne segh wyth syght.   582   *saw*
    And er than they togedere mette,   *ere*
Hys lordes helm he on sette,
Fayre and well adyght.   *bedecked, adorned*
Tho was Launfal glad and blythe
And thonkede Gyfre mauy sythe   *(a) time*
For hys dede so mochel of myght.   588
    Syr Valentyne smot Launfal soo
That hys scheld fel hym fro,
Anoon ryght yn that stounde.   *"Straightaway"*
And Gyfre the scheld up hente   *snatched*
And broughte hyt hys lord to presente
Er hyt cam doune to grounde.   594
    Tho was Launfal glad and blythe
And rode ayen the thridde sythe.   *again/third/time*
As a knyght of mochell mounde.   *strength*
Syr Valentyne he smot so there
That hors and man bothe deed were,
Gronyng wyth grysly wounde.   600
    Alle the lords of Atalye
To Syr Launfal hadde greet envye   *hatred*
That Valentyne was yslawe,   *slain*
And swore that he schold dye
Er he wente out of Lumbardye,
And be hongede and todrawe.   606   *hanged/drawn to
                                                       bits*

    Syr Launfal brayde out hys fachon   *drew/sword, fal-
                                                       chion*

And as lyght as dew he leyde hem doune
In a lytyll drawe,   *while*
And whan he hadde the lordes sclayn
He wente ayen ynto Bretayn
Wyth solas and wyth plawe.   612   *"With pleasure and
                                                       joy"*

    The tydyng com to Artour the kyng
Anoon, wythout lesyng,   *lie*
Of Syr Launfales noblesse.
Anoon a let to hym sende   *he had*

That Launfale schuld to hym wende
At Seynt Jonnys Masse.   618   *St. John's*
  For Kyng Artour wold a feste holde
Of erles and of barouns bolde,
Of lordynges more and lesse.
Syr Launfal schud be stuward of halle
For to agye hys gestes alle,   *direct/guests*
For cowthe of largesse.   624   *Because/(his)gen-*
                                                     erosity

  Launfal toke leve at Tryamour,
For to wende to Kyng Artour
Hys feste for to agye.
Ther he fond merthe and moch honour,
Ladyes that wer well bryght yn bour,
Of knyghtes greet companye.   630
  Fourty dayes leste the feste,   *lasted*
Ryche, ryall, and honeste.   *royal*
What help hyt for to lye?
And at the fourty dayes ende
The lordes toke har leve to wende,
Everych yn hys partye.   636   *Each (one)/into/*
                                                     part (of the
                                                     world)

  And aftyr mete Syr Gaweyn,
Syr Gyeryes, and Agrafayn,
And Syr Launfal also,
Wente to daunce upon the grene
Under the tour ther lay the quene
Wyth syxty ladyes and mo.   642
  To lede the daunce Launfal was set.
For hys largesse he was lovede the bet   *better*
Sertayn of alle tho.
The quene lay out and beheld hem alle.   *leaned*
"I se," sche seyde, "daunce large Launfalle.   *generous*
To hym than wyll Y go.   648
  Of all the knyghtes that Y se there
He ys the fayreste bachelere.   *young knight*
He ne hadde never no wyf.
Tyde me good other ylle,   *(Whether) betides/*
                                                    or/ill, bad
  I wyll go and wyte hys wylle.   *know*
Y love hym as my lyf."   654
  Sche tok wyth her a companye,

The fayrest that sche myghte aspye,	*espy, find*
Syxty ladyes and fyf,	*five*
And wente hem doun anoon ryghtes,	*right away*
Ham to pley among the knyghtes	*(For) them*
Well stylle wythouten stryf.	660
The quene yede to the formeste ende	*went "most important place"*
Betwene Launfal and Gauweyn the hende,	
And after, here ladyes bright	
To daunce they wente alle yn same.	*together*
To se hem play, hyt was fayr game,	
A lady and a knyght.	666
They hadde menstrales of moch honours,	
Fydelers, sytolyrs, and trompours,	*citole-players/ trumpeters*
And elles hyt were unryght.	
Ther they playde, for sothe to say,	
After mete the somerys day	
All-what hyt was neygh nyght.	672 *Until/nearly*
And whanne the daunce began to slake,	
The quene gan Launfal to counsell take,	
And seyde yn thys manere,	
"Sertaynlyche, Syr Knyght,	*Certainly*
I have the lovyd wyth all my myght	
More than thys seven yere.	678
But that thou lovye me,	
Sertes Y dye for love of the,	*Certainly*
Launfal, my lemman dere."	*lover*
Thanne answerede the gentyll knyght,	
"I nell be traytour, day ne nyght,	*will not (neg. + will)*
Be God that all may stere!"	684
Sche seyde, "Fy on the, thou coward!	
Anhongeth worth thou hye and hard!	*You shall be hanged*
That thou ever were ybore!	*born*
That thou lyvest, hyt ys pyté!	
Thou lovyst no woman, ne no woman the.	
Thou wer worthy forlore!"	690 *worthily/done away with*
The knyght was sore aschamed tho.	
To speke ne myght he forgo,	
And seyde the quene before,	
"I have loved a fayryr woman	

Than thou ever leydest thyn ey upon
Thys seven yer and more. 696
    Hyr lothlokste mayde, wythoute wene, *loathliest/doubt*
Myght bet be a quene *better*
Than thou, yn all thy lyve!"
Therfore the quene was swythe wroth. *very*
Sche taketh hyr maydenes and forth hy goth *they*
Into her tour al so blyve. 702 *tower/quickly*
    And anon sche ley doun yn her bedde.
For wreth syk sche hyr bredde *"She made herself*
      sick with wrath"

And swore, so moste sche thryve, *must, might*
Sche wold of Launfal be so awreke *avenged*
That all the lond shuld of hym speke
Wythinne the dayes fyfe. 708 *five*
    Kyng Artour com fro huntynge,
Blythe and glad yn all thyng.
To hys chamber than wente he.
Anoon the quene on hym gan crye,
"But Y be awreke, Y schall dye!
Myn herte wyll breke athre! 714 *in three*
    I spak to Launfal yn my game
And he besofte me of schame, *besought*
My lemman for to be.
And of a lemman hys yelp he made, *boast*
That the lothlokest mayde that sche hadde
Myght be a quene above me!" 720
    Kyng Artour was well wroth,
And be God he swor hys oth
That Launfal schuld be sclawe. *slain*
He wente aftyr doghty knyghtes
To brynge Launfal anoon ryghtes *right away*
To be hongeth and todrawe. 726
    The knyghtes softe hym anoon, *sought*
But Launfal was to hys chaumber gon
To han hadde solas and plawe. *have/pleasure/joy*
He softe hys leef, but sche was lore *love, beloved/lost*
As sche hadde warnede hym before.
Tho was Launfal unfawe! 732 *miserable*
    He lokede yn hys alner, *purse*
That fond hym spendyng all plener *supplied/plente-*
      ously

Whan that he hadde nede,

And ther nas noon, for soth to say, *neg. + was*
And Gyfre was yryde away *ridden*
Up Blaunchard, hys stede. 738 *Upon*
　All that he hadde before ywonne, *won*
Hyt malt as snow agens the sunne, *melted*
In romaunce as we rede.
Hys armur that was whyt as flour,
Hyt becom of blak colour,
And thus than Launfal seyde: 744
"Alas," he seyde, "My creature,
How schall I from the endure, *(away) from*
Swetyng Tryamour? *Sweeting*
All my joye I have forlore, *lost*
And the (that me ys worst fore) *"which is the worst loss"*

Thou blysfull berde yn bour!" 750 *lady (l. 548)*
　He bet hys body and hys hedde ek, *beat/also*
And cursede the mouth that he wyth spek
Wyth care and greet dolour;
And for sorow yn that stounde, *time*
Anoon he fell aswowe to grounde. *swooning*
Wyth that come knyghtes four 756
　And bond hym and ladde hym tho— *led*
Tho was the knyghte yn doble wo—
Before Artour the kyng.
Than seyde Kyng Artour,
"Fyle ataynte traytour, *Vile/tainted*
Why madest thou swyche yelpyng? 762 *such/boasting*
　That thy lemmanes lothlokest mayde
Was fayrer than my wyf, thou seyde.
That was a fowll lesynge! *lie*
And thou besoftest her befor than *besought (l. 716)*
That sche schold be thy lemman.
That was mysprowd lykynge!" 768 *misproud, over-proud/desire*

　The knyght answerede with egre mode, *eager, fierce*
Before the kyng ther he stode,
The quene on hym gan lye. *about*
"Sethe that Y ever was yborn, *Since*
I besofte her here beforn
Never of no folye. 774
　But sche seyde Y nas no man,
Ne that me lovede no woman,

Ne no womannes companye.
And I answerede her and sayde
That my lemmannes lothlokest mayde
To be a quene was better worthye.   780
    Sertes, lordynges, hyt ys so.   *Certainly*
I am aredy for to do
All that the court wyll loke."   *order*
To say the sothe, wythout les,   *lie*
All togedere how hyt was,
Twelve knyghtes wer dryve to bok.   786   *driven/(the) Book*
                                                              (for oath-swear-
                                                              ing?)

    All they seyde ham betwene,   *"among themselves"*
That knewe the maners of the quene   *habits*
And the queste toke,   *inquest, "took up the*
                                                              question"

The quene bar los of swych a word   *reputation*
That sche lovede lemmannes wythout her   *besides*
    lord.
Har never on hyt forsoke.   792   *"Nobody denied it"*
    Therfor they seyden alle
Hyt was long on the quene and not on   *It (the guilt)/be-*
    Launfal.   *longed*
Therof they gonne hym skere.   *acquit*
And yf he myghte hys lemman brynge,
That he made of swych yelpynge,
Other the maydens were   798   *Or/(who) were*
    Bryghter than the quene of hewe,
Launfal schuld be holde trewe
Of that yn all manere.
And yf he myghte not brynge hys lef,   *beloved*
He schud be hongede, as a thef,
They seyden all yn fere.   804   *together*
    Alle yn fere they made proferynge   *proposal*
That Launfal schuld hys lemman brynge.
Hys heed be gan to laye.   *head/(as a pledge)*
Than seyde the quene, wythout lesynge,
"Yyf he bryngeth a fayrer thynge,
Put out my eeyn gray!"   810   *eyes*
    Whan that wajowr was take on honde,   *wager*
Launfal therto two borwes fonde,   *guarantors*
Noble knyghtes twayn.
Syr Percevall and Syr Gawayn,

They wer hys borwes, soth to sayn,
Tyll a certayn day.   816
 The certayn day, I yow plyght,
Was twelve moneth and fourtenyght,
That he schuld hys lemman brynge.
Syr Launfal, that noble knyght,
Greet sorow and care yn hym was lyght.
Hys hondys he gan wrynge.   822
 So greet sorowe hym was upan
Gladlyche hys lyf he wold a forgon.   *Gladly/have*
In care and in marnynge,   *mourning*
Gladlyche he wold hys hed forgo.
Everych man therfore was wo   *Every*
That wyste of that tydynge.   828 *knew*
 The certayn day was nyghyng;
Hys borowes hym broght befor the kyng.
The kyng recordede tho
And bad hym bryng hys lef yn syght.   *beloved*
Syr Launfal seyde that he ne myght,
Therfore hym was well wo.   834
 The kyng commaundede the barouns alle
To yeve jugement on Launfal   *give*
And dampny hym to sclo.   *condemn/(be) slain*
Than sayde the Erl of Cornewayle,   *Cornwall*
That was wyth ham at that conceyle,   *council*
"We wyllyth naght do so.   840
 Greet schame hyt wer us alle upon
For to dampny that gantylman
That hath be hende and fre;
Therfor, lordynges, doth be my reed.   *"act according to my*
              advice"*

Our kyng we wyllyth another wey lede:
Out of lond Launfal schall fle."   846
 And as they stod thus spekynge,
The barouns sawe come rydynge
Ten maydenes, bryght of ble.   *face*
Ham thoghte they wer so bryght and schene   *fair*
That the lothlokest, wythout wene,   *doubt*
Har quene than myght be.   852
 Tho seyde Gawayne, that corteys knyght,
"Launfal, brothyr, drede the no wyght.   *whit/"not a bit"*
Her cometh thy lemman hende."
Launfal answerede and seyde, "Ywys,   *Certainly*

Non of ham my lemman nys,   neg. + *is*
Gawayn, my lefly frende!" 858 *beloved*
 To that castell they wente ryght;
At the gate they gonne alyght.
Befor Kyng Artour gonne they wende
And bede hym make aredy hastyly
A fayr chamber for her lady   *their*
That was come of kynges kende. 864 *kin*
"Ho ys your lady?" Artour seyde. *Who*
"Ye schull ywyte," seyde the mayde, *know*
"For sche cometh ryde."   *riding*
The kyng commaundede for her sake
The fayryst chaunber for to take *to be taken, readied*
In hys palys that tyde. 870
 And anon to hys barouns he sente
For to yeve jugemente   *give*
Upon that traytour full of pryde.
The barouns answerede anoon ryght,
"Have we seyn the maydenes bryght, *"We have seen"*
Whe schull not longe abyde." 876 *We*
 A newe tale they gonne tho, *(?)tally, vote*
Some of wele and some of wo,
Har lord the kyng to queme. *please*
Some dampnede Launfal there, *condemned*
And some made hym quyt and skere. *paid up/without*
        debt

Har tales wer well breme. 882 *intense*
 Tho saw they other ten maydenes bryght,
Fayrer than the other ten of syght,
As they gone hym deme.   *judge*
They ryd upon joly moyles of Spayne, *mules*
Wyth sadell and brydell of Champayne.
Har lorayns lyght gonne leme. 888 *reins/(to) gleam*
 They wer yclothed yn samyt tyre. *silk/attire*
Ech man hadde greet desyre
To se har clothynge.
Tho seyde Gaweyn, that curtayse knyght,
"Launfal, her cometh thy swete wyght, *one, creature*
That may thy bote brynge." 894 *boot, remedy*
 Launfal answerede wyth drery thoght,
And seyde, "Alas, Y knowe hem noght,
Ne non of all the of sprynge." *none/"they come of"*
Forth they wente to that palys

And lyghte at the hye deys   *dais*
Before Artour the kynge.   900
    And grette the kyng and quene ek,   *also*
And oo mayde thys wordes spak
To the kyng, Artour:
"Thyn halle agraythe and hele the walles   *prepare/cover*
Wyth clothes and wyth ryche palles   *cloths/hangings*
Agens my lady Tryamour."   906   *Against (the coming*
                                                of), in preparation
                                                for

    The kyng answerede bedene,   *at once*
"Wellcome, ye maydenes schene,   *fair*
Be our Lord, the Savyour!"   *By*
He commaundede Launcelot du Lake to   *together*
    brynge hem yn fere
In the chamber ther har felawes were,   *where/companions*
Wyth merth and moche honoure.   912   *much*
    Anoon the quene supposed gyle—   *suspected/guile*
That Launfal schulld yn a whyle
Be ymade quyt and skere   *free/clear (1. 881)*
Thorugh hys lemman that was commynge.
Anon sche seyde to Artour the kyng,
"Syre, curtays yf thou were,   918
    Or yf thou lovedest thyn honour,
I schuld be awreke of that traytour   *avenged (1. 706)*
That doth me changy chere.   *makes/change/com-*
                                                plexion, disposi-
                                                tion

To Launfal thou schuldest not spare.
Thy barouns dryveth the to bysmare.   *scorn*
He ys hem lef and dere."   924   *beloved (to them)*
    And as the quene spak to the kyng,
The barouns seygh come rydynge   *saw*
A damesele alone
Upoon a whyt comely palfrey.
They saw never non so gay
Upon the grounde gone: 930   *traveling on earth*
    Gentyll, jolyf as bryd on bowe,   *bird/bough*
In all manere fayr inowe   *enough, indeed*
To wonye yn wordly wone.   *dwell/worldly/*
                                                dwelling, i.e., "to
                                                be human"

The lady was bryght as blosme on brere,   *blossom/briar*

Wyth eyen gray, wyth lovelych chere. *eyes*
Her leyre lyght schoone. 936 *face*
   As rose on rys her rode was red. *branch/complexion*
The her schon upon her hed *hair*
As gold wyre that schynyth bryght.
Sche hadde a crounne upon here molde *crown/head*
Of ryche stones and of golde,
That lofsom lemede lyght. 942 *lovesomely, beautifully/gleamed*

   The lady was clad yn purpere palle, *purple/cloth*
Wyth gentyll body and myddyll small,
That semely was of syght.
Her mantyll was furryd wyth whyt ermyn,
Ireversyd jolyf and fyn. *Lined*
No rychere be ne myght. 948
   Her sadell was semyly set. *"adorned in seemly manner"*

The sambus wer grene felvet, *saddle covers/velvet*
Ipaynted wyth ymagerye. *pictures*
The bordure was of belles
Of ryche gold, and nothyng elles,
That any man myghte aspye. 954
   In the arsouns, before and behynde, *saddlebows*
Were twey stones of Ynde, *India*
Gay for the maystrye. *"Most beautiful"*
The paytrelle of her palfraye *breast armor*
Was worth an erldome, stoute and gay,
The best yn Lumbardye. 960
   A gerfawcon sche bar on her hond, *gyrfalcon*
A softe pas her palfray fond, *gentle/pace*
That men her schuld beholde.
Thorugh Karlyon rood that lady. *rode*
Twey whyte grehoundys ronne hyr by. *ran beside her*
Har colers were of golde. 966
   And whan Launfal sawe that lady,
To alle the folk he gon crye an hy, *out loud*
Bothe to yonge and olde,
"Here," he seyde, "comyth my lemman
   swete!
Sche myghte me of my balys bete, *"remedy my woes"*
Yef that lady wolde!" 972
   Forth sche wente ynto the halle,
Ther was the quene and the ladyes alle,

And also Kyng Artour.

Her maydenes come ayens her ryght,   *toward*
To take her styrop whan sche lyght,   *alighted*
Of the lady, Dame Tryamour.   978
   Sche dede of her mantyll on the flet   *took off/floor*
That men schuld her beholde the bet,   *better*
Wythoute a more sojour.   *further/hesitation*
Kyng Artour gan her fayre grete,   *fairly*
And sche hym agayn wyth wordes swete   *(greeted) him*
                                       (back) again

That were of greet valour.   984
   Up stod the quene and ladyes stoute,   *stately*
Her for to beholde all aboute,
How evene sche stod upryght.
Than wer they wyth her al so donne   *(in comparison)*
                                   with/dun, sallow

As ys the mone ayen the sonne,
Aday whan hyt ys lyght.   990   *In the daytime*
   Than seyde sche to Artour the kyng,
"Syr, hydyr I com for swych a thyng   *hither/such*
To skere Launfal the knyght;   *secure (the freedom*
                                   of)

That he never, yn no folye,
Besofte the quene of no drurye,   *love-making*
By dayes ne be nyght.   996
   Therfor, Syr Kyng, good kepe thou myne.   *"take good heed of*
                                   my words"

He bad naught here, but sche bad him   *bade not her*
Here lemman for to be.
And he answerede her and seyde
That hys lemmannes lothlokest mayde
Was fayryr than was sche."   1002
   Kyng Artour seyde, wythouten othe,
"Ech man may yse that ys sothe,   *see*
Bryghtere that ye be."   *(The) fairer*
Wyth that, Dame Tryamour to the quene   *went*
   geth
And blew on her swych a breth
That never eft myght sche se.   1008   *afterward*
   The lady lep an hyr palfray,   *leaped on*
And bad hem alle have good day.
Sche nolde no lengere abyde.   *neg. + would/*
                                     longer

Wyth that com Gyfre all so prest,   *fast*
Wyth Launfalys stede out of the forest
And stode Launfal besyde.   1014
  The knyght to horse began to sprynge
Anoon, wythout any lettynge   *hesitation*
Wyth hys lemman away to ryde.
The lady tok her maydenys achon   *each one*
And wente the way that sche hadde er gon *ere, formerly*
Wyth solas and wyth pryde.   1020 *pleasure*
  The lady rod thorugh Cardevyle
Fer ynto a jolyf ile,   *Far*
Olyroun that hyghte.   *was called*
Every yer, upon a certayne day
Me may here Launfales stede nay,   *Men, one (may*
                                     hear)
And hym se wyth syght.   1026
  Ho that wyll ther axsy justus,   *Whoever/ask a joust*
To kepe hys armes fro the rustus,   *rust*
In turnement other fyght,   *or*
Dar he never forther gon:
Ther he may fynde justes anoon
Wyth Syr Launfal the knyght.   1032
  Thus Launfal, wythouten fable,
That noble knyght of the Rounde Table,
Was take unto fayrye.   *taken/fairydom*
Sethe saw hym yn thys lond no man, *Since*
Ne no more of hym telle Y ne can
For sothe, wythoute lye.   1038
  Thomas Chestre made thys tale
Of the noble knyght Syr Launfale,
Good of chyvalrye.
Jhesus, that ys Hevenekyng,
Yeve ys alle Hys blessyng
And Hys Modyr Marye. AMEN   1044
   explicit Launfal

SUPPLEMENTARY MATERIAL

Lucy A. Paton, *Studies in the Fairy Mythology of Arthurian Romance,*
New York, 1903; reprinted, 1959.

LE MORTE DARTHUR

William Caxton's Edition

[Book XVII, Chapters 19–23, "Thachyevyng of the Sangreal"]

Soo departed he from thens and commaunded the bretheren to God.
And soo he rode fyve dayes tyl that he came to the maymed kynge.
And ever folowed Percyval the fyve dayes, askynge where he had
ben and soo one told hym how the adventures of Logrys were encheved. So on a daye it befelle that they cam oute of a grete foreste   5
and there they mette at travers with sir Bors, the whiche rode alone.
Hit is none nede to telle yf they were glad and hem he salewed and
they yelded hym honour and good adventure and everyche told
other. Thenne said Bors, hit is more than a yere and an half
that I ne lay ten tymes where men dwelled but in wylde forestes   10
and in montayns but God was ever my comforte.
   Thenne rode they a grete whyle tyl that they came to the
castel of Carbonek, and whan they were entryd within the castel,
kynge Pelles knewe hem. Thenne there was grete Ioye, for they
wyst wel by theire comynge that they had fulfylled the quest of the   15
Sancgreal. Then Elyazar, kynge Pelles sone, broughte to fore
hem the broken suerd where with Ioseph was stryken thurgh
the thygh. Thenne Bors sette his hand therto yf that he myght
have souded hit ageyne but it wold not be. Thenne he took it
to Percyval but he had no more power therto than he. Now have   20
ye hit ageyne, sayd Percyvall to Galahad, for and it be ever
encheved by ony bodely man, ye must doo hit. And thenne he
took the pyeces and sette hem to gyders and they semed that
they had never ben broken and as well as hit had ben fyrst forged.
And whanne they within aspyed that the adventure of the suerd was   25
encheved, thenne they gaf the suerd to Bors, for hit myght not be
better set, for he was a good knyghte and a worthy man. And a
lytel afore even the suerd arose grete and merveyllous and was ful

5 *achieved*

7 *them/saluted*
8 *everyone*

13 *entered*
14 *joy*
15 *knew*
16 *Holy Grail/before*
17 *sword/Joseph of Arimathea*
18 *(to see) if*
19 *soldered/again*

21 *and* = *if* (here and freq. following)
22 *any/bodily*
23 *together*

of grete hete, that many men felle for drede. And anone alyght a voys
amonge them and sayd: they that ought not to sytte at the table of 30
Ihesu Cryst aryse, for now shalle veray knyghtes ben fedde. Soo
they wente thens, all sauf kynge Pelles and Elyazar his sone, the
whiche were holy men, and a mayde which was his nece. And soo
these thre felawes and they thre were there, no more. Anone they
sawe knyghtes al armed came in at the halle dore and dyd of their 35
helmes and their armes and sayd unto Galahad, Sire we have hyed
ryght moche for to be with yow at this table where the holy mete
shalle be departed. Thenne sayd he, ye be welcome, but of whens
be ye? So thre of them sayd they were of Gaule and other thre sayd
they were of Irland and the other thre sayd they were of Denmarke. 40
So as they satte thus there came oute a bed of tree of a chamber,
the whiche four gentylwymmen broughte, and in the bed lay a good
man seke and a crowne of gold upon his hede. And there in the myddes
of the place they sette hym doune and wente ageyne their waye.
Thenne he lyfte up his hede and sayd: Galahad knyght, ye be wel- 45
    come,
for moche have I desyred your comynge, for in suche payne and in
suche anguysshe I have ben longe. But now I truste to God the terme
is come that my payn shall be alayed, that I shall passe oute of this
world so as it was promysed me longe ago. There with a voyce sayd:
ther be two amonge you that be not in the quest of the Sancgreal 50
and therfor departe ye.
Chap. XX. Thenne kynge Pelles and his sone departed and there
with alle besemed that there cam a man and four angels from
heven clothed in lykenes of a Bisshop and had a crosse in his
hand and these foure angels bare hym up in a chayer and sette 55
hym doune before the table of sylver where upon the Sancgreal
was and it semed that he had in myddes of his forhede letters
the whiche sayd, See ye here Ioseph, the fyrst Bisshop of
Crystendome and the same whiche our lord socoured in the
Cyté of Sarras in the spyrytuel place. Thenne the knyghtes 60
merveylled for that Bisshop was dede more than thre honderd
yere to fore. O knyghtes, sayde he, merveyle not, for I
was somtyme an erthely man. With that they herde the chamber
dore open and there they sawe Angels and two bare candels of
waxe and the thyrd a towel and the fourthe a spere whiche bled 65
merveillously, that thre droppes felle within a boxe whiche he
helde with other hand. And they sette the candels upon the table
and the thyrd the towel upon the vessel and the fourth the holy

31 *true*
32 *save, except*
33 *niece*

35 *took off*
36 *hastened*
37 *food*
38 *divided*

41 *wooden* (*bed*)

43 *sick*

47 *anguish*

54 *likeness*
55 *chair*

58 (son of Jos. of Ar., above)
59 *succored*
60 *spiritual*
61 *marveled*

spere even up ryghte upon the vessel. And thenne the Bisshop
made semblaunt as though he wold have gone to the sacrynge   70
of the masse, and thenne he tooke an ubblye whiche was made
in lykenes of breed and at the lyftynge up there came a fugur in
lykenes of a chyld and the vysage was as reed and as bryghte
as ony fyre and smote hym self in to the breed so that they
all sawe hit, that the breed was formed of a flesshely man.   75
And thenne he putte hit in to the holy vessel ageyne. And thenne
he dyd that longed to a preest to doo to a masse. And thenne
he wente to Galahad and kyssed hym and badde hym goo and
kysse his felawes and soo he dyd anone. Now sayd he: servauntes of Ihesu Cryste ye shall be fedde afore this table with   80
swete metes that never knyghtes tasted. And whanne he had
sayd, he vanysshed awey. And they sette hem at the table in
grete drede and made their prayers. Thenne loked they and
sawe a man come oute of the holy vessel that had alle the
sygnes of the passion of Ihesu Cryste, bledynge alle openly,   85
and sayd: my knyghtes and my servauntes and my true
children whiche ben come oute of dedely lyf in to spyrytual lyf,
I wyl now no lenger hyde me from you, but ye shal see now a
parte of my secretes and of my hydde thynges. Now holdeth
and receyveth the hyghe mete which ye have soo moche desyred.   90
Thenne took he hym self the holy vessel and came to Galahad
and he kneled doune and there he receyved his saveour and
after hym soo receyved alle his felawes and they thoughte
it soo swete that hit was merveillous to telle. Thenne sayd
he to Galahad: sone, wotest thow what I hold betwixe my   95
handes? Nay, sayd he, but yf ye will telle me. This is, sayd he,
the holy dysshe wherin I ete the lambe on sherthursdaye. And
now hast thou sene that thou most desyred to see, but yet haste
thou not sene hit soo openly as thow shalt see it in the Cyté of
Sarras in the spyrituel place. Therfore thow must go hens   100
and bere with the this holy vessel, for this nyght it shalle departe from the Realme of Logrys, that it shalle never be sene
more here. And wotest thou wherfor? For he is not served nor
worshypped to his ryghte by them of this land, for they be torned
to evylle lyvynge. Therfor I shall disheryte them of the honour   105
        whiche
I have done hem. And therfore goo ye thre to morowe unto the see
where ye shal fynde your shyp redy and with you take the suerd with
the straunge gyrdels and no mo with yow but sire Percyval and syre
Bors. Also I will that ye take with you of the blood of this spere

70 *semblance/consecration*
71 *wafer*
72 *bread/figure*
73 *face/red*

77 *what belonged, was fitting/at*

85 *signs*

87 *deadly*
88 *longer*
89 *hidden*

95 *son/know*
96 *unless*
97 *ate/*(Thurs. before Easter)

103 *know*
104 *turned*

108 *strange girdles*

for to enoynte the maymed kynge, bothe his legges and alle his body   110
and he shalle have his hele. Sire, sayd Galahad, why shalle not
these other felawes goo with us? For this cause: for ryght as I departed my postels, one here and another there, soo I wille that ye
departe and two of yow shalle dye in my servyse, but one of yow
shal come ageyne and telle tydynges. Thenne gaf he hem his bless-   115
ynge and vanysshed awaye.
Chap. XXI. And Galahad wente anone to the spere whiche lay upon
the table and touched the blood with his fyngers and came after to
the maymed kynge and anoynted his legges and there with he clothed
hym anone and starte upon his feet oute of his bedde as an hole man   120
and thanked oure lorde that he had helyd hym. And that was not to
the world-ward, for anone he yelded hym to a place of relygyon of
whyte monkes and was a ful holy man. That same nyghte aboute
mydnyght came a voyce amonge hem whiche sayde: my sones and
not my chyef sones, my frendes and not my werryours, goo ye   125
hens where ye hope best to doo and as I bad yow. A, thanked be
thou, lord, that thou wilt vouchesaufe to calle us thy synners. Now
maye we wel preve that we have not lost our payncs.
    And anone in alle haste they took their harneis and departed.
But the thre knyghtes of Gaule, one of them hyghte Claudyne,   130
kynge Claudas sone, and the other two were grete gentylmen.
Thenne praid Galahad to everyche of them that yf they come to
kynge Arthurs court that they sholde salewe my lorde sir Launcelot, my fader and of hem of the round table, and prayed hem yf
that they cam on that party that they shold not forgete it. Ryght   135
soo departed Galahad, Percyval and Bors with hym and soo they
rode thre dayes and thenne they came to a ryvage and fonde the
shyp wherof the tale speketh of to fore. And whanne they cam
to the borde they fonde in the myddes the table of sylver whiche
they had lefte with the maymed kynge and the Sancgreal whiche   140
was coverd with rede samyte. Thenne were they gladde to have
suche thynges in theyr felaushyp and soo they entryd and maade
grete reverence ther to and Galahad felle in his prayer longe
tyme to oure lord, that at what tyme he asked, that he shold
passe out of this world. Soo moche he prayd tyl a voyce sayd   145
to hym: Galahad, thou shalt have thy request and whan thow ask-
est the dethe of thy body thou shalt have it and thenne shalt thow
fynde the lyf of the soule. Percyval herd this and prayd hym of
felaushyp that was bitwene them to telle hym wherfor he asked
suche thynges. That shalle I telle yow said Galahad: thother   150
day whanne we sawe a parte of the adventures of the Sancgreal

110 *anoint*
111 *health*

113 *apostles*

115 *(the) news/gave*

121 *healed*
122 *yielded himself*

125 *chief/warriors*
126 *Ah*
127 *vouchsafe*
128 *prove*
129 *harness*
130 *called*

132 *each, every(one)*
133 *salute, greet*

137 *riverbank*

141 *samite, rich cloth*
142 *fellowship*

150 *the + other*

I was in suche a Ioye of herte that I trowe never man was that
was erthely. And therfore I wote wel whan my body is dede,
my sowle shalle be in grete Ioye to see the blessid Trynyté every
day and the magesté of oure lord Ihesu Cryst. Soo longe were   155
they in the shyp that they sayd to Galahad: syr, in this bedde
ought ye to lye for soo saith the scrypture. And soo he leyd
hym doune and slepte a grete whyle and whan he awaked he
loked afore hym and sawe the Cyté of Sarras. And as they wold
have landed they sawe the shyp wherein Percyval had putte his   160
syster in. Truly, sayd Percyval, in the name of God, wel
hath my syster holden us covenaunt. Thenne toke they out of
the ship the table of sylver and he tooke it to Percyval and to
Bors to goo to fore and Galahad came behynde and ryght soo they
went to the Cyté and at the gate of the Cyté they sawe an old man   165
croked. Thenne Galahad called hym and bad hym helpe to bere
this hevy thynge. Truly, said the old man, it is ten yere ago
that I myght not goo but with crouchys. Care thou not, sayd
Galahad, and aryse up and showe thy good wille and soo he assayed
and fonde hym self as hole as ever he was. Thenne ranne he to   170
the table and took one parte ageynst Galahad. And anone arose
there grete noyse in the Cyté that a cryppyl was maade hole by
knyghtes merveyls that entryd in to the cyté. Thenne anon after
the thre knyghtes wente to the water and broughte up in to the
paleys Percyvals syster and buryed her as rychely as a kynges   175
doughter oughte to be. And whan the kynge of the Cyté whiche
was cleped Estorause, sawe the felaushyp, he asked hem of
whens they were and what thyng it was that they had broughte
upon the table of sylver. And they told hym the trouthe of the
Sancgreal and the power whiche that God had sette there. Thenne   180
the kynge was a Tyraunt and was come of the lyne of paynyms
and toke hem and putte hem in pryson in a depe hole.
Chap. XXII. But as soone as they were there oure lord sente
hem the Sancgreal thorow whoos grace they were al waye
fulfylled whyle that they were in pryson. Soo at the yeres ende   185
hit befelle that this kynge Estourause lay seke and felte that he
shold dye. Thenne he sente for the thre knyghtes and they
came afore hym and he cryed hem mercy of that he had done
to them and they forgaf hit hym goodely and he dyed anone.
Whanne the kynge was dede alle the Cyté was desmayed and   190
wyst not who myghte be her kynge. Ryght soo as they were in
counceille there came a voyce amonge them and badde hem
chese the yongest knyght of them thre to be her kynge: for he

152 *joy/swear*

157 *laid*

166 *(an old) crooked (man)*

168 *crutches*
169 *tried*

171 *opposite*

173 *marvels*

175 *palace*

177 *called*

181 *tyrant/pagans*

184 *through*

186 *sick*

190 *dismayed*
191 *knew*
192 *council*
193 *choose*

shalle wel mayntene yow and all yours. Soo they made Galahad
kynge by alle the assente of the hole Cyté and els they wold have   195
slayne hym. And whanne he was come to beholde the land he
lete make above the table of sylver a cheste of gold and of
precyous stones that hylled the holy vessel. And every day
erly the thre felawes wold come afore hit and make their
prayers. Now at the yeres ende and the self daye after Galahad   200
had borne the croune of gold, he arose up erly and his felawes
and came to the palais and sawe to fore hem the holy vessel and
a man knelynge on his knees in lykenes of a Bisshop that had
aboute hym a grete felaushyp of Angels, as it had ben Ihesu
Christ hym self. And thenne he arose and beganne a masse of   205
oure lady. And whan he cam to the sacrament of the masse and
had done anone, he called Galahad and sayd to hym: come forthe,
the servaunt of Ihesu Cryst, and thou shalt see that thou hast
moche desyred to see. And thenne he beganne to tremble ryght
hard whan the dedely flesshe beganne to beholde the spyrytuel   210
thynges. Thenne he helde up his handes toward heven and sayd:
lord I thanke the, for now I see that that hath ben my desyre many
a daye. Now blessyd lord, wold I not lenger lyve yf it myghte
please the, lord. And there with the good man tooke oure lordes
body betwixe hys handes and proferd it to Galahad and he receyved   215
hit ryghte gladly and mekely. Now wotest thow what I am, sayd the
good man. Nay, said Galahad. I am Ioseph of Armathye, the
whiche oure lord hath sente here to the to bere the felaushyp and
wotest thou wherfor that he hath sente me more than ony other?
For thou hast resemblyd me in to thynges: in that thou hast sene   220
the merveyles of the Sancgreal; in that thou hast ben a clene mayden
as I have ben and am. And whanne he had said these wordes Galahad
went to Percyval and kyssed hym and commaunded hym to God and
soo he wente to sire Bors and kyssed hym and commaunded hym to
God and sayd: fayre lord, salewe me to my lord, syr Launcelot,   225
my fader, and as soone as ye see hym byd hym remembre of this
unstable world. And there with he kneld doune tofore the table and
made his prayers and thenne sodenly his soule departed to Ihesu
Crist and a grete multitude of Angels bare his soule up to heven,
that the two felawes myghte wel behold hit. Also the two felawes   230
sawe come from heven an hand, but they sawe not the body. And
thenne hit cam ryght to the vessel and took it and the spere and soo
bare hit up to heven. Sythen was there never man soo hardy to saye
that he had sene the Sancgreal.

194 *maintain*
195 *or else*

197 *had made*
198 *covered*

200 *same*

204 *as* (*if*)

216 *know*
217 (Josephes, the son of Jos. of Ar.)

220 *two*

233 *Afterward/hardy enough*

[Book XXI, Chapters 3–7, 9–10, "The deth of Kynge Arthur and how Quene Guenever made hir a nonne in Almesburye"]

And thenne the kyng lete serche all the townes for his knyghtes that were slayne and enteryd them and salved them with softe salves that so sore were wounded. Thenne moche peple drewe unto kynge Arthur and thenne they sayd that sir Mordred warred upon kyng Arthur with wronge. And thenne kynge Arthur drewe hym with his   5 hoost doune by the see syde westward toward Salysbury. And ther was a day assygned betwixe kyng Arthur and sire Mordred that they shold mete upon a doune besyde Salysbury and not ferre from the see syde, and this day was assygned on a monday after Trynyté sonday, wherof kyng Arthur was passyng glad that he myghte be avengyd   10 upon sire Mordred. Thenne syr Mordred areysed moche peple aboute London, for they of Kente, Southsex and Surrey, Estsex and of Southfolke and of Northfolk held the most party with sir Mordred. And many a ful noble knyghte drewe unto syr Mordred and to the kynge, but they loved sir Launcelot drewe unto syr   15 Mordred. Soo upon Trynyté sonday at nyghte kynge Arthur dremed a wonderful dreme and that was this: that hym semed he satte upon a chaflet in a chayer and the chayer was fast to a whele and therupon satte kynge Arthur in the rychest clothe of gold that myghte be made and the kyng thoughte   20 ther was under hym fer from hym an hydous depe blak water and there in were alle maner of serpentes and wormes and wylde bestes, foule and horryble. And sodenly the kynge thoughte the whele torned up-soo- doune and he felle amonge the serpentys and every   25 beest took hym by a lymme. And thenne the kynge cryed, as he lay in his bedde and slepte: helpe. And thenne knyghtes, squyers and yomen awaked the kynge and thenne he was soo amased that he wyst not where he was and thenne he felle on slomberynge ageyn, not slepynge nor thorouly wakynge. So the kynge semed veryly   30 that there came syr Gawayne unto hym with a nombre of fayre ladyes with hym. And whan kynge Arthur sawe hym thenne he sayd: welcome my systers sone. I wende thou haddest ben dede and now I see the on lyve, moche am I beholdynge unto almyghty Ihesu. O fayre nevewe and my systers sone, what ben these   35 ladyes that hydder be come with yow? Sir, said sir Gawayne, alle these ben ladyes for whome I have foughten whanne I was man lyvynge and alle these are tho that I dyd batail for in ryghteuous quarel. And God hath gyven hem that grace at

1 had searched
2 interred

8 far

11 raised/many
12 Sussex/Essex
13 Suffolk/Norfolk/part

15 they (who)

17 "it seemed to him"
18 platform/chair/fastened

21 far/hideous
22 (body of) water
23 beasts

25 upside down

28 amazed
29 slumbering
30 "it seemed to the king"

33 thought
34 alive/beholden
35 nephew
36 hither

38 alive/those/battle

their grete prayer by cause I dyd bataille for hem that they   40
shold brynge me hydder unto yow. Thus moche hath God
gyven me leve for: to warne yow of youre dethe, for and ye
fyghte as to morne with syre Modred as ye bothe have
assygned, doubte ye not ye must be slayne and the moost
party of your peple on bothe partyes. And for the grete grace   45
and goodenes that almyghty Ihesu hath unto yow, and for pyté
of yow and many moo other good men there shalle be slayne,
God hath sente me to yow of his specyal grace to gyve yow
warnynge, that in no wyse ye doo bataille as to morne but
that ye take a treatyce for a moneth day and profer yow largely,   50
so as to morne to be putte in a delaye. For within a monethe
shalle come syr launcelot with alle his noble knyghtes and rescowe
yow worshipfully and slee sir Mordred and alle that ever wylle hold
with hym.

Thenne syr Gawayne and al the ladyes vaynquysshed and anone   55
the kyng callyd upon hys knyghtes, squyers and yemen and charged
them wyghtly to fetche his noble lordes and wyse bysshoppes unto
hym. And whan they were come, the kyng tolde hem his avysyon,
what sir Gawayn had tolde hym and warned hym that yf he faught
on the morne he shold be slayn. Than the kyng comaunded syr   60
Lucan de butlere and his broder syr Bedwere with two bysshoppes
wyth hem and charged theym in ony wyse, and they myght, take a
traytyse for a monthe day wyth syr Mordred where he had a grymme
hoost of an hondred thousand men. And there they entreted syr
Mordred longe tyme and at the laste Syr Mordred was agreyd for   65
to have Cornwayl and Kente by Arthures dayes; after, alle Englond
after the dayes of kyng Arthur.
Chap. IV. Than were they condesended that Kyng Arthure and syr
Mordred shold mete betwyxte bothe theyr hoostes and everyche
of them shold brynge fourtene persones, and they came wyth thys   70
word unto Arthure. Than sayd he: I am glad that thys is done. And
so he wente in to the felde. And whan Arthure shold departe he
warned al hys hoost that: and they see ony swerde drawen, look
ye come on fyersly and slee that traytour syr Mordred for I in
noo wyse truste hym. In lyke wyse syr Mordred warned his   75
hoost that: and ye see ony swerde drawen look that ye come on
fyersly and soo slee alle that ever before you stondeth, for in
no wyse I wyl not truste for thys treatyse. For I knowe wel my
fader wyl be avenged on me. And soo they mette as theyr poyntemente
was and so they were agreyd and accorded thorouly and wyn was sette   80

40 *because*

42 *permission/(for) if*

45 *part/sides*

47 *(who) shall*

50 *treaty*

52 *rescue*
53 *slay*

55 *vanished*
56 *yeomen*
57 *swiftly*
58 *vision*

62 *any way/if (they)*

65 *agreed*
66 *in (Arthur's)*

68 *agreed*
69 *each*

73 *if/any*
74 *fiercely/slay*

79 *appointment*
80 *wine*

and they dranke. Ryght soo came an adder oute of a lytel hethe busshe
and hyt stonge a knyght on the foot and whan the knyght felte hym
    stongen
he looked doun and sawe the adder and than he drewe his swerde to slee
the adder and thought of none other harme. And whan the hoost on bothe
partyes saw that swerde drawen than they blewe beamous, trum-   85
    pettes
and hornes and shouted grymly, and so bothe hoostes dressyd hem
to gyders. And kyng Arthur took his hors and sayd: Allas thys
unhappy day; and so rode to his partye. And syr Mordred in
like wyse. And never was there seen a more doolfuller bataylle
in no crysten londe, for there was but russhyng and rydyng, fewnyng   90
and strykyng, and many a grymme worde was there spoken eyder to
other and many a dedely stroke. But ever kyng Arthur rode thorugh
oute the bataylle of syr Mordred many tymes and dyd ful nobly as a
noble Kyng shold and at al tymes he faynted never and syr Mordred
that day put hym in devoyr and in grete perylle.   95
    And thus they faughte alle the longe day and never stynted
tyl the noble knyghtes were layd to the colde erthe and ever they
faught stylle tyl it was nere nyghte and by that tyme was there an
hondred thousand layed deed upon the down. Thenne was Arthure
wode wrothe oute of mesure whan he sawe his peple so slayn from   100
hym. Thenne the kyng loked aboute hym and thenne was he ware of
al hys hoost and of al his good knyghtes were lefte no moo on lyve
    but two knyghtes,
that one was Syr Lucan de butlere and his broder Syr Bedwere.
And they were full sore wounded. Ihesu mercy, sayd the kyng,
where are al my noble knyghtes becomen? Alas that ever I shold   105
see thys dolefull day, for now, sayd Arthur, I am come to myn ende.
But wolde to God that I wyste where were that traytour Syr Mordred
that hath caused alle thys meschyef. Thenne was kyng Arthure ware where
syr Mordred lenyd upon his swerde emonge a grete hepe of deed men.
Now gyve me my spere, sayd Arthur unto Syr Lucan, for yonder I   110
have espyed the traytour that alle thys woo hath wrought. Syr, late
hym be, sayd Syr Lucan, for he is unhappy. And yf ye passe thys
unhappy day he shalle be ryght wel revengyd upon hym. Good lord,
remembre ye of your nyghtes dreme and what the spyryte of Syr

82 *stung*

85 *beams (battle trumpets)*

87 *addressed themselves to each other*

90 *foining, thrusting*
91 *either, each*

95 *devoir, duty*

99 *dead*
100 *madly*
101 *aware*
102 *alive*

111 *woe/let*

Gauwayn tolde you this nyght, yet God of his grete goodnes hath pre-   115
served you hyderto. Therfore for Goddes sake, my lord, leve of
by thys, for blessyd by God, ye have wonne the felde. For here we
ben thre on lyve and wyth syr Mordred is none on lyve. And yf ye
leve of now thys wycked day of desteynye is paste. Tyde me deth
betyde me lyf, sayth the kyng, now I see hym yonder allone he   120
shal never escape myn handes, for at a better avaylle shal I never
have hym. God spede you wel, sayd syr Bedware. Thenne the
kyng gate hys spere in bothe his handes and ranne toward syr Mordred,
cryeng: Tratour, now is thy deth day come. And whan syr Mordred
herde syr Arthur he ranne untyl hym with his swerde drawen in his   125
hande. And there kyng Arthur smote syr Mordred under the shelde
with a foyne of his spere thorughoute the body more than a fadom.
And whan syr Mordred felte that he had hys dethes wounde, he thryst
hym self wyth the myght that he had up to the bur of kynge Arthurs
spere, and right so he smote his fader, Arthur, wyth his swerde   130
holden in bothe his handes on the syde of the heed that the swerde
persyd the helmet and the brayne panne and therwythall syr
Mordred fyl starke deed to the erthe. And the nobyl Arthur fyl in
a swoune to the erthe and there he swouned ofte tymes and syr
Lucan de butlere and syr Bedwere oftymes heve hym up. And soo   135
waykely they ledde hym betwyxte them bothe to a lytel chapel not
ferre from the see syde. And whan the kyng was there he thought
hym wel eased. Thenne herde they people crye in the felde. Now
goo thou, syr Lucan, sayd the kyng, and do me to wyte what by-
tokenes that noyse in the felde. So syr Lucan departed, for he   140
was grevously wounded in many places. And so as he yede he
sawe and herkened by the mone lyght how that pyllars and
robbers were comen in to the felde to pylle and robbe many a
ful noble knyghte of brochys and bedys, of many a good rynge
and of many a ryche Iewel, and who that were not deed al oute   145
there they slewe theym for theyr harneys and theyr rychesse.
Whan syr Lucan understode thys werke he came to the kyng
assone as he myght and tolde hym al what he had herde and
seen. Therfore, be my rede, sayd syr Lucan, it is beste
that we brynge you to somme towne. I wolde it were soo, sayd   150
the kyng.
Chap. V. But I may not stonde, myn hede werches soo. A,
Syr Launcelot, sayd kyng Arthur, thys day have I sore myst the.
Alas that ever I was ayenst the, for now have I my dethe, wherof syr

116 *leave off*
117 *blessed be God*

119 *destiny/"Whether death or life befalls me"*

121 *advantage*

123 *got*

127 *foin* (l. 90)/*fathom*
128 *thrust*

131 *held/head/(so) that*
132 *pierced/brain pan, skull*
133 *fell*

135 *lifted*
136 *weakly*
137 *far*

139 *"find out for me"*
140 *betokens*
141 *went*
142 *pillagers*
143 *plunder*
144 *brooches/beads*
145 *jewel/those who/completely*
146 *harness/riches*

148 *as soon*
149 *"in my opinion"*

152 *works/Ah*
153 *missed*

Gauwayn me warned in my dreme. Than syr Lucan took up the kyng   155
the one parte and Syr Bedwere the other parte and in the lyftyng
the kyng sowned and syr Lucan fyl in a sowne wyth the lyfte, that
the parte of his guttes fyl oute of his bodye. And therwyth the
noble knyghtes herte braste and whan the kyng awake he behelde
syr Lucan how he laye foomyng at the mowth and parte of his guttes   160
laye at his feet. Alas, sayd the kyng, thys is to me a ful hevy syght,
to see thys noble duke so deye for my sake, for he wold have holpen
me that had more nede of helpe than I. Alas he wold not complayne
hym, hys herte was so sette to helpe me. Now Ihesu have mercy
upon hys soule. Than syr Bedwere wepte for the deth of his brother.   165
Leve thys mornyng and wepyng, sayd the kyng, for al this wyl not
avaylle me, for wyte thou wel and I myght lyve my self the deth of
syr Lucan wolde greve me ever more, but my tyme hyeth fast, sayd
the kyng. Therfore, sayd Arthur unto syr Bedwere, take thou Excalybur, my good swerde, and goo with it to yonder water syde and   170
whan thou comest there I charge the throwe my swerde in that water
and come ageyn and telle me what thou there seest. My lord, sad
Bedwere, your commaundement shal be doon and lyghtly brynge
you worde ageyn. So syr Bedwere departed and by the waye he
behelde that noble swerde that the pomel and the hafte was al of   175
precyous stones and thenne he sayd to hym self, yf I throwe this
ryche swerde in the water, therof shal never come good but harme
and losse. And thenne syr Bedwere hydde Excalybur under a tree
and so as sone as he myght he came ageyn unto the kyng and sayd he
had ben at the water and had throwen the swerde in to the water.   180
What sawe thou there, sayd the kyng. Syr, he sayd, I sawe no thynge
but wawes and wyndes. That is untrewly sayd of the, sayd the
kynge. Therfore goo thou lyghtelye ageyn and do my commaundemente, as thou arte to me leef and dere; spare not but throwe
it in. Than syr Bedwere returned ageyn and took the swerde in   185
hys hande and than hym thought synne and shame to throwe awaye
that nobyl swerde and so efte he hydde the swerde and retorned
ageyn and tolde to the kyng that he had ben at the water and done
his commaundemente. What sawe thou there, sayd the kyng. Syr,
he sayd, I sawe no thynge but the waters wappe and wawes wanne.   190
A traytour untrewe, sayd kyng Arthur, now hast thou betrayed me
twyse. Who wold have wente that thou that hast been to me so leef
and dere and thou arte named a noble knyghte and wold betraye
me for the richesse of the swerde. But now goo ageyn lyghtly for
thy longe taryeng putteth me in grete Ieopardye of my lyf, for I   195
have taken colde. And but yf thou do now as I byd the, yf ever

157 *swooned/swoon/(so) that*

159 *burst/awoke*
160 *foaming*

162 *die so/helped*

166 *mourning*
167 *know/if (I might)*
168 *hastens*

172 *said*
173 *quickly, lively*

182 *waves*

184 *beloved*

187 *again*

190 *lap/waves/wane*

192 *thought/beloved*

194 *quickly*
195 *jeopardy*
196 *Unless*

I may see the I shal slee the myn owne handes, for thou woldest
for my ryche swerde see me dede. Thenne Syr Bedwere departed
and wente to the swerde and lyghtly took hit up and wente to the
water syde and there he bounde the gyrdyl aboute the hyltes and   200
thenne
he threwe the swerde as farre in to the water as he myght and there
cam an arme and an hande above the water and mette it and caught
it and so shoke it thryse and braundysshed and than vanysshed awaye
the hande wyth the swerde in the water. So syr Bedwere came
ageyn to the kyng and tolde hym what he sawe. Alas, sayd the   205
kyng, helpe me hens, for I drede me I have taryed over longe.
Than syr Bedwere toke the kyng upon his backe and so wente wyth
hym to that water syde and whan they were at the water syde, evyn
fast by the banke hoved a lytyl barge wyth many fayr ladyes in hit
and emonge hem al was a quene and al they had blacke hoodes and   210
al they wepte and shryked whan they sawe Kyng Arthur. Now put
me in to the barge, sayd the kyng, and so he dyd softelye. And there
receyved hym thre quenes wyth grete mornyng and soo they sette hem
doun and in one of their lappes kyng Arthur layed hys heed and than
that quene sayd, A, dere broder, why have ye taryed so longe from   215
me?
Alas, this wounde on your heed hath caught overmoche colde. And soo
than they rowed from the londe and syr Bedwere cryed, A, my lord
Arthur, what shal become of me now ye goo from me and leve me
here allone emonge myn enemyes. Comfort thy self, sayd the kyng,
and doo as wel as thou mayst, for in me is no tryste for to truste in.   220
For I wyl in to the vale of Avylyon to hele me of my grevous wounde.
And yf thou here never more of me, praye for my soule, but ever the
quenes and ladyes wepte and shryched that hit was pyté to here.
And assone as syr Bedwere had loste the syght of the baarge he wepte
and waylled and so took the foreste and so he wente al that nyght and   225
in the mornyng he was ware betwyxte two holtes hore as a chapel and
an ermytage.
Chap. VI. Than was syr Bedwere glad and thyder he wente and whan
he came in to the chapel he sawe where laye an heremyte grovelyng
on al foure there fast by a tombe was newe graven. Whan the Eremyte   230
sawe syr Bedwere he knewe hym wel for he was but lytel tofore
bysshop of Caunterburye that syr Mordred flemed. Syr, sayd Syr Bedwere, what man is there entred that ye praye so fast fore? Fayr sone,

197 *slay*

203 *brandished*

221 (*I will*) *go/Avalon*

223 *shrieked*
224 *as soon*
225 (*took*) *to*
226 *aware . . . of*

227 *hermitage*
229 *hermit*

231 *before*
232 *put to flight*
233 *interred*

sayd the heremyte, I wote not verayly but by my demyyng, but thys
nyght at mydnyght here came a nombre of ladyes and broughte hyder   235
a deed cors and prayed me to berye hym and here they offeryd an
hondred tapers and they gaf me an hondred besauntes. Alas,
sayd syr Bedwere, that was my lord kyng Arthur that here lyeth
buryed in thys chapel. Than syr Bedwere swowned and whan he
awoke he prayed the heremyte he myght abyde wyth hym stylle   240
there, to lyve wyth fastyng and prayers. For from hens wyl I
never goo, sayd syr Bedwere, by my wylle, but al the dayes of
my lyf here to praye for my lord Arthur. Ye are welcome to
me, sayd the heremyte, for I knowe you better than ye wene
that I doo. Ye are the bolde Bedwere and the ful noble duke   245
Syr Lucan de butlere was your broder. Thenne syr Bedwere
tolde the heremyte alle as ye have herde to fore. So there
bode syr Bedwere with the hermyte that was tofore bysshop
of Caunterburye and there syr Bedwere put upon hym poure
clothes and servyd the hermyte ful lowly in fastyng and in   250
prayers. Thus of Arthur I fynde never more wryton in
bookes that been auctorysed nor more of the veray certenté
of his deth herde I never redde, but thus was he ledde aweye
in a shyppe wherin were thre quenes: that one was kyng
Arthurs syster, quene Morgan le fay; the other was the   255
quene of North galys; the thyrd was the quene of the waste
londes. Also there was Nynyue, the chyef lady of the lake
that had wedded Pelleas, the good knyght, and this lady had
doon moche for kyng Arthur, for she wold never suffre syr
Pelleas to be in noo place where he shold be in daunger of   260
his lyf and so he lyved to the uttermest of his dayes wyth
hyr in grete reste. More of the deth of kyng Arthur coude
I never fynde but that ladyes brought hym to his buryellys
and suche one was buryed there that the hermyte bare wytnesse that
somtyme was bysshop of Caunterburye, but yet the heremyte knewe   265
not in certayn that he was verayly the body of kyng Arthur, for thys
tale syr Bedwer knyght of the table rounde made it to be wryton.
Chap. VII. Yet somme men say in many partyes of Englond that kyng
Arthur is not deed, but had by the wylle of our lord Ihesu in to another
place. And men say that he shal come ageyn and he shal wynne the   270
holy crosse. I wyl not say that it shal be so, but rather I wyl say
here in thys world he chaunged his lyf, but many men say that there
is wryton upon his tombe this vers: *Hic iacet Arthurus Rex quondam
Rex que futurus.* Thus leve I here syr Bedwere with the hermyte

234 *know/truly/judgment*

236 *corpse*
237 *gold coins*

244 *think*

252 *authorized*
253 *nor read*

256 *Northgalis*

261 *utmost*

263 *burial*

269 *dead*

273 *"Here lies Arthur, a king of old, and a king to be"*

that dwellyd that tyme in a chapel besyde Glastynburye and there   275
    was
his ermytage and they lyvyd in theyr prayers and fastynges and
grete abstynence. And whan quene Guenever understood that kyng
Arthur was slayn and al the noble knyghtes, syr Mordred and al the
remenaunte, than the quene stale aweye and v ladyes wyth hyr. And
soo she wente to Almesburye and there she let make hir self a nonne   280
and ware whyte clothes and blacke and grete penaunce she toke as
ever dyd synful lady in thys londe. And never creature coude make
hyr mery, but lyved in fastyng, prayers and almes dedes, that al
maner of peple mervaylled how vertuously she was chaunged. Now
leve we quene Guenever in Almesburye, a nonne in whyte clothes   285
    and
blacke, and there she was abbesse and rular as reason wolde and torne
we from hyr and speke we of Syr Launcelot du Lake.
Chap. IX. Than came syr Bors de ganys and sayd, my lord syr
Launcelot, what thynke ye for to doo now? To ryde in this royame?
Wyt you wel ye shal fynde fewe frendes. Be as be may, sayd Sry   290
Launcelot, kepe you stylle here, for I wyl forth on my Iourney
and noo man nor chylde shall goo with me. So it was no bote to
stryve, but he departed and rode westerly and there he sought
a vij or viij dayes and atte last he cam to a nonnerye. And than
was quene Guenever ware of sir Launcelot as he walked in the   295
cloystre and whan she sawe hym there she swouned thryse that
al the ladyes and Ientyl wymmen had werke ynough to holde the
quene up. So whan she myght speke she callyd ladyes and Ientyl
wymmen to hir and sayd: ye mervayl, fayr ladyes, why I make this
fare. Truly, she said, it is for the syght of yonder knyght that yender   300
standeth. Wherfore I praye you al calle hym to me. Whan syr Launcelot was brought to hyr, than she sayd to al the ladyes: thorowe this man
and me hath al this warre be wrought and the deth of the moost
noblest knyghtes of the world, for thorugh our love that we have loved
to gyder is my moost noble lord slayn. Therfor, syr Launcelot, wyt   305
thou wel I am sette in suche a plyte to gete my soule hele and yet I
truste thorugh Goddes grace that after my deth to have a syght of the
blessyd face of Cryst and at domes day to sytte on his ryght syde for
as synful as ever I was are sayntes in heven. Therfore, syr Launcelot,
I requyre the and beseche the hertelye for al the love that ever was   310
betwyxte us that thou never see me more in the vysage. And I

275 *Glastonbury*

279 *rest/stole/five*
280 *became a nun*
281 *wore*

289 *realm*
290 *Know/Be as it may*
291 *(will) go/journey*
292 *boot, benefit*

294 *seven/eight/nunnery*

296 *swooned/so (that)*
297 *gentlewomen/enough*

300 *yonder*

302 *through*

comaunde the on Goddes behalfe that thou forsake my companye
and to thy kyngdom thou torne ageyn and kepe wel thy royame from
warre and wrake. For as wel as I have loved the, myn hert wyl
not serve me to see the, for thorugh the and me is the flour of   315
kynges and knyghtes destroyed. Therfor, sir Launcelot, goo to
thy royame and there take the a wyf and lyve with hir with Ioye and blysse
and I praye the hertelye praye for me to our lord that I may amende my
myslyvyng. Now swete madam, sayd, syr Launcelot, wold ye that I
shold torne ageyn unto my cuntreye and there to wedde a lady? Nay,   320
Madam, wyt you wel that shal I never do, for I shall never be soo fals
to you of that I have promysed. But the same deystenye that ye have
taken you to, I wyl take me unto for to plese Ihesu and ever for you I
cast me specially to praye. Yf thou wylt do so, sayd the quene, holde
thy promyse, but I may never beleve but that thou wylt torne to the   325
world ageyn. Wel, madam, sayd he, ye say as pleseth you, yet wyst
you me never fals of my promesse and God defende but I shold forsake
the world as ye have do, for in the quest of the sank greal I had fosaken
the vanytees of the world had not your lord ben, and yf I had done so
at that tyme wyth my herte, wylle and thought, I had passed al the   330
knyghtes that were in the sanke greal excepte syr Galahad, my sone.
And therfore, lady, sythen ye have taken you to perfeccion, I must
nedys take me to perfection of ryght. For I take recorde of God, in
you I have had myn erthly Ioye and yf I had founden you now so
          dysposed
I had caste me to have had you in to myn owne royame.   335
Chap. X. But sythen I fynde you thus desposed I ensure you faythfully
I wyl ever take me to penaunce and praye whyle my lyf lasteth yf
that I may fynde ony heremyte, other graye or whyte, that wyl receyve
me. Wherfore madame I praye you kysse me and never nomore. Nay,
sayd the quene, that shal I never do, but absteyne you from suche   340
werkes. And they departed, but there was never so harde an herted
man but he wold have wepte to see the dolour that they made, for there
was laementacyon as they had be stungyn wyth sperys and many tymes
they swouned. And the ladyes bare the quene to hir chambre and syr
Launcelot awok and went and took his hors and rode al that day and   345
al nyght in a forest, wepyng. And atte last he was ware of an ermytage
and a chappel stode betwyxte two clyffes and than he herde a lytel
belle rynge to masse. And thyder he rode, and alyght, and teyed
his hors to the gate, and herd masse; and he that sange masse was
the bysshop of Caunterburye. Bothe the bysshop and sir Bedwer   350
          knewe

313 *realm*
314 *wrack*

317 *joy*

319 *misliving*

322 *destiny*

326 *knew*

328 *Holy Grail/forsaken*

330 *would have surpassed*

332 *since*

336 *assure*

338 *any/either*

340 *abstain*

343 *lamentation/spears*

347 *that (stood)*
348 *tied*

syr Launcelot and they spake to gyders after masse, but whan syr Bedwere had tolde his tale al hole syr Launcelottes hert almost braste for
sorowe. And sir Launcelot threwe hys armes abrode and sayd, alas,
who may truste thys world. And than he knelyd doun on his knee and
prayed the bysshop to shryve hym and assoyle hym, and than he be   355
sought the bysshop that he myght be hys brother. Than the bysshop
sayd, I wyll gladly. And there he put an habyte upon Syr Launcelot,
and there he servyd God day and nyght with prayers and fastynges.

Thus the grete hoost abode at Dover and than sir Lyonel toke
fyftene lordes with hym and rode to London to seke sir Launcelot and   360
there syr Lyonel was slayn and many of his lordes. Thenne Syr
Bors de ganys made the grete hoost for to goo hoome ageyn. And
syr Boors, syr Ector de maris, Syr Blamour, syr Bleoboris with
moo other of syr Launcelottes kynne toke on hem to ryde al
Englond overthwart and endelonge to seek syr Launcelot. So syr   365
Bors by fortune rode so longe tyl he came to the same chapel
where syr Launcelot was and so syr Bors herde a lytel belle knylle
that range to masse and there he alyght and herde masse. And whan
masse was doon the bysshop, syr Launcelot and sir Bedwere came
to syr Bors and whan syr Bors sawe sir Launcelot in that maner   370
clothyng, than he preyed the bysshop that he myght be in the same sewte.
And so there was an habyte put upon hym, and there he lyved in
prayers
and fastyng, and wythin halfe a yere there was come syr Galyhud, syr
Galyhodyn, sir Blamour, syr Bleoheris, syr Wyllyars, syr Clarras
and sir Gohaleaniyne. So al these vij noble knyghtes there abode styll   375
and whan they sawe syr Launcelot had taken hym to suche perfeccion,
they had no last to departe but toke suche an habyte as he had. Thus
they endured in grete penaunce syx yere and than syr Launcelot took
thabyte of preesthod of the bysshop and a twelve monthe he sange masse.
And there was none of these other knyghtes but they redde in bookes   380
and
holpe for to synge masse and range bellys and dyd bodoly al maner of
servyce. And soo their horses wente where they wolde, for they
toke no regarde of no worldly rychesses, for whan they sawe syr
Launcelot endure suche penaunce in prayers and fastynges they toke
no force what payne they endured for to see the nobleste knyght of   385
the world take suche abstynaunce that he waxed ful lene. And thus
upon a nyght there came a vysyon to syr Launcelot and charged hym
in remyssyon of his synnes to haste hym unto Almysbury and by thenne
then come there, thou shall fynde quene Guenever dede. And therfore

351 *together*
352 *burst*

355 *absolve*

364 *themselves*

367 *knell*

375 *Gahalantine*

379 *the + habit*
380 *who did not read*

381 *bodily*

385 *account*

take thy felowes with the, and parcvey them of an hors bere, and 390
fetche thou the cors of hir, and burye hir by her husbond, the noble
kyng Arthur. So this avysyon came to Launcelot thryse in one nyght.

SUPPLEMENTARY MATERIAL

1. Comparison with the Winchester text in *The Works of Sir Thomas Malory*, ed. Eugène Vinaver, Oxford, 1947, 3 vols., or *King Arthur and His Knights*, edited by Vinaver, Boston, 1956 [1 vol., paper].
2. R. S. Loomis, *The Development of Arthurian Romance*, New York, 1963.
3. William Matthews, comp., *Old and Middle English Literature* (New York, 1968), pp. 59–60 [bibliography].
4. Jessie L. Weston, *From Ritual to Romance*, New York, 1957.
5. Arthur B. Ferguson, *The Indian Summer of English Chivalry: Studies in the Decline and Transformation of Chivalric Idealism*, Durham, N.C., 1960.
6. Caxton bibliography in H. S. Bennett, Section A, Bibliography.
7. Richard L. Brengle, *Arthur, King of Britain*, New York, 1964.

APPENDIX 1.

The Rules of Courtly Love,
based on the De Amore of Andreas Capellanus

1. Marriage should not be a deterrent to love.
2. Love cannot exist in the individual who cannot be jealous.
3. A double love cannot obligate an individual.
4. Love constantly waxes and wanes.
5. That which is not freely given by the object of one's love loses its savor.
6. It is necessary for a male to reach the age of maturity in order to love.
7. A lover must observe a two-year widowhood after his beloved's death.
8. Only the most urgent circumstances should deprive one of love.
9. Only the insistence of love can motivate one to love.
10. Love cannot coexist with avarice.
11. A lover should not love anyone who would be an embarrassing marriage choice.
12. True love excludes all from its embrace but the beloved.
13. Public revelation of love is deadly to love in most instances.
14. The value of love is commensurate with its difficulty of attainment.
15. The presence of one's beloved causes paleness of complexion.
16. The sight of one's beloved causes palpitation of the heart.
17. A new love brings an old one to a finish.
18. Good character is the one real requirement for worthiness of love.
19. When love grows faint its demise is usually certain.
20. Apprehension is the constant companion of the true lover.
21. Love is reinforced by jealousy.
22. Suspicion of the beloved generates jealousy and therefore intensifies love.
23. Eating and sleeping diminish greatly when one is aggravated by love.
24. The lover's every deed is performed with the thought of his beloved in mind.
25. Unless it please his beloved, no act or thought is worthy to the lover.
26. Love is powerless to withhold anything from love.

27. There is no such thing as too much of the pleasure of one's beloved.
28. Presumption on the part of the beloved causes suspicion in the lover.
29. Aggravation of excessive passion does not usually afflict the true lover.
30. Thought of the beloved never leaves the true lover.
31. Two men may love one woman or two women one man.

REFERENCES:

A. J. Denomy, "Courtly Love and Courtliness," *Speculum*, XXVIII (1953), 44–63.

————, *The Heresy of Courtly Love*, New York, 1947.

E. T. Donaldson, "The Myth of Courtly Love," *Ventures*, V (1965), 16–23.

W. T. H. Jackson, "The *De Amore* of Andreas Capellanus and the Practice of Love at Court," *Romanic Review*, XLIX (1958), 243–51.

C. S. Lewis, *The Allegory of Love*, New York, 1958.

J. J. Parry, trans., *The Art of Courtly Love*, New York, 1941 (*Records of Civilization*, No. 33).

APPENDIX 2.

The Significance of Numbers

In common with all medieval art, Middle English literature shows a concern for what Mâle has christened "a kind of sacred mathematics."[1] The order of the natural world was observable proof of the existence of God, and numbers, the key to that order, inspired awe. There were traditional meanings for the numbers, well known and, in some instances, still in use today. But there were also believed to be secrets hidden in numbers which could be revealed only if one were diligent, faithful, or, so it would sometimes seem, inventive enough to unlock them. Numbers were combined to give complex meanings, i.e., 4 + 3 = not only the meanings for 7, but the significance of its components 3 and 4 as well. And multiples of important numbers gave intensified significance, i.e., if 3 = Trinity, 9 = triple Trinity. Further, interpreters manipulated the components of large numbers in all possible fashions. (For example, see *144,000* below.) The letters of the alphabet would be assigned numerical value, i.e., $A = 1$, $B = 2$, etc., to give mathematical significance to specific words, or the number of letters in a word, i.e., *Adam* = 4, could yield meaning.

A sample of the Kalandar and Compost of Shepherds well illustrates the medieval numbers game:

> "We Shepherds say that the age of a man is seventy-two year, and that we liken but to one whole year. For evermore we take six year for every month, as January or February and so forth: for as the year changeth by the twelve months into twelve sundry manners, so doth a man change himself twelve times in his life, so be that he live to seventy-two, for three times six maketh eighteen, and six times six maketh thirty-six, and then is man at the best and also at the highest, and twelve times six maketh seventy-two and that is the age of a man.
>
> Thus must ye reckon for every month six year or else it may be understood by the four quarters and seasons of the year. So is divided man into four parts as to youth, strength, wisdom, and age; he to be eighteen

---

[1] Emile Mâle, *The Gothic Image*, trans. Dora Nussey (New York, 1958), p. 5.

year young, eighteen year strong, eighteen year in wisdom, and the fourth eighteen year to go to the full age of seventy-two."[2]

Some of the simple medieval meanings of numbers are listed below.

ONE = Unity, God

TWO = Incarnation, Jesus Christ as God and Man

THREE = Holy Trinity, three persons in one God
    three Magi
    three periods in time before Law (Adam to Noah, to Abraham, to Moses)

FOUR = Blessings (Clarity, Impassivity, Knowledge, Delectation)
    four rivers of paradise
    four cardinal virtues
    four seasons
    four humors
    four corners of the earth with their four winds
    four elements (earth, air, fire, water)

FIVE = Sacrifice, five wounds of Christ
    five senses
    five points to a star, pentangle (*Gawain*, II, 6)

SIX = Imperfection (one less than 7, perfection)
    six days of creation of the world

SEVEN = Perfection (sum of 3 and 4), Universality, Man (4 = body, 3 = soul)

seven planets	seven ages of the world
seven days	seven journeys of Christ
seven churches	seven parts of the mass
seven sorrows of Mary	seven ages of man
seven Deadly Sins	seven sacraments
seven Virtues	seven last words of Christ
seven petitions of Lord's Prayer	seven tones of the scale

EIGHT = Regeneration (seven days of creation plus following time of grace)
    eight souls in Noah's ark

NINE = Mystery (3 × 3)
    nine moving heavens (see Appendix 3)

TEN = Completion
    Ten commandments, outlining man's complete duty to God and fellow man

TWELVE = Universal number (3 × 4, spirit penetrating matter)
    twelve apostles
    twelve signs of the Zodiac
    twelve tribes of Israel

---

[2] Quoted by Vincent Hopper in *Medieval Number Symbolism* (New York, 1958), p. 91, n. 11.

twelve parts of man
twelve articles of the Apostles' Creed
THIRTEEN
  thirteen days for three kings' journey to Christ child
  thirteen at Last Supper
TWENTY-FOUR
  twenty-four elders
  twenty-four hours of natural day
THIRTY = Christ's age when he began to preach
FORTY
  forty days of Lent
  forty days of Christ in wilderness
  forty days of Moses on Mount Sinai
ONE HUNDRED = Completeness (10 × 10)
TWO HUNDRED FORTY-EIGHT = bones of the body
ONE THOUSAND = Perfection
  one thousand acts of Devil
SEVEN THOUSAND = Universal perfection (perfection, 1000 × universality, 7)
ONE HUNDRED FORTY-FOUR THOUSAND = All of God's created people receiving spiritual blessing
    (12 × 12 × 1000) = (Trinity, 3, × parts of the earth, 4, × apostles or tribes, 12, × perfection, 1000) = 144,000

APPENDIX 3.

The Planets: Their Relation to the Days and Hours

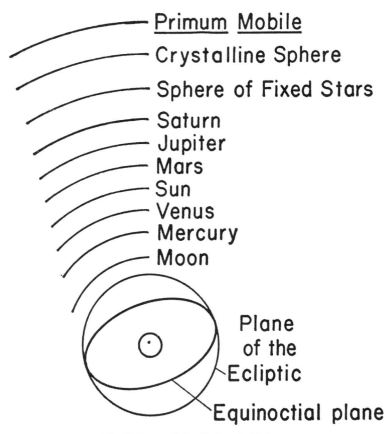

The Spheres of the Ptolemaic Universe

Primum Mobile—gave motion to the other spheres

Equinoctial plane—celestial equator

Ecliptic plane—belt in which planets move, annual course of the sun, and the line of the Zodiac, divided into its twelve signs
(the autumnal and vernal equinoxes occurred when the annual course of the sun, in the ecliptic plane, crossed the equinoctial plane in March and September)

On this scheme of the planets rested the control of the 168 hours of the week (page 520)

The Hours of the Week and Their Controlling Planets

	12 to 1 am	2	3	4	5	6	7	8	9	10	11	12 noon	1	2	3	4	5	6	7	8	9	10	11	12 pm
Saturday (Saturn, ♄)	♄	♃	♂	☉	♀	☿	☽	♄	♃	♂	☉	♀	☿	☽	♄	♃	♂	☉	♀	☿	☽	♄	♃	♂
Sunday (Sun, ☉)	☉	♀	☿	☽	♄	♃	♂	☉	♀	☿	☽	♄	♃	♂	☉	♀	☿	☽	♄	♃	♂	☉	♀	☿
Monday (Moon, ☽)	☽	♄	♃	♂	☉	♀	☿	☽	♄	♃	♂	☉	♀	☿	☽	♄	♃	♂	☉	♀	☿	☽	♄	♃
Tuesday* (Mars, ♂)	♂	☉	♀	☿	☽	♄	♃	♂	☉	♀	☿	☽	♄	♃	♂	☉	♀	☿	☽	♄	♃	♂	☉	♀
Wednesday* (Mercury, ☿)	☿	☽	♄	♃	♂	☉	♀	☿	☽	♄	♃	♂	☉	♀	☿	☽	♄	♃	♂	☉	♀	☿	☽	♄
Thursday* (Jupiter, ♃)	♃	♂	☉	♀	☿	☽	♄	♃	♂	☉	♀	☿	☽	♄	♃	♂	☉	♀	☿	☽	♄	♃	♂	☉
Friday * (Venus, ♀)	♀	☿	☽	♄	♃	♂	☉	♀	☿	☽	♄	♃	♂	☉	♀	☿	☽	♄	♃	♂	☉	♀	☿	☽

* cf. Tuesday—Mars: Fr. *mardi;* Wednesday—Mercury: Fr. *mercredi;* Thursday—Jupiter, Fr. *jeudi;* Friday—Venus, Fr. *vendredi*

REFERENCES:

John Livingstone Lowes, *Geoffrey Chaucer*, Chapter I, "Backgrounds and Horizons," Bloomington, Ind., 1958 [originally printed as *Geoffrey Chaucer and the Development of His Genius*, Boston, 1934].

Thorndike (see Bibliography).

For a short, concise discussion and further references, consult Ackerman, Chapter V, "The World View of the Middle Ages" (see Bibliography).

BIBLIOGRAPHY

A. Selected References for Middle English Literature and Its Background

(See also the items under "Supplementary Material," listed at the end of each text, and bibliographies such as William Matthews' *Old and Middle English Literature*, New York, 1968.)

Ackerman, Robert W., *Backgrounds to Medieval English Literature*, New York, 1966.

Baugh, Albert C., *A Literary History of England*, 2nd ed. (New York, 1967), I, "The Middle English Period," pp. 109–312.

Bennett, H. S., *Chaucer and the Fifteenth Century*, Oxford, 1947.

Bird, Ruth, *The Turbulent London of Richard II*, London, 1949.

Blades, William, ed., *Boke of St. Albans*, London, 1901 [treatises on hunting, hawking and heraldry].

Blanch, Robert J., ed., *Piers Plowman: Critical Essays*, Knoxville, Tenn., 1968.

———, ed., *Sir Gawain and Pearl: Critical Essays*, Bloomington, Ind., 1966.

Bloomfield, Morton W., *The Seven Deadly Sins*, East Lansing, Mich., 1952.

Bosman, Anthony, *Hieronymus Bosch*, New York, 1962.

Carroll, William M., *Animal Conventions in English Renaissance Non-Religious Prose (1550–1600)*, New York, 1954.

Chambers, E. K., *The Medieval Stage*, 2 vols., London, 1903.

———, *The English Folk-Play*, Oxford, 1933.

Chaytor, H. J., *From Script to Print*, Cambridge, 1945.

Coulton, G. G., *Medieval Panorama*, 2nd ed., 2 vols., London, 1961.

Craig, Hardin, *English Religious Drama of the Middle Ages*, Oxford, 1955.

Curtius, Ernst R., *European Literature and the Latin Middle Ages*, trans. W. R. Trask, New York, 1953.

Davis, Charles T., ed., *Western Awakening*, Sources of Medieval History, Vol. II, New York, 1967.

Diamond, Naomi, and Mary Kirby, "From Every Shire's End: The World of Chaucer's Pilgrims," *Pilgrim Films*, London, 1968 [film].

Dronke, Peter, *Medieval Latin and the Rise of the European Love Lyric*, Vol. I, Oxford, 1965.

Dunbar, Helen F., *Symbolism in Medieval Thought and Its Consummation in the Divine Comedy*, New Haven, 1929.

Evans, J., *Dress in Medieval France*, Oxford, 1952.

Fisher, John H., ed., *The Medieval Literature of Western Europe: A Review of Research, Mainly 1930–1960*, New York, 1966.

Flores, Angel, ed., *Medieval Age*, New York, 1963 [comparative medieval literature].

Ford, Boris, ed., *The Age of Chaucer*, rev. ed., Harmondsworth, 1963.

Frank, Grace, *The Medieval French Drama*, Oxford, 1954.

Furnivall, F. J., ed., *Early English Meals and Manners*, EETS 32, London, 1868.

Hassall, W. O., ed., *Medieval England: As Viewed by Contemporaries*, New York, 1965.

Hopper, Vincent F., *Medieval Number Symbolism*, New York, 1958.

Howard, Donald R., *The Three Temptations: Medieval Man in Search of the World*, Princeton, 1966.

Huizinga, Johan, *The Waning of the Middle Ages*, New York, 1954; Harmondsworth, 1924.

Hussey, Maurice, *Chaucer's World: A Pictorial Companion*, Cambridge, England, 1967.

Jackson, W. T. H., *Medieval Literature, A History and A Guide*, New York, 1966 [comparative medieval literature].

Jones, Gwyn, and Thomas, trans., *The Mabinogion*, New York/London, 1949.

Kelly, Amy, *Eleanor of Aquitaine*, Cambridge, Mass., 1950.

Knowles, Dom David, *The English Mystics*, London, 1927.

———, *The Evolution of Medieval Thought*, New York, 1964.

Leff, Gordon, *Medieval Thought, St. Augustine to Ockham*, Baltimore, 1958.

Lipson, Ephraim, *An Introduction to the Economic History of England*, London, 1915, Vol. I, *The Middle Ages*.

Mâle, Emile, *The Gothic Image*, trans. Dora Nussey, New York, 1958 (previously published as *Religious Art in France of the Thirteenth Century*, New York, 1913).

Matthews, William, ed., *Later Medieval English Prose*, New York, 1963.

Muntz, Hope, *The Golden Warrior*, New York, 1949.

Owst, G. R., *Preaching in Medieval England*, Cambridge, 1933.

———, *Literature and Pulpit in Medieval England*, Cambridge, Mass., 1950.

Patch, H. R., *The Other World, According to Descriptions in Medieval Literature*, Cambridge, Mass., 1950.

Quennell, Marjorie, and Ch. H. B., *A History of Everyday Things in England*, Vol. I, New York, 1956.

Reese, Gustave, *Music in the Middle Ages*, New York, 1940.

Rickert, Edith, "Travel," *Chaucer's World*, ed. C. C. Olson and M. M. Crow, New York, 1948.

Ross, James B., and Mary M. McLaughlin, eds., *The Portable Medieval Reader*, New York, 1949.

Sarton, George, *Introduction to the History of Science*, 3 vols., Washington, 1927–48, reissued 1947–50.

Spearing, A. C., *Criticism and Medieval Poetry*, New York/London, 1964.

Speirs, John, *Medieval English Poetry, The Non-Chaucerian Tradition*, London, 1957.

Taylor, H. O., *The Classical Heritage of the Middle Ages*, 3rd ed., New York, 1911.

Thorndike, Lynn, *A History of Magic and Experimental Science During the First Thirteen Centuries of Our Era*, 8 vols., New York, 1923–58.

Trevelyan, George M., *Illustrated English Social History*, Vol. I, London, 1949.

Utley, Francis L., *The Crooked Rib*, Columbus, Ohio, 1944.

Vasta, Edward, ed., *Middle English Survey: Critical Essays*, Notre Dame, Ind., 1965.

Vossler, Karl, *Medieval Culture*, New York, 1929, 2 vols.
Wells, J. E., *A Manual of the Writings in Middle English, 1050–1400*, supps. I–IX, New Haven, 1916–51.
Weston, Jessie L., *From Ritual to Romance*, Cambridge, 1920; New York, 1957.
Young, Karl, *The Drama of the Medieval Church*, 2 vols., Oxford, 1933.

B. Selected References for Middle English Language

Baugh, Albert C., "Middle English," *A History of the English Language*, 2nd ed. (New York, 1963), pp. 189–239.
Bennett, J. A. W., and G. V. Smithers, "Early Middle English," *Early Middle English Verse and Prose* (Oxford, 1966), pp. xviii–lviii.
Dickens, Bruce, and R. M. Wilson, "Characteristics of Early Middle English," *Early Middle English Texts* (New York, 1951), pp. 136–50.
Kurath, Hans, and Sherman M. Kuhn, eds., *Middle English Dictionary*, Ann Arbor, Mich., 1954– (in progress).
Mossé, Fernand, *A Handbook of Middle English*, trans. James A. Walker, Baltimore, 1952.
Nist, John, *A Structural History of English* (New York, 1966), pp. 141–209.
Roseborough, Margaret M., *An Outline of Middle English Grammar*, New York, 1938.
Sisam, Kenneth, "The English Language in the Fourteenth Century," *Fourteenth Century Verse and Prose* (Oxford, 1925), pp. 265–92.
Wardale, Edith E., *An Introduction to Middle English*, London, 1937.
Wright, Joseph and Elizabeth M., *An Elementary Middle English Grammar*, London, 1932.

C. Bibliography of Texts

1. *Sir Gawayn and the Grene Knyght*
   (based on British Museum MS. Cotton Nero A. x.)
Cawley, A. C., ed., *Pearl and Sir Gawain and the Green Knight*, Everyman's Library 346, New York, 1962.
Ford, Boris, ed., *The Age of Chaucer* (above).
Gollancz, Israel, ed., *Pearl, Cleanness, Patience, and Sir Gawain*, reproduced in facsimile, EETS 162, London, 1923.
Morris, R., ed., *Sir Gawayne and the Green Knight*, revised edition of I. Gollancz, EETS 4, London, 1912.
Tolkien, J. R. R. and E. V. Gordon, eds., *Sir Gawain and the Green Knight*, 2nd ed., revised by Norman Davis, Oxford, 1968.
Translations:
   Banks, T. H., *Sir Gawain and the Green Knight*, New York, 1929.
   Borroff, Marie, *Sir Gawain and the Green Knight*, New York, 1967.
   Gardner, John, *The Complete Works of the Gawain Poet*, Chicago, 1965.
   Stone, Brian, *Sir Gawain and the Green Knight*, rev. ed., Baltimore, 1964.

2. *Piers Plowman*, selections from the A-text
   (based on the Oxford Vernon MS.)
Langland, William, *Piers Plowman: The A Version*, ed. George Kane, London, 1960.

——, *Piers the Plowman: A Critical Edition of the A-Version*, T. A. Knott and D. C. Fowler, eds., Baltimore, 1952.

——, *The Vision of William Concerning Piers the Plowman*, ed. W. W. Skeat, 2 vols., Oxford, 1886.

Translations:

Attwater, D. and R., *Piers Plowman*. London/New York, 1957.

Burrell, A., *Piers Plowman*, London/New York, 1912, reprinted 1931.

Goodridge, *Piers Plowman*, Harmondsworth, 1959.

Warren, Kate M., *Piers Plowman*, London, 1913.

Wells, H. W., *Piers Plowman*, London, 1938; reissued 1959.

Willard, R., and R. S. Loomis, *Medieval English Verse and Prose*, New York, 1948.

3. *Mandeville's Travels*, selections
   (based on Cotton MS. Titus C xvi.)

Hamelius, Paul, ed., *Mandeville's Travels*, EETS 153, 154, London, 1919–23.

Sisam, K., *Fourteenth Century Verse and Prose* (above).

Translated in Willard and Loomis (above).

4. *Second Shepherds' Play*
   (based on the Towneley MS., now Huntington MS. HM I)

Adams, J. Q., *Chief Pre-Shakespearean Dramas*, Cambridge, Mass., 1924.

Cawley, A. C., ed., *Everyman and Medieval Miracle Plays*, London, 1956.

——, *The Wakefield Pageants in the Towneley Cycle*, Manchester, 1958.

England, G., and A. W. Pollard, eds., *The Towneley Plays*, EETSes 71, London, 1897; reprinted 1952.

Translations:

Gassner, John, *A Treasury of the Theatre*, rev. ed., Vol. I, New York, 1951.

Hopper, Vincent, and G. B. Lahey, *Medieval Mystery Plays*, Woodbury, N.Y., 1962.

Rose, Martial, *The Wakefield Mystery Plays*, New York, 1961.

Willard and Loomis (above).

5. *Everyman*
   (based on Skot's Britwell copy)

Adams, J. Q., *Chief Pre-Shakespearean Dramas* (above).

Cawley, A. C., *Everyman* (above).

Greg, W. W., *Materialien zur Kunde des älteren englischen Dramas*, Vols. 4, 24, 28, Louvain, 1904–10.

Pollard, A. W., *English Miracle Plays, Moralities and Interludes*, 8th ed., rev., Oxford, 1927.

Translations:

Gassner (above).

Hopper and Lahey (above).

Willard and Loomis (above).

6. *The Play of Noah*
   (based on the Towneley MS., see 4., above)

Adams (above).

Cawley, *Wakefield Pageants* (above).

England and Pollard (above).

Sisam (above).

7. *Sir Orfeo*
(based on the Auchinleck MS.; emendations from Harley 3810)
Bliss, A. J., *Sir Orfeo*, London, 1954.
Ford, *Age of Chaucer* (above).
French, Walter H., and Charles B. Hale, *Middle English Metrical Romances*, Englewood Cliffs, N.J., 1930.
Sands, Donald B., *Middle English Verse Romances*, New York, 1966 [reprints French and Hale's *Sir Orfeo*].
Sisam (above).
Translations:
Rickert, Edith, *Early English Romances* . . . , London/New York, 1908.

8. *The Owl and the Nightingale*, selections
(based on the Jesus College, Oxford 29 MS.)
Atkins, J. W. H., *The Owl and the Nightingale*, Cambridge, 1922.
Ker, N. R., *The Owl and the Nightingale, reproduced in facsimile from the surviving manuscripts, Jesus Coll. Oxford 29 and B. M. Cotton Caligula A. IX*, EETS 251, London, 1963.
See also:
Bennett, J. A. W., and G. V. Smithers, *Early Middle English Verse and Prose*, Oxford, 1966 [Cotton MS.].
Dickens, B., and R. M. Wilson, *Early Middle English Texts*, New York, 1951 [also Cotton MS.].
Grattan, J. H. G., and G. F. H. Sykes, *The Owl and the Nightingale*, EETSes 119, London, 1935 [diplomatic edition].
Translations:
Atkins (above).
Eggers, Graydon, *The Owl and the Nightingale*, Durham, N.C., 1955.
Willard and Loomis (above).

9. *Pearl*
(based on Cotton Nero A. x.; see *Gawain*, above)
Cawley (see *Gawain*, above).
deFord, Sara, *The Pearl*, New York, 1967.
Gollancz, facsimile edition (see *Gawain*, above).
——, *Pearl*, London, 1921.
Gordon, E. V., *Pearl*, Oxford, 1953.
Hillman, Mary Vincent, *The Pearl: Mediaeval Text with a Literal Translation and Interpretation*, New York, 1959.
Osgood, C. G., *The Pearl*, Boston, 1906.
Translations:
deFord (above).
Gardner (see *Gawain*, above).
Gollancz, 1921 ed. (above).
Hillman (above).

10. Lyrics
Somewhat greater liberty with normalization has been taken with this section of texts than with others throughout the book; the leeway in dealing with the following basic manuscripts is, in some cases, considerable: "The Blacksmiths," Arundel 292; "Sumer Is Icumen In," Harley 978; "I Syng of a Mayden," Sloane 2593; "The Corpus Christi Carol," Balliol College, Oxford, 354; "Of a Rose, a

Lovely Rose," Sloane 2593 and Balliol College, Oxford, 354; "The Mourning of an Hare," Porkington 10; "Alas, alas the wyle, that ever I cowde daunce," Gonville and Caius Colleges, Cambridge, 383; "Holly and Ivy," Harley 5396; "Foweles in the Frith," Bodl. Douce 139; "Now Springs the Spray," Lincoln Inn MS., Hale 135; "Ubi sunt qui ante nos fuerunt?" Bodl. Digby 86; "Nou goth sonne under wod," Bodl. Arch. Selden, supra 74; "Erthe toc of erthe," Harley 2253; "The Agincourt Carol," Bodl. Arch. Selden B. 26 (3340).
For more comprehensive information on the lyrics consult *The Index of Middle English Verse*, ed. Carleton Brown and Rossell Hope Robbins, New York, 1943.
A partial list of popular lyric collections includes the following:
Bennett and Smithers (above).
Brook, George L., *The Harley Lyrics*, 2nd ed., Manchester, 1956.
Brown, Carleton, *English Lyrics of the XIIIth Century*, Oxford, 1932.
——, *Religious Lyrics of the XIVth Century*, 2nd ed., rev. G. V. Smithers, Oxford, 1952.
——, *Religious Lyrics of the XVth Century*, Oxford, 1939.
Chambers, E. K., and F. Sidgwick, *Early English Lyrics*, London, 1907.
Davies, R. T., *Medieval English Lyrics, A Critical Anthology*, Evanston, Ill., 1964.
Dickens and Wilson (above).
Greene, R. L., *The Early English Carols*, Oxford, 1935.
——, *A Selection of English Carols*, Oxford, 1962.
Halliwell, J. O., *Early English Miscellany*, Publications of the Warton Club, II, pp. 43–46 [lyric no. 6].
Hartshorne, C. H., *Ancient Metrical Tales*, London, 1829 [Cambridge MS., lyric no. 6].
Kaiser, Rolf, *Alt-und-mittelenglische Anthologie*, 2nd ed., Berlin, 1955.
Ker, N. R., *Facsimile of British Museum MS. Harley 2253*, EETS 255, London, 1965.
Murray, Hilda, *Earth upon Earth*, EETS 141, London, 1911.
Rickert, Edith, *Ancient English Christmas Carols*, 1400–1700, London, 1914.
Robbins, R. H., *Secular Lyrics of the XIVth and XVth Centuries*, 2nd ed., Oxford, 1956.
——, *Historical Poems of the XIVth and XVth Centuries*, New York, 1959.
Stevens, J., *Musica Britannica, iv, Mediaeval Carols*, London, 1952.
Stevick, Robert D., *One Hundred Middle English Lyrics*, New York, 1964.

11. *Brut*, selections
    (based on Cotton Caligula A IX; emendations from Cotton Otho C XIII)
Bennett and Smithers (above), selections [Otho MS.].
Brooks, G. L., and R. F. Leslie, *Layamon's Brut*, Vol. I, EETS 250, London, 1963.
Dickens and Wilson (above), selections.
Madden, Frederic, *Layamon's Brut*, 3 vols., London, 1847.
Translations of several selections from the *Brut* appear in Willard and Loomis' anthology (above).

12. Richard Rolle, *"Love Is Life That Lasts Ay,"* *The Form of Living*, Chapter XII (based on Cambridge Dd. 5. 64)
Allen, Hope E., *Writings Ascribed to Richard Rolle*, New York/London, 1927.
Comper, F. M. M., *The Life of Richard Rolle, Together with an Edition of His English Lyrics*, London/New York, 1929.
Hodgson, G. E., *The Form of Perfect Living*, London, 1910.
Horstman, Carl, *Yorkshire Writers*, 2 vols., London, 1895–96.

Sisam (above), selections.
Translations:
"Love Is Life That Lasts Ay," Comper (above).
The Form of Living, Chapter XII, Willard and Loomis (above).

13. *The Land of Cokaygne*
    (based on Harleian MS. 913)
Bennett and Smithers (above).
Heuser, W., *Die Kildare-Gedichte*, Bonner Beiträge zur Anglistik, XIV (1904),
    pp. 141–50.
Mätzner, E., *Altenglische Sprachproben*, I. i, p. 147ff.
Robbins, *Historical Poems* (above).
Translations:
    Donaldson, E. T., *The Norton Anthology of English Literature*, rev. ed., Vol. I,
        New York, 1968.
    Willard and Loomis (above).

14. *Wynnere and Wastoure*
    (based on British Museum Add. MS. 31042)
Ford, *Age of Chaucer* (above).
Gollancz, Israel, *Wynnere and Wastoure*, London, 1920.

15. *The Parlement of the Thre Ages*
    (based on British Museum Add. MS. 31042; see item 14, above)
Ford (above).
Gollancz, Israel, *The Parlement of the Thre Ages*, London, 1915.
Offord, M. Y., *The Parlement of the Thre Ages*, EETS 246, London, 1959.

16. Robert Mannyng, *Handlyng Synne*, selections
    (based on Harley MS. 1701)
Ford (above), selections.
Furnivall, F. J., *Handlyng Synne*, EETS 119, 123, London, 1901–3.
Sisam (above), selections.

17. Thomas Chestre, *Sir Launfal*
    (based on Cotton Caligula A. II.)
Bliss, A. J., *Thomas Chestre: Sir Launfal*, London, 1960.
French and Hale (see *Sir Orfeo*, above).
Rumble, Thomas C., *The Breton Lays in Middle English*, corr. ed., Detroit, 1967.
Sands (reprints French and Hale; see *Sir Orfeo*, above).

18. Syr Thomas Malory, *Le Morte Darthur*, Caxton edition, selections
Pollard, A. W., *The Romance of King Arthur and His Knights of the Round
    Table*, New York, 1917 [abridged]; 2 vols., 1900.
Sommer, Oskar, *Le Morte Darthur*, 3 vols., London, 1889–91.
Strachey, Edward, *Le Morte Darthur*, London, 1907.
Modernized selections:
    Donaldson (above).
    Willard and Loomis (above).

D. Addendum, 1965–85

Anderson, Earl R., "The Structure of Sir Launfal," *Papers on Language and Literature* 13 (1977), 115–24.
Andrews, Malcolm, *The Gawain Poet: An Annotated Bibliography, 1829–1977*, New York/London, 1979.
Boase, Roger, *The Origin and Meaning of Courtly Love: A Critical Study of European Scholarship*, Manchester/Totowa, N.J., 1977.
Brody, Saul Nathaniel, *The Disease of the Soul: Leprosy in Medieval Literature*, Ithaca, N.Y./London, 1974.
Burrow, J. A., *Richardian Poetry*, London/Boston, 1971.
Campbell, Josie P., "Farce as Function in the Wakefield Shepherd's Plays," *Chaucer Review* 14 (1980), 336–43.
Capellanus, Andreas, *Andreas Capellanus on Love*, trans. P. G. Walsh, London, 1982.
Colaianne, A. J., *Piers Plowman: An Annotated Bibliography of Editions and Criticisms, 1550–1977*, New York/London, 1978.
Cooper, Geoffrey, and Christopher Worthem, eds., *The Summoning of Everyman*, Nedlands, Australia, 1980.
Cosman, Madeleine P., *Fabulous Feasts: Medieval Cookery and Ceremony*, New York, 1976.
———, *Medieval Holidays and Festivals*, New York, 1981.
Davenport, W. A., *The Art of the Gawain Poet*, Humanities Press, 1978.
———, *Fifteenth-Century English Drama: The Early Moral Plays and Their Literary Relationships*, Cambridge/Totowa, N.J., 1982.
Doob, Penelope B. R., *Nebuchadnezzar's Children: Conventions of Madness in Middle English Literature*, New Haven/London, 1974.
Emmerson, Richard Kenneth, *Antichrist in the Middle Ages: A Study of Apocalypticism, Art and Literature*, Seattle, 1981.
Friedlander, Carolyn Van Dyke, "The First English Story of King Lear: Layamon's Brut, Lines 1448–1887," *Allegorica* 3 (1978), 42–76.
Gardener, John, *The Alliterative Morte Arthure, The Owl and the Nightingale, and Five Other Middle English Poems in a Modernized Version with Comments on Poems and Notes*, Carbondale, Ill./London, 1971.
———, *The Construction of the Wakefield Cycle*, Carbondale, Ill., 1974.
Goldhamer, Allen D., "Everyman: A Dramatization of Death," *Quarterly Journal of Speech* 59 (1973), 87–98.
Green, Richard Firth, *Poets and Princepleasers: Literature and the English Court in the Late Middle Ages*, Toronto/Buffalo, 1980.
Greene, Richard L., ed., *The Early English Carols*, 2nd ed., rev. and enl., Oxford/New York, 1977.
Helterman, Jeffrey, *Symbolic Action in the Plays of the Wakefield Master*, Athens, Ga., 1981.
Henisch, B. A., *Fast and Feast: Food in Medieval Society*, University Park, Pa./London, 1976.
Houle, Peter J., *The English Morality and Related Drama: A Bibliographical Survey*, Hamden, Ct., 1972.
Howard, Donald R., *Writers and Pilgrims: Medieval Pilgrim Narratives and Their Posterity*, Berkeley/Los Angeles, 1980.
Hume, Kathryn, *The Owl and the Nightingale: The Poem and Its Critics*, Toronto/Buffalo, 1975.

Jeffrey, David L., "Literature in an Apocalyptic Age; or, How to End a Romance," *Dalhousie Review* 61 (1981), 426–46.

Kane, George, and E. Talbot Donaldson, eds., *Piers Plowman: The B Version*, London, 1975 (2nd vol. of *Piers Plowman: The Three Versions*).

Lampe, David E., "The Poetic Strategy of the Parlement of the Thre Ages," *Chaucer Review* 7 (1973), 173–83.

Lane, Daryl F., Jr., "Conflict in Sir Launfal," *Neuphilologische Mitteilungen* 10 (1973), 283–87.

Logorio, Valerie M., and Ritamarie Bradley, *The 14th Century English Mystics: A Comprehensive Annotated Bibliography*, New York/London, 1981.

Longsworth, Robert M., "Sir Orfeo, the Minstrel and the Minstrel's Art," *Studies in Philology* 79 (1982), 1–11.

Mack, Maynard, Jr., "The Second Shepherd's Play: A Reconsideration," *PMLA* 93 (1978), 78–85.

Pearsall, Derek, ed., *Piers Plowman: An Edition of the C-Text*, Berkeley/Los Angeles, 1979.

Peck, Russell A., "The Careful Hunter in The Parlement of the Thre Ages," *ELH* 39 (1972), 333–41.

Potter, Robert A., *The English Morality Play: Origins, History and Influence of a Dramatic Tradition*, London/Boston, 1975.

Riehle, Wolfgang, *The Middle English Mystics*, trans. Bernard Strandring, London/Boston, 1981.

Rigg, A. G., and Charlotte Brewer, *Piers Plowman: The Z Version*, Toronto, 1983.

Rowland, Beryl, "The Three Ages of the Parlement of the Three Ages," *Chaucer Review* 9 (1975), 342–52.

Spearing, A. C., *Medieval Dream Poetry*, Cambridge/London, 1976.

Stokstad, Marilyn, and Jerry Stannard, *Gardens of the Middle Ages*, Lawrence, Kan., 1983.

Wakefield, Walter L., and Austin P. Evans, eds. and trans., *Heresies of the High Middle Ages*, New York, 1969.

INDEX